Reform and Insurrection
in Bourbon New Granada
and Peru

Reform and Insurrection in Bourbon New Granada and Peru

EDITED BY

John R. Fisher
Allan J. Kuethe and
Anthony McFarlane

Louisiana State University Press
BATON ROUGE AND LONDON

Manufactured in the United States of America
First printing
99 98 97 96 95 94 93 92 91 90 5 4 3 2 1

Typeface: Linotron Bembo
Typesetter: G&S Typesetters, Inc.
Printer and binder: Thomson-Shore, Inc.

Library of Congress Cataloging-in-Publication Data
Reform and insurrection in Bourbon New Granada and Peru / edited by
John R. Fisher, Allan J. Kuethe, and Anthony McFarlane.
p. cm.
Includes bibliographical references and index.
ISBN 0-8071-1569-X (alk. paper). ISBN 0-8071-1654-8 (pbk.: alk. paper)
1. Colombia—Politics and government—To 1810. 2. Colombia—History—War of Independence, 1810–1822. 3. Peru—Politics and government—1548–1820. 4. Peru—History—War of Independence, 1820–1829. 5. Spain—Colonies—America—Economic policy. 6. Government, Resistance to—Colombia—History. 7. Government, Resistance to—Peru—History. 8. Colombia—Economic conditions. 9. Peru—Economic conditions. I. Fisher, John Robert. II. Kuethe, Allan J., 1940– . III. McFarlane, Anthony, 1946– .
F2272.R34 1990
986.1'02—dc20 90-35704
CIP

This book is published with the generous assistance of The Program for Cultural Cooperation Between Spain's Ministry of Culture and United States Universities.

Chapter 8, by Anthony McFarlane, appeared in a somewhat different form in the *Hispanic American Historical Review,* LXIX (May, 1989), 283–330.

The paper in this book meets the guidelines for permanence and durability of the Committee on Production Guidelines for Book Longevity of the Council on Library Resources. ♾

Contents

Part Two: Commercial and Economic Overviews

Part Three: Resistance and Rebellion

Maps

Acknowledgments

The editors thank the individuals and institutions that have contributed to the preparation of this volume. The Graduate School of Texas Tech University, the Research and Innovations Fund of the University of Warwick, and the Institute of Latin American Studies of the University of Liverpool contributed funds for the typing of the original text. In addressing that task, Mrs. Joan Weldon went well beyond the call of duty in her patient deciphering of editorial attempts to harmonize multinational footnoting and spelling styles. Allan J. Kuethe is grateful to the United States–Spanish Joint Committee for Cultural and Educational Cooperation, whose support for his research in Spain during the academic year 1983–1984 made his contributions to this volume possible. John Fisher's contributions result primarily from research undertaken in Spain in 1982–1984 with the assistance of a grant from the British Academy and from research in Peru undertaken with David Cahill and supported by a subsequent award from the Economic and Social Research Council (award no. RG/00/23/2117).

Abbreviations

AAE	Archives des Affaires Etrangères, Paris
CPE	Correspondance Politique Espagne
ACHSC	*Anuario colombiano de historia social y de la cultura*
ADC	Archivo Departamental, Cuzco
AEA	*Anuario de estudios americanos*
AGI	Archivo General de Indias, Seville
IG	Indiferente General
SD	Santo Domingo
SF	Santa Fe
AGN	Archivo General de la Nación, Lima
AGS	Archivo General de Simancas
AHN	Archivo Histórico Nacional, Madrid
AHNC	Archivo Histórico Nacional de Colombia, Bogotá
ANHE	Archivo Nacional de Historia del Ecuador, Quito
PQ	Presidencia de Quito
RC	República de Colombia
BHA	*Boletín de historia y antigüedades*
BNM	Biblioteca Nacional, Madrid
SM	Sección de Manuscritos

BP	Biblioteca del Palacio, Madrid
SMA	Sección Miscelánea Ayala
HAHR	*Hispanic American Historical Review*
JLAS	*Journal of Latin American Studies*

Reform and Insurrection in Bourbon New Granada and Peru

NEW GRANADA AND PERU IN THE LATE EIGHTEENTH CENTURY

Introduction

Historical myths are more pernicious than other forms of fantasy, primarily because they tend to be rooted in not only dogma but also a degree of reality, no matter how distorted or misunderstood. Their eradication requires patient investigation, analysis, and elucidation rather than dramatic denouements. One of the most pervasive myths in the field of Spanish-American history is that identifying the eighteenth century as a period of unhindered progress and prosperity, when the implementation of a rational imperial reform program awakened Spain and its imperial possessions from their Hapsburg slumber, though with the unintended result of giving the American colonies the maturity and confidence required for their transition to independence.

New Spain, it has been traditionally argued, was the greatest beneficiary of the material success story of the Bourbon era, followed by Cuba, Venezuela, and the Río de la Plata, formerly neglected frontier or peripheral regions, which expanded their economies rapidly in the late colonial period in response to programs of commercial liberalization, tax reform, and administrative reorganization. The differing responses of these regions to the movements for independence in the period 1808–1824—New Spain's grudging acceptance, Cuba's opposition, and the enthusiastic support of dominant groups in Venezuela and the Río de la Plata—have, with the partial exception of Cuba's, been explained primarily in terms of social and strategic factors, rather than political or regional considerations.

Historians who have attempted grand syntheses of the Spanish-American history of this period have found it difficult to interpret developments and attitudes in the viceroyalties of New Granada and Peru. The former, established in 1739 by its definitive separation from the viceroyalty of Peru, finally succeeded in turning the historical tables in 1824 when a Colombian army at Ayachucho secured South American independence by defeating a Peruvian force still struggling to preserve royalist authority in the highlands of the southern Andes. In that sense New Granada ultimately aligned itself with the progressive tendencies revealed in Caracas and Buenos Aires by 1810.[1] However, the factors that lay behind New Granadan responses during 1810–1822 have remained obscure, primarily because the viceroyalty's relative uniqueness—it was, for example, the only major jurisdiction not to be administered by intendants from the 1780s—and its intense regional differentiation have tended to frighten off the generalizers, whose syntheses, accordingly, have proved incapable of accommodating the New Granadan experience.

New Granada also presented profound difficulties for the royal officials who attempted to understand and govern it from Santa Fe. Despite its geographical extent, a population of well over one million, and a reasonably favorable endowment of natural resources, the colony failed throughout most of the eighteenth century to pay the cost of its own government and defense. It depended upon subsidies from Peru and, on at least one occasion, even far-away Mexico. The inhabitants showed a distinct aversion to honoring imperial commercial law and to paying taxes, and they much preferred local political arrangements to systems imposed from Spain or, for that matter, even the colonial capital. The frustration of the royal administration as, decade after decade, it vainly attempted to

1. In this text, the administrative division "New Granada" is understood to exclude the captaincy general of Caracas, which enjoyed an autonomous status.

assert effective control left it with no illusions about the allegiance to the crown of the kingdom's inhabitants: in 1772 Viceroy Pedro Messía de la Cerda warned his successor, Manuel Guirior, that their obedience "has no other support, except the armed forces, than the free will and pleasure with which they accept directives, because, without their approval, there is no force, weapon, or authority that their superiors can use to gain respect and compliance; hence command is very uncertain, and the success of measures taken is excessively tenuous; by the same token, this lack of confidence requires treading lightly and, at times, without complete freedom, trying to accommodate circumstances."[2] The viceroy might have added that, owing to the paucity of royal revenues, the armed forces remained hopelessly small and seldom influenced events beyond the colonial capitals or military strongpoints.

Geography posed a fundamental problem in New Granada. The northern reach of the Andes Mountains, which extended almost to the Caribbean coast, was divided into three ranges by the fast-flowing Cauca and Magdalena Rivers. Crossed by the equator, the fractured terrain varied from dense, impenetrable jungle-covered lowlands to snow-capped peaks. To the east lay the Llanos, a vast, sprawling, and lightly populated tropical savanna. Swamps and tropical vegetation bordered most of the coast on both the Caribbean and the Pacific, and coves and inlets abounded. Much of the coastline lay in the hands of unpacified Indians or semicivilized outlaw communities, very frequently the descendants of unions between escaped slaves and aboriginals. To reach Santa Fe from Cartagena, a traveler had to navigate up the treacherous Magdalena River, disembark at Honda, and then ascend into the Eastern Cordillera. This trip took about five or six weeks, roughly the same time it took to sail from Cádiz to Havana. To reach Quito in the far southwest, a traveler from Santa Fe had to descend the Eastern Cordillera into the Magdalena Valley, cross the Central Cordillera through the difficult Quindío Pass, advance through the Cauca Valley, and finally negotiate the western range. This trip took eight to ten weeks, providing, of course, that the individual

2. Pedro Messía de la Cerda, "Relación del estado del Virreinato de Santafé . . . 1772," in E. Posada and P. M. Ibañez (eds.), *Relaciones de mando: Memorias presentadas por los gobernantes del Nuevo Reino de Granada* (Bogotá, 1910), 113.

did not fall ill upon the way owing to the harsh variations of climate that he endured. Guayaquil, the port and shipbuilding center in the south of the kingdom of Quito, was entirely cut off from even its own audiencia capital during the rainy season, a factor which, with other considerations, provoked its formal return to the viceroyalty of Peru in 1803. Under these circumstances, it is hardly surprising that the authorities in Santa Fe found themselves remote from the governed or that the populations of distant coasts and plains or isolated valleys assumed an independent attitude in their relationships with the viceregal capital, not to mention Madrid, and that very frequently local administrative authorities shared this perspective.

It is, of course, commonplace that despite pretenses toward an increased centralization of authority, the eighteenth-century monarchies suffered from very real limitations in actual power. Administrative authority was often compromised or still structurally weak; finances were fragile; and innovative capacity was obstructed by traditional liberties, special arrangements, and privileged orders. Yet New Granada took this reality a step or two further. The root problem of the Bourbon monarchy in New Granada was its inability to harness the flow of commerce, much to the chagrin of both royal treasury officials and Spanish merchants who watched helplessly as smugglers denied them the profits of colonialism. It was a vicious circle. Without revenue the authorities lacked the means to maintain the troops, the coast guard, and the police force necessary to exact compliance in the midst of most difficult geographic conditions, and without such enforcement revenues continued to languish.

Despite an inauspicious beginning, however, the record of the viceroys who served the crown in New Granada showed them on the whole to be capable men. The administration of Philip V first upgraded New Granada to the status of a viceroyalty in 1719. The inaugural viceroy, Jorge de Villalonga, was not a fortunate choice. He was proud, vain, avaricious, and personally implicated in the contraband trade, and his ill-managed administration resulted in the abandonment of the viceregal experiment upon his recall in 1724. It took an international crisis to resurrect the idea, and in 1739, on the eve of the War of Jenkins' Ear, Philip reestablished the viceroyalty under the leadership of Sebastián de

Eslava. Eslava presided at Cartagena when Spain's armed forces repulsed the British attack led by Admiral Edward Vernon, and the crown decided that the viceroyalty should remain extant. Thereafter, a respectable array of administrators occupied the viceregal office, and men such as Manuel Antonio Flores (1776–1782) and José de Ezpeleta (1789–1796) showed considerable ability. Moreover, the famous Antonio Caballero y Góngora (1782–1789), though in some respects a mediocre administrator, is well remembered for his enlightened vision and his skillful management of the Comunero affair. It is evident, nevertheless, that none of these individuals, no matter how experienced and dedicated, was able to alter tangibly the political culture of New Granada, particularly insofar as that culture expressed itself in commercial practices.

Part of the difficulty arose from the attitude of the crown itself. Accustomed to ruling from above and determined, come what may, to improve imperial efficiency, the royal authorities in Madrid and the inspectors whom they dispatched to America in the 1770s, showed little inclination to consult with and learn from their subjects. Initiatives in policy were therefore often misguided and met at the local level with indifference or hostility. The best example of this phenomenon in New Granada was the ill-fated reform mission of Regent-Visitor Juan Francisco Gutiérrez de Piñeres. Sent to New Granada by Minister of the Indies José de Gálvez on the eve of Spain's intervention in the American War of Independence, Gutiérrez de Piñeres faced the Herculean task of reorganizing the colonial administration and sharply increasing local revenues to pay for improved imperial defenses. Harsh methods, rather than consultation and compromise, were the order of the day. Gutiérrez abruptly replaced creole officeholders with Spaniards, reorganized the instruments of revenue collection, and raised taxes and royal monopoly prices. The result was armed resistance and an unprecedented humiliation of the royal administration in Santa Fe as it found itself compelled to capitulate to an angry Comunero army. The regent-visitor had to flee to the coast to escape assassination.

A measure of royal control was eventually reasserted with the arrival of an army from Cartagena—this in the midst of war with Britain—but it was fragile from the start. True, the Comuneros went home and a few token reprisals, including the execution of one leader, were effected. Moreover, although Gutiérrez de Piñeres' revenue reforms were modified to placate the populace, enforcement continued to be pursued vigorously, and royal income increased impressively, surging from just under 1,000,000 pesos in 1772 to approximately 3,350,000 by the end of the 1780s. Much of this growth came from the profits of the royal aguardiente and tobacco monopolies, which could be enforced with some efficiency in the major population centers. It should be remembered, however, that these taxes were collected at the point of a bayonet and at a terrible political price. Gálvez, working through Archbishop Antonio Caballero y Góngora, who had negotiated the capitulations and who was now rewarded with appointment as viceroy, established a garrison of 1,300 men in Santa Fe—a force larger than that deployed in the traditional military strongpoint of Cartagena—and raised an interior disciplined militia under the leadership of Spanish officers. He also advanced plans to fortify the colonial capital and establish a gunpowder factory. The cost of maintaining the army of occupation and the expanded bureaucracy, as well as a concurrent attempt to seal gaping avenues for the contraband trade through the forced pacification of the Cuna Indians of Darién and the Guajiros of Río Hacha, further depleted the treasury. The practical-minded, moderate authorities who assumed control of the colonial administration in Madrid after the death of Gálvez in 1787 dismantled much of this apparatus in the name of harmony and economy and discarded Gálvez' plan to introduce the unpopular intendant system of provincial administration in New Granada. Thereafter, the upward curve in revenue collection first leveled out and then waned: treasury income stood at slightly over three million pesos in 1810.[3] The new emphasis on cost consciousness, however, reduced expenses enough to enable the colony to produce a small surplus for Spain by the end of the century.

3. These figures are based on the calculations of Francisco Antonio Moreno y Escandón, "Estado del Virreinato de Santafé, Nuevo Reino de Granada . . . 1772," *BHA,* XXIII (1936), 603–605; Antonio Caballero y Góngora, "Relación del estado del Nuevo Reino de Granada . . . 1789," in Posada and Ibañez (eds.), *Relaciones de mando,* 258–61; and José Manuel Restrepo, *Historia de la revolución de la República de Colombia en la América meridional* (8 vols.; Bogotá, 1942–50), I, xxxi.

There were, of course, alternatives to mere retrenchment. A liberalization of commercial policy to make the Spanish trade more competitive might, simply on free-market principles, undercut contraband. The 1778 Regulation of Free Trade came too late to be of much political help to Gutiérrez de Piñeres in his attempt to advance administrative and revenue reform, but it broke the legal monopoly of the Consulado de Cádiz and eventually drew a larger percentage of the viceroyalty's trade into imperial channels. Customs receipts accordingly showed a modest increase over the years, but nevertheless accounted for only the humiliatingly small sum of 258,000 pesos in 1810.

Another alternative was the search for material progress through scientific and technological innovation, a process that, it was hoped, would generate a larger tax base. A case in point was the botanical expedition headed by José Celestino Mutis. Although dedicated to the general study of botany, it sustained a continuing interest in the location and identification of commercially important vegetable resources, such as the quinine-producing cinchona tree. More ambitious was the mining reform mission led by Juan José D'Elhúyar, who was charged with attempting to regenerate silver mining through modernized mining and refining techniques. Sponsored by Archbishop-Viceroy Caballero y Góngora, this mission was nevertheless destined to fail for a multiplicity of reasons, not the least of which was the failure to consult with the colonists in advance to determine realistic goals and approaches.

The crown's limited successes in diverting a larger portion of New Granada's trade to legal channels, and the general increase in royal income largely due to the aguardiente and tobacco monopolies, should not lead the historian to the false conclusion that Madrid had somehow brought its wayward colony to heel. Most goods still left and entered the viceroyalty through contraband channels. Local elites continued to enjoy regional autonomy. And much of the coastline and the vast eastern plains remained outside of effective royal control. As Viceroy Pedro Mendinueta perceptively lamented in 1797, "I will never be persuaded that these municipalities sustain in them the most dutiful submission and obedience that they should; they will continue their superficial tranquillity until an opportunity arises to throw off the gentle yoke that governs them."[4] The yoke was indeed gentle because Bourbon colonialism had been able to advance very little. And the colony, which had largely been beyond effective royal control, was prepared by 1810 to break relatively easily its ties with the mother country. The independence process was, however, predictably complicated by regional rivalries and jealousies that played into imperial hands and turned an uncomplicated birth into a lengthy ordeal.

Eighteenth-century Peru has seemed to historians to offer a more coherent, comprehensible profile than New Granada, from which it differed, of course, in a number of important respects. Traditionally regarded as a more effective administrative entity than its northern counterpart, Peru was governed in the late Bourbon period from Lima, the historic seat of Spanish power in South America, by powerful viceroys who succeeded in imposing their authority over the interior provinces, despite the trauma of the Indian rising of 1780–1783 initiated by the *cacique* José Gabriel Túpac Amaru. Its relative political quiescence thereafter, particularly after 1810, has usually been attributed to both the social conservatism of its creole population, who feared further Indian uprisings, and to the economic and political decline ushered in by the imperial reforms of the 1770s. According to this interpretation, these events left Peru's sullen, despondent inhabitants hanging on in the 1820s with only the memories of former glories, as they grimly struggled to preserve the imperial connection for want of any acceptable alternative. Research during the last two decades has peeled away the layers of ignorance obscuring the reality of Peru in the last fifty years of the colonial period to substantially revise this picture of unity of purpose within a context of genteel decadence. It is now clear that, despite the obstruction of vested interests within and outside the viceregal court of Lima, the financial, commercial, and administrative reforms implemented during the *visita general* of José Antonio de Areche and Jorge de Escobedo (1777–1785) were much more effective and productive—for both crown and colony—than the parallel program in New Granada. Royal revenues increased dramatically after the introduction of the intendant system in 1784, and, after initial difficulties caused by wartime interrup-

4. Pedro Mendinueta to the Príncipe de la Paz, Santa Fe, May 19, 1798, AGI, Estado, leg. 52.

tions and market saturation, legal commerce, too, expanded impressively in the 1780s, despite the opening of other ports in the Río de la Plata and in the Pacific to the direct trade with Spain formerly monopolized by Callao. Even the mining mission led by Thaddeus von Nordenflicht, unlike the D'Elhúyar expedition to New Granada, seemed somewhat successful, though the doubling of silver production to six million pesos a year in the truncated viceroyalty in the quarter century following the loss of Upper Peru (1776) owed more to economic and commercial forces than to technical innovation.[5]

The achievements of Charles III did not mean, of course, that Bourbon reformism encountered no resistance in the Peruvian viceroyalty. The shattering disorders of 1780–1783, which began as a creole protest against the reform mission of Areche and quickly turned into a mass Indian uprising, defined very real limits to the crown's ability to effect change. In some respects, however, the uprising represented a protest against local abuses permitted by the unreformed system of administration, and, after order was restored, the crown moved quickly to use the insurrection as a springboard for launching its newly constructed program of administrative reform. After an impressive beginning, the intendant system, introduced in 1784, had lost its impetus at the local level by the end of the century, and in the long run did little to alter Peruvian political culture. Yet, while the fragile bonds that tied New Granada to Madrid shattered quickly under the force of the Napoleonic invasion of Spain, Peru held fast, honoring a long-standing tradition of obedience to colonial authority, partly because the emancipation movements that surfaced in the viceroyalty in 1810–1814 came primarily from its interior and thus resurrected the regional and racial challenges to *limeño* authority that had been implicit in the Túpac Amaru movement.

It is not surprising that New Granada has been the least studied of the major jurisdictions of the Spanish empire. If the viceroys in Santa Fe and their masters in Madrid experienced difficulty in ascertaining the reality of the colony, the task has been no less

5. For general discussions of Bourbon policies and their results in post-1776 Peru, see J. R. Fisher, *Government and Society in Colonial Peru: The Intendant System, 1784–1814* (London, 1970); and J. R. Fisher, *Silver Mines and Silver Miners in Colonial Peru, 1776–1824* (Liverpool, 1977).

daunting for the historian. Yet in recent years a flurry of research has opened new perspectives into the historical experience of the Granadine viceroyalty. We resolved to bring together as much of this expertise as possible at the Forty-fifth International Congress of Americanists, which met in Bogotá in 1985, with the hope of advancing knowledge and debate. We also hoped that in crucial areas new perspectives on the history of the Peruvian viceroyalty might provide useful points of comparison. This book is the product of that gathering.

The book's ten essays are grouped in three sections. The first encompasses studies of different dimensions of imperial policy in eighteenth-century New Granada and Peru, ranging from the broad context of policy formulation and development by Spain to the application and effects of its reformist principles in areas of economic and military organization. The second section focuses more closely on the economic sphere, in essays that are, in turn, directed toward investigating the conditions of New Granadan commerce under the early Bourbons, assessing the comparative impact of Bourbon commercial reform on Peruvian and New Granadan trade with Spain, and tracing the outlines of New Granadan agricultural production at the end of the colonial period. The third part examines colonial protest and rebellion, bringing together studies of resistance to Bourbon reform in each of the viceroyalties during the eighteenth century with an exploration of the role of popular insurrection in New Granada's wars of independence.

The four essays of Part One address a fundamental theme of Spanish-American history in the Bourbon period: the efforts of the Bourbon monarchy to rationalize colonial government, to strengthen colonial defenses, and to bolster imperial finances. In Chapter 1, Allan Kuethe introduces this theme by defining the character and limitations of early reformist initiatives under Charles III and placing New Granada in the wider context of policies developed in Madrid following Spain's humiliation in the Seven Years' War. Under the influence of the Marqués de Esquilache, who emerged as the dominant figure in Charles's postwar cabinet, the need to base the reconstruction of Spanish power on the reorganization of colonial commerce became the cornerstone of a fresh initiative in imperial policy. Although this need had long been recognized by Spanish political economists and tentatively acknowledged in the earlier reforms of the transatlantic fleet system, the momentum of reform was not long sustained, as Kuethe shows, and its impact was much greater in Cuba than in New Granada. With the collapse of the Esquilache government, and reassertion of the political influence of the Cádiz monopoly, the new thrust of policy was blunted and delayed. In New Granada, the early Caroline commercial reforms were limited in their extent and effect, and internal reorganization was confined to piecemeal extensions of royal monopolies and a partial reordering of the military establishment.

These measures did, however, contain the seeds of later, more dramatic developments. In the late 1770s and early 1780s, New Granada was to feel the full force of Bourbon reformism when, together with the viceroyalty of Peru, it was subjected to a swingeing review of its government and finances, and affected by the great reforms to the transatlantic trading system brought by the 1778 Regulation of Free Trade.

Some of the implications of the later reforms of Charles III are described and discussed in the subsequent essays in Part One. In Chapter 2, Sandra Montgomery Keelan examines state intervention in a sector of the New Granadan mining industry, showing how an "enlightened" attempt to apply new technology to silver mining failed to achieve its purpose. In New Granada, as in Peru, the Spanish authorities failed to recognize that traditional techniques, though apparently primitive, were often well adapted to local needs and conditions. Doomed by too much planning and too little practical input from below, and plagued by unfortunate timing and weak financial support, not even one of Spain's most brilliant scientific stars, Juan José D'Elhúyar, could rescue the silver mines of New Granada.

An aspect of Bourbon reformism that left a far deeper imprint on colonial politics was the military reorganization undertaken in the later eighteenth century. In Chapter 3, Juan Marchena Fernández advances a social analysis of the veteran and volunteer forces of Peru and New Granada during the period after 1750 and demonstrates the power that the elites of both viceroyalties came to exert over the colonial armed forces. In this comparative study, he not only draws attention to important differences between Peru and New Granada, but also points out significant variations within the latter viceroyalty, distinguishing between the different roles of the elites in the major cities of Santa Fe and Cartagena. Although Marchena Fernández argues generally that the militia remained the traditional stronghold of the landed upper class and urban merchants in both its pre-reform and post-reform "disciplined" configurations, he shows that in the garrison of politically volatile Santa Fe, the crown tailored its officer corps to ensure peninsular Spanish superiority. Elsewhere, the officer corps of the regular army, though initially dominated by Europeans, also succumbed to American majorities as powerful creoles deployed their economic and political influence to secure appointments for their sons. Inevitably, therefore, by 1810, militias and regulars alike responded to local rather than inperial needs. In Peru, the two coincided, but the crown was to be less fortunate in other areas, where the local military forces it had created were often to be turned against Spain.

In Chapter 4, the section's closing essay, Jacques Barbier returns to that vital current in Bourbon reformism, the attempt to reanimate the Spanish mercantilist system persistently threatened by foreign penetration and recurrent interimperial warfare. In particular, he deals with metropolitan attempts during the reign of Charles IV to stimulate coastal agriculture through a liberalization of slave-trade legislation and to bring New Granada back into an imperial commercial network increasingly undermined by British blockade and foreign contraband incursions. When these strategies failed, peninsular government could do little more than attempt to squeeze a revenue surplus from New Granada to help subsidize an embattled metropolis embroiled in the maelstrom of European wars. At the end of the colonial period, he shows, New Granada still directly contributed little to the sustenance of the imperial center.

A recurring theme in these essays on Bourbon reformism in Peru and New Granada is the crown's determination to fortify the structures of the empire by shoring up its economic underpinnings. In Part Two the opening essays address this theme more directly and explicitly, exploring the weaknesses of the imperial commercial nexus and the efficacy of measures employed to repair its flaws.

In Chapter 5, Lance Grahn provides a detailed account of the debilities of the Spanish commercial system in New Granada during the first half of the Bourbon century. He shows how, on the Caribbean coast of New Granada, great gaps in Spain's mercantilist shield admitted a flourishing smuggling trade that competed with Spanish imports. In Riohacha, contraband involved strategic as well as economic problems because the smugglers maintained contacts with the indomitable, still unpacified Indians of the Guajiro Peninsula. Even in areas closer to the seat of effective government, in Santa Marta and Cartagena, contraband could not be contained. For not only did local demand for smuggled imports encourage illegal trade, but the very officials responsible for arresting such commerce colluded in its commission and operation.

The deep inroads made by foreign contraband, especially in the Caribbean region, were, of course, a major reason for the introduction of *comercio libre* in 1778, and John Fisher's essay addresses the impact of this reform on Peruvian and Neogranadian trade. In Chapter 6, Fisher analyzes the effects of the Regulation of Free Trade of 1778 in the Spanish empire, with particular reference to Peru and New Granada. Fisher's statistical data show the striking extent of Spain's success in recapturing a larger portion of the American trade through its reformist strategy. He explores in depth the ramifications of this phenomenon for Peruvian domestic industry, which, he suggests, underwent a period of change rather than simple decline. His findings confirm the continuing dominance of Peru in South America as both a market for exports from Spain and a supplier of colonial products to the metropolis. Equally striking is the relative and continuing insignificance of Spanish trade with New Granada, seen within the broad context of Spanish Atlantic commerce. Fisher concludes that, although its total value modestly increased during the *comercio libre* period, the viceroyalty had ceased to be of any major importance to the overall imperial economy long before 1810.

After these reflections on the workings of the imperial mercantile system, Chapter 7 examines the New Granadan economy, offering a statistical perspective on the workings of its agrarian sector at the end of the colonial period. Using tithe revenues as his measurement, Maurice Brungardt presents a wealth of data on the agricultural bases of the regional economies in the New Granadan interior. The isolation of much of this economic activity is a striking theme, as is the ability of the Socorro textile industry to sustain its position in the face of the expanding commercial network of the world economy. This latter point reinforces Fisher's argument that colonial industry was generally much more resilient to European competition in the era of Hispanic free trade than has hitherto been acknowledged.

The studies in Part Three focus on another, equally fundamental aspect of the Bourbon century in the Peruvian and New Granadan viceroyalties. Adopting the perspective of the governed rather than the government, these essays explore expressions of colonial opposition to imperial innovation, both during the late eighteenth century and at the moment of Spain's great crisis after 1810.

Two of the essays deal directly with specific episodes of colonial resistance to Bourbon fiscal innovation. In Chapter 8, Anthony McFarlane reconstructs the insurrection of the city of Quito in 1765, a major urban rebellion precipitated by changes in taxation. Triggered by the attempt of the viceroy of New Granada to extend the royal liquor monopoly and to alter the sales tax in Quito, this uprising united different social groups in a common reaction against royal policy and prefigured the great cluster of riots and uprisings in Peru and New Granada during the early 1780s. One of these later uprisings—that of the Peruvian city of Arequipa in 1780—is the subject of David Cahill's essay in Chapter 9, which carries the analysis of colonial obduracy in the face of fiscal reorganization into the opening phase of the great southern Andean insurrection known as the Rebellion of Túpac Amaru.

These rebellions are of manifold interest. Not only do they reflect the powerful opposition to the Caroline reforms in the colonies, but, by focusing on such episodes of conflict, these essays also illuminate the attitudes and beliefs that shaped colonial political culture at different social levels. Both essays start with an analysis of the socioeconomic context of the rebellions; equally, however, they suggest that to explain such conflicts in purely economic terms is to see them in only one dimension. Far from being the actions of heedless mobs driven by deprivation to violent acts of vengeance, the extraordinary popular mobilizations that took place in Quito and Arequipa reveal latent structures of organization and discipline informing crowd actions and reflect allegiances to shared interests, values, and beliefs among common people. The temporary uniting of patrician elites, anxious to protect their own privileges, with the laboring classes shows, moreover, how cross-class alliances could be forged. Together, patricians and populace constituted a force sufficiently powerful to lay bare the fragility of royal government. But, in both Quito and Arequipa—as in the more far-reaching rebellions of Túpac Amaru and the Comuneros—the deep divisions of race and class precluded durable opposition to Spanish rule, and these movements fractured along the lines of their internal contradictions. Nonetheless, though these movements reflected the narrow limits of popular political consciousness, they reminded the crown of the limits to its practical authority, and the elites of the social dangers of rousing the lower orders.

In Chapter 10, the final essay, Brian Hamnett pursues the thematic of rebellion, carrying it into the context of the broader conflicts that surfaced in New Granada during the period of imperial crisis from 1810 through the early 1820s. Hamnett explores provincial politics in the independence period, turning from the traditional focus on interelite competition and concentrating on the effects of social tensions and the role of popular participation in the civil struggles that beset New Granada. He shows that if viceregal government had failed to fully impose itself on New Granada's complex concatenation of regions and peoples, the creole separatists of 1810 were to fare no better. In a struggle in which regional loyalties generally outweighed larger political considerations, and social conflict emerged as a persistent theme, both republican and royalist commanders sought to control popular militancy for their distinct ends. Indeed, the Spanish authorities were able to exploit internal rivalries to sustain a strong presence into the early 1820s and, though popular discontents were harnessed to the insurgent cause in some regions, in the south the royalist cause was long sustained by popular allegiance to the crown. Moreover, not only did the social and regional conflicts inherited from the colonial period intensify during the Wars of Independence, but during the nineteenth century, republican governments found it even more difficult than had their viceregal predecessors to fully control the state and its territory.

Our final observation is that, notwithstanding our generally critical analysis of the efficacy of the Bourbon reforms in both viceroyalties, the one unquestioned monument to the profundity of the attempts of Charles III in particular to improve and monitor the performance of Spain's imperial possessions is the extraordinary richness of documentary materials available in Spanish and Spanish-American archives. If the essays in this volume attract more scholars to take advantage of their availability, superficial generalizations about Spanish America in the Bourbon era are likely to be pushed even farther into the realms of mythology, which is where they belong.

Part One

Colonial Policy and Reform

ALLAN J. KUETHE

Chapter 1

The Early Reforms of Charles III in the Viceroyalty of New Granada, 1759–1776

"The Royal Treasury is the means to satisfy the public necessities of the kingdom. Through it, defense is sustained during wartime, and all that ensures tranquillity, security, and good government is provided during peacetime, maintaining troops and fortifications for protection and ministers to impart proper justice; and the most scrupulous care is required of the viceroys as superintendents general of the Royal Treasury in knowing how to distribute the revenues properly and, perhaps even more important, to see that the royal officials collect and administer them with the necessary integrity and fidelity, which is difficult to achieve.

"To this point, therefore, I have suggested to your excellency that in a kingdom where there is no active commerce [legal], navigation has no function, and the inhabitants are poor, it can neither produce to enrich the Royal Treasury nor sustain the many responsibilities that must be met for its preservation and well-being. The clamor and representations of the governors and [their] subordinates cause the greatest distress, now manifesting the importance of various projects, [and] again the need to pay the troops and employees, without finding the means to realize the former nor to satisfy the latter. And from this situation, it results that dedication sometimes cools and the best intentions of a zealous viceroy remain fruitless, as he finds himself stretched because of the lack of funds. Indeed, a recourse to loans is not even an alternative where there is no one who can make them."[1]

With these plaintive remarks to his successor, Manuel Antonio Flores, Viceroy Manuel de Guirior in 1776 eloquently summarized the dilemma that royal government faced in the viceroyalty of New Granada. Although Guirior's affection for courtly diversion at the viceregal palace in Santa Fe hardly justified his self-description as "a zealous viceroy," the problems he identified were authentic and stood as major obstacles to the realization of the reformist Bourbon program.[2]

It is evident that the colonial reorganization initiated by Charles III and sustained by his son had only a relatively minor impact on New Granada. The disciplined militia system, among the most important of the Bourbon reforms, was applied mainly on the coast—albeit with some noteworthy short-term exceptions—and had little long-range influence on the institutional history of Colombia.[3] Royal revenues peaked during the late 1780s and had leveled off by the end of the colonial period at just under three million pesos, a modest sum that eloquently expressed the frustrations experienced in the area of revenue reform.[4] The structure of royal administration remained essentially unchanged. And the modernized mercantilism of the late Bourbons did very little to alter the established patterns of commerce.[5] Finally, despite a bold, promising beginning, an ambitious attempt at mining re-

1. Manuel de Guirior, "Relación del estado del Nuevo Reino de Granada . . . 1776," in Gabriel Giraldo Jaramillo (comp.), *Relaciones de mando de los virreyes de la Nueva Granada: Memorias económicas* (Bogotá, 1954), 87.

2. Vicente Palacio Atard, "Areche y Guirior: Observaciones sobre el fracaso de una visita al Perú," *AEA*, III (1946), 294; José Manuel Pérez Ayala, "Aspectos desconocidos de la vida del virrey don Manuel de Guirior, co-fundador de la Biblioteca Nacional de Bogotá," *BHA*, XLIII (1956), 170–82.

3. Allan J. Kuethe, *Military Reform and Society in New Granada, 1773–1808* (Gainesville, 1978), chap. 9.

4. Restrepo, *Historia de la revolución*, I, xxxi.

5. Luis Ospina Vásquez, *Industria y protección en Colombia, 1810–1930* (Medellín, 1955), 38–39.

form failed.[6] Indeed, except for the ill-fated mission of Regent-Visitor Juan Francisco Gutiérrez de Piñeres, Colombian historians have hardly taken notice of the Bourbon reforms, presumably because of the lack of tangible results. Yet from a broader imperial perspective, the experience of New Granada assumes importance because its unusual character provides clues to the workings of the late Spanish empire and the challenge faced by the statesmen who attempted to rebuild and sustain it. An examination of this experience also suggests explanations for the behavior of Colombians in 1810 and after.

Although a proven reformer as king of the Two Sicilies, the circumstances under which Charles III inherited the Spanish throne mitigated against ambitious innovations during the earliest years of his reign. His half-brother, Ferdinand VI (1746–1759), had lingered in a hopeless state for months before his death at Villaviciosa on August 10, 1759, a situation that in turn influenced the character of the governmental transition. Charles's mother, Isabel Farnese, had been a major force during the reign of her husband, Philip V (1700–1746), but in effect had been banished to Río Frío when her stepson ruled. As Ferdinand lay on his deathbed, she reported with alarm that the affairs of state were adrift and that she feared opportunists were taking advantage of the political vacuum. And despite repeated medical reports predicting his imminent demise, Ferdinand, who had gone quite mad, clung to life.[7] Because the laws of propriety demanded that Charles stand off at a prudent, respectable distance, the best he could do under the circumstances was issue a proclamation, dated February 13, 1759, that accorded his mother the power of regent in the event of Ferdinand's death.[8] Isabel, who was impatiently, if not indiscreetly, hovering about nearby La Granja, was thus able to rule indirectly, but she was forced to do so through the existing cabinet.

Fortunately, Isabel was able to work with Minister of State Ricardo Wall, the dominant figure in Ferdinand's government, both to stabilize the royal administration during his final days and

6. Sandra Cornell Montgomery, "The Bourbon Mining Reform in New Granada, 1783–1796" (M.A. thesis, Texas Tech University, 1984).

7. Isabel's correspondence with Charles can be found in the AHN, Estado, leg. 2548.

8. Proclamación, Caserta, February 13, 1759, AHN, Estado, leg. 2850.

to smooth the way for Charles's arrival from Italy in October. This arrangement, however, in effect committed the new monarch to the cabinet that he inherited. Apart from Wall, these men included Bailío Frey Julián de Arriaga, minister of the navy and the Indies, and the Marqués del Campo de Villar, who held the portfolio for the Ministry of Grace and Justice. Wall himself had become minister of war, an office that became vacant with the death of Sebastián de Eslava in June. The sole casualty of the transition was Minister of Finance Conde de Valparaíso, whom Charles replaced with a favorite from Italy, the Marqués de Esquilache, who had held the portfolios for the Ministries of Finance, War, and the Navy in Naples.[9]

Although moderately reformist, this government did not attempt major initiatives in colonial affairs. Building upon work that had begun under Ferdinand in the viceregal capital, for example, the Ministry of the Indies pressed ahead with modest plans in New Granada to tighten control over the aguardiente monopoly by replacing private concessionaires with salaried officials and in 1760 extended the modernized system to Mompós. Nothing, however, was done to address the complex question of commercial policy, the area of imperial administration most visibly demanding reform.[10] Spain's American trade remained the property of the Consulado de Cádiz, which held a legal monopoly over transactions between the colonies and the peninsula. Originally established more than two centuries earlier when the consulado resided in Seville, this system had obviously outlived its economic usefulness. The plan to liberalize commercial practices that has erroneously been attributed to José Campillo y Cossío appeared in the highest levels of government by the mid-1740s, and a host of new proposals greeted Charles upon his accession to the throne, including one by a young, still relatively unknown lawyer in Madrid, José de Gálvez.[11] In the face of the powerful vested interests

9. Allan J. Kuethe and Lowell Blaisdell, "The Esquilache Government and the Reforms of Charles III in Cuba," *Jahrbuch für Geschichte von Staat, Wirtschaft und Gesellschaft Lateinamerikas*, XIX (1982), 120–29.

10. Miklos Pogonyi, "The Search for Trade and Profits in Bourbon Colombia, 1765–1777" (Ph.D. dissertation, University of New Mexico, 1978), 163.

11. Luis Navarro García, "Campillo y el nuevo sistema: Una atribución dudosa," in

that influenced the politics at court, however, change was most difficult, as the consulado's history of survival surely shows. Minister of the Indies Julián de Arriaga, moreover, was not at all inclined to alter the existing arrangement. Apart from his naturally conservative instincts, Fray Arriaga had served during the early 1750s as president of the Casa de Contratación in Cádiz, the regulatory body that supervised the American trade, and he had developed strong personal ties to the merchant guild. Breaking the impasse on commercial policy would require a major jolt to the imperial system that might justify a sweeping reevaluation of existing regulations. Precisely such a blow was, of course, just around the corner, for on August 14, 1762, a triumphant British army marched into Havana, turning Charles's ill-advised intervention in the Seven Years' War into ignominious defeat.

Spain's reverses in the Seven Years' War, as confirmed by the Treaty of Paris, February 10, 1763, have often been characterized as a humiliation. This description is difficult to challenge, but the Spanish armed forces did hold out for over two months in Havana (longer than the much-heralded victors of 1741 at Cartagena) and suffered an incredible number of casualties. In the face of massive British striking power, the garrison simply lacked enough trained men to sustain a successful defense. As in the case of Cartagena, the invaders outnumbered the defenders roughly six to one, but the British, who had learned from their earlier defeat, curtailed the danger posed by disease through regular resupply and reinforcement from the North American colonies.[12] Spain emerged from the war still united with France under the Third Family Compact, and both powers resolved to seek revenge at the first opportunity. Even before the peace treaty was signed, the government of Charles III had initiated plans to place the American army on a competitive footing through a fundamental reorganization.

Appropriately, the crown's initial experiment with military reform and the fiscal, commercial, and administrative measures

---

Temas americanistas (Seville, 1983), II, 22–29. Proposals for commercial reorganization can be found in the BP, SMA, including the "Discurso y reflecciones" of Gálvez, Madrid, n.d., sig. 2816, fols. 109–32.

12. Allan J. Kuethe, *Cuba, 1753–1815: Crown, Military, and Society* (Knoxville, 1986), chap. 1.

that necessarily accompanied it were conducted in Cuba after Spain retrieved Havana in exchange for Florida. Because these reforms set the standard for the larger empire and offer an instructive contrast to later reforms implemented in New Granada, they require brief consideration. Accepting a plan devised by the Conde de Ricla to introduce the disciplined militia system into the island, Charles made the momentous decision to arm his colonists effectively in order to even the odds in the event of another invasion. This new militia system provided volunteer units with standardized tables of organization, uniforms and equipment, veteran officers and enlisted men integrated into the chain of command, weekly drills and bimonthly unit tactical maneuvers, and military corporate privileges. Ricla's plan also entailed a substantial strengthening of the veteran garrison. The cost of properly equipping and training the disciplined militia placed new demands upon the royal treasury as, to a greater extent, did the salaries and support expenses of the additional components of the regular army. On another level, fortification costs added more weight to the burden of military expenditures. It was thus understood when Charles sent Ricla to Cuba as governor and captain general that ambitious parallel reforms must accompany the military reorganization.[13]

Personnel adjustments in the royal cabinet paved the way for colonial reform. Minister of State and War Ricardo Wall was encouraged to resign because of his age. Minister of the Treasury Esquilache, who with the support of the queen mother quickly emerged as the dominant figure in the royal cabinet, acquired the Ministry of War, and the Marqués de Grimaldi, another Italian, ambassador to Paris, and coauthor of the Third Family Compact, returned to assume responsibility for the Ministry of State, also with Isabel's support. Arriaga survived as minister of the Indies, perhaps because of his reputation as an honest and reasonably competent administrator and because he offered a native presence in the government, but his influence with the king had diminished noticeably. His decline was confirmed when Charles established the Junta de Ministros upon Grimaldi's return in October. An interministerial commission consisting of Esquilache, Grimaldi,

13. Allan J. Kuethe and G. Douglas Inglis, "Absolutism and Enlightened Reform: Charles III, the Establishment of the Alcabala, and Commercial Reorganization in Cuba," *Past and Present*, no. 109 (November, 1985), 119–23.

and Arriaga, the junta assumed jurisdiction over the process of colonial reform, and thereafter the minister of finance and war, not the minister of the Indies, became the primary force behind the emerging colonial reorganization.[14]

In Esquilache's mind, commercial reform was the key to a resurgence of Spanish military power, or, to state the proposition more concretely, the destruction of the Cádiz monopoly, the opening of the American trade to additional Spanish ports, and a rationalization of customs duties and licensing procedures were indispensable steps toward rebuilding the colonial armies. These measures would amount to a modernization of mercantilistic arrangements and, he hoped, permit Spain to recapture that portion of the American trade lost to contraband as well as stimulate economic growth, all, of course, to the obvious advantage of the royal treasury and in turn military reform.

The question arises whether military necessities were the actual cause for the momentum behind commercial reorganization or simply the pretext, especially in light of the growing pressures for a liberalization of the trade laws that had emerged well before the war. It is doubtful, however, that the two issues were separable in either Esquilache's or Grimaldi's mind, or for most of the others committed to a modernization of the colonial system. Given the crisis mentality that enveloped the court after the losses suffered at Havana, the debate surrounding the implementation of reform in Cuba plainly showed that military necessity served as the rationale for nearly everything. But at least by the beginning of the new year, Esquilache contemplated a liberalization of commercial policy for all of the American empire except Mexico, and this included New Granada.[15] The Italian was clearly eager to exploit the opportunities of the moment to go beyond immediate military necessities.

Esquilache manipulated the Cuban situation skillfully to advance his larger purpose. Governor Ricla, as instructed by the minister of war and finance, consulted with the Havana elite during 1763–1765, declaring the administration's determination to raise taxes but alluding to commercial reform as a possible pal-

14. Kuethe and Blaisdell, "The Esquilache Government," 120–29.

15. Marquis d'Ossun to Duc de Choiseul, Madrid, January 23, 1764, AAE, CPE, Vol. 540, fols. 64–69.

liative. The *habaneros,* predictably, urged a liberalization of the trade laws and in particular the abolition of the Cádiz monopoly, but within the framework of a political trade-off they showed a willingness to accept a substantial increase in local taxation. They also understood that creole patricians would enjoy the honor of commands in the disciplined militia that the new revenues would support. Moreover, in another attempt to co-opt the Havana elite, the crown awarded four new titles of Castile over this same period while two more were in process.[16]

On another level, Field Marshal Alejandro O'Reilly, commissioned to Cuba with Ricla to effect the actual military reorganization, conducted a general *visita* of the island in conjunction with his other responsibilities. Returning to Havana in April, 1764, O'Reilly issued a comprehensive report blaming most of Cuba's ills on the inflexibility of the commercial system and made the outlandish claim that some one thousand British ships had called at Havana during the ten-month occupation. His central point—that commercial reform would benefit defense—could not be missed. A liberalized trade system would undercut contraband and stimulate economic growth, lead to a strengthening of the royal treasury, and therefore ultimately ensure a stronger military establishment.[17]

Soon after O'Reilly's report reached Spain, Esquilache acted to extend the Cuban question to the larger empire. On July 31, 1764, the Junta de Ministros appointed a select committee of five to examine the whole question of imperial commercial policy. Appointed to the committee were Francisco Craywinckel, Simón de Aragorri, the Marqués de los Llanos, Pedro Goosens, and Tomás Ortiz de Landazuri. The committee had a strong liberal orientation, for the latter three men were already on record as favoring a modernization of the existing system.[18] The Consulado de Cádiz attempted to bring its best political influence to bear in defense of its privileges, particularly through Manuel de Larrarte, its lobbyist at court, but Esquilache refused the monopoly guild entrance to

16. Kuethe and Inglis, "Absolutism and Enlightened Reform," 123–34.

17. A copy of the report from O'Reilly's *visita* is in the AGI, SD, leg. 1509.

18. The ideas of Ortiz de Landazuri and the Marqués de los Llanos can be found in BP, SMA, sig. 2867, fols. 49–53 and 101–15, and those of Goosens in AHN, Estado, leg. 2944.

the deliberations of the Junta de Ministros. In the political chemistry that prevailed after the Seven Years' War, the concerns of Havana carried more weight than those of Cádiz. Arriaga remained sympathetic to the consulado, but he was consistently outvoted in the Junta's proceedings.[19]

The report of the Committee on Commerce, dated February 14, 1765, leveled a deadly broadside at the prevailing commercial order. Blaming the loss of trade on the monopoly port system, irrational taxation based on weight and volume instead of value, and the delay and expense occasioned by the seemingly endless paperwork, inspections, and petty fees, the committee proposed sweeping changes. The most important suggestions were that colonial trade should be opened to all the provinces of Spain, licensing and inspection procedures simplified, and customs duties rationalized and converted to an ad valorem basis.[20]

In the politics at court, the report by the Committee on Commerce, as reinforced by the voice of Havana, provided Esquilache with the leverage he needed to overcome the opposition of the consulado. During the summer and early fall, Fray Arriaga did his best to block the extension of commercial concessions to Cuba, which was the immediate issue at hand but obviously just the first, politically expedient step in what promised to be a comprehensive reordering of the colonial commercial structure. Nevertheless, backed by Grimaldi, Esquilache prevailed before the king. Through the royal decree of October 16, 1765, the Cuban trade was opened to Alicante, Málaga, Cartagena, Barcelona, Santander, Gijón, La Coruña, and Seville in addition to Cádiz; most duties were consolidated and placed on an ad valorem basis; and Cubans were permitted to conduct trade on their own ships. In return, however, a royal order of that same date, building upon an earlier decree of April 25, 1764, raised the *alcabala* from 2 to 6 percent and confirmed new levies on colonial liquors. And an *intendente de ejército* had just arrived to streamline the collection and disbursement of royal revenues, this also an innovation from Es-

19. The resistance of the consulado to the prospect of commercial reform has been treated in G. Douglas Inglis and Allan J. Kuethe, "El Consulado de Cádiz y el Reglamento de Comercio Libre de 1765," in Bibiano Torres Ramírez and José Hernández Palomo (eds.), *Andalucía y América en el siglo XVIII* (Seville, 1985), I, 79–89.

20. This document can be found in the AHN, Estado, leg. 2314.

quilache's desk. On the other hand, much to the pleasure of the growing planter component in the Havana elite, the October order reduced export taxes on sugar, while conserving the Spanish ports' duty-free access to that same product.[21]

The government of Charles III, acting through the Junta de Ministros and in particular Esquilache, thus fashioned a politically workable reform package for Cuba. Military expenditures were increased through the establishment of a disciplined militia and an expansion of the regular army as well as by a commitment to repair and improve fortifications. To help defray these expenses, the crown raised taxes substantially but ameliorated this burden through timely revisions of the trade laws, a process conducted in consultation with Havana, whose pressing needs were played politically against the pretenses of Cádiz. The establishment of the intendant system promised efficiency in the execution of the new regulations.

Seen from a political perspective, commercial reform was the motor that made the rest work. Serving as compensation for tougher taxation, it laid the foundation for recapturing the Cuban trade, stimulating the island's economy, and structuring a cooperative relationship with the creole elite. The local patricians, after all, were expected to provide officers for the new militia, to sustain enlistments and provide uniforms through the *ayuntamientos,* and to accommodate the pretenses of military justice as exercised by the new volunteer units in their communities. The reforms implemented by Ricla, O'Reilly, and the Marqués de Esquilache created the framework for cooperation between crown and colony that endured well into the nineteenth century, and during the American Revolution, this relationship greatly contributed to Spanish revenge upon the British in the Gulf of Mexico.[22] In these respects, Cuba had little in common with New Granada.

The Spanish crown rarely legislated for its empire as a whole. Given the size and complexity of its dominions, good sense dictated that major initiatives in colonial policy proceed by trial and error and with adjustments for local realities. Within this context, the Caribbean islands were normally treated as a unit; accordingly,

21. Kuethe and Inglis, "Absolutism and Enlightened Reform," 138–40.

22. Kuethe, *Cuba, 1753–1815,* chaps. 4, 6.

the royal decree of October, 16, 1765, also encompassed Puerto Rico, Santo Domingo, Trinidad, and Margarita, and intercolonial trade in non-European commodities was permitted among the islands. Moreover, after leaving Cuba, Alejandro O'Reilly extended the disciplined militia system to Puerto Rico.

Given the expectation of another war, the Esquilache government also moved with dispatch in other areas. A joint expedition headed by Lieutenant General Juan de Villalba y Angulo and Francisco Armona left for New Spain in 1764 to introduce military, financial, and administrative reform. Armona's death aboard ship, however, led to the appointment of the famous José de Gálvez as his replacement. This expedition, significantly, did not anticipate commercial reform, for the royal administration hoped at this stage to develop first the peripheries of the empire, lest they otherwise be overwhelmed by competition from Mexico, the wealthiest of the American colonies. The authorities also seemed to fear contraband less in New Spain than in most other colonies, and, in any event, the results of the Cuban experiment would need to be weighed before further advances were attempted.[23] In Peru, where the respected Viceroy Manuel de Amat had already labored long and hard to bring order to the colony's defenses, the crown issued an order in 1763 to standardize the militia system. Eventually, copies of the regulation drafted for the militia of Cuba arrived.[24]

In the midst of all of this activity, New Granada was an anomaly in several important respects. It was the only one of the three viceroyalties not to undertake military reform during 1763–1764, despite Cartagena's status as the second or third most important military stronghold in Spanish America as well as Panama's lingering, if declining, significance as an interoceanic crossroads. Nor was the viceroyalty subject to a reformist *visita* such as that of O'Reilly in Cuba or Gálvez in New Spain. Peru, of course, had no such mission either, but in a practical sense it was much more remote from military danger and therefore, presumably, could make do with less. In any event the southern viceroyalty enjoyed the dy-

23. John Fisher, "Imperial 'Free Trade' and the Hispanic Economy, 1778–1796," *JLAS*, XIII (1981), 21–23. See also n. 15 above.

24. Leon G. Campbell, *The Military and Society in Colonial Peru, 1750–1810* (Philadelphia, 1978), chaps. 2–3.

namic military leadership of Manuel Amat. The neglect of New Granada during these early years arose from a lack of royal revenues and any immediate hope of correcting that deficiency on a short-term basis.

Viceroy Pedro Messía de la Cerda (1761–1772), proud of his achievements in improving the condition of the royal treasury despite formidable odds, reported in 1767 that the income for New Granada during the first six years of his administration had averaged 693,398 silver pesos and 41,252 golden *castellanos* annually as compared to the average of 481,506 pesos and 36,309 *castellanos* that his predecessor, José de Solís, had registered. The colonial treasury had indeed made a relatively important advance, but compared to other jurisdictions, it was poverty-stricken. Peru's treasury, for example, collected about five times what Messía claimed and New Spain's, ten.[25] Revealingly, the Mexican subsidy to Cuba during 1763–1769 averaged more than twice the sum Messía raised in New Granada.[26] The central difficulty in Santa Fe was the paucity of tax revenues from commerce and mining. Mining revenues went far to sustain Peru and help explain the relative affluence of the royal administration there. Viceroy Guirior, distressed by the lack of alternatives, hoped that mining might someday do as much for New Granada.[27] For the moment, however, the main problem was the inability of the royal administration to harness, manipulate, and tax the commerce of New Granada, which flowed in and out with little interference and seldom paid any duties.

This sort of predicament was, of course, exactly what Esquilache's program as developed in Cuba was intended to remedy. Local elites, tempted by liberalized trade laws, possible tax incentives, and the prospect of personal and military honors for those willing to serve the king, might well be drawn into a constructive relationship with the royal administration both to promote eco-

25. Treasury Report, Messía de la Cerda, Santa Fe, September 27, 1767, AGI, SF, 576; Campbell, *The Military and Society*, 71; D. A. Brading, *Miners and Merchants in Bourbon Mexico, 1763–1810* (Cambridge, England, 1971), 53.

26. The *situado* data for Cuba are reproduced in Allan J. Kuethe, "Guns, Subsidies, and Commercial Privilege: Some Historical Factors in the Emergence of the Cuban National Character, 1763–1815," *Cuban Studies*, XVI (1986), 130.

27. Guirior, "Relación," in Jaramillo (comp.), *Relaciones de Mando*, 65.

nomic growth and legal trade and to structure an effective defense against the British foe. Major initiatives, however, would have to await positive results from the experiment in the islands to sway sympathy away from the Consulado de Cádiz. Above all, it would be politically hazardous to tighten revenue collection too radically without first reaching a political understanding with the colonial elites.

Under these circumstances, the Esquilache government found itself compelled to operate within limited spheres in promoting revenue reform in New Granada and forced to delay indefinitely the reorganization of the viceregal army. The program to place the aguardiente monopoly under the control of salaried officials was extended to Cartagena and Honda, and Viceroy Messía de la Cerda sent a special agent, Juan Díaz de Herrera, to Popayán and Quito in 1764 to advance that same process in those jurisdictions and to convert the administration of the *alcabala* from tax farmers to salaried officials. More ambitious was Esquilache's plan for a royal tobacco monopoly. Such monopolies had earlier been established in Cuba (1717), Peru (1752), and Chile (1753–1754).[28] Esquilache, who was himself a connoisseur of the Cuban-grown leaf, assumed personal control over the monopoly through the Ministry of Finance and envisioned extending the scheme throughout the empire. Introduced on a limited basis in New Granada in 1764, the tobacco monopoly became an important contributor to the treasury as early as 1772. It was destined to become the single most lucrative source of royal income in the viceroyalty.[29]

The limits of the crown's ability to alter quickly the character of royal revenue collection was exposed graphically by the dramatic upheaval that erupted in Quito during 1765 and swept through the Cauca Valley into the Chocó in reaction to the revenue reform initiatives of Díaz Herrera.[30] Quito had been depressed economically owing to the long-term effects of epidemics among the Indian population during the 1690s and to the legalization of the Cape

28. Pogonyi, "The Search for Trade," 161–63, 180–82.

29. Royal Cedula, El Pardo, January 25, 1766, AHNC, Reales Cédulas, tomo 17, fols. 40–41; Margarita González, "El estanco colonial del tabaco," *Cuadernos colombianos,* no. 8 (1975), 649–50, 685; Moreno y Escandón, "Estado del Virreinato," 605.

30. Anthony McFarlane, "Civil Disorder and Popular Protests in Late Colonial New Granada," *HAHR,* LXIV (1984), 23–27.

Horn shipping route to the Pacific in mid-century and would have been a problem colony under any circumstance, but the gravity of the upheaval pointed to the political difficulty of raising revenues in the uplands to sustain faraway military bases. Surplus *quiteño* revenues were destined for Cartagena, whose connection to the Ecuatorial highlands must have seemed remote indeed. What sort of political arrangement, if any, might have forestalled this confrontation is difficult to gauge, but as is well known, consultation and compromise were not part of the reform program. The Quito rebellion surely dampened hopes at court that revenue reform could be advanced very far on its own terms. It is highly instructive that during the remainder of the decade and into the early 1770s, the royal administration made no further attempt to modernize the operations of the aguardiente monopoly in New Granada.[31]

As explained earlier, the Esquilache government fully understood the connection between commercial reform, revenue reform, and military reform, and it stood poised to extend the decree of October, 1765, at the first opportunity, presumably as soon as the Cuban experiment had shown positive results. Such hopes and plans, however, were shattered by the famous Madrid riots of March, 1766, and the resulting fall and exile of the Italian minister. What role, if any, the Consulado de Cádiz might have had in the revolution against the Esquilache government is uncertain, but it is perfectly clear that the guild sought to exploit the situation to limit the damage to its commercial privileges and, at least in the short-term, did so effectively. The smoke had hardly cleared in Madrid before the consulado's lobbyist, Manuel de Larrarte, had cornered Minister of the Indies Arriaga at Aranjuez to press the guild's case. The departure of Esquilache, soon followed by the death of Isabel Farnese, permitted Fray Arriaga to regain his stature in the royal cabinet. He remained a friend of the consulado until his death in January, 1776.[32]

The ten-year interlude between the fall of Esquilache and the appointment of José de Gálvez to succeed Arriaga was a period characterized by conservatism in colonial policy. In the troubled

31. A limited innovation occurred in 1774 when Guirior placed the monopoly of Zipaquirá under the administration in Santa Fe, but this was the only such step until the arrival of Regent-Visitor Gutiérrez de Piñeres. Pogonyi, "The Search for Trade," 162–64.

32. Inglis and Kuethe, "El Consulado de Cádiz," 90–91.

days following the Madrid riots, Charles found no one of Esquilache's stature to renew the cause of imperial reform. Neither Juan Gregorio Muniain, who succeeded to the Ministry of War, nor Miguel de Múzquiz, who took the Ministry of Finance, asserted a strong hand in colonial affairs. The consulado's access to the central government, which had in practice been closed during Esquilache's time, became intimate indeed. Prior Francisco Montes, for example, was appointed royal treasurer in 1770, and although a sense of propriety ultimately led him to take leave of his official position with the merchant guild, he nevertheless continued to sustain contact with his old friends and business associates.[33] Talk even circulated at court for a time that the October, 1765, decree for the Caribbean Islands might be withdrawn, but given the commitments made in Cuba and the system already in place, such dreams were unrealistic.[34] So too, on the other hand, were hopes that the liberalized structure might be extended very far, though several limited advances occurred. These included the incorporation of Yucatán into the Caribbean system in 1770, as well as a 1774 regulation legalizing intercolonial commerce in the Pacific.[35] The Cádiz monopoly, nevertheless, remained essentially unscathed.

Within this framework, the colonial reorganization in New Granada languished. Without the revenues and political arrangements that might have accompanied a modernization of the trade laws, little could be done in other spheres. Viceroy Guirior's lamentation, quoted at the beginning of this essay, pinpointed eloquently the predicament of the royal government in Santa Fe. He might have added that the viceroyalty was a sieve through which trade entered and left on its own terms, quite independent of royal policy, and that without fundamental readjustments little improvement could be expected.[36] Meanwhile, revenues from the aguardiente and the tobacco monopolies continued to grow, although

33. AGI, Consulado de Cádiz, libro 84, esp., the consulado to Arriaga, Cádiz, January 23, 1770.

34. Inglis and Kuethe, "El Consulado de Cádiz," 91.

35. J. Muñoz Pérez, "La publicación del Reglamento de Comercio Libre de Indias, de 1778," *AEA*, IV (1947), 640–42.

36. Guirior's frustrations are treated in Manuel Lucena Salmoral, "Apuntes para un diálogo sobre el Virreinato del Nuevo Reino de Granada en 1776," in *Hispanoamérica hacia 1776* (Madrid, 1980), 210–13.

the gains in the liquor monopoly came principally from Cartagena. In the interior, where the royal officials found themselves compelled to tread lightly, income showed signs of stagnating.[37] The staid pattern of the post-Esquilache period was broken only when an international crisis unexpectedly intervened, bringing the empire to the brink of war.

Spain's hopes for a reckoning with the United Kingdom had faded by the late 1760s as France cooled toward the idea of an early confrontation. Frustrated by its inability to use the Third Family Compact to gain special access to the American trade and skeptical about Spain's progress in preparing its empire for another war, the French were reluctant to commit themselves where little national advantage seemed likely. Under these circumstances, the Spanish crown was able to make do in New Granada with the seriously flawed army that Charles had inherited from his half-brother. Cartagena was garrisoned by one fixed battalion and two artillery companies, and Santa Marta by two infantry companies and one-half artillery company. Panama's fixed battalion had disintegrated, leaving only an artillery company. In the commandancy general of Quito, five small infantry companies established after the 1765 uprising garrisoned Guayaquil (one), Quito (three), and Popayán (one). The viceregal guard completed the army of New Granada. As a result of the Quito affair, two battalions from the Regiment of the Queen had also been deployed in Panama and Quito in 1766, and in 1769 they were replaced by single battalions from the Regiments of Murcia and Naples, both of which stayed in Panama. Significantly, the militia remained undisciplined.[38] During late 1770 and early 1771, the furor that resulted from Governor Francisco Bucareli's expulsion of an attempted British settlement in the Falkland (Malvinas) Islands changed much of this.

Charles, who seemed perfectly prepared to use British behavior in the incident as proper cause for war, named Alejandro

37. For statistics on the aguardiente monopoly, see Gilma Mora de Tovar, "La política fiscal del estado colonial y el monopolio de la industria del aguardiente en la Nueva Granada durante el siglo XVIII," *Desarollo y sociedad,* no. 10 (1983), 100; for tobacco, see Pogonyi, "The Search for Trade and Profits," 198. The *conservador de rentas reales,* Francisco Moreno y Escandón, reported in 1772 that the two monopolies had already become major sources of income for the viceroyalty (Moreno y Escandón, "Estado del Virreinato," 605).

38. Kuethe, *Military Reform and Society,* table 1.

O'Reilly inspector general of the army of America and directed him to supervise the emergency deployment of Spanish troops in the colonies. This buildup included a battalion from the Regiment of Savoy to reinforce the Cartagena garrison. The crisis passed, however, when Louis XV, troubled by severe internal problems, withdrew his kingdom's support and urged his cousin to seek peace.[39] Nevertheless, by bringing the empire to the verge of international conflict, the incident had served as a reminder of the unattended problems exposed by the last war.

The furor had also led to the elevation of the dynamic O'Reilly. Vested with powers that made him virtually autonomous within the Ministry of the Indies, O'Reilly in effect acted as minister of war for the colonies, and he used his power accordingly, resuming work on the military reform that he had begun in Cuba and Puerto Rico, but that had languished elsewhere since the fall of Esquilache.[40] Because New Granada lacked the funds requisite for a comprehensive program, the inspector general was compelled to proceed piecemeal, focusing upon the most vital strongpoints and operating through the local authorities rather than a specialized, high-level commission. Moreover, military reform, though conveying coveted corporate privileges, was not sweetened through a connection to commercial concessions or an effort to draw local elites into a kind of practical understanding with the crown. Consequently, although a measure of progress would occur in the regular army, the attempt to establish a disciplined militia was not destined to enjoy much immediate success.

Beginning preparations in mid-1771, O'Reilly officially initiated the reform process through a series of orders dating from late 1772 through early 1773. These measures doubled Cartagena's fixed infantry to a regiment of two battalions, reestablished a fixed battalion in Panama, and authorized a disciplined militia of three battalions and twelve separate companies for the isthmus and for Cartagena at a level that the local authorities might find appropriate, judged in Spain to be about four battalions. In fact, the officials of Cartagena went well beyond that mark, raising two bat-

39. Julius Goebel, *The Struggle for the Falkland Islands: A Study in Legal and Diplomatic History* (New Haven, 1927), 271–410.

40. Expediente, inspector generalship, 1770–1771, AGI, IG, leg. 1885.

talions and 62½ separate companies. Although the municipalities were normally expected to equip the militiamen, O'Reilly, for obvious reasons, sent the supplies for the new units from Spain. He also sent cadres of veteran officers and enlisted men to train New Granada's volunteers, though not enough; theoretically the remainder were to come from the expanded veteran garrisons.

Not surprisingly, the woes of the reorganized militia of Panama and Cartagena were many. The number of units exceeded what the supplies sent from Spain could equip, what the veteran cadres could instruct, and what the population could realistically sustain. Part of the problem was that Viceroy Guirior chose to remain in Santa Fe, thus permitting the governors a free hand. Unfortunately, deaths had left both governorships in the hands of interim administrators, neither of whom managed the reorganization with skill or a proper sense of responsibility. Moreover, ordinary justices in both Cartagena and Panama balked at the intrusion of the *fuero militar* into the everyday life of their communities, and they engaged the reformed army in a series of jurisdictional disputes.

When Viceroy Flores descended to the coast in 1779 to assume personal command of Cartagena upon the outbreak of war, he found that the two battalions based in the city of Cartagena itself showed a measure of proficiency but that nearly all of the backland units of the province lacked training, if they even existed at all, and many of the units in Panama had completely disintegrated. Although Flores, assisted by Lieutenant Colonel Anastasio Zejudo, would impose order in the city's volunteer units, the early years of military reform on the coast were obviously an overall failure.[41]

The work in Cartagena, nevertheless, was a first-class operation compared to the extension of the military reform to Guayaquil and Popayán that followed. This phase of the colonial reorganization came at the initiative of the colonial authorities without proper support at any level. In 1775, Guirior, acting with royal approval, commissioned Captain Víctor Salcedo y Somodevilla to organize a disciplined militia in Guayaquil using officers and enlisted men from the fifty-man veteran garrison to train it and ask-

41. Kuethe, *Military Reform and Society*, chaps. 1–2.

ing volunteer officers to uniform their own companies in return for their commissions. His successor Flores launched a similar project for Popayán. In both instances, the want of proper support showed in unfulfilled objectives, but in the absence of adequate revenues and a comprehensive reform package, little more was possible.

In this respect, Popayán is particularly instructive. Raised in the interest of internal security at the initiative of Captain Diego Antonio Nieto of the Fixed Infantry Company, the Popayán militia consisted of fourteen poorly equipped companies. When it became evident in the city of Popayán that the municipality's companies would be commanded by Spaniards and employed to sustain the governor's authority in the area of revenue collection, the reformers encountered persistent obstructionism. At the behest of patricians like Don Pedro Valencia and Francisco Basilio de Angulo, young creoles refused subordinate commissions, the *ayuntamiento* waged jurisdictional challenges to the *fuero militar,* and the popular voice demeaned those who were willing to serve as soldiers for the king.[42] The experience of Popayán contrasted with that of Cuba, where crown and creole cooperated toward mutually acceptable goals. Perhaps such cooperation was intrinsically impossible in an interior province where military spending patterns were bound to be unfavorable, but no attempt was made to define an acceptable common ground. With the trade laws still subordinate to the interests of Cádiz, the possibility of ambitious pragmatism was remote.

An intriguing outgrowth of the military reorganization emerged in an attempt by Viceroys Guirior and Flores to secure effective control over the Guajiro Peninsula and thus seal off the important contraband route that passed through Riohacha. The Guajiro Indians had recently expelled the Capuchin missionaries from their lands, openly defying the Spanish authorities. Soon after the Falkland Islands crisis abated, Viceroy Messía de la Cerda had sent 400 men from the Regiment of Savoy, 300 regulars from the garrisons of Cartagena and Santa Marta, and 340 untrained militiamen to punish the Guajiros for their outrageous treatment of the Capuchin fathers, but when confronted by overwhelming,

42. *Ibid.*, chap. 3.

well-armed Indian forces, the commander of the expedition prudently withdrew. With the use of direct military force no longer an option, Guirior attacked the problem by establishing four fortified, strategically located outposts. Staffed by missionaries and populated by small numbers of settlers, these strongpoints were sustained by detachments from the garrison of Cartagena, which had just undergone the reorganization ordered by O'Reilly. The fortified outposts, it was hoped, would obstruct the flow of contraband and, through a combination of intimidation and evangelization, woo the aboriginals into the Spanish imperial system.

For a time, this strategy seemed marginally successful, but in late 1775, the Guajiros, who had lost patience with Spanish meddling in their affairs, demolished the fortified outpost of Apiesi. Although a general uprising accompanied this blow to the pacification strategy, the royal administration could do precious little about it. To subdue the peninsula would require thousands of troops, something that Cartagena did not possess, and, in any event, the outbreak of the American Revolution with all its attendant international implications dictated that Cartagena retain its main force. After the Spanish declaration of war on Great Britain, Viceroy Flores recalled the bulk of the expeditionary army, and thereafter the colonial authorities sustained only a token force in the Guajiro territory, this in a relatively safe stronghold. Years later, in 1790, the last of the troops were finally withdrawn. Without the requisite finances and military forces, the Guajiro Peninsula was destined to remain outside effective royal control, and its function as a major conduit for contraband ensured that the royal authorities would continue to lack the financial and military means to subdue it.[43]

It is evident, then, that the early reforms of Charles III only negligibly affected the viceroyalty of New Granada. Moderate exceptions were the gains made by the tobacco monopoly and by eliminating tax farming in other areas. Total royal revenues had risen to roughly 950,000 pesos by 1772.[44] A case can also be made

43. This subject is treated in greater depth in Allan J. Kuethe, "The Pacification Campaign on the Riohacha Frontier, 1772–1779," *HAHR,* L (1970), 467–81.

44. Moreno y Escandón, "Estado del Virreinato," 602–606.

that the military improved. The veteran garrison was expanded, which surely counted for something. Moreover, a battalion or so of Cartagena's disciplined militia developed a measure of proficiency as shown a bit later when the volunteer units contributed some 250 men to the force that marched from the coast to contain the Comunero Rebellion.[45] Nevertheless, in the larger sense these achievements amounted to very little and left José de Gálvez a very poor hand to play when he became minister of the Indies in 1776.

Lexington and Concord, Bunker Hill, and the approach of war opened the way for a resumption of the work that the exile of Esquilache had left undone. With so little time and only a limited foundation to work from in New Granada, however, Gálvez' men, especially Juan Francisco Gutiérrez de Piñeres, had to operate under highly unfavorable conditions as they financially prepared the colony for war. Gutiérrez' radical, intemperate measures are notorious, but it is important to remember that he was asked to initiate a reform of the tax structure before the Regulation of Free Trade was finally promulgated, and that despite the unfavorable political circumstances that he confronted, he operated without appropriate military support. These difficulties were further complicated by the intrinsic hostility that the highlands harbored for the outflow of monies for remote coastal defenses. The ensuing catastrophe is well known.

The scars of the Comunero Rebellion would remain, and despite the commercial reorganization of 1778, an accommodation to bring the colony into a satisfactory, workable relationship with the mother country failed to emerge. The military reform was extended to the key inland district of Santa Fe and was renewed in Popayán, but the army never found acceptance in these areas, where it stood behind unpopular fiscal policies. Although royal revenues reached an all-time high during the 1780s, the inland garrison cost more than its presence contributed to the royal coffers. When moderate men withdrew much of the military from the interior after the death of Gálvez, revenue collection quickly waned.[46]

45. Kuethe, *Military Reform and Society,* 86–87.

46. Allan J. Kuethe, "More on the 'Culmination of the Bourbon Reforms': A Perspective from New Granada," *HAHR,* LVIII (1978), 477–80.

During the 1790s, moreover, the creole elite's ready acceptance of the ideals of the French Revolution exposed the tenuousness of Spain's grip on the colony. Given the utter failure of Bourbon colonialism in New Granada, one is tempted to wonder what might have happened had Esquilache had more time. Unfortunately, history does not disclose its alternatives.

SANDRA MONTGOMERY KEELAN

Chapter 2

The Bourbon Mining Reform in New Granada, 1784–1796

The silver-mining reform mission to New Granada was the product of an age of reform and enlightenment. The Spanish crown sought a more efficient exploitation of the mines to increase royal revenue, a commodity in short supply in the colony, owing, at least in part, to the royal administration's inability to harness trade and thereby generate acceptable levels of taxation. The idea of applying science to the economy gained prominence during the eighteenth century.[1] The mining reform was a striking instance of invoking this new approach to achieve royal objectives. Yet it was also an experiment that revealed the limitations of reform imposed from above without proper preparation at the local level.

Despite its reputation as one of the empire's more backward colonies, New Granada shared in the course of the Spanish-American enlightenment, thanks largely to the beliefs and actions of Archbishop Antonio Caballero y Góngora who served as vice-

1. Frank Safford, *The Ideal of the Practical: Colombia's Struggle to Form a Technical Elite* (Austin, 1976), 92.

roy from 1782 to 1789.[2] Best known for his ability to maintain political harmony between the crown and creoles in the troubled aftermath of the Comunero Rebellion of 1781, Caballero y Góngora was intellectually an apostle of the modern age. He viewed knowledge as a useful tool for progress and prosperity, or more specifically, as the means to please the crown by making economic enterprises more profitable through scientific and technological advancement.

One means by which the archbishop-viceroy called attention to the importance of science was through his patronage of New Granada's famous botanical expedition, organized in 1783 under the leadership of José Celestino Mutis, which won acclaim for its achievements throughout the scientific world.[3] Another example of his commitment to science was his sponsorship of the mineralogical expedition headed by Juan José D'Elhúyar.

On the European side, the D'Elhúyar mining expedition's roots can be traced to the navy's decision in 1777 to revitalize Spain's weapons factories. The navy had been procuring its gunnery from Scotland, but with the peace of Europe threatened by the American Revolution, the crown hoped to identify experts who could reform the domestic industry. An elaborate interviewing process led to the selection of two Basque brothers from Logroño in northern Spain, Juan José and Fausto D'Elhúyar, who had studied chemistry in Paris. Both were sent to top European schools of mining and metallurgy, and Juan José was expected to continue on to Scotland to pirate British technology.[4]

At Freiberg, Juan José studied under some of the best scholars in Europe, establishing himself as an expert in metallurgy and mining. He then journeyed to Sweden to study under the famous professor and chemist in Uppsala, Torbern Olaf Bergmann, under whom he hoped to further his education, but also to verify what he had heard about Swedish arms. Along with Bergmann, Karl Wilhelm Scheele, one of the discoverers of oxygen, was especially

2. José Manuel Pérez Ayala, *Antonio Caballero y Góngora, virrey y arzobispo de Santa Fe, 1723–1796* (Bogotá, 1951), 126, 150.

3. A. Federico Gredilla, *Biografía de José Celestino Mutis con relación de su viaje y estudios practicados en el Nuevo Reino de Granada* (Madrid, 1911), 104–106.

4. Arthur P. Whitaker, "The Elhúyar Mining Missions and the Enlightenment," *HAHR,* XXXI (1951), 560–65, 571.

helpful and encouraging. This stimulating education led D'Elhúyar to the discovery of tungsten in 1783 soon after his return to Spain. He made this discovery with the help of his brother, Fausto, who, though a valuable assistant, did not possess the expertise that Juan José had gained from his stint in Sweden. Unfortunately, the young Spaniard never received the credit he deserved for his discovery, because he was in New Granada by the time the publications about the element appeared. Further, his shy and reticent personality did not lend itself to the pursuit of fame.[5] Fausto, who was still in Spain when the news became public in Europe, received most of the credit, but it had been Juan José's expertise that led to the discovery.

Juan José returned to Spain without attempting his mission to Scotland, which he viewed as useless, given what he had learned in Uppsala, and he informed the navy that the Swedish technique for making cannons was superior to that of the Scots. This assertion, after the crown had plans well underway to convert to the Scottish method, coupled with his refusal to spy in Scotland, led Minister of the Navy Marqués González de Castejón to dismiss him in February, 1783. Castejón died soon thereafter, however, and D'Elhúyar was rehired, this time as an employee of José de Gálvez, the minister of the Indies.[6]

In New Granada, the archbishop-viceroy had written to Gálvez in 1782 analyzing the condition of silver mining in his kingdom and holding out hope that a revival of the industry might produce badly needed revenues. Despite the recent low yields, he believed that the mines had great potential if exploited properly. He also suggested trying smelting rather than amalgamation, the method that had been used in the past.[7]

Caballero y Góngora's hypothesis regarding the advantage of smelting over amalgamation seemed timely since that same issue had been debated at length in Europe during the years immediately preceding his report. The patio amalgamation method was widely used in Spanish America, though in general modern Euro-

5. Stig Ryden, *Don Juan José de Elhúyar en Suecia (1781–1782)* (Madrid, 1963), 26; Bernardo J. Caycedo, *D'Elhúyar y el siglo XVIII neogranadino* (Bogotá, 1971), 38.

6. Caycedo, *D'Elhúyar,* 572.

7. Antonio Caballero y Góngora to José de Gálvez, Santa Fe, October 14, 1782, AGI, SF, leg. 837.

pean thinkers favored smelting. The archbishop-viceroy's recommendation was enthusiastically received by Gálvez, who had written a paper on gold and silver mining in Spanish America in 1760 advocating smelting over amalgamation.[8]

A switch to smelting also made strategic sense because the amalgamation process required mercury, which was difficult to obtain in Spanish America. The colonies acquired much of their supply from Spain, which both mined mercury domestically and imported it. In times of war, however, this source often proved unreliable. Currently, only one mercury mine was worth exploiting in all of Spanish America, that in Huancavelica, Peru. This mine was heavily worked in connection with the recent boom in silver mining in Mexico, but was showing disturbing signs of decline. Experts had been searching for a new source of mercury in Spanish America in the hope of establishing the capacity to sustain uninterrupted mining by reducing dependence on imported mercury, but this search had not been fruitful.[9]

The basic difficulty with the patio amalgamation process was that it wasted mercury. Baron von Born was later to develop a much more efficient amalgamation process, but not until 1785, shortly after Juan José D'Elhúyar had launched the mining reform mission in New Granada. In the meantime, Gálvez did not consider finding a local source of mercury the most feasible way of exploiting the Spanish-American mines. It was instructive that the royal administration selected the mining technique prior to the D'Elhúyar mission rather than after a scientist or technician had examined the mines. Despite Gálvez' exposure to science, which far exceeded that of most royal administrators, he failed to observe during his visit to Mexico that the mining areas lacked enough fuel to sustain smelting.[10] Unfortunately, this reality prevailed in most of the mining regions of Spanish America.

Gálvez, who had seen the Comuneros blunt his ambitious plans to increase royal revenues in New Granada, acted quickly on Caballero y Góngora's proposal. In early 1783, he wrote the viceroy that his proposal on mining reform was "consistent with royal

8. Whitaker, "Elhúyar Mining Missions," 574–75; Herbert Ingram Priestley, *José de Gálvez, Visitor-General of New Spain, 1765–1771* (Berkeley, 1916), 321.

9. Whitaker, "Elhúyar Mining Missions," 574–77.

10. *Ibid.*, 577.

intentions" and that he would seek a scientist qualified to upgrade the industry in New Granada. He named Juan José D'Elhúyar director of the reform mission soon thereafter.[11] Having just discovered tungsten, Juan José was ready for a new challenge.

D'Elhúyar received his instructions to regenerate the silver-mining industry in New Granada through the use of smelting in December, 1783. Although he now enjoyed the security of a contract, he was also limited by its provisions. His method was predetermined even though he had never seen the mines to ascertain which technique would be preferable. He was sent to institute a specified system, not to experiment and innovate. This arrangement represented a departure from his earlier experiences since he had customarily enjoyed a certain amount of academic freedom to investigate the new technologies being developed throughout Europe and to select the ideas that seemed the most feasible. Now he was to act as a technician rather than an innovator. The contract also stipulated that he was to teach his technology to the colonists so that they could use the smelting method to expand the mining industry.[12]

That his mission was so clearly defined might well have been the result of the royal administration's previous experience with D'Elhúyar's independence of mind. He had earlier advocated Swedish over Scottish technology after plans had already been made to convert the Spanish munition works to the Scottish method. In the present instance, the crown, wanting its preconceived ideas brought to fruition, took a highly competent scientist and ordered him to administer a method which, as fate would have it, soon became outdated. D'Elhúyar's earlier attempt at evaluating European technology had cost him his job and, unfortunately, his experience with cannonry was to foreshadow his destiny with the mining mission. Whatever the reason for the clear delineation of his duties in the New World, he left Europe on an assignment fraught with limitations.

In 1785, after innumerable complications and delays, D'Elhúyar and his staff reached the royally owned silver mines in the

11. Gálvez to Caballero y Góngora, El Pardo, January 31, 1783, AGI, SF, leg. 837; Juan José D'Elhúyar to Gálvez, San Ildefonso, September 22, 1783, in Caycedo, *D'Elhuyar,* 68.

12. Royal Order, December 31, 1783, AGI, SF, leg. 837.

province of Mariquita, which after a period of exploitation in the seventeenth century had fallen into disuse. This site had been chosen for him by Caballero y Góngora and José Celestino Mutis, leader of the famous botanical expedition. Mutis had acquired a small amount of mining experience during 1766–1770 at the royal mines of Montuosa in Pamplona. He also had knowledge of a mining project undertaken in the province of Ibagué that had ended in failure, largely because of insufficient funding.[13]

The archbishop-viceroy wrote Mutis concerning the mining reform project while he was doing botanical research in the province of Mariquita. Caballero y Góngora, who respected Mutis as a friend as well as a scientist, asked him to conduct a secret investigatory mission to ascertain the condition of the mines in that province and determine which were being worked, which had been abandoned, and which seemed to hold the most potential. He emphasized the confidential nature of the mission, admonishing him to maintain secrecy at all costs.[14]

Mutis reported to Caballero y Góngora on May 25, 1784, describing the mines as rich in potential. He attributed their decadence to a lack of labor, not a deficiency of minerals. The abolition of the *mita* early in the century, he argued, had led to the current lack of productivity. Implying strongly that a revival was feasible, he described at length the mines' potential and lamented that the crown had abolished the *mita* "without contemplating beforehand the mortal blow that the whole kingdom would suffer." Mutis closed his letter with the recommendation that the incoming experts themselves decide which mines to work since so many appeared to have potential. Thus, although he obeyed his instructions to investigate, he showed respect for technological opinion by leaving the choice of mines to the experts themselves.[15] Unfor-

13. José Celestino Mutis to Caballero y Góngora, Mariquita, May 25, 1784, in Vicente Restrepo, *Estudios sobre las minas de oro y plata de Colombia* (2nd ed.; Bogotá, 1888), 300–301; Gredilla, *Biografía de José Celestino Mutis*, 142, 146.

14. Charles H. Bowman, "Antonio Caballero y Góngora y Manuel Torres: La cultura en la Nueva Granada," *BHA*, LVIII (1971), 427; Caballero y Góngora to Mutis, Santa Fe, March 30, 1783, in Guillermo Hernández de Alba (comp.), *Archivo epistolar del sabio naturalista Don José Celestino Mutis* (Bogotá, 1968–1975), III, 35–36.

15. Mutis to Caballero y Góngora, Mariquita, May 25, 1784, in Restrepo, *Minas de Colombia*, 300–301.

tunately, his assertion that the Mariquita silver mines had great potential effectively limited the geographic focus of the reform mission's work.

Mutis sent a second communication dated May 26, 1784, further expressing his eagerness to contribute to the fomentation of the Mariquita mines.[16] He wrote to Caballero y Góngora as a colleague and a friend. It is important to remember, however, that his scientific background in mining was limited. The archbishop-viceroy and Mutis had thus laid the groundwork for the mining mission long before D'Elhúyar and his brother-in-law, Angel Díaz, reached New Granada. Although well intentioned, the decision to locate the expedition in Mariquita province would have unfortunate results.

When D'Elhúyar arrived in Mariquita in February, 1785, he surveyed royal mines designated for his direction and sent the archbishop-viceroy an encouraging preliminary report. He observed, however, that water blocked many veins and that other entrances had broken down with the passage of time. Soon afterward, matters became further complicated as rain caused regular, often lengthy, delays.[17]

Labor, like rain, presented a chronic problem for the mining mission, even to the extent that a worker would eventually contribute to the demise of Juan José D'Elhúyar's career. When the mining mission first arrived in Mariquita, the local *alcalde* hired day laborers to work the mines. They were not permanent, however, nor were there enough of them. Indians, blacks, and whites alike all found the work involved in mining repugnant. It was not only dangerous, but distasteful, and most considered it a last resort. Moreover, since the *mita* had been abolished, forced labor was no longer a legal option. Caballero y Góngora eventually supplied the expedition with slaves, but they were few, and revolt and escapes presented new problems.[18] This situation dictated that work

16. Mutis to Caballero y Góngora, Mariquita, May 26, 1784, in Restrepo, *Minas de Colombia,* 232.

17. D'Elhúyar to Caballero y Góngora, Mariquita, May 25, 1785, and "Extractos de las cartas de D. Juan José D'Elhúyar a los virreyes," April 1, 1785, to July 20, 1790, in Restrepo, *Minas de Colombia,* 300–305.

18. Caycedo, *D'Elhúyar,* 27, 156, 178.

on the mines, which were in poor condition anyway, could progress only slowly and erratically.

In June, 1786, just when it appeared that the project was finally starting to take shape, D'Elhúyar informed Caballero y Góngora that the crown had commissioned his brother, Fausto, to study a new method of amalgamation that had recently been discovered by Baron von Born in Vienna. This method was reported to be both less expensive and more efficient than smelting.[19] After D'Elhúyar recommended delaying the construction of foundries for smelting until his brother sent further information, operations were stalled indefinitely.

In December, Fausto confirmed his earlier report concerning the Born discovery. He remained in Vienna to master the new amalgamation procedure and promised to convey specific information as quickly as possible. Fausto's confidence convinced Juan José that the Born method was indeed superior to smelting, and in January, 1787, he began to collect the materials that would be needed to apply the new system. These preliminary preparations occupied him for several months, but once he had done everything possible within the limitations imposed by his equipment, as well as his official orders to smelt rather than to amalgamate, he was again forced to wait. In July, 1787, both D'Elhúyar and Mutis received a royal order acknowledging the likely superiority of Born's method over smelting, but specifying that nothing be done toward instituting the new procedure until a properly trained specialist could be sent from Europe to teach the method to D'Elhúyar.[20] The waiting had become official.

Almost a year after the royal order instructed him to suspend operations, D'Elhúyar received a full report on Born's discovery from his brother. Stretching his orders a bit, he began experimenting at once. After three months of trials, he accommodated the new amalgamation method to conditions in the Mariquita mines. Indeed, with the Born method, silver could be extracted in a mere

19. D'Elhúyar to Caballero y Góngora, Santa Ana, June 17, 1786, in Restrepo, *Minas de Colombia,* 234.

20. Fausto D'Elhúyar to Juan José D'Elhúyar, Vienna, December 18, 1786, in Caycedo, *D'Elhuyar,* 150, 151; Caballero y Góngora to D'Elhúyar and Mutis, Turbaco, July 3, 1787, in Hernández de Alba (comp.), *Archivo epistolar,* III, 72–73.

three or four hours, whereas smelting required at least ten days.[21]

Meanwhile, plans were developing in Europe for ambitious assistance to the American mines. After sending Fausto D'Elhúyar to Vienna to study the Born method, Gálvez named him director of the mines of New Spain. He also arranged for the recruitment of Saxon technicians for Mexico, New Granada, and other mining missions to America.[22] While these preparations were being made, however, Gálvez died in June, 1787. His successor, Antonio Valdés, was neither familiar with the American colonies nor with the background of the mining mission, but he nevertheless continued support for the reform program.

The newly hired Saxon specialists were divided into four groups. The largest was assigned to New Spain and the others to New Granada, Peru, and Chile, though an expedition for the last never materialized. Juan José was not pleased by this turn of events. He was confident of his understanding of the Born method and did not believe that additional personnel were necessary. When the mission arrived in December, 1788, moreover, he discovered that only one of the seven Saxons possessed technological expertise; the others were simply skilled workers. To make matters worse, the expert became gravely ill soon after his arrival and eventually died. When D'Elhúyar wrote to Santa Fe asking for guidance, his letter was received by Francisco Gil y Lemos, who had replaced Caballero y Góngora in January, 1789.[23]

Very soon after taking office, Gil y Lemos abruptly altered the mining reform situation. Inheriting a huge debt from his spendthrift predecessor and under instructions from Valdés to economize wherever possible, he withheld the fresh instructions sought by D'Elhúyar, instead ordering yet another suspension of operations.[24] In that the reform mission had not yet yielded a profit, Gil

21. "El método de amalgamación del Barón de Born, descrito por Don Juan José D'Elhúyar," Santa Ana, September 17, 1788, in Restrepo, *Minas de Colombia,* 305–306.

22. Walter Howe, *The Mining Guild of New Spain and Its Tribunal General, 1770–1821* (New York, 1968), 306.

23. Whitaker, "Elhúyar Mining Missions," 584; Caycedo, *D'Elhúyar,* 171.

24. Francisco Gil y Lemos, "Relación del estado del Nuevo Reino de Granada que hace el exmo. Sr. D. Francisco Gil y Lemos a su sucesor excmo. Sr. D. José de Ezpeleta, 1789," in Jaramillo (ed.), *Relaciones de mando,* 144.

y Lemos resolved to discontinue work until he could visit the mines personally to determine the worth of the reform expedition.

While he awaited the visit of Gil y Lemos, D'Elhúyar wrote him, submitting a plan for the establishment of a *cuerpo de minería* (mining guild) in New Granada. He argued that although the natives wanted to foment the mines, they lacked the necessary knowledge. To solve the dilemma, he recommended that a system be instituted similar to that in New Spain, namely that the entire industry be organized as a formal body with a *tribunal de minería* at its head. This institution would be in charge of financing mining enterprises, educating miners, and administering justice within the industry.[25] Unfortunately, owing to the uncertain political support that would plague D'Elhúyar's work in the future, this far-sighted plan would never be implemented.

When Gil y Lemos eventually visited the mines personally, he quickly reversed his position. They still seemed to hold promise, and practical political considerations intervened as well. To totally discontinue support for the undertaking entailed the risk of antagonizing the inhabitants of the mining district, for it would appear that the reform had been undertaken solely to enrich the royal treasury, rather than also to assist local producers. Any implementation of the new policy had to be weighed against this consideration because of lingering anti-administration sentiments dating back to at least the Comunero Rebellion. Gil y Lemos recommended to Valdés that the crown continue its support of D'Elhúyar.[26] Unfortunately, he was never able to put action behind his words of confidence because the crown transferred him to Peru, replacing him with José de Ezpeleta on July 31, 1789.

The Ezpeleta administration reflected Spain's continuing strategy of fiscal and political restraint. The new viceroy, who remained in office until 1796, immediately summoned D'Elhúyar to Santa Fe to report fully on the mines and their potential. In the meantime, the work of the mining mission would remain sus-

25. D'Elhúyar, "Plan para el establecimiento del cuerpo de minería en este Reino de Granada, a imitación del que se halla establecido en Nueva España," in Restrepo, *Minas de Colombia,* 306–15.

26. Francisco Gil y Lemos to Antonio Valdés, Cartagena, February 28, 1789, and Santa Fe, May 15, 1789, AGI, SF, leg. 838.

pended. And although Ezpeleta cautiously permitted activity to be resumed after his interview with D'Elhúyar, the reform mission plainly operated on shaky ground. Mutis, however, assured the viceroy that patience would be rewarded and urged him not to abandon D'Elhúyar.[27]

After years of delay and labor and weather problems, the mining mission produced its first silver in 1791. Ezpeleta, however, had grown increasingly skeptical about the worth of the mines and their director as well. The reform mission had not lived up to royal expectations even though six years' worth of time and some 137,000 pesos had been invested. Ezpeleta wanted tangible results, especially in the face of the royal administration's continued emphasis on financial restraint. D'Elhúyar attempted to reassure the viceroy through optimistic reports and again urged the organization of a guild. He also petitioned for an increase in his salary, which appalled the viceroy, who was tiring rapidly of spending money on the mines and seeing meager results.[28]

At this juncture, events took a bizarre, fateful turn that would deal a mortal blow to D'Elhúyar's career and eventually the mining mission. For unknown reasons, Isidro Jaramillo, one of the mining mission's day laborers, attempted to beat D'Elhúyar to death in mid-1793.[29] The employee was jailed, and D'Elhúyar given a leave of absence in Santa Fe to recover from the incident. Unfortunately, D'Elhúyar selected José Caycedo y Flórez as his attorney to represent him in the proceedings against Jaramillo. Caycedo was a close personal friend of Antonio Nariño, the famous precursor of the independence movement. It was at this time that Nariño published the Declaration of the Rights of Man and the Citizen, causing hysteria among the colonial authorities. Nariño was promptly arrested, but his deed cast suspicion on his associates, including Caycedo and even D'Elhúyar, though the latter did

27. Caycedo, *D'Elhúyar,* 175; Restrepo, *Minas de Colombia,* 240–42; Mutis to D'Elhúyar, Santa Fe, February 9 and July 9, 1791, in Restrepo, *Minas de Colombia,* 240–41.

28. Mutis to D'Elhúyar, Santa Fe, February 9 and July 9, 1791, and "Parte final del informe de D. Juan José D'Elhúyar sobre las minas de Santa Ana," in Restrepo, *Minas de Colombia,* 241–42, 315–16; "Informe de J. J. D'Elhúyar," February 1, 1793, in Caycedo, *D'Elhúyar,* 219.

29. Restrepo, *Minas de Colombia,* 242.

not appear to take an interest in politics.[30] The audiencia promptly denounced D'Elhúyar to Spain, urging the crown to suspend the mining mission in view of his questionable associations. And in mid-1795, Ezpeleta finally relieved D'Elhúyar as director of the mines, replacing him with his brother-in-law, Angel Díaz, with whom he no longer enjoyed cordial relations.[31]

Without D'Elhúyar's leadership, the mining operations quickly deteriorated. Ezpeleta tried to locate a private owner for the mines with the hope that someone would be able to exploit profitably the vast riches that supposedly existed in them. When this strategy failed, he recommended that the government simply abandon them and award them free to anybody who was willing to work them.[32]

D'Elhúyar died soon afterward, without ever ridding himself of his legal and political problems, though his difficulties arose through association only. Once a well-respected scientist, he had become an isolated administrator who knew no end to frustration. He died in relative obscurity without ever having received just recognition for his scientific achievements.

The mining reform exemplifies the crown's attempt to find solutions to New Granada's financial dilemma through scientific progress. The experiment, however, suffered from too much planning from above and too little input from below. The mines of Mariquita were not a fortunate choice. Plagued by labor problems and a poor choice of location, D'Elhúyar failed to produce results that might have encouraged continued governmental support.

The accident of timing posed, perhaps, an even greater obstacle. The work had begun before von Born's discovery, and smelting was the royal administration's preference until the new amalgamation technique became known. The circumstances sur-

30. In 1790, for example, when news of the French Revolution arrived in New Granada, D'Elhúyar did not even reply to Mutis' comments about it. Mutis to D'Elhúyar, Mariquita, 1790, in Hernández de Alba (comp.), *Archivo epistolar,* I, 159, 161, 163.

31. Restrepo, *Minas de Colombia,* 243.

32. José de Ezpeleta, "Relación del estado del Nuevo Reino de Granada que hace Sr. D. José de Expeleta a su sucesor Sr. D. Pedro de Mendinueta, año de 1796," in Posada and Ibáñez (eds.), *Relaciones de mando,* 344–46; Ezpeleta to Valdés, September 19, 1796, in Caycedo, *D'Elhúyar,* 286.

rounding the transition to the von Born method occasioned extensive delays that were in turn exacerbated by the process of political reassessment and adjustment after the death of Gálvez. Eager to consolidate the gains that Gálvez had made in colonial reform, but at the same time determined to bring the colonial budget under control through fiscal restraint, both Gil y Lemos and Ezpeleta continued the mining reform, but only cautiously. Caballero y Góngora's unrestrained enthusiasm contrasted markedly with the prudent attitude of the more skeptical Gil y Lemos and even more sharply with the critical view of Ezpeleta, who faced the mines' continuing lack of financial productivity. Yet the innumerable delays and resulting losses, even during the latter years, were at least as much the result of royal indecision as of the shortcomings of the reform expedition itself. D'Elhúyar perhaps never really had a fair chance to succeed. His legal difficulties posed a final, fatal complication. In his absence, the mining reform drifted hopelessly, and Ezpeleta had little practical choice but to terminate it.

JUAN MARCHENA FERNÁNDEZ

Chapter 3

The Social World of the Military in Peru and New Granada: The Colonial Oligarchies in Conflict, 1750–1810

Between 1750 and 1810, a complex interplay of internal and external forces reshaped the Spanish colonial system. Such forces as the beginnings of the Industrial Revolution in Europe, the French Revolution, the slow death of the Spanish mercantilist system, and the growth of the colonial economy contributed to a fundamental transformation of Spanish America. In this process, the elites played a role of unquestionable importance.

During the final decades of the eighteenth century, the elites were the main catalyst in the social and economic processes that led to the destruction of the Spanish colonial system and the establishment of the new republics in the early nineteenth century. This transformation did not, however, eliminate all colonial structures. On the contrary, the same groups that had monopolized political power before independence remained in power afterward. Their dominance of decision making in their local economies perpetuated an intermediary role that promised handsome benefits. Furthermore, a repressive control over the popular sectors of society, which constituted the labor force, was consolidated and sustained. This control ensured continued exports of raw materials, the traditional basis of Spanish-American economic activity, while simultaneously permitting the elites to perpetuate their preeminent position.

The counterpoint to this phenomenon came from the popular sectors, which entered into a complex chain of actions and reactions in attempting to escape—albeit without much success—the pressures imposed upon them from above. These pressures came on the one hand from the colonial administration, which tried to protect the interests of the crown, and on the other from the American oligarchies or, more specifically, the groups with capital among the creoles, who sought to advance their own welfare. These creoles expanded their landholdings, frequently at the cost of indigenous farming communities, and aggressively attempted to increase production, which would in turn allow them to augment their income via exportation.[1]

Although I have researched these issues for some years, my conclusions cannot be carried too far at this point owing to a host of complicating variables.[2] The local American oligarchies functioned within the same general framework, but were sufficiently diverse to justify an infinite number of studies. Moreover, one must distinguish between urban and rural elites while remembering that their attitudes, whether progressive or conservative, were often subject to change and ill-defined. Further, the differences between merchant oligarchs and land-owning oligarchs must be treated cautiously, because the aspirations of these groups, as expressed by behavior and attitudes, often overlapped. Finally, the available sources are so numerous and diverse that a single researcher simply cannot do more than sample them. My aim, therefore, is to address the questions that seem most important with the hope of advancing the current level of debate and encouraging others to undertake detailed local studies.[3]

1. *Exportation* is used here in a broad sense to include trade reaching beyond local markets well into other zones of the territory, other areas of the continent, and Europe, either via legal or contraband transatlantic commerce.

2. Juan Marchena Fernández, *Oficiales y soldados en el ejército de América* (Seville, 1983).

3. This essay addresses the military, but I have also examined the elites from the perspective of the Church. See Paulino Castañeda Delgado and Juan Marchena Fernández, "La iglesia americana en la segunda mitad del siglo XVIII," in Demetrio Ramos (ed.), *Historia general de España y América* (Madrid, 1989), XI, 498–521.

This essay examines the place of the local oligarchies in the colonial army as well as the socioeconomic role played by that institution during the final decades of Spanish dominion in continental America. After a brief general overview, the analysis focuses on the experiences of both Peru and New Granada and in particular upon the diversity and competition between the different groups that constituted what was called the "American army." During the second half of the eighteenth century, the officer corps of the colonial army was progressively Americanized, and the creole elites had firmly established their domination by the end of the century. Although the royal authorities attempted to arrest this process, their efforts were singularly unsuccessful.[4]

The term *officer corps* here refers to not only the ranks from sublieutenant to brigadier, but to those of sergeant and cadet as well. This approach permits the broadest possible analysis of the collective military experience. Moreover, during this period military law did not clearly distinguish between commissioned and noncommissioned officers. Service records were maintained for sergeants and cadets, and sergeants enjoyed corporate privileges on the same basis as those serving in the higher ranks. The inclusion of sergeants in the collective analysis leads to a statistical bias in favor of Europeans since nearly all were Spanish; the inclusion of cadets, on the other hand, has the opposite effect since nearly all were Americans.

The data presented in Table 1 reveal the extent to which Americans dominated the veteran officer corps during the final years of the eighteenth century. Most of these officers were from wealthy families of the principal cities of the empire, from Mexico City in the north to Buenos Aires and Santiago de Chile in the south. The growing strength of the American elites, whose claims of noble status reflected their burgeoning economic power, shifted control of the military apparatus from peninsular officers to local cliques with disposable capital.[5] This group could readily provide the loans that the crown depended upon to alleviate the chronic

4. Marchena Fernández, *Oficiales y soldados*.

5. *Ibid.* According to prevailing legislation, these were not nobles by birthright but by reputation and culture in most instances. In Spain, the same thing occurred. Antonio Domínguez Ortiz, *Sociedad y estado en el siglo XVIII* (Barcelona, 1976).

TABLE 1
The Veteran Officer Corps of the Army of America

	1740–49	1750–59	1760–69	1770–79	1780–89	1790–99	1800–10
Geographic origins (%)							
Peninsulars	62.9	63.4	63.5	54.9	47.6	43.1	36.4
Creoles	34.6	34.3	33.8	39.8	48.5	52.7	60.1
Foreigners	2.5	2.3	2.7	5.3	3.9	4.2	3.5
Social origins (%)							
Nobles	12.5	7.1	28.3	51.6	48.6	50.5	51.1
Officers' sons	15.4	20.7	8.2	10.2	11.4	15.5	17.3
Known	72.1	61.0	40.8	21.7	22.3	17.3	17.5
Humble	—	11.2	22.7	16.5	17.7	16.7	14.1

SOURCE: Data from Juan Marchena Fernández, *Oficiales y soldados en el ejército de América* (Seville, 1983). This work also contains a detailed analysis of the methodology employed to define the various social categories within the officer corps and provides the locations of the primary sources (service records) upon which the analysis depends.

financial deficits that plagued the American army.[6] Thus, "nobles' constituted 70 percent of the officer corps by 1800–1810.[7] These developments go far to explain why Spain had such enormous difficulty in sustaining its dominion in its overseas colonies after 1810.

An undeclared but nevertheless very real struggle between the creole oligarchy and the colonial administration for control of the opportunities associated with the American army precipitated a series of power struggles between different sectors of the American elite. In Peru and New Granada, as in other areas, confrontation of this sort, though barely visible to society at large, had both spatial and economic dimensions, reflecting, for example, rivalries between the coast and the interior and between the political center and the periphery. Ultimately, the struggle hinged upon rivalry between the commercial and the landed oligarchies.

American control of the military institution, though certainly evident in the regular army, was both more visible and sociologically interesting in the militia owing to the peculiar role of the

6. Juan Marchena Fernández, "La financiación militar en Indias: Introducción a su estudio," *AEA*, XXXVI (1979), 81–110.

7. Included in this percentage are many sons of officers, who might be identified in their service records as "nobles" or as "sons of officers."

militiamen and in particular of their officers. Because their duties were fewer and their activities much less limited by the rigors of military life, they enjoyed greater personal opportunity than the regulars to seek social, legal, and economic privileges.

José de Gálvez, writing in 1779, succinctly summarized the predicament of the royal administration: "Even if the king of Spain possessed all the treasuries, the armies, and the storehouses in Europe, it would be an impossible task to construct all the necessary fortifications, to send the number of troops needed to defend the localities exposed to invasion, and to provide sufficient equipment for all the strongpoints." Faced with the impossibility of defending its colonies with the regular army alone, the crown was forced to resort to options that in effect transferred a major portion of this burden to its American subjects. They had to be convinced that "the defense of the king's rights was linked to that of their own properties, the security of their families, their homeland, and their happiness."[8]

The result was the establishment of a vast militia system, a gigantic paper army theoretically composed of regiments, battalions, and separate companies comprising all the able-bodied males between the ages of fifteen and forty-five and placed under the command of the most distinguished leaders from each locality and its environs: "The colonels will be selected from amongst the most qualified and highly titled in each district . . . the other leaders and officers from amongst the lesser nobility [*caballeros hidalgos*] and others who live decently, even though they might be merchants . . . the sergeants from those men who are the most suitable, without requiring any other qualification from them . . . the soldiers from the subjects of any status or condition."[9] Units might be organized by occupation (e.g., Battalion of Commerce, Companies of Tailors), by ethnic origin (whites, *pardos,* and free *morenos,* or "all colors"), or by jurisdiction, including urban and rural areas.

8. José de Gálvez to Viceroy Manuel Antonio Flores, Aranjuez, May 15, 1779, AGI, SF, leg. 577A.

9. Royal Cedula, November 8, 1704, for the army of Spain, in Domínguez Ortiz, *Sociedad y estado,* 78. See, too, Santiago Gerardo Suárez, *Las milicias: Instituciones militares hispanoamericanas* (Caracas, 1985), 57.

Analyzing the militia from a sociological perspective yields a wealth of information about the character of colonial life. The creation of volunteer units offered opportunities for both the urban and rural elites. The crown granted privileges, most notably the *fuero militar,* and social reputations might be reinforced or enhanced through the prestige of the uniform, military rank, and the authority they represented. Opportunities arose to secure control over large segments of the population—sometimes entire communities—as well as to employ men at arms to defend personal interests.

In describing the Peruvian militia, Alexander von Humboldt observed:

> It is not the military spirit of the nation but the vanity of a small number of families—the heads of which aspire to the ranks of colonel or brigadier—that has nourished the militia in the Spanish colonies. . . . It is amazing to see, even in the small provincial towns, all the businessmen transformed into colonels, captains, and *sargentos mayores*. . . . Because the rank of colonel provides the right to seignorial prerogatives and title, something the people discuss endlessly in daily conversation, it is commonplace that this sort of honor contributes greatly to domestic felicity, and for this the creoles invest the most extraordinary sums of money.[10]

A global analysis reveals that over 90 percent of the militia officers were American-born and recruited from the most important merchant and landowning groups of their respective cities and districts. Virtually all enlisted men were Americans. Apart from providing insights into the socioeconomic spectrum of the eighteenth century, an analysis of the officer corps and the soldiery of the American army brings into focus one of the principal vehicles through which the American oligarchy manipulated power between 1780 and 1820.

Although it is very difficult to establish comparative parameters for the viceroyalties of New Granada and Peru, partly because the relationships between Santa Fe and Lima and their respective

10. See Jean Descola, *La vida cotidiana en el Perú en tiempos de los españoles* (Lima, 1962), 98.

hinterlands were quite different, I will compare and contrast on the one hand Santa Fe and its relationship with Cartagena and, on the other, Lima and its problems with Cuzco-Arequipa. The analysis will focus on both the relationships and the individual characteristics of each of these four centers.

Basic Structures in New Granada and Peru

Although both viceroyalties operated within the same institutional and legal structures, their armies differed considerably because the royal administration as a matter of course pursued policies in each jurisdiction designed to recognize their distinctive geographic conditions and strategic needs. These differences in policy in turn influenced the roles of the local oligarchies. The distinct courses of military development pursued during the second half of the eighteenth century are illustrated in Table 2, which lists the military units of Peru and New Granada.

In Peru, the regular army was concentrated in the capital and its port, Callao. Only a few, scattered outposts existed in the Sierra. The figure of 1,681 soldiers for all of Peru is surprisingly small and suggests the extent to which military responsibility rested with the militia. In the case of New Granada, the diffusion of the principal units is important. The viceroyalty's location at the vital triangle of peninsular-American communications, and its greater exposure to enemy attacks, demanded larger coastal defenses. Santa Fe, the inland capital and theoretically the focus of political power, did not acquire a fixed garrison until the rising of Socorro's Comuneros demonstrated its vulnerability, not to foreign invasion, but to the wrath of the local population. The largest units were garrisoned on the coast, where they performed social and military functions quite distinct from those of the garrison eventually deployed in Santa Fe. This dichotomy, arising from the differing character and interests of the local oligarchies, created innumerable conflicts before, during, and after the Wars of Independence. The militia of New Granada was less important than that of Peru and served principally as a coastal reserve. In Peru the roles of the regular army in providing coastal defense and bolstering administrative and political power in the viceregal capital coin-

TABLE 2
The Regular Armies of Peru and New Granada

Place	Unit	Authorized Strength
Peru		
Lima	Halberdier company of the Viceregal Guard	24
Lima	Cavalry company of the Viceregal Guard	34
Lima	Royal Infantry Regiment of Lima	1,468
Tarma	Cavalry detachment of Tarma	25
Cuzco	Dragoon detachment of Cuzco	36
Lima	Artillery company	94
	Total	1,681
New Granada		
Cartagena	Fixed infantry regiment	1,400
Cartagena	Artillery companies (two)	200
Santa Marta	Fixed infantry companies (two)	132
Panama	Fixed infantry battalion	600
Panama	Artillery company	100
Santa Fe	Halberdier company of the Viceregal Guard	24
Santa Fe	Cavalry company of the Viceregal Guard	30
Santa Fe	Auxiliary regiment	500
Popayán	Fixed infantry company	80
Quito	Company of Presidential Guards	30
Quito	Fixed infantry companies (four)	320
Guayaquil	Fixed infantry company	60
	Total	3,476

SOURCE: See Table 1.

cided, whereas these roles were divided spatially and, as a consequence, socially in New Granada.

Before 1780, the militia in New Granada was widely dispersed throughout the viceroyalty. Units were established in all towns and localities of moderate or greater size and importance in proportion to the male population. The system operated with the cooperation of the municipal authorities or through the services of the *capitán a guerra,* a type of militia organizer in each jurisdiction. The local unit—detachment, company, battalion, or regiment—thus stood ready, replete with drum, banner, and, most important, a prominent local leader, to serve the king, despite the fact that in most cases arms and uniforms were virtually nonexistent, instruction was lacking, and military discipline was still worse. In strictly military terms, little was achieved except, of course, for the dust raised in the plazas after Sunday Mass when a sort of sad parody of a military parade took place.

It is instructive, nevertheless, to note the way in which the officers were selected under the provisions of the militia regulations specifically drafted for New Granada, but also applied in Peru: "The officials will be chosen by reason of birthright, good conduct, the concept and sound promise of spirit and utility . . . paying more attention to the public renown and opinion than to the certificates and papers that can be acquired through favors and friendship." In other words, in the city as well as in the country, the elites would dominate the enormous and heterogeneous aggregate constituting the American militia and thus gain the official recognition and status conveyed by the uniform, the selection process itself, and the countless privileges received through the *fuero militar*.[11]

In the majority of the companies and battalions, except for those of Cartagena, Santa Fe, Santa Marta, Quito, and Guayaquil, the rural element was prominent in that the units were composed of men from not only the towns but also the rural districts. Even in the case of Cartagena, the viceroyalty's major port city, some of the companies of the Regiments of Whites, Pardos, and All Colors were filled by people from the outlying areas, from Baru to Sabanalarga or Mahates. In addition, the province's interior militia extended into three districts: Lorica (ten villages), Mompós (eight), and Barranquilla (fourteen). Militiamen came from 110 localities, ranging from significant urban centers like Mompós, Tolu, or Barranquilla, to villages lost in the swamps, stockades, ranches, or haciendas whose landowners sent peons to join the companies they commanded.[12] In the rural districts, the landed oligarchy controlled the militia, whereas in urban centers, where troops were raised according to race and by neighborhoods and streets, merchants or financiers prominent in the urban patriciate commanded.

11. AGI, IG, leg. 1885; Lyle N. McAlister, *The "Fuero Militar" in New Spain, 1764–1800* (Gainesville, 1957).

12. See Juan Marchena Fernández, *La institución militar en Cartagena de Indias, 1700–1810* (Seville, 1982).

Following the Comunero Rebellion of Socorro, this vast aggregate of militia units suffered a major reduction. The insurgents had appropriated the militia system to organize the rebel army, and the royal authorities had been reluctant to mobilize units from other areas to contain the movement for fear that the Socorro example might cause the revolts to spread even farther. It was necessary, therefore, to turn to the regular army when the elites of Santa Fe called for assistance, and the Fixed Regiment of Cartagena was brought up, though the port's militia provided some support.

In that the militia was of little use in this case, and a veteran regiment had to be organized in the viceregal capital—the Auxiliary Regiment of Santa Fe—the colonial authorities subsequently decided to dismantle much of the interior militia system through the regulation of 1794, which eliminated more than 60 percent of its strength. The displaced militia officers retained their ranks, privileges, and the use of the uniform.

Peru's experience was both similar and unique. On the one hand, the militia, compared to the regular army, was massive. The responsibility for defending Peru fell mainly upon volunteer units, which were positioned over a much greater geographic area than in New Granada. The system of recruitment for troops and officers was the same, but here the rural communities played a more important role, contributing most of the manpower. The landowners had greater control over the units because many of the communities lay completely within their properties. They practically owned their units, body and soul.

The Túpac Amaru uprising also showed that these militia forces maintained by the landowners were devastatingly effective as natives fought natives and rural laborers other rural laborers. The suppression of the Sierra uprising was largely the work of these landowners and their militia. We will see how these creole oligarchies, relishing their triumph, went so far as to return to the king unclaimed salaries as well as monies paid for the food and gunpowder of the Indian soldiery, who brought about the bloody end to the rebellious cry of their brothers. The Regiment of Soria, practically the only regular unit sent into the fight, remained inactive in Cuzco most of the time, serving principally as a defensive force.

Much the same thing occurred during the Arequipa disorders. Although the local oligarchy initially contributed actively to the protests against royal policy, it did not hesitate to mobilize its militia when finding its interests threatened by the pretensions of the angry populace. This militia was already on the verge of becoming a "private army," and with the support of the colonial administration, it suppressed the threat to the stability of the system.

Therefore, a study of the militia at the level of both officers and troops, or of the regular army itself, involves an analysis of the social structures of Peru and New Granada in all their aspects, substances, and realities. The most important urban oligarchical groups found representation in the officer corps, as did the owners of vast rural properties, while the ordinary soldiers, whom the elites exploited to their own advantage, were recruited from the Indians, peons, and the lower classes of urban society.

Lima at the End of the Eighteenth Century: A City of Officers and Merchants

Ricardo Palma, describing the capital city of republican Peru, observed that the sons of the great families of Lima were practically born in uniform: "Above all, the militia had the attraction of the uniform. A young blueblood, rich and good looking, or the son of an officer, had with only these qualities more than it took to become at least a general within a few years."[13] This tendency originated in the eighteenth century, when a man bedecked with his brilliantly colored uniform, golden stripes, and shiny buttons had widespread social influence. The aspiration of many a young man was to become a lieutenant or a captain in the Royal Infantry Regiment of Lima, the most important unit in the viceroyalty, the largest of the American army in the south of the continent, and the only regular unit of any significance in Peru. Its officers commanded real troops rather than paper units of militiamen, and they were full members of the king's army, resident in the capital, with all the privileges that this status entailed. Given the smallness of their number, they could boast of being part of the military elite par excellence, notwithstanding the increase in their numbers dur-

13. Ricardo Palma, *Tradiciones peruanas* (Buenos Aires, 1942), 167.

TABLE 3
The Veteran Officers of Lima, 1760–1810

Dates	Number
1760–1769	27
1770–1779	77
1780–1789	120
1790–1799	138
1800–1810	144
Total	506

SOURCE: Marchena Fernández, *Oficiales y soldados*. The data in this table and in Tables 4–8 are derived from the service records of the 506 officers, from brigadiers to sergeants, who served in Lima between 1760 and 1810.

ing this period owing to the transformation of the unit from a battalion to a regiment (Table 3).[14]

In the interior of Peru, the only garrisons of regular troops were the small unit posted in Tarma near the fortress of Chanchamayo, which was demolished in 1784,[15] and that in Cuzco with its store of arms, which caused more than a few problems.[16] An additional component of the veteran officer corps was the personnel

14. During the first half of the eighteenth century, the veteran troops consisted of 500 soldiers on salary in Callao organized as separate companies (AGI, Lima, leg. 1489). In 1753, the Regulation for the Garrison of the Plaza del Real Felipe del Callao established a fixed battalion for the defense of Lima and its port consisting of 421 soldiers and an artillery squadron of 21 men (AGI, IG, leg. 1337), to which an additional company of infantry was attached later (AGN, Superior Gobierno, leg. 13, C-286, fol. 2). In 1775, another company of artillery was created (AGI, Lima, legs. 1499–1500). In 1782, the Royal Infantry Regiment of Lima was established by combining the battalion of El Callao with a new battalion (AGI, Lima, leg. 1501). More reforms occurred in 1787 (Biblioteca Nacional, Lima, Sección Investigaciones Históricas, MS C-557).

15. Expediente, AGI, Lima, leg. 1494.

16. Beyond its responsibility for defense, this detachment also had the mission of guarding the Cuzco gunpowder magazine. Since the expulsion of the Society of Jesus, the gunpowder, unbelievably, had been placed in the sacristy of the Jesuit church. A plot of land was bought in San Sebastián for the magazine with contributions of *vecinos* who were frightened because of the danger posed by lightning at the church's location. In fact, the gunpowder did nearly explode, though not owing to the lightning but to some lighted candles that tipped over. Some daring *vecinos*, however, saved the day by managing to carry it out in time.

attached to peninsular units deployed in Peru as reinforcements. Such deployments, however, occurred only during emergencies such as during the rebellion of Túpac Amaru when the Regiments of Soria and Extremadura were deployed in the viceroyalty. Similar steps had been taken in 1746 and 1769.[17]

We now turn to the question of birthplace. *Limeños* constituted 37 percent of all of the regular officers who served in Peru, and creoles as a whole constituted nearly 45 percent (see Table 4). Moreover, *limeños* constituted a majority in the officer corps from the 1780s, except in the years 1790–1795, when many officers were transferred from the departing Regiments of Soria and Extremadura (see Table 5). These officers, already connected to local interests and married to Peruvian women, joined the Royal Regiment of Lima in order to remain in Peru. By the late 1790s, a creole majority had emerged again.

Table 6 shows the different descriptions of social status found in the service records of the Lima officer corps. Table 7 aggregates these categories into five groups (nobles, sons of officers, known, humble, and unknown), and both tables identify geographic origins and indicate chronological development.[18] Beginning in the late 1770s, nobles were the largest single component of the officer corps; the number of peninsular nobles was maintained by the transfer of officers from the two Spanish regiments that arrived in the 1780s. Peninsulars also constituted a majority among those of humble birth, particularly because of the policy of recruiting them as sergeants. Preference was given to peninsulars at this level because their greater experience in managing soldiers was considered crucial. The last thing a higher-ranking officer wanted was a distracting lack of discipline among his troops.

Safeguards imposed by the colonial authorities prevented

17. See the Expedientes on these missions in AGI, Chile, leg. 433, and Lima, legs. 1491, 1494. No more expeditions occurred until 1813–1818 (Marchena Fernández, *Oficiales y soldados*, 341).

18. The noble category includes not only those with titles but also persons of social distinction in their localities, such as descendants of old families, prominent merchants, landowners, and financiers. One consequence is that sons of officers are underrepresented because of their inclusion in the noble category. The "decent" category shown in Table 6 comprised mainly sergeants, who were unable to claim noble status because of their rank. For further details of the typology employed, see Marchena Fernández, *Oficiales y soldados*.

TABLE 4
Geographic Origins of the Lima Officer Corps

Birthplace	Number	Percentage
All Lima officers		
Andalusia	88	17.4
Aragón	9	1.8
Asturias	12	2.4
Balearic Islands	2	0.4
Castile	50	9.9
Catalonia	21	4.2
Galicia	19	3.8
Extremadura	17	3.4
Levante and Murcia	12	2.4
Navarre	18	3.6
North Africa	7	1.4
Basque Country	4	0.8
Antilles and Florida	1	0.2
New Spain	1	0.2
New Granada	7	1.4
Peru	220	43.5
Foreigners	12	2.4
Unknown	6	1.2
Total	506	
Peruvian officers		
Lima	187	85.0
Arequipa	8	3.5
Cuzco	6	2.5
Tarma	4	1.9
Piura	5	2.2
Trujillo	4	1.8
Chincha	3	1.3
Oropesa	1	0.4
Moquegua	1	0.4
Tacna	1	0.4
Total	220	

SOURCE: See Table 3.

creoles from holding the highest offices. Nevertheless, they were the majority in the middle ranks of captain and lieutenant and by 1810 had gained access to the position of colonel. Over 90 percent of the cadets were creoles. It is evident, then, that the creole elite had significant power over the regular army. That power is also visible in the creole ability to gain promotions (Table 8).

TABLE 5
Social Composition of the Lima Officer Corps by Decade

	1760–69	1770–79	1780–89	1790–99	1800–10
Peninsulars	14	49	57	73	66
Creoles	13	22	59	58	77
Foreigners	—	6	4	1	1

SOURCE: See Table 3.

TABLE 6
Social Status of the Lima Officer Corps

Status	Total	Number of Creoles	Percentage Creoles
Titled or illustrious	13	7	53.8
Nobles	328	178	54.2
Hidalgos	9	—	—
Caballeros	2	—	—
Sons of officers	9	5	55.5
Known	1	—	—
Good	6	—	—
Decent	93	37	39.7
Clear ancestry	2	—	—
Soldier of fortune	1	—	—
Humble	1	—	—
Sons of merchants	4	—	—
Sons of farmers	34	2	5.8
Unknown	4	—	0.7

SOURCE: See Table 3.

Peninsular nobles needed an average of 3.2 promotions on the military scale to secure their rank, while the creoles needed only 1.8. The average age of the peninsulars at the beginning of their military service was twenty, but of creoles, only sixteen. And the average number of years in service for peninsulars was about 16.9; that of creoles was twelve. Finally, while the peninsulars served in an average of 3.4 regiments during their military careers, 174 of the 220 creoles served in only the Royal Infantry Regiment of Lima, and another forty in only the fixed Battalion of Callao. Only eight creoles had performed part of their service in units outside of the capital and its environs.

TABLE 7
Social Status of the Lima Officer Corps by Decade

	Nobles		Sons of Officers		Known		Humble		Unknown		
	no.	%	no.	%	no.	%	no.	%	no.	%	Total
1760s											
Peninsulars	5	38	0	0	0	0	9	64	0	0	14
Creoles	8	62	0	0	0	0	5	36	0	0	13
Foreigners	0	0	0	0	0	0	0	0	0	0	0
Total	13		0		0		14		0		27
1770s											
Peninsulars	29	63	1	100	8	73	11	58	0	0	49
Creoles	14	30	0	0	0	0	8	42	0	0	22
Foreigners	3	7	0	0	3	27	0	0	0	0	6
Total	46		1		11		19		0		77
1780s											
Peninsulars	39	44	1	100	2	33	13	57	2	100	57
Creoles	47	53	0	0	2	33	10	43	0	0	59
Foreigners	2	2	0	0	2	33	0	0	0	0	4
Total	88		1		6		23		2		120
1790s											
Peninsulars	40	45	2	33	16	100	14	74	1	100	73
Creoles	49	55	4	66	0	0	5	26	0	0	58
Foreigners	1	1	0	0	0	0	0	0	0	0	1
Total	89		6		16		19		1		132
1800–1810											
Peninsulars	41	38	0	0	9	100	16	64	0	0	66
Creoles	67	61	1	100	0	0	9	36	0	0	77
Foreigners	1	1	0	0	0	0	0	0	0	0	1
Total	109		1		9		25		0		144

SOURCE: See Table 3.

An analysis of marital status is also revealing. Whereas 70 percent of the creoles remained single owing to age factors and the lack of economic and social incentives, more than 70 percent of the peninsulars were married, and of these more than 80 percent to local women. In view of the substantial dowries that the future

TABLE 8
Average Ages of the Lima Officer Corps, 1760–1810

Group	Average Age
Total	36
Peninsular	42
Creole	30

SOURCE: See Table 3.

fathers-in-law had to pay before the military authorities would authorize wedding licenses, the brides belonged to the best families of the colony. The peninsular officer, who had previously found himself obliged to live off his modest salary, thus became a part of the local oligarchy. The sons of these couples would be nobles and officers through their fathers and landowners or merchants through their mothers' inheritances.[19]

The peninsular self-identity of these officers and their role as a political interest group at the end of the century were substantially modified by these local connections. Evidence, moreover, indicates that many of them left the royal service to manage landed properties or businesses obtained through marriage. Nor did the troops they commanded show strong peninsular representation (Table 9).[20]

In sum, the regular army, which was at least theoretically the strongest military force in Peru, was dominated by creoles, who served under the command of men situated at the highest level of *limeño* society, and was manipulated by a small group of administrators that was itself very much compromised by local circumstances. Moreover, the immediate economic necessities of the military institution were frequently financed by creole capital through loans, a process that had become routine by the end of the eighteenth century. Private capital had become one of the keys to military finance and kept a system costing the crown almost two million

19. They were known in Lima as *mamones*. See Palma, *Tradiciones*.

20. This conclusion is supported by data on 561 men derived from troop reviews showing names, ages, heights, years of service, and other details; the nature and location of these sources are explained in Marchena Fernández, *Oficiales y soldados*.

TABLE 9
Soldiery of the Regular Army of Peru

General Origin		Percentage
Peninsulars		11.9
Creoles		85.2
Foreigners		2.8
Birthplaces	**Number**	**Percentage**
Castile	18	3.2
Andalusia	23	4.0
Galicia	9	1.6
Asturias	2	0.3
Levante	7	1.2
Catalonia	4	0.7
Extremadura	4	0.7
Peru	354	63.1
Chile	94	16.7
Río de la Plata	8	1.4
New Granada	22	3.9
Portugal	5	0.8
Italy	9	1.6
Germany	2	0.3

SOURCE: Marchena Fernández, *Oficiales y soldados*. Data on these 561 men were derived from troop reviews showing names, ages, heights, years of service, and other details.

pesos yearly from collapsing. The social and political role, then, played by the regular army after 1780 was one determined by the elites, as later events would forcefully demonstrate.

Hacendados, Merchants, and Peasant Communities in the Militia of Peru

Given late-eighteenth-century realities, the rural oligarchy assumed control of the militia system within distinct regional power centers, which, when necessary, clashed with the *limeño* oligarchy. The Peruvian militia traced its roots far back in the viceroyalty's history. For two centuries, the base of the Peruvian defense system had been the obligatory military service that required the encomenderos to provide men and arms when called upon to do so. The corregidores and some communities also had prominent roles in this mission. Essentially two distinct zones were involved: the coast, where the towns were assaulted by pirates and corsairs, and the Sierra, which included in the east the border with the Portuguese territories, the so-called "Tarma frontier," beyond which lived "uncivilized" lowland Indians, and Upper Peru in the southeast.

During the first half of the eighteenth century, the militia had functioned much as it did in other parts of Spanish America, but in 1763 Viceroy Manuel de Amat, operating under orders from Madrid instructing him to defend Peru with all the means at his disposal, reformed the system completely. This viceroy, who liked to be pictured in uniform with military plans in hand and with a besieged European fortress in the background, issued decrees and secured the resources to ready the viceroyalty for war. When word first arrived of the rupture with England during the Seven Years' War, he dictated a general edict urging the population to prepare itself for combat, "to mount the most vigorous defense possible, with the valor and constancy that characterize the Spanish nation."[21] He mobilized the troops; summoned the patricians of Lima, Cuzco, Arequipa, and all the other jurisdictions, naming them captains, colonels, and *sargentos mayores* of mythical regiments; and commanded them to shape an army able to resist surprise attack by the "perfidious Albion" and her Portuguese ally.

Filled with patriotic fervor, undoubtedly seasoned with a desire to break the chronic boredom that enveloped their lives, the creole nobility, the merchants, and the hacendados assumed control over the general mobilization, heeding the call of the viceroy. "This order deeply moved men of position—those with titles and other persons of splendor, who with instant zeal hastened to enlist, offering their lives, those of their sons, and . . . arms, horses, and whatever their resources permitted in sacrifice for the defense of religion, king, and country." Dragooned by these men, and placed under their command, "the plebeians and those of common

21. "Compendio de las prevenciones . . . ," Manuel de Amat, 1763, AGI, Lima, leg. 1490.

estate, mainly Indians, *pardos,* and *morenos,* demonstrated on this occasion a very obliging compliance."[22]

The corregidores were ordered to implement similar policies in the interior of the colony, as well as to provide reliable accounts concerning the general state of preparation in the kingdom and of all noblemen who raised, funded, and commanded militia units so that a review and inspection might be made throughout Peru. No surprises appear about the manner in which the urban and rural oligarchies—the patricians of Lima and Cuzco and the hacendados of the Sierra—shaped the leadership of these units. The landlord was the colonel, his sons the captains, the foremen the sergeants, and the peons and peasants the troops. Thus, Amat "envisioned the most glorious military project that had ever been seen in Peru and in all the rest of America," and he "involved the nobility fully to concur personally in defense of the lands that had been conquered by their ancestors."[23]

The Peruvian oligarchy figures prominently in the military records. "Don Felix de Encalade, following the footsteps of his ancestors, provided the uniforms for a company entitled Grenadiers of the Queen Mother, most illustrious and replete with select noblemen who could shine among the best of Europe." Don Francisco Micheu raised another company of "the most important merchants of this city," followed by nine more "that formed the Battalion of Commerce." All the notables, including the likes of Francisco Merino, the Torre-Tagle family, Pedro José de Zarate, and Lucas de Vergara, rounded up *pardos, morenos,* or Indians in the neighborhoods of Lima to fill their companies and hold troops under their command. Carabaillo, Lurigancho, Bellavista, and the haciendas in the outskirts of Lima soon followed, the owners forming units with their farmhands, paying for their uniforms and arms, assisting at the reviews, and making the soldiery march under their command to the beat of the drum. Finally, "since it was necessary to recruit officers from the nobility for the companies, His Excellency reserved the most esteemed for the formation of the highly select Regiment of Nobles." The first company of this regiment comprised "only those holding titles of Castile,"

22. *Ibid.*

23. *Ibid.*

and the other companies, only "those from the most illustrious families of the kingdom."[24]

Thus, the officer rolls from Piura to Tacna provide a superb representation of the Peruvian patriciate of 1763, from members of the creole elite such as the Marqués de Moscoso to Indian nobles like Carlos Chuquihuanca, Felipe Huaman Condon, and Simón Cayro. Amat believed that as a consequence the coast stood defended and that he had even "closed the doors to the vast countryside that lies between Tucumán, Potosí, and Chuquisaca."[25]

A regulation for the militia promulgated to refine and codify these measures included definitions of the *fuero militar,* promotion policy, official honors, etc., and consolidated the oligarchy's command and control over this immense establishment.[26] All of this remained during and after the war as an essential component of the colonial defense system, and the militia thus became one of the key institutions of the viceroyalty.[27]

Two decades later, when insurgency erupted in the Sierra immediately before and during the rebellion of Túpac Amaru, the militia was the landowners' most effective instrument against the dissidents, first in Arequipa in early 1780 and subsequently in the Cuzco region. John Fisher has clearly shown that the true enemies of the peasantry in 1780–1783 were not peninsular Spaniards but those who controlled the economic and social life within the viceroyalty and especially in the rural areas, that is, the creole oligarchy. Leon Campbell has demonstrated the role of the militia, which the creole elites controlled, in repressing the threat to their socioeconomic interests that the rebellion represented.[28] The following discussion will provide a general analysis of the militia, designed first to identify the roles of the various social sectors in its structure and second to assess the social consequences of the disturbances of 1780–1783 and the role of the militia in their suppres-

24. *Ibid.*

25. Expediente, general defense of Peru. AGN, Superior Gobierno, leg. 12, C-265, fol. 12.

26. AGI, Lima, leg. 654.

27. See the Inspection Reports in AGI, Lima, leg. 1490, and AGN, Superior Gobierno, leg. 17, C-448, fol. 120.

28. John Robert Fisher, "La rebelion de Túpac Amaru y el programa de la reforma imperial de Carlos III," *AEA,* XXXVIII (1971), 405–21; Leon G. Campbell, "The Army of Peru and the Túpac Amaru Revolt," *HAHR,* LVI (1976), 31–57.

sion. However, neither the cycle of events that culminated in the Túpac Amaru rebellion nor the military campaigns that ended it will be addressed directly.[29]

Between 1780 and 1800, the Peruvian militia was positioned, albeit in a somewhat dispersed manner, in five specific zones. The Lima area, from Santa to Chincha, had units based in the viceregal capital as well as in the coastal haciendas and native communities. In the Tarma area, which encompassed the territory from Huánuco to Huamanga, the officers were hacendados and merchants from the Sierra, and the enlisted men Indian peasants taken from the haciendas and native communities. In the Arequipa and Moquegua area of southern Peru, hacendados and merchants served as officers, and the troops, both urban and rural, were Indians. The Cuzco area extended to the Urubamba frontier, and hacendados and merchants commanded peasants. The north, including the zone from Piura to Cajamarca, featured hacendado and merchant officers and a soldiery of peasants from the haciendas and Indians from the native villages. An analysis of these units within the context of their respective regions provides important information about how members of the local oligarchies controlled them. The service records of the officers and sergeants for 1780–1810 are highly instructive.

The Lima Area and Its Coast

The predominance of the local elites in the Lima area is clearly evident (see Table 10). The lower social sectors provided not only the common soldiers but also the sergeants and adjutants, who usually emerged from the ranks. In the case of Lima proper, the "soldiers of fortune" were discharged enlisted men of peninsular origin from the regular army who had adopted diverse occupations since being discharged (tailor, barber, book dealer, etc.). The creole "nobility" continued to provide the core of the officer corps, even after the rebellion in the Sierra.

29. The abundant literature on the participation of the militia in these campaigns includes Leon G. Campbell, "Social Structure of the Túpac Amaru Army in Cuzco," *HAHR,* LXI (1981), 675–93; Leon G. Campbell, "The Changing Racial and Administrative Structure of the Peruvian Military Under the Later Bourbons," *Americas,* XXXII (1975), 117–33; and Juan José Vega and Alejandro Seraylan Leiva, *Historia general del ejército peruano* (Lima, 1981).

TABLE 10
Militia Officers of the Lima Region

Officer Characteristics	Number	Percentage
Lima		
Officers analyzed	246	100
Birthplace		
Lima	118	48
Spain	80	32
Other Peruvian places	48	20
Total Americans	166	68
Social status		
Titles, nobles, distinguished	107	43.4
Soldiers of fortune	41	16.6
Commoners, *morenos, pardos*	98	39.8
Lima outskirts and the coast		
Officers analyzed	44	100
Birthplace		
Local area	28	64
Spain	15	34
Other Peruvian places	1	2
Social status		
Titles, nobles, distinguished	43	98
Soldiers of fortune	1	2

Source: Service Records, AGI, Lima, legs. 1500–1503.
Note: The units analyzed include the Infantry Battalion of Spanish Militia of Lima, the Battalion of Free Pardos of Lima, the Regiment of Provincial Dragoons of Lima, the Immemorial Militia Companies of the King (tailors), the Militia Artillery Companies, the Militia Cavalry Squadron of Lima (free *pardos*), the Company of Lancers (free *morenos*), and the Separate Companies of Free Morenos of Lima. The units from the coast and the outskirts of the city include the Volunteer Cavalry of Santa, the Cavalry Regiment of Carabaillo, and the militia of the Districts of Ica and Chincha.

The officers were members of the cabildo, the consulado, and the customs and monopoly administrations (*i.e.*, the whole patrician sector of the city). Before 1784 some of the officers had been corregidores or held other public offices in Tinta, Cuzco, Collado, and Tarma. Among their contributions were funding for uniforms, mounts, and armaments for their militiamen, as well as the payment of the salaries for "soldiers" employed to repair the cathedral or to conduct other public works.

Almost to the man, the colonels and captains included in their campaign records the suppression of the Huarochirí Revolt of

TABLE 11
The Militia Officers of Tarma and the Central Sierra

Officer Characteristics	Number	Percentages
Officers analyzed	94	100
Birthplace		
Local area	46	49.0
Spain	40	42.5
Other Peruvian places	8	8.5
Social status		
Titles, nobles, distinguished	82	87.2
Mestizos	12	12.8

SOURCE: Service Records, AGI, Lima, legs. 1503–1504.
NOTE: Included are the Regiment of Dragoons of the Tarma Frontier and the separate militia companies of Jauja, Moyobamba, Huanta, and Huamanga.

1784 (a local movement led by *caciques*), and a goodly number of them also listed their performance in the expedition against Túpac Amaru under the command of Don José del Valle, which took place in Cuzco, Yanquipampa, Llocllora, Combapata, and Condorcuyo. Some also mentioned the repression of the disturbances led by Puma Catari in Omasuyu.

The documentation for the officers of the coastal units reveals that some had been active in the expulsion of the Jesuits and in crushing the Trujillo Revolt of 1770. They paid for the uniforms and, as they put it, "the up-keep of my soldiers in campaign."[30]

The Tarma Area and Central Sierra

The landowners constituted the most important officer group in the Tarma and central Sierra locality, and more than four thousand peasants served in their units (Table 11). They claimed to have funded their companies during various operations against internal rebellions. All of them served against Túpac Amaru, taking prominent prisoners, and they occupied the five fortresses of Paucartambo. Most of the Spanish officers (70 to 80 percent) were married to women from the region and had lived there for many years.[31]

30. AGI, Lima, legs. 1500–1503.

31. AGI, Lima, legs. 1503–1504.

TABLE 12
The Militia Officers of Arequipa and Moquegua

Officer Characteristics	Number	Percentage
Officers analyzed	203	100
Birthplace		
Local area	162	80
Spain	31	15
Other Peruvian places	10	5
Social status		
Titles, nobles, distinguished	169	83
"Good" and American Spaniards[a]	28	14
Mestizos	6	3

SOURCE: Service Records, AGI, Lima, leg. 1504.
NOTE: Included are the Cavalry Regiment of Arequipa, the Provincial Infantry Regiment of Arequipa, the Moquegua Dragoons, the Cavalry Regiment of Moquegua, and the Infantry Regiment of Moquegua.
[a]The categories "Good" and "American Spaniards" are translated literally from the service records. They denote intermediate social groups not considered "noble" or "distinguished," but of Spanish descent—"poor white" would be an equivalent.

Arequipa and the Moquegua Area

The service records of the Moquegua officers literally classified them as "hacendados" or as "nobles" and "hidalgos" (Table 12). After the Arequipa and Cuzco campaigns, they forgave the salaries owed them by the king, defrayed the cost of their "banners as well as the festivities to bless them," provided sustenance for their troops while on campaign, and lent the crown considerable sums. All of them fought in the Arequipa rebellion, and their service records describe these actions precisely. They also fought against Túpac Amaru in Lampa, Puno, Chucuito, La Paz, Juli (classified as a "great battle"), Moho, Huaycho, and Carumas.[32]

The Cuzco Area

The percentage of Spaniards in the Cuzco area was quite small during this period, and the oligarchy came strictly from the city of Cuzco (Table 13). Nearly all were characterized as "land-

32. AGI, Lima, leg. 1504.

TABLE 13
The Militia Officers of Cuzco

Officer Characteristics	Number	Percentage
Officers analyzed	88	100
Birthplace		
Local area	73	82.9
Spain	5	5.6
Other Peruvian places	10	11.3
Social status		
Titles, nobles, distinguished	47	53
Honorable	41	47

SOURCE: Service Records, Cavalry and Infantry Regiments of Cuzco, AGI, Cuzco, leg. 63.

owners," or "from commerce." The service records of the sergeants described them as "honorable," though in later years simply as "mestizos." Some held the title of marqués; and a number were corregidores. Various hacendados had been born in localities adjoining the city, such as San Sebastián, Accha, Paruro, Coporque, Tinta, and Checacope. Their service records enumerated familiar merits: uniforming their troops; contributing mules; purchasing arms, cannons, gunpowder, and gun carriages; constructing storehouses; feeding the troops on expedition; and making donations to the king. They served under the command of José del Valle in all the campaigns against Túpac Amaru, including the siege of Cuzco in 1781 and the general offensive, and the actions at Calca, Vilcanota, Chitapampa, Pisac, Tinta, and Ocongate, on up to Puno. They also related how these officers personally assumed responsibility for the imprisonment of the leader and took part in the trials of the insurgents.[33]

The Northern Region

In the northern region, the number of officers described as "landowners" is rather high, as is the portion that appears as "from commerce" (Table 14). The majority of these units were mobilized during the Cuzco disorders; some troops from Cajamarca were

33. AGI, Cuzco, leg. 63.

TABLE 14
The Militia Officers of the North

Officer Characteristics	Number	Percentage
Officers analyzed	345	100
Birthplace		
Local area	313	90.7
Spain	25	7.2
Other Peruvian places	7	2.0
Social status		
Titles, nobles, distinguished	197	57.1
"Good"[a]	42	12.1
Honorable and humble	106	30.7

Source: Service Records, AGI, Lima, leg. 1504.
Note: Included are the Infantry Regiment of San Antonio, Dragoons of Guambos, Dragoons of Celendin, Cavalry Regiment of San Pablo de Chalaquez, all from the District of Cajamarca; the Dragoon Regiment of Chota, the Infantry Battalion of Piura, the Cavalry Squadrons of Huancabamba and Chalaco, all of the District of Piura; and the Infantry Regiment of San Juan de la Frontera and the Cavalry of Luya and Chillaos, both from the Province of Chachapoyas.
[a] "Good" denoted an intermediate social group.

quartered in Trujillo. They intervened directly in the repression of other popular revolts, including that of the Hualgayoc mining camp in 1778 and that against the "Juez Real." They also put down a rising of peasants in Sangana (Chota) who were attempting to reclaim lands usurped by hacendados.[34]

The histories of these five regions as a whole reveal the manipulative behavior of the dominant rural oligarchies. Disenchanted with the reform program advanced by Charles III, they were the first to show opposition by encouraging popular protest movements, as in Arequipa and Cuzco; but when they saw their interests threatened from below they did not hesitate to use the militia system to sustain their power and privileges. They were able to use peasant against peasant because their grip on the peons of their haciendas and on the communities under their jurisdictions was so

34. AGI, Lima, leg. 1504.

complete that the Indians could scarcely refuse to cooperate, selling themselves for the pay and food that the landowner supplied them as militiamen. Once again the worst enemies of the peasantry were other peasants manipulated by the landed elite. This story would be repeated again and again in the history of Peru, before, during, and after the Independence period.

The duplicity of the Sierra oligarchy was plainly evident during 1760–1800. Moreover, during these years, which are the key to understanding later events, the landed elite engaged in the massive acquisition of new properties by exploiting the permissiveness of the royal administration. The vast holdings of the Jesuits were placed on the market, as were the lands of Indian communities that lay in ruins after the rebellions of 1780–1783. The expanding mining production of the same period also advanced private landownership by encouraging increased capitalization. Throughout this process, the hacendados used the militia to crush any kind of resistance to their interests and at the same time gain the favor of the king through the claim that they were thwarting dangerous insurrections that might threaten viceregal authority. A further factor of fundamental importance was the increased social conservatism of the patricians of the Sierra as a consequence of the insurrection of Túpac Amaru.[35]

The other side of the coin was that the royal administration acceded to many of the demands of those who had rebelled. Reform measures introduced in the early 1780s included the abolition of the *repartos* and the establishment of an audiencia in Cuzco. The presence of peninsular civil authorities in the zone was increased, while the local oligarchies were ousted from juridical posts that had given them responsibility over the peasants, all of which provoked protests from the landed elite. Overall, nevertheless, the degree of real change was not profound. The militia, one of the most important instruments of political pressure and control, remained in the hands of the patricians of the Sierra, and the reform measures, though extensive in theory, were not fully enforced.

At another level, the oligarchy of the Sierra, after asserting its dominion through bloody repression and by monopolizing the

35. Campbell, "The Army of Peru."

land as well as public and ecclesiastical offices, was drawn into conflict with the *limeño* financiers. The producers of the interior believed, perhaps incorrectly, that the relative unimportance of agricultural products among Peru's exports resulted from the indifference of the merchants in the viceregal capital, whereas the merchants attributed the problem to factors outside their control, such as high prices charged by producers. The *limeños* themselves, though deeply divided over the issue of free trade, ultimately had no option but to make the best of it. The even more conservative hacendados of the Sierra, for their part, were afraid to permit the slightest reduction in their power or to tolerate modern ideas during the relatively enlightened period of the early 1790s because they thought the native communities under their control might attempt to reassert their legal claims. Their fears were realized in 1814, with the outbreak of revolution in Cuzco, and again in 1821, as the Wars of Independence finally reached the interior of Peru.

These factors left the *limeño* elite undecided about which side to support between 1810 and 1818, while the *serranos,* for their part, took a clearly conservative direction. As late as 1817, the latter continued supporting the army of Upper Peru with manpower and money. With the support and collaboration of the landed elite, six thousand men a year were recruited from Puno, Huamanga, Cuzco, and Arequipa, to oppose revolution in Upper and Lower Peru, according to the prominent creole royalist Pío Tristán. And in 1815, the commander of the royalist army, Juan Ramírez, recaptured Arequipa from Pumacahua as the inhabitants, including the oligarchy, shouted "long live Fernando VII!" The *arequipeños,* like the patriarchs of Cuzco, regarded the "patriots" as the real invaders and believed that a rebel triumph would bring an end to their own power. Between 1818 and 1820, therefore, the contributions of money and men from Cuzco, Suipacha, and Trujillo continued.[36] By the end of this period, with San Martín's arrival on the coast, the war had become a direct confrontation between the Sierra and the coast, the former waving the royal banner and the latter, albeit reluctantly, committing itself to the course of independence.

36. Biblioteca Nacional (Lima), Sección Investigaciones Históricas, ms. D6649; AGI, Panama, leg. 257; Biblioteca Nacional (Lima), Sección Investigaciones Históricas, MS D12361, D12364, D12365.

In 1820, after the liberal restoration in Spain, Cuzco and its district swore allegiance to the constitution of 1812.[37] The oligarchies of the Sierra, however, felt threatened by the provisions of the constitution, which, from their viewpoint, appeared excessively progressive, and confronted by the fact that they had lost the struggle for the political future of Peru, they began the process of disengagement.[38] They not only had lost the support of the peninsular forces, which were in any event already small and of poor quality, but the power structure of Lima had begun to construct a Peruvian republic from the capital, almost completely ignoring the Sierra. The elites withdrew within themselves and their immediate interests, enclosing themselves behind the secure walls of their vast haciendas.

The Rivalry Between Cartagena and Santa Fe

The characterization of Cartagena de Indias as a military city in the eighteenth century is widely accepted. Certainly, the city was designed with defensive considerations uppermost. Almost from its beginnings, however, it also functioned as the principal port for New Granada through which the districts of the Audiencia of Santa Fe sent their surpluses onto the transatlantic market, receiving a broad variety of imports in return. It was the central commercial entrepôt for the economy of New Granada.

Santa Fe, on the other hand, played a very different role. As the colonial administrative center, first of the audiencia and then of the viceroyalty, Santa Fe attempted to exercise jurisdiction over a vast territory ranging hundreds of kilometers in every direction. This was an impossible task. Neither the Atlantic nor the Pacific ports, which grew rapidly during the eighteenth century, accepted the situation. Nor did the areas surrounding Santa Fe itself or the more remote regions of the interior. Quito always attempted to be—and in reality was—another major nucleus of power, and it perceived the viceregency in Santa Fe as a serious impediment to its development. Popayán also enjoyed extensive autonomy and

37. Archivo Diocesano, Cuzco, XII, 1, 12, XVI, 3, 5, 42, 100.

38. See the "Libro mayor de operaciones del ejército del Alto Perú," Biblioteca Nacional (Lima), Sección Investigaciones Históricas, MS D12431.

viewed skeptically the power structure emerging in Santa Fe. The same was true of Antioquia and the Llanos.

Santa Fe, aspiring to act as the redistribution center for the viceregal economy, envied the real successes of Cartagena in this respect, but the power it could amass from its function as the colonial administrative center was insufficient to counteract the power of the coastal oligarchy. This rivalry lay deeply rooted in the past and would continue into modern times.

The military documentation provides important insights into the personalities of the power groups at both centers. After the creation in 1784 of the Santa Fe Regiment, the regular army unit of Cartagena had 363 officers, and that of Santa Fe, 121.[39]

Although each garrison had a strong nucleus of peninsular officers, the characteristics of the two corps varied significantly. The officer corps of the Auxiliary Regiment of Santa Fe served principally in the viceregal capital, where they had the promise of better assignments and more rapid promotions. A portion of the hacendados of the Santa Fe district, as well as of the outlying savanna, together with some merchants from the capital, eventually acquired commissions in the auxiliary regiment, though they never came to dominate it. Between 1790 and 1810, Cartagena's merchant oligarchy, as well as landowners from Mompós, Lorica, and Sinú, by contrast, established a strong presence in the fixed regiment established in the port. The peninsular officers stationed in Cartagena, moreover, forged strong links with the local oligarchy, through both marriage and investments in business and land. On the whole, these men had little desire to leave Cartagena, if only because their businesses did not permit them to do so, though some of their sons went to the capital in search of advancement. These two units sustained an open rivalry, as shown by innumerable disputes over troop levels, materiel, and prestige. When one gained some small advantage, the officers of the other inevitably complained about inequities.

A significant portion of the Spanish officers of the auxiliary regiment obtained positions in the bureaucratic apparatus of the viceregal administration and played important roles in the reform

39. For details of these establishments, see Kuethe, *Military Reform and Society*.

program. Many married creoles or managed to acquire haciendas in the savanna, in places such as Tunja or Villa de Leiva, thus transforming themselves into landed magnates. At the same time they formed the politico-military elite around the viceroy. These relationships made them and their creole comrades antagonistic toward the coastal groupings of officer-merchants and officer-landowners, men who in any event were inclined to get on with their business with or without the approval of the viceregal authorities.

Table 15 lists the birthplaces of all officers of the Cartagena and Santa Fe garrisons, and Table 16 details the birthplace distribution of those born in New Granada. The latter shows, perhaps not surprisingly, that natives of Cartagena and Santa Fe constituted the largest elements among the creole officials in their respective garrisons. This pattern was reinforced by the local ties of the Spanish-born officers. Obviously these units were rooted deeply in their respective localities.

Adding the variable of rank to that of birthplace reveals that the quantitative superiority of peninsulars was not fully reflected in qualitative terms (see Table 17). In Cartagena and Santa Fe between 1800 and 1810, creoles dominated the officer corps to an even greater extent than they had in the 1780s and 1790s: in Cartagena, 80 percent of the middle-rank officers were natives of the city, as were almost all the cadets and sublieutenants; nearly all the peninsulars occupied the lower ranks of sergeant or unit commander. In 1810, the cabildo summoned Cartagena's military leadership to dispossess the governor, who had refused to come to acceptable political terms. The leaders called were Diego Marazona, colonel of artillery; Manuel de Anguiano, colonel of engineers; José del Castillo, colonel of the fixed infantry regiment; Eduardo Llamas, lieutenant colonel of the pardo battalion; Felipe García del Río, captain commander of the white regiment; and Mateo Manrique, the *sargento mayor* of the plaza. They responded promptly, naming Lieutenant Colonel Blas de Soria as provisional governor. Although not a creole by birth, Soria was a *cartagenero* by adoption. All these officers had lived in Cartagena for many years and developed innumerable family and personal interests. During a review of the fixed regiment in 1811, they informed the troops of their decision to declare the city independent of Santa Fe

TABLE 15
Geographic Origins of the Officer Corps of Cartagena and Santa Fe

Birthplace	Number	Percentage
Cartagena officers, 1760–1810		
Andalusia	68	19.0
Aragón	6	2.0
Asturias	5	1.0
Balearic Islands	3	1.0
Canary Islands	7	2.0
Castile	44	12.0
Catalonia	19	5.0
Galicia	11	3.0
Extremadura	12	3.0
Levante and Murcia	8	2.0
Navarre	1	0
North Africa	23	6.0
Basque Country	6	2.0
Caribbean and Florida	4	1.0
New Spain	3	0.8
New Granada	127	34.9
Foreigners	12	3.3
Unknown	4	1.1
Santa Fe officers, 1780–1810		
Andalusia	17	14.0
Aragón	2	2.0
Balearic Islands	1	1.0
Canary Islands	1	1.0
Castile	36	30.0
Catalonia	4	3.0
Galicia	1	1.0
Extremadura	10	8.0
Levante and Murcia	1	1.0
North Africa	1	1.0
Basque Country	2	2.0
Caribbean and Florida	1	1.0
New Spain	3	2.4
New Granada	38	31.4
Foreigners	3	2.4

SOURCE: Service Records, which are dispersed between the AGI and AGS. For full details of the locations, see Marchena Fernández, *Oficiales y soldados,* Appendix I. The exact archival locations are AGI, SF, leg. 1156, Chile, leg. 438; and AGS, Guerra Moderna, legs. 7280–82.

TABLE 16
The Native-born Officers of Cartagena and Santa Fe

Birthplace	Number	Percentage
Cartagena officers		
Cartagena and its district	84	66.1
Santa Fe	12	9.4
Santa Marta	11	8.6
Cartago	2	1.5
Honda	4	3.0
Ocaña	1	0.7
Río Hacha	1	0.7
Popayán	1	0.7
Other	11	8.6
Santa Fe officers		
Santa Fe	22	57.8
Cartagena	9	23.6
Charala	1	2.6
Antioquia	2	5.2
San Juan de Girón	1	2.6
Popayán	2	5.2
Honda	1	2.6

SOURCE: See Table 15.

TABLE 17
The Officers of Cartagena and Santa Fe by Grade, 1780–1810

	Cartagena (%)		Santa Fe (%)	
Grade[a]	Peninsulars	Creoles	Peninsulars	Creoles
High	81.3	17.7	88.7	11.3
Middle	42.1	57.9	54.2	45.8
Junior	30.0	70.0	27.7	72.3
Sergeants	84.0	16.0	73.0	27.0

SOURCE: See Table 15.
[a]High-grade officers are brigadiers, colonels, *sargentos mayores,* and lieutenant colonels; middle-grade officers are captains, lieutenants, and adjutants; lower-grade officers are sub-lieutenants and cadets.

as well as Madrid. Only a few voiced disagreement, and no conflict whatever occurred.[40]

In Santa Fe, though peninsulars were proportionately more numerous, a similar situation developed. The declining prestige of the viceroy and the strengthening of the cabildo, combined with the offenses believed to have been committed by the colonial administration against the interests of Santa Fe in favor of Cartagena, and the tempting possibility of organizing the state of Cundinamarca, induced the local oligarchy, despite its ties with the viceregal institutions, to replace them with a self-proclaimed power that extended throughout the whole territory of the audiencia.

Although in Santa Fe and Cartagena some officials were expelled, they were a minority. The vast majority supported the establishment of the juntas. They included the chief of engineers in Cartagena, Manuel Anguiano, who wrote in 1810 saying that he would not leave the city. "In this situation, it is necessary for me to remain here where destiny has taken me."[41] He eventually became one of the martyrs of Cartagena when it was reconquered by Spanish troops.

The social status of the officer corps provides insights into the configuration of the urban patriciate (Table 18). Almost all the creoles were members of the urban oligarchy; nobles and the sons of military officers represented over 90 percent. This was as much the case in Cartagena as in Santa Fe. Peninsulars were prominent in the humble category (approximately one-third), but most of these men were sergeants, as already shown.

The rest of the variables, such as years of service, promotion rates, mobility, etc., reveal that in general the officer group basically did not leave the city (except in the case of the transfer of the auxiliary regiment to Santa Fe) and that their dedication to military duty was seldom strong. Their multiple outside interests did not permit undivided commitments. Many of the peninsulars were married, and their wives had come from Cartagena or Santa Fe, depending upon their station.

What emerges throughout the rivalry between the fixed regiment and the auxiliary regiment, between José Bernet (colonel in

40. G. Porras Troconis, *Cartagena hispánica, 1533–1810* (Bogotá, 1954), 47. See, too, Marchena Fernández, *La institución militar.*

41. Servicio Histórico Militar, Madrid, doc. 5-2-12-11.

TABLE 18
The Social Standing of the Officer Corps of
Cartagena and Santa Fe, 1780–1810

Status	Cartagena (%)		Santa Fe (%)	
	Creoles	Peninsulars	Creoles	Peninsulars
Nobles	67.7	51.1	73.6	56.4
Sons of officers	23.6	11.1	23.6	11.5
Commoners	8.6	37.8	2.6	32.0

SOURCE: See Table 15.

Cartagena) and Anastasio Cejudo (colonel in Santa Fe), and between the officers of the port and the military leadership of the viceroyalty is the tremendous desire of each garrison to dominate the other. This phenomenon should not be perceived solely in military terms, however, but in the broader context of a *cartagenero* elite that had wearied of competing with Santa Fe over questions of internal and external commercial traffic, while the oligarchs from the city of Tequendama resisted the pervasive erosion of their control over the viceroyalty owing to Cartagena's ability to dominate the market. To the chagrin of Santa Fe, moreover, the major portion of the monies that paid for the fortifications, troops, and officer salaries in Cartagena came from the royal treasury in the capital. And because the port habitually complained that it did not have the funds needed to meet these expenses—roughly half a million pesos every year—the king ordered the royal coffers in Santa Fe to provide annual subsidies. In other words, the revenues raised through taxation in the upland districts of the viceroyalty served, among other things, to create monetary liquidity on the coast, thus stimulating businesses that competed with those of the interior.[42]

When Santa Fe protested this state of affairs, alleging that a rebellion had occurred in Socorro because of these taxes and that tensions remained high in all upland jurisdictions, Cartagena complained about its "defenselessness" and a lack of funds to complete "necessary repairs" and to meet other needs. Conscious of the city's status as the most important naval base in Spanish America

42. Kuethe, *Military Reform and Society*, 89.

after Havana, the royal administration routinely ordered Santa Fe and Quito to increase the subsidies. This was a primary reason why the oligarchy of Santa Fe sought at every opportunity to humble the arrogance of the patricians of the north.[43]

A Profile of the Militia of New Granada

New Granada, like Peru, had a long-standing tradition of militia service. In Cartagena, volunteer units dated back to the seventeenth century, even though their inefficiency was proverbial and frequently referred to, as, for example, when Baron de Pointis attacked the city and when Admiral Edward Vernon in his turn assaulted its fortresses. One witness related some years later that the fear of the poor militiamen, when faced by a real army, was sobering. In the course of the Battle of Cartagena, the men of the Battalion of Pardos had to be wedged between the Regiments of Aragon and Spain with their officers standing behind them under orders "to slash in the chest whomever might flee, by which means they managed to hold more troops in place."[44]

The militia system in this jurisdiction did not, therefore, differ substantially from that of the rest of the continent. Moreover, the same general legislation was applied: the Regulation for the Disciplined Militia of Cuba in 1772, the modifications for Puerto Rico, the Regulation for the Militia of Yucatán and Campeche in 1778, and in 1794, a specific regulation for New Granada.[45]

Under the arrangements that prevailed before 1772, the militia was scattered throughout the province's municipalities and their districts in a multitude of companies, ranging in size from twenty to two hundred men, depending upon the population of the city, village, or hacienda that supported them. The *capitanes a guerra* reported every year that all was in proper order. Reality, however, was something else. In 1736, for example, the force of 1,421 men raised in San Benito Abad possessed a total weaponry of 125 rifles, 187 lances, 12 swords, and 3 pistols. The six companies scattered throughout the Savanna of Tolú had never mustered as a tactical

43. *Ibid.*

44. Report, Antonio de Salas, AGI, SF, leg. 948A.

45. These regulations are in AGI, IG, leg. 1885; and AGI, SF, leg. 948A.

unit, each drilling separately on Sundays when the local hacendado had no harvest underway.[46]

After the reforms of 1772 and the application of a formal regulation, the situation changed somewhat on the coast. Under the new system, the militia of the cities, towns, and other localities were organized into regiments or battalions of whites, *pardos,* and all colors; separate companies; and detachments under a scheme that, on paper, seemed to represent an improvement. In reality, everything continued much as before for the militia of the interior districts, which was commanded by hacendados. But the militia of the city was in fact upgraded. The merchants and financiers were responsible for filling the units, uniforming them, instructing them, and building barracks, roles that gave them the opportunity to challenge other authorities on questions of rank and preeminence in the city's processions, fiestas, and assorted soirees.

A typical example of these urban patricians, suddenly converted into colonels and sporting greatcoats, wigs, batons, cravats, and multicolored cockades, was Juan Fernández de Moure, colonel of the White Infantry Regiment of Cartagena toward the end of the eighteenth century. Born in Galicia, he was more *cartagenero* than the Cerro de la Popa. A prosperous merchant, he was a member of the cabildo with various properties in the Mompós district. Persistent rumors that part of his fortune had accrued from smuggling repeatedly drove him to offer gifts and loans to the royal treasury. The former included bridges and roads constructed at his personal expense, and sometimes straight cash. He also lent money to the royal treasury without demanding interest when it came due. His regiment was his pride and joy, and he dedicated himself to it passionately. Lawsuits to advance corporate privileges abounded, and he claimed his unit to be far superior to the fixed regiment. His troops stood guard duty and conducted night patrols, all funded by Don Juan. The governor described him as "haughty, prideful, and ungovernable." Businessmen criticized him for leaving them without help for their stores because, regulation in hand, Fernández de Moure would not permit a single white to evade the weekly military drills. Moure went so far as to solicit the rank of colonel in the regular army, but this honor the crown

46. AGI, SF, leg. 939.

apparently refused him.[47] There were many such officers in the American militia because the uniform accorded high prestige in urban society. Moreover, most of those who embraced the militia system did so to enjoy the benefits accorded by the *fuero militar.*

On the coast, the presence of large units from the regular army overshadowed the presence of the militia. In the interior, by contrast, this was not the case during the 1760s and 1770s. From Santa Fe to Ocaña, in Antioquia, or in the south, around Popayán, Cali, and Pasto, the grip that the oligarchies held on the militia was typical as was the effect this institution in turn had on the whole of society. In Popayán, for example, the most select of the city were present at Sunday reviews, and in the viceregal capital, the unit commanders were the flower of the Santa Fe elite.

In 1781, when the Comuneros of Socorro advanced on Zipaquirá, thus threatening the capital, it was militiamen at arms who challenged the colonial establishment. This movement was directed not only against the authorities who had increased taxation, but also against the hacendados of the area and the rentiers from Santa Fe. The cry "Long live the king, death to bad government," clearly implied an attack on the landed magnates, who were actually the individuals exercising power and ruling over the populace.[48] Although the origin of the conflict lay in the interior elites' discontent with the Bourbon reforms, the elites very quickly realized, as in the Peruvian case, that popular mobilization was a cure far worse than the disease because it threatened their interests directly.

After the movement was extinguished, with the head and hands of José Antonio Galán affixed to poles positioned at popular crossroads, the lesson was learned. The traditional militia was disbanded while the new units were established in Santa Fe under the provisions of the Cuban regulation and under tight control.[49] The Auxiliary Regiment of Santa Fe was created, establishing a permanent force of regular troops in the capital. And the militia of Popayán, which had been reorganized just before the rebellion,

47. AGI, SF, leg. 949, 948A–948B, 636.

48. Pablo G. Cárdenas Acosta, *El movimiento comunal de 1781 en Nueva Granada* (Bogotá, 1960).

49. AGI, SF, leg. 948B.

was retained.[50] The peasants at last understood that they had little chance of overcoming the abuses inflicted by the hacendados, who were even more firmly entrenched in their positions of privilege and power.

As events developed, the patriciate would not use the militia as an overt political instrument until 1810. It was then employed in Santa Fe to undermine the power of the viceroy, and in Cartagena, together with the fixed regiment, to overthrow the governor and declare the city independent. Thereafter, in serving as the soldiery of the patriot armies of the centralists and the federalists, the militia became the cannon fodder of the civil wars.[51]

Whereas the struggle between 1810 and 1815 can be characterized as primarily an affair of the elites, the heightened military pressure that followed the arrival from Spain in 1815 of General Pablo Morillo's royalist forces led the patriciate to draw the popular sectors—that is, the militia—into the action. Hermes Tovar has documented the participation of the hacendados in these conflicts with, of course, their militia.[52] The ambivalent behavior of the oligarchies was evident when, as in Peru, the elites defended their interests by repressing the peasantry and the village Indians who attempted to reclaim their rights and usurped lands. Later, however, they did not hesitate to put them in the firing line against the peninsular invaders. After the final triumph, however, the peasants and Indians were not permitted to participate in the construction of their nation.

Throughout the preceding decades, the *cartagenero* oligarchy had stood united in defense of its interests. Creoles and penin-

50. Unfortunately, the service records for this militia cannot be analyzed because none exist for Santa Fe and Popayán. Records do, however, exist for Cartagena. Analysis of them (AGI, SF, leg. 1156, and Chile, leg. 438) reveals that conclusions identical to those drawn for Peru are justified. A high percentage of *cartageneros* and regional groups appear as "nobles," "small farmers" (*labradores*), and "honorable."

51. In the lists of prisoners of the several armies that devastated the territory well into the nineteenth century, individuals continue to appear who maintained their militia ranks. For example, in 1813, among those captured and tried by Antonio Nariño were three captains, a lieutenant, and an ensign, all militiamen. Hermes Tovar Pinzón, "Guerras de opinión y represión en Colombia durante la Independencia, 1810–1820," *ACHSC*, XI (1983), 207.

52. *Ibid.*, 208.

sulars, who in any event were interrelated through marriage and commercial ties, sustained "harmonious unity that brought imponderable benefits."[53] In Santa Fe, by contrast, friction between peninsular administrators and creole merchants appeared at an early date. However, when Cartagena obtained a consulado in 1795 and Santa Fe did not, despite much effort to do so, and the capital found itself almost completely dependent upon the port, earlier signs of discord within the Santa Fe elites began to dissipate. The resulting unity would eventually contribute to the movement against the figure of the viceroy.

In reality, with some exceptions, the primary economic role of Santa Fe was that of an interior distribution center, its merchants buying goods on credit from Cartagena for subsequent sale throughout the viceroyalty. "The commerce between New Granada and the metropolis, as well as with the other dominions in America, is done through the port of Cartagena, where the true merchants are found, who receive merchandise on their accounts and from there market it in the inland provinces, where normally there are only encomenderos and merchants functioning as second and third hands [in this trade]."[54]

Santa Fe's intermediary role, in turn, alienated the other centers of the interior, including Popayán, Tunja, Pasto, and Antioquia, which never accepted their dependency upon the viceregal capital. Besides increasing their taxes and attempting to impose political centralization, Santa Fe controlled the prices of merchandise that, especially in the case of Antioquia, could be acquired directly from Cartagena. Thus, apart from the inherent rivalry that characterized the relationship between Santa Fe and Cartagena, a secondary series of jealousies simmered between the elites of the interior provinces and those of the capital.

From 1810 on, the hacendados of Popayán, who controlled a well-armed and substantial militia, made good their regional pretenses, first in the face of the Junta of Bogotá, then before the central government. In Tunja, Pasto, Buga, Socorro, and other locali-

53. Anthony McFarlane, "Comerciantes y monopolio en la Nueva Granada: El Consulado de Cartagena de Indias," *ACHSC*, XI (1983), 47–48.

54. *Ibid.*, 64.

ties, similar situations developed.[55] The Pasto militia stood against the national government not only after 1815, but also after the declaration of Colombian independence, as the oligarchy marshaled squadrons of tenants and peasants to defend local interests. In the Llanos, Cúcuta, and the Cauca Valley, much the same thing occurred.

The origins of the bloody conflicts that emerged in Colombia during the nineteenth century are to be found in the rivalries during the late colonial and Independence periods between the various local elites, in the roles of the popular sectors in these conflicts, and in the popular sectors' dissatisfaction with the social outcome of independence. Those who lost out to the triumphant elites in the late 1820s simply awaited the first opportunity to turn the tables.

55. AGI, SF, legs. 602, 949; AGI, Quito, leg. 574; AGI, SF, leg. 577A; AHNC, Miscelánea, tomo 138, fols. 246ff., tomo 116, fols. 418–20.

JACQUES A. BARBIER

Chapter 4

Commercial Reform and *Comercio Neutral* in Cartagena de Indias, 1788–1808

The commercial policy of Spain toward its Indies, and with it that toward Cartagena de Indias, took a dramatic turn with the end of the Seven Years' War. The loss of Havana drove home the lessons that the empire's security could not be sustained by traditional means and that far-reaching military reforms were necessary.[1] Such a course of action involved great expense and, to avoid the risks inherent in imposing new taxes on an unwilling colonial population, the crown decided to raise the necessary funds by stimulating economic growth through a limited deregulation of the economy. A broader tax base, it was reasoned, would provide the revenues needed for military reform.

It was in this context that the monarchy launched its mail-boat service in 1764 and decreed the establishment of *comercio libre* for Cuba and the other West Indian islands in 1765.[2] This policy

The author wishes to thank the Social Sciences and Humanities Research Council of Canada for funding his research.

1. Kuethe, *Cuba, 1753–1815*, 24.

2. *Reglamento provisional del correo marítimo de España a sus Indias Occidentales* (Madrid, 1764), AGI, IG, leg. 1586; *Reglamento para el comercio libre, 1778* (Seville, 1978), 1.

was slowly extended to other Caribbean and Gulf ports in the years following and in 1778 was applied to most of the rest of the empire—including the port of Cartagena de Indias.[3] This new trading structure was completed in 1789 when Venezuela was brought into the system, and a somewhat mitigated version of *comercio libre* was imposed on Veracruz.[4] Only the Philippines, whose trade was in the hands of a newly formed chartered company and of the traditional Manila Galleon, remained an exception to the universally applied policy. Everywhere else, freer trade, albeit within what remained an essentially mercantilist framework, had become the general rule.[5]

Nonetheless, despite the crown's apparent simplicity of purpose, the Bourbon reforms are not easily grasped. To properly understand them, one must have a holistic view of the renewal effort—a perspective that goes beyond bureaucratic imperatives and seeks to capture the sociopolitical realities that shaped Spanish and American motivations and reactions. The program (despite the constant complaints of the Consulado de Cádiz) was acceptable to most peninsular interest groups.[6] The elaborate military and fiscal establishments reformers called for were obvious founts of patronage, which Spaniards hoped to monopolize. Most importantly, the mercantilist foundations of the economic program held out the promise of larger colonial markets for the manufactured goods and agricultural products of the peninsula and opened wider perspectives for its reexports. The reforms bore the hopes of the monarchy, but were also a vehicle for the aspirations of much of Spain.[7]

3. The only exceptions were Mexico, the Philippines, and Venezuela.

4. Jacques A. Barbier, "The Culmination of the Bourbon Reforms, 1787–1792," *HAHR*, LVII (1977), 51–68. For Veracruz, see Javier Ortiz de la Tabla, *Comercio exterior de Veracruz, 1778–1821: Crisis de dependencia* (Seville, 1978).

5. On the Philippines, see María Lourdes Díaz-Trechuelo Spínola, *La Real Compañía de Filipinas* (Seville, 1965).

6. On consulado opposition, see Inglis and Kuethe, "El Consulado de Cádiz." For a case study of policy formation in these years, see Jacques A. Barbier, "Imperial Policy Towards the Port of Veracruz, 1788–1808: The Struggle between Madrid, Cádiz and Havana Interests," in Nils Jacobsen and Hans-Jurgen Puhle (eds.), *The Economies of Mexico and Peru During the Late Colonial Period, 1760–1810* (Berlin, 1986), 240–51.

7. For a general discussion of the dynamics of colonial policy-making in Spain during these years, see Jacques A. Barbier, "Silver, North American Penetration and the Span-

Similarly, although the reform program was clearly a peninsular and crown initiative, Spanish Americans were deeply implicated in its implementation. *Indianos* were not passive when faced with far-reaching change. Indeed, in the first flush of reform, the Cuban elite was told that it had to tolerate a greater military and fiscal burden, but that it would be rewarded by economic growth. The colonial upper classes had every intention of holding the crown to this type of bargain, even in areas where the monarchy was less forthright about its plans than it had been in Spain's "ever faithful isle." Moreover, despite some Spanish opposition, the Spanish-American elites expected to benefit from the services and opportunities derived from a more complex state structure, as the dominant groups in Cuba and Chile clearly managed to do.[8] The colonial population accepted reform if it brought benefits and opposed it otherwise. The local elites perverted crown desires to their own advantage whenever they could. Faced with change, they reacted vigorously to protect their own interests and those of the societies whose natural leaders they were.

Clearly, some measure of political conflict between imperial officialdom and colonials was inevitable; the interests of the motherland and its overseas domains were not so similar as to preclude it. Logically, struggle tended to arise where contradictions were most acute, and as one might expect of a far-reaching program, the Bourbon reforms carried within themselves the seeds of a number of contradictions. Some were general and brought to the fore only by adversity, as in the case of the conflict between Madrid's hunger for treasure and the peninsular periphery's need for trade. Others were particular but structural, as with the specie shortage of the Venezuelan economy.[9]

The most poignant, however, involved those cities or interests which, given their circumstances, could not benefit greatly from the reform effort. In those cases, the crown's economic in-

---

ish Imperial Economy, 1760–1800," in Jacques A. Barbier and Allan J. Kuethe (eds.), *The North American Role in the Spanish Imperial Economy, 1760–1819* (Manchester, England, 1984), 6–12.

8. Kuethe and Inglis, "Absolutism and Enlightened Reform"; Jacques A. Barbier, *Reform and Politics in Bourbon Chile, 1755–1796* (Ottawa, 1980).

9. See Jacques A. Barbier, "Peninsular Finance and Colonial Trade: The Dilemma of Charles IV's Spain," *JLAS,* XII (1980), 21–37; and Jacques A. Barbier, "Venezuelan 'Li-

junctions were much like Shakespeare's tale told by an idiot, full of sound and fury but signifying nothing. This is quite evidently the case with Cartagena—a port profoundly marked by the role it had once played in the Indies trade, a commercial city saddled with a predominantly military vocation. Together, historical and strategic factors prevented the chief entrepôt of New Granada from responding positively to the commercial aspects of the reforms.

Commercial Reform in Cartagena

With the decline and end of the *galeones,* Cartagena lost much of its commercial *raison d'être.*[10] Given Spain's reluctance to legalize the Cape Horn route into the Pacific, however, it did not lose all importance as an entry point for the Andean zone.[11] Indeed, the gradual decline of the Hapsburg trading system, as it left the traditional commercial structure in place but undersupplied with goods, tended to transform the habitual trade routes into channels of contraband. Cartagena shared in this evolution. Soldiers and officials, badly and irregularly paid, supplemented their official incomes as best they could, shielding and indulging in illegal trade. Crown agencies did no less. In the time of the British *asiento,* the South Sea Company (in which the king himself was a shareholder) used the port, covering contraband with the cloak of the legal slave trade. Indeed, as other commentators, including contributors to this collection, have indicated, contraband had become the principal engine driving the local economy by the early eighteenth century. A port whose prosperity had been founded on Spanish exclusivism now became wedded to covert contacts with its monarch's foreign competitors and enemies.

Nor was the *asiento de negros* the only such cover. Keeping the garrison and field forces fed and supplied was of such importance that occasional recourse to foreign markets was condoned even

branzas,' 1788–1808: From Economic Nostrum to Fiscal Imperative," *Americas,* XXXVII (1981), 457–78.

10. See Geoffrey J. Walker, *Spanish Politics and Imperial Trade, 1700–1789* (Bloomington, 1979); and George Robertson Dilg, "The Collapse of the Portobelo Fairs: A Study in Spanish Commercial Reform, 1720–1740" (Ph.D. dissertation, Indiana University, 1975).

11. Use of the Cape Horn route was not legalized until 1740, and Spanish vessels began to use it only after the end of the War of Austrian Succession.

into the late eighteenth century. In this regard, Cartagena was no different from Spain's other Caribbean forts and outposts. Eventually, under Archbishop-Viceroy Caballero y Góngora, exceptions extended even to allowing trade with the newly independent United States.[12] Here again, a licensed trade could serve as a cover for illegal commerce, and the military functions of the harbor blunted the force of mercantilism. In fact, the case just cited is peculiarly significant because the "abuse" was instituted in the name of reform. The archbishop-viceroy who allowed direct commercial contact with Anglo-Americans saw it as a useful support for a much-desired objective: the pacification of Darién.[13] To other reformers, however, such measures were no more than a betrayal of deeply held mercantilist principles.

Yet, it must be recognized that keeping to the pure mercantilist faith was extraordinarily difficult. As noted, local interests could be depended upon to use liberalizing legislation as a cover for contraband. Moreover, the crown itself seemed to hold to mercantilism in a rather Jesuitical way. In this regard, there were two major areas of contention. The first had to do with Madrid's willingness to compromise economic principles to developmentalist objectives. Perhaps the best example of this tendency comes with *comercio libre de negros,* which gave foreigners access to Spanish-American ports provided that they sailed in with Negro slaves to sell. Convinced that the economy of New Granada would not respond adequately to the input of additional slave labor, local reformers objected to the implementation of this scheme. The crown, however, proved adamant, for it was convinced that intelligent deregulation would bring economic growth, which could then be exploited by the motherland through intelligent mercantilism.

Second, sustaining seaborne trade in wartime was a critical problem. Recourse to so-called *comercio neutral* was one of the more contentious issues for Spanish mercantilists. Yet, the crown's

12. Viceroy José Manuel Ezpeleta to Conde de Lerena, Santa Fe, March 19, 1792, AGI, SF, leg. 641. This matter was discussed at the cabinet level in Spain. See the minutes of the meeting of May 9, 1791, AHN, Estado, libro 4. For the far-reaching character of these types of "exceptions," see Ezpeleta to Diego de Gardoqui, July 19, 1794, AGI, SF, leg. 643.

13. For the military circumstances in the Cartagena area, see Kuethe, "The Pacification Campaign"; and Kuethe, *Military Reform and Society.*

acceptance of this measure was merely the logical application of mercantilism under difficult circumstances. Indeed, because the Real Armada could not be expected to keep the sea-lanes clear in time of war against Great Britain, some means of transporting needed supplies to public agencies on both sides of the Atlantic and of continuing private commercial traffic had to be found.[14] Given the great number of wars in the eighteenth century, and the perception that frequent wars were "natural," it would have been irresponsible not to recognize the need for contingency plans.

In fact, the reforms were designed to produce an economy far more dependent upon overseas trade than had previously been the case. If the crown's plans were to be successful, transatlantic and pan-Caribbean transport had to be guaranteed, even in time of war. In many ways, the adequacy of wartime trade policy, which was most often based on variants of *comercio neutral,* was the acid test for the success or failure of the Bourbon reforms in imperial trade.

It is well known, of course, that no permanent legislation allowing recourse to neutral and friendly flags in fact existed and that such legislation was always opposed by powerful interests, such as those of Cádiz. Nonetheless, such circumstances should not mislead anyone. The crown could hardly publicize its belief that the Real Armada could not keep the sea-lanes open, nor could it know in advance what the most advantageous form of neutral trade might be, given the transient circumstances of war. Thus, no contingent legislation existed. Nonetheless, the history of Spanish imperial trade in the Wars of Spanish Succession, Austrian Succession, and American Independence, and in Charles IV's two successive conflicts with Great Britain, is quite clear on the subject. Again and again, the crown resorted to foreign-flag vessels. The Ministry of the Indies, and later that of Finance, clearly understood that wartime made alien ships the lifeblood of the empire.

I will examine how the Spanish crown attempted to continue the policy orientations of Charles III (1759–1788) in the war-torn

14. On the Spanish navy in this period, see José Patricio Merino Navarro, *La armada española en el siglo XVIII* (Madrid, 1981); and Jacques A. Barbier, "Indies Revenues and Naval Spending: The Cost of Colonialism for the Spanish Bourbons, 1763–1805," *Jahrbuch für Geschichte von Staat, Wirtschaft und Gesellschaft Lateinamerikas,* XXI (1984), 171–88.

reign of Charles IV (1788–1808). Although the success of the monarchy's wartime course is a fair index of what the Bourbon reforms achieved in the major port of the viceroyalty, an analysis of their success must also consider the continuity that characterized Spanish colonial policy in the late eighteenth century. Indeed, although *comercio libre* was an initiative of the reign of Charles III, neither the policy nor the orientation that spawned it disappeared with his death.[15] The ministers of Charles IV continued the old king's trade policies through, for example, the establishment of a comprehensive network of consulados (including that of Cartagena in 1795), legislation concerning *puertos menores,* and laws allowing *comercio libre de negros.*

Comercio Libre de Negros

The ongoing liberalization of trade legislation was a deeply ambiguous development in the viceroyalty of New Granada. The crown's agents there, men whose original service usually dated back to the tenure of José de Gálvez as minister of the Indies, tended to react negatively to the spectacle provided by Cartagena de Indias. In the major port of the viceroyalty, contraband was a way of life for private individuals and a valuable income supplement for the king's agents. Nor was legal trade always better. To the problems implicit in such mores were added those deriving from royal legislation. Indeed, when reformers spoke of destroying illicit commerce they often meant not only clearly illegal trade, but also trade that ought to have been because it was contrary to mercantilist principles.

Given the importance of illicit commerce in the economy of Cartagena, *comercio libre* was a two-edged sword. Indeed, freer trade made contraband less necessary, thereby threatening the despised industry. Yet, if it were implemented too liberally, it could just as easily subvert mercantilist principles or provide a cover for trade that would infringe upon them. Reformers well knew that contraband could bloom under the cover of licensed trade. The result was that officials on the scene often seemed more intent on mercantilism than did ministers back in Madrid, even as they

15. See Barbier, "Culmination of the Bourbon Reforms."

manifested a marked reticence about certain aspects of the reform effort.

In fact, reformers actually in the colonies readily identified direct trade with foreigners as the chief obstacle to achieving Spain's mercantilist ambitions in New Granada and tended to condemn all such contacts. As they became aware of the limited degree to which the local economy could respond to the deregulation emanating from Madrid, these officials found it rather difficult to see the difference between crown-sanctioned trade with aliens and that resulting from the exercise of purely local initiative.

Indeed, it could well be argued that the New Granada reform effort was based upon a series of ill-founded hopes. For the projected changes to be successful in the Cartagena region, they had to produce a great increase in the number of Spanish vessels calling at the port. Such a development could only be related to the development of local production for export or the capture of the markets of the interior. These phenomena do not seem to have occurred on a very large scale (see the figures provided in Chapter 6).

In any case, formidable obstacles stood in the way of such ambitions. Other Caribbean zones were better placed than distant Cartagena to penetrate the highly competitive European market for tropical products, particularly if it had to be done through peninsular harbors. Transport costs to and from the interior were relatively high. The eventual rise of Baranquilla speaks volumes about Cartagena's potential as a dominant port for the interior. Contraband, which brought in goods that even *comercio libre* discouraged and took out goods that still could not be sold otherwise for lack of economical transport, remained an essential element in Cartagena's trade.

The attitudes of colonial officials toward allowing foreigners access to the Cartagena market is revealed in their reaction to *comercio libre de negros*. In February, 1791, the crown extended its new regulations concerning this trade to Cartagena.[16] The policy had been instituted by a royal cedula of February 28, 1789, largely in response to Cuban demands for easier access to sources of slave labor, and policymakers in the colonial ministry saw it as a means

16. Circular Royal Order, February 23, 1791, AGI, Ultramar, leg. 722.

of fomenting export-oriented agriculture.[17] Unfortunately, the fighting against France and the two wars with Great Britain never allowed the legislation to produce its intended effect, even assuming that it could have. Further, the new law was met with a great deal of resistance in certain colonies, notably in New Granada.

Applying the new law in this viceroyalty proved very difficult because colonial authorities protested and sabotaged the initiative from the very start. Indeed, as early as December, 1791, Viceroy Ezpeleta informed Madrid that he had ordered the suspension of compliance on the grounds that the law served to shield contrabandist activities. The viceroy's attitudes did not readily change. The following year, he informed Madrid that he had suspended the cedula of November 24, 1791, which further extended the trade, using the same reasoning as before.[18]

Madrid did not react well to this attitude. The desk officer of the Indies Department of the Ministry of Finance who handled the dossier advised the minister that if precautions were taken, the dangers could be obviated without forcing the crown to abandon a dearly held policy. An order to that effect was drafted and approved, and the viceroy felt compelled to issue a *bando* implementing Madrid's decision throughout New Granada. As in most such cases, in the face of a ministry determined to reform, the use of the *obedezco pero no cumplo* formula proved to be no more than a suspensive veto. This original acquiescence was followed by further compliance, this time to a directive of June 9, 1792, allowing French vessels to bring *negros bozales* to Cartagena. Lastly, in April, 1793, the viceroy confirmed that he had proclaimed and publicized the order of January 24, 1793, by which the crown offered further concessions to Spaniards who were prepared to undertake direct trade with the Guinea coast.[19]

17. The Ministry of War and Finance for the Indies first took this stance, which was later adopted by the Indies Department of the Ministry of Finance when it inherited the former ministry's trade jurisdiction.

18. Ezpeleta to the Ministry of Finance, Extract of Letter, December 19, 1791, AGI, IG, leg. 2823; Ezpeleta to Lerena, Santa Fe, March 19, 1792, AGI, SF, leg. 641.

19. Ezpeleta to the Ministry of Finance, Extract of Letter, December 29, 1791, AGI, SF, leg. 641; Ezpeleta to Gardoqui, Santa Fe, September 19, 1792, AGI, IG, leg. 2823; Ezpeleta to Gardoqui, Santa Fe, October 19, 1792, AGI, SF, leg. 641; Ezpeleta to Gardoqui, Santa Fe, April 19, 1793, AGI, SF, leg. 642.

Nonetheless, despite compliance, the viceregal mind was not changed in any way. As late as October, 1794, Ezpeleta was still insisting that the *informes* he had gathered on the subject all led to the same conclusion: "Everything shows that the inhabitants of this kingdom are not disposed to take advantage of the freedom conceded by the royal cedula that permits this commerce and that it has served only as a pretext for contraband." Madrid, however, was equally intent upon its point of view. With the temporary end of the struggle with Great Britain, the imperial administration renewed its favorable policy towards *comercio libre de negros*.[20] The fact that such a measure might not be completely applicable to a zone like Cartagena, where the transition to export-oriented agriculture had been slow, was not considered.

In any event, the statistics of the trade led to some obvious conclusions. The discrepancy between the number of vessels employed and the number of slaves brought in reveals that few of these ships were full-fledged slavers. Rather, many captains brought in a small number of blacks so as to be allowed to enter port and benefit from the franchises allowed under *comercio libre de negros*. Some undoubtedly engaged in contraband trade, but even if they did not, their presence was not welcomed by mercantilists. Indeed, the crown legislation covering this trade allowed those who practiced it to bring in a series of other "related" goods, to the detriment of merchants who engaged in the ordinary *comercio libre*. The large proportion of Spanish vessels involved also merits discussion. *Comercio libre de negros* legalized access to foreign colonies, albeit under stringent conditions. The potential for contraband was obvious to everyone. Lastly, it should be noted that only slightly more than half of the imported slaves remained in the port region. Others were shipped out to other Spanish American cities, mute witness to Cartagena's limited potential as an export-producing area (See Table 1).

Still, by no means were all of the mercantile elements of the city determined to abuse the crown's confidence. A distinction must be made between better-capitalized long-distance mercantile firms, which gambled on the success of the reform effort, and

20. Ezpeleta to Gardoqui, Santa Fe, October 19, 1794, AGI, SF, leg. 643; Royal Cedula, April 22, 1804, AGI, IG, leg. 1707.

TABLE 1
Comercio Libre de Negros in Cartagena, 1791–1796

	Number of Slaves	Number of Vessels[a]
Spanish ships	882	71
Foreign ships	598	17[b]
Total slaves	1,480	
Reexported slaves	721	
Net in Cartagena	759	

SOURCE: Commandant General of Cartagena to Marqués de las Hormazas, Cartagena, January 3, 1798, AGI, IG, leg. 2824.
[a] The number of vessels is actually the number of *entradas*.
[b] Of these 17 ships, 3 were American, 8 Danish, 3 Dutch, and 3 English.

other local houses. By the 1790s the merchants of the Consulado of Cartagena were demanding that the coast guard become more active against contraband and insisting upon protection for the coastal trade that brought cotton to Cartagena for eventual shipment to Europe. Similarly, some Cartagena merchants bought foreign vessels in these years to use in the export trade.[21] Others secured licenses allowing them to export tropical goods to Spain duty-free.[22] The results of this trading activity, however, were not particularly distinguished.

Cartagena's legal exports did not react particularly well to *comercio libre*. Between 1784 and 1788, the average yearly exports amounted to 2,163,422 pesos, and that amount declined in the succeeding quinquennium to 2,047,096 pesos. Treasure accounted for some 91 percent of this (Table 2). Admittedly, the proportion of goods in the export balance increased from 6.4 percent in the first quinquennium to 11.2 percent in the second. This phenomenon, however, was mostly the product of the stagnation of treasure shipments due to the troubles in the Caribbean brought on by the

21. Letter of the Consulado of Cartagena de Indias, October 31, 1795, cited in Informe of Francisco de Viana, April 16, 1807, AGI, SF, leg. 960; Ministry of Finance, Letter of Ezpeleta, Santa Fe, September 19, 1795, AGI, SF, leg. 957.

22. Ezpeleta to Miguel Cayetano Soler, Santa Fe, July 19, 1794, AGI, SF, leg 643. The product involved was dyewood (*palo brasilete*), but *canela de Quito* was also favored. See the Royal Order of April 16, 1792, in AGI, Ultramar, leg. 723.

TABLE 2
Exports from Cartagena, 1784–1793

Year	Treasure	Goods	Total
1784	1,570,217	80,308	1,650,525
1785	1,817,098	164,635	1,981,733
1786	372,156	89,942	462,098
1787	4,424,081	224,150	4,648,231
1788	1,939,462	135,059	2,074,521
1789	2,114,290	186,418	2,300,708
1790	2,108,328	203,773	2,312,101
1791	2,558,245	285,273	2,843,518
1792	1,634,037	225,843	1,859,880
1793	671,117	248,155	919,272
Average	1,920,903	184,356	2,105,259
Percentage	91	9	

SOURCE: AGI, SF, leg. 957.
NOTE: All money amounts are in pesos.

TABLE 3
Imports into Cartagena, 1784–1793

Year	Total (pesos)
1784	1,543,648
1785	2,584,896
1786	2,155,797
1787	1,644,501
1788	3,363,937
1789	2,593,647
1790	1,233,525
1791	1,677,260
1792	1,462,840
1793	1,296,473
Average	1,955,652

SOURCE: AGI, SF, leg. 957.

onset of the French Revolution. Regarding imports, the situation was even worse. The average yearly value of legal imports was reported as having been 2,258,559 pesos in 1784–1788 and only 1,652,749 pesos in 1789–1793 (Tables 3, 4). It was only natural that these results be ascribed to the continuing inroads of contra-

TABLE 4
Balance of Payments, Cartagena, 1784–1793

Year	Total (pesos)
1784	106,877
1785	(603,163)
1786	(1,693,699)
1787	3,003,730
1788	(1,289,416)
1789	(292,939)
1790	1,078,576
1791	1,166,258
1792	397,040
1793	(377,201)
Average	149,606

SOURCE: AGI, SF, leg. 957.

band, and this may well account for the skepticism of local reformers faced with what they saw as Madrid's overly liberal attitude.

Here again, however, imperial and colonial institutions were working at cross-purposes. The crown repeatedly reaffirmed its faith in *comercio libre de negros,* and some of its officials were prepared to go further yet. As they began to suspect that the struggle against contraband could not be won in time of war through repression or restriction, they pushed for the legalization of *comercio neutral*. This attitude was eloquently expressed in 1807 by Francisco de Viana, by then *contador general de Indias.* Viana had been a key official in the Indies Department of the Ministry of Finance for many years, and the views that he expressed on that occasion were identical to those he had been thrusting on the ministry for some time. He pointed out that South America's coastal geography made it difficult to prevent contraband and that clandestine trade was inevitable as long as the shortage of capital and vessels left Spanish shipping unequal to its assigned task. He concluded: "Commerce will be conducted in times of peace, and of war, not only with friendly colonies but also with enemies. . . . The means to manage it are absolute freedom, abandoning all restrictions, lowering duties, expanding the [list of] articles permitted in the commerce with [other] colonies. . . . Neutral trade during wartime (and in peacetime an amplification of the imports permitted in the [commerce] with foreign colonies to [include] all that the metropolis does not provide) will be the measures most effective in reducing contraband."[23]

Comercio Neutral

Spain's brief, albeit costly, war with revolutionary France was not of such a nature as to force the crown to have recourse to *comercio neutral.*[24] Anglo-Spanish forces were overwhelming at sea, and convoys and patrols largely kept the sea-lanes open. Still, until British forces were able to capture the principal French colonial ports later in the war, privateering remained a serious obstacle to trade. This was particularly true for those Spanish ports, like Cartagena, that were not important enough commercially to obtain much protection from the Real Armada. Contacts with Europe declined, and local pressure for access to foreign and overseas markets began to build.

Viceroy Ezpeleta gave in somewhat to such pressure and allowed some merchants to buy ships in allied colonies and others to redeem vessels captured by French privateers.[25] In the first case, he said that ships were needed to sustain the export trade. In the second, the viceroy pointed out that redeeming the vessels was part of a prisoner exchange and would also bring, among other benefits, revenue-producing sealed paper and scarce European goods.

Such special favors, however, could not satisfy the local mercantile community once war broke out with Great Britain, as this threatened to bring a general breakdown of seaborne trade. At first, Viceroy Mendinueta refused to hear such demands, had the matter squashed by a Junta de Tribunales convoked for the purpose, and warned the crown against granting such concessions once he knew that Cartagena's merchants had appealed directly to the throne.[26] This harsh stand could not be maintained long, how-

23. Informe of Francisco de Viana, April 16, 1807, AGI, SF, leg. 960.

24. On the cost of Spain's war with France, see Jacques A. Barbier and Herbert S. Klein, "Revolutionary Wars and Public Finances: The Madrid Treasury, 1794–1807," *Journal of Economic History,* XLI (1981), 315–39.

25. Ezpeleta to Gardoqui, Santa Fe, September 19, 1795, AGI, SF, leg. 644.

26. Viceroy Pedro de Mendinueta to Gardoqui, Santa Fe, June 19, 1797, Mendinueta

ever, for Madrid itself was about to legalize what Mendinueta resisted, and the viceroy himself was soon to see the necessity of having some access to foreign ports.

The significance of *comercio neutral* changed over time. The policy came to be closely wedded to the need to repatriate crown silver.[27] At first, however, it was purely a trade policy, launched with several objectives in mind, including keeping the colonial export-oriented economies working, providing an alternative way of getting Spanish production to market, and preventing the development of colonial manufactures.

Madrid legalized neutral trade on November 18, 1797, though the measure covered only ships sailing from Europe to America. The delay was due to the strong opposition of the Consulado de Cádiz, to the dithering of the monarch, and to the residual hope that the Spanish navy might keep the sea routes open. This first phase of *comercio neutral* was brief and therefore did not greatly affect Cartagena de Indias. Some foreign ships did make it to port under the aegis of that order—such as the American merchant frigate *Flora* inbound from New York.[28] Such, however, were the exceptions. Indeed, on April 20, 1799, Cádiz interests secured the repeal of the legislation.[29]

More meaningful than this ephemeral trade was the change in Viceroy Mendinueta's attitude. He found himself having to obtain paper for his secretariat and china for his table from foreign colonies. Compelled by his own circumstances, he asked the crown to first legalize trade with foreign colonies and then allow direct commerce with the United States. By early 1800, however, such requests could hardly be considered very significant—two British frigates blocked the port of Cartagena, and its trade was firmly oriented towards Jamaica.[30]

to Marqués de las Hormazas, Santa Fe, December 19, 1797, both in AGI, SF, leg. 646; Mendinueta to Francisco de Saavedra, Santa Fe, August 19, 1798, AGI, SF, leg. 647.

27. Barbier, "Peninsular Finance and Colonial Trade"; Barbier, "Venezuelan 'Libranzas.'"

28. Petition of Lizaur, November 4, 1796, AGI, IG, leg. 535, 2466; Letter of Mendinueta, Santa Fe, July 29, 1799, AGI, SF, leg. 648.

29. See the documentation in AGI, IG, legs. 2466–67.

30. Mendinueta to Soler, Santa Fe, February 19, 1799, Mendinueta to Soler, Santa

Reflecting upon these events, the Consulado of Cartagena reported that in the first war with Great Britain, considerable quantities of fresh meat and foodstuffs were exported to Jamaica and New Providence. Over the course of the war, New Granadine exports to these enemy ports were reputedly worth twenty million pesos.[31]

The merchant guild reported that only *comercio neutral* could have decreased the value of that trade, but that the measures announced in the royal order of November 18, 1797, were so limited and applied so briefly that they had no real impact. The same could be said of the brief restoration of neutral trade in January, 1801. Thus, on purely commercial questions the views of Cartagena's consulado merchants and of the Ministry of Finance's trade officials had begun to coincide. By then, however, this was almost irrelevant since the crown had begun to give more thought to purely fiscal issues than to economic ones.

The viceroyalty of New Granada was never one of the principal revenue producers of the empire. Mexico and Peru were always far more important. Nor did its relative importance greatly change during the course of the eighteenth century. The political consequences of the Comunero Rebellion, failure of the Gutiérrez de Piñeres *visita,* expensive military reforms, and the overly ambitious administration of Archbishop-Viceroy Caballero y Góngora all threatened to keep the colonial government in a state of penury.[32] Despite such circumstances, however, the viceroyalty began to produce surpluses by the last decade of the eighteenth century. The reasons for this are not entirely clear, though the economical administration that followed the death of José de Gálvez in 1787 and the patient work of the fiscal cadres (the largely anonymous treasurers, comptrollers, administrators, and their minions) undoubtedly played a role. In any event, by the 1790s the viceroys

Fe, July 19, 1799, both in AGI, SF, leg. 648; Mendinueta to Soler, Santa Fe, January 19, 1800, AGI, SF, leg. 649.

31. Consulado of Cartagena de Indias to the Minister of Finance, Extract of a Letter, July 24, 1805, AGI, SF, leg. 956.

32. John Leddy Phelan, *The People and the King: The Comunero Revolution in Colombia, 1781* (Madison, 1978), 3–186; Kuethe, *Military Reform and Society,* 79–144.

had been driven by Madrid's urgent pleas to look for ways to ship their spare cash, and whatever they could borrow, to the metropolis.

In the early 1790s, ships of the Real Armada were commonly used. The availability of such vessels during the war with France was, in fact, one of the limits on New Granada's capacity to respond to Madrid's desires in this matter.[33] Tables 5 and 6 provide some indication of the amounts involved, and these sums must be taken into consideration when discussing the overall deficit in the balance of payments (see Table 4).

When Charles IV began his first war with Great Britain, enemy domination of the seas accentuated these difficulties. By 1799, Viceroy Mendinueta had tentatively offered to send as much as 1 million pesos to Spain, if means could be found to transport them. He was subsequently forced to report, however, that war-related expenses had reduced the amount he could transfer. Further efforts subsequently brought the sum back up to the million promised.[34] With the temporary return of peace late in 1802, Mendinueta was able to dispatch a considerable sum on the war frigate *Sabina*.[35] The lesson, however, was clear. If the crown could not find more reliable means of transferring its wealth, it would have to run the risk that colonial officials would find justifiable ways in which to spend it.

After Charles IV began a second war with Great Britain, *comercio neutral* was reestablished in December, 1804, but under very different circumstances from those of 1797. To begin with, the economy of New Granada had hardly had time to recover from the previous war. The wartime pattern of trade now threatened to become structural, and this could not help but affect mercantile attitudes. Secondly, the crown was now far more concerned with its

33. Ezpeleta to Gardoqui, Santa Fe, July 19, 1793, AGI, SF, leg. 643. The problem of secure passage for the king's treasure also arose on the Pacific side of the viceroyalty. There it led to delays in the remission of the *situado* Peru traditionally paid to Panama. See Mendinueta to Soler, Santa Fe, May 19, 1799, AGI, SF, leg. 648, and May 19, 1799, AGI, SF, leg. 650. The latter deals with the loss of the frigate *Sta. Elena* with 130,000 pesos on board.

34. Mendinueta to Soler, Santa Fe, April 19, 1799, and August 19, 1799, AGI, SF, leg. 648; Mendinueta to Soler, Santa Fe, November 19, 1800, and April 19, 1802, AGI, SF, leg. 649, 651.

35. Some 29,997,780 *reales de vellón* (1,499,889 pesos) reached Spain. Mendinueta to Soler, Santa Fe, January 8, 1802, AGI, SF, leg. 651.

TABLE 5
Royal Treasure Shipped from Cartagena, 1792–1796

Ship Name	Type	Year	Crown (pesos)	Ageno (pesos)	Total (pesos)
Agueda	Fragata	1792	106,685	11,792	118,477
		1792	150,015	6,192	156,207
Famoso Sevillano	Paquebote	1792	44,766	0	44,766
		1792	277,400	0	277,400
Gloria, Agueda	Fragatas	1794	611,177	50,690	661,867
Pallas	Fragata	1796	360,840	0	360,840

SOURCES: Ezpeleta to Gardoqui, Santa Fe, March 19, June 19, and November 19, 1792, October 19 and December 19, 1794, January 19 and October 19, 1794, AGI, SF, leg. 641, 643, 645.

TABLE 6
Funds of Known Geographical Provenance, 1792–1796

City	Amounts (pesos)	Percentage
Quito	239,854	33.30
Popayán	43,725	6.07
Santa Fe	235,815	32.74
Cartagena	200,793	27.88
Total	720,187	100.00

SOURCES: See Table 5.

immediate financial problems than with Spain's economic future. Its trade policy in this war was going to be based on political rather than commercial considerations.

Cartagena's trade figures for 1805, the first full year of the new war, are difficult to compare to those available for the late 1780s and early 1790s because they are not presented in the same way. They also reflect the viceroy's political interference in commercial affairs. Using these figures to isolate the consequences of warfare with any degree of exactitude is therefore difficult, and they must be used with prudence.

TABLE 7
The Trade of Cartagena in 1805

	No. of Ships	Specie	Spanish Goods	Foreign Goods	Colonial Goods	Total
Spain						
Imports	3	0	26,449	14,387	0	40,836
Exports	8	2,821	0	0	128,888	131,709
Total						172,545
America						
Imports	31	69,079	8,256	101,146	56,217	234,698
Exports	6	0	160	57	61,039	61,256
Total						295,954
All exports		2,821	160	160	189,927	192,965
All imports		69,079	34,705	115,533	56,217	275,534
Total						468,499
Bal. payments						(82,569)
Bal. trade						(16,311)

SOURCE: AGI, SF, leg. 960.
NOTE: All money amounts are in pesos. Ships arriving from Spain were from Cádiz, Barcelona, Málaga, and Sanlúcar de Barrameda. Ships leaving for Spain were cleared to Cádiz, La Coruña, and Santander. Ships arriving from America were from Maracaibo, Trinidad, Santa Marta, Portobello, Santiago, Ríohacha, Nicaragua, Coro, New York, Alexandria, Philadelphia, Havana, and Veracruz. Ships leaving for America were cleared to Trinidad, Philadelphia, Santiago de Cuba, Batabanó, Havana, and San Andrés.

Nonetheless, the figures given in Table 7 do reveal the new economic reality. The most striking aspect of these statistics is the almost complete absence of specie import and export. It was simply too dangerous to set out on the high seas with such cargo, and the monarchy discouraged it. Another conclusion that can be drawn concerns the export of tropical products. Given the relatively scant value of European goods reexported from Cartagena, the change in value of shipments of colonial products from the base level of the 1780s and 1790s must have been relatively small. Indeed, exported goods of all sorts, excluding specie, were worth 190,144 pesos in 1805, compared with 248,155 pesos in the first year of the war with France (1793) and a yearly average of 184,356 pesos in 1784–1793 (see Tables 2, 7). Lastly, the area of commerce that suffered the greatest damage was clearly the import sector, which declined from an average yearly value of 1,955,652 pesos for 1784–1793 to a mere 275,534 pesos in 1805. This decline must overwhelmingly reflect the collapse in the legal importation of European goods (see Tables 3, 7). These figures suggest that trade must have been massively redirected into contraband channels, and most particularly into illegal trade with Jamaica.

Under the circumstances, the most logical posture for Cartagena's merchants would have been to obtain direct access to the European market, via *comercio neutral*. If such a trade succeeded, it would either cut out the Jamaican contrabandists and their profits or, by bringing competition to the marketplace, lower prices to Cartagena's wholesalers. Interest in having the crown legalize trade with friendly nations and colonies per se was relatively muted. The previous war had shown that all of these were destined to fall into British hands relatively quickly and that the United States was likely to be treated as "European" by Madrid policymakers.

With the renewal of war, the Consulado of Cartagena insisted anew upon the need to allow trade under neutral flags. Responding to a royal order of August 26, 1802, that asked the consulado to report "the causes of the excessive contraband in the Indies," that body insisted that in time of war contraband was the result of "necessity rather than avarice." Significantly, the consulado did not see fit to respond to this order until a new war began: it foresaw that in the renewed conflict contraband would be fueled by a pent-up demand resulting from inadequate levels of legal trade during the brief peace. Further, it insisted that even if wartime contraband could be prevented, the results would be disastrous for the peninsular-oriented trade because such action would diminish long-term demand for European goods. Indeed, the consulado predicted that under such circumstances import substitution in such domains as textiles, edible oils, and alcoholic beverages was inevitable, and that in warm climates the population would return to its previously "naked" state. Thus, it concluded: "After a war of six or seven years, Spanish commerce will discover that the towns of America will have regressed a good many steps toward a state of incivility [*incivilidad*], and that three-fourths of the consumers of products and goods from the metropolis will have been lost."[36]

From the consulado's perspective, the major obstacle to implementing *comercio neutral* was not Madrid, but the viceroy of New Granada. Indeed, Viceroy Amar y Borbón closed the ports of the viceroyalty as a device for preventing contraband.[37] After eight months of enforced closure, Amar y Borbón then relented to the point of granting licenses to favored individuals. These allowed their recipients to export goods to Cuba if they carried official correspondence. The policy brought renewed protest from the merchants, who objected to such patronage. The viceroy then received a royal order of November 8, 1805, to open the ports, but other crown actions prevented business from returning to normal.[38]

Indeed, the consulado merchants escaped the viceroy's unfair treatment only to fall victim to the king's. From 1805 to 1808, the Spanish monarch largely turned the legal trade of Cartagena over to agents and partners of the infamous Caja de Consolidación de Vales Reales. To pursue his objectives, the head of that agency, Manuel Sixto Espinosa, at first made use of Juan José Marco del Pont, an unsavory Spanish merchant adventurer, and a German mercantile house. Ultimately, however, the trade came into the hands of an essentially British firm, that of Gordon-Murphy, who briefly dominated the trade of New Granada.[39]

To understand the situation, one must recall that the crown hoped to finance its new war by applying the so-called *consolidación de vales reales* to the Americas. As is well known, this measure involved two different types of exactions in the New World: the sale of the properties and forced repayment of the borrowed capital of colonial *obras pías,* and a series of special taxes on the clergy's revenues. The income in both cases was meant to pay interest on, and

36. Consulado of Cartagena de Indias to the Ministry of Finance, Extract of Letter, July 24, 1805, AGI, SF, leg. 956.

37. This was in consequence of circular orders, dated November 8 and 23, 1804, sent by Manuel de Godoy to all Spanish-American ports but ignored in most of them. The crown subsequently advised its colonies on September 17, 1805, that they had interpreted the original orders inappropriately. See Ministry of Finance, Note of Mesa, circa February 26, 1806, AGI, SF, leg. 960.

38. Consulado of Cartagena de Indias to the Ministry of Finance, Extract of Letter, October 20, 1805, AGI, SF, leg. 960.

39. For an overview of Cartagena's neutral trade, see "Razón de las expediciones neutrales a Cartagena de Indias," AGI, Ultramar, leg. 742.

eventually pay off, the *vales reales*—interest-bearing, moneylike bills issued by the crown. The policy was a logical extension of similar measures already applied in Spain. Since devaluation of the *vales* threatened the liquidity of Spain's treasury, the monarchy had an obvious interest in ensuring that Espinosa receive in Madrid the funds raised the America. It soon became obvious that using neutral-flag vessels was the most natural way to repatriate the desired cash.[40]

Two other considerations further enhanced the Caja de Consolidación's interest in *comercio neutral*. The first was that the crown's penury compelled it to "borrow" cash from Espinosa's Spanish revenues. It "repaid" the Caja with *libranzas* (bills of exchange) drawn on the royal treasuries of Spanish America. Thus, part of the ordinary surplus of the colonial treasury came into the hands of Espinosa, thereby increasing the problem posed by the repatriation of funds. For Cartagena, the amounts involved are indicated in Table 8.[41] In addition, given the uncertainties surrounding royal bills of exchange, the Caja decided it needed independent revenues to carry out its mandated tax. It therefore embarked upon a series of trading operations in the New World, under the cover of trading licenses bought from the Marqués de Branciforte (brother-in-law of the royal favorite, Godoy) and of contracts approved by the crown.

The result was that Cartagena's *comercio neutral* never corresponded to the official policy proclaimed on December 24, 1804. Instead of relatively free trade in the hands of a select number of firms, New Granada's trade was handed over to a series of shadowy constructs. In 1806, two vessels were successfully sent from the Elbe to Cartagena and back. The *William and Albert* and *Juana Adriana* were dispatched by the Hamburg merchant house of M. Van Heiningen and Company, with the Caja de Consolidación as a silent but equal participant. All capital was provided by the

40. For a discussion of this issue, see Barbier, "Peninsular Finance and Colonial Trade," 32–34.

41. The system did not always work as anticipated. In New Granada, the viceroy used the sums gathered from the revenues alloted to *consolidación* to repay the sums owed to that agency by the Spanish treasury. In fact, Manuel Sixto Espinosa was literally repaid with his own money. See Viceroy Ántonio Amar y Borbón Amar to Soler, March 19, 1807, AGI, SF, leg. 653.

TABLE 8
Consolidacion's *Libranzas* on Cartagena, 1804–1805

Purpose	Date of Issue	Amount (pesos)
Real Servidumbre	August 2, 1804	212,766
Empréstito de Holanda	August 8, 1804	175,000
Real Servicio	March 8, 1805	71,758[a]
El Ferrol (Real Armada)	May 18, 1805	112,000[a]
Real Servicio	June 11, 1805	44,870[a]
Ouvrard Loan	June 16, 1805	1,270,800
Empréstito de Holanda	August 16, 1805	200,000[a]
Real Giro	October 6, 1805	217,000[a]
Total		2,304,194

SOURCE: AGI, Ultramar, leg. 833.
NOTE: Most, and perhaps all, of these *libranzas* were for Manuel Sixto Espinosa, head of the Caja de Consolidación de Vales Reales.
[a] Viceroy Amar knew of these through the kindness of the British who sent him some of his captured mail. By September of 1806 he had paid all but the last (428,628 pesos out of 645,628 pesos). See Amar to Soler, Santa Fe, September 19, 1806, AGI, SF, leg. 653. To pay *libranzas,* Amar had to borrow 100,000 pesos from the consulado. See Amar to Soler, Santa Fe, December 19, 1807, AGI, SF, leg. 654.

Hamburg merchants; the Spaniards "borrowed" their half (at interest) from their partners. To further magnify the difficulties, both the firm and the ship pretended to be domiciled in Altoona, in Danish-controlled Holstein, because Hamburg was occupied by the French.[42] These were relatively significant voyages: the *William and Albert* sailed outbound with a cargo worth 46,599 *marcos banco,* and *Juana Adriana* with one valued at 59,748, mostly composed of manufactured goods in each case. Interestingly, the return cargo largely consisted of tropical goods, for which there may have been a good market in Europe at that time because of the so-called "continental blockade." The ships carried back a variety of dyewoods plus cacao, cotton, sugar, quinine, balsam, sarsaparilla, and hides. Whether the expeditions were a commercial success is not known, however, because the Hamburg firm suspended payments early in 1806, having been involved in the bankruptcy of the

42. The contracting parties were brought together by the shadowy Juan José Marco del Pont. See Manuel Sixto Espinosa to Soler, Madrid, September 23, 1805, AGI, Ultramar, leg. 839.

Dutch merchant-banking firm, Ed. Croese and Company, to which it was closely allied.[43]

As might have been expected, Francisco de Viana (whose interest in trade and development was always paramount) objected to the privileges accorded the Caja de Consolidación, reporting that only two vessels of the neutral trade entered Cartagena in 1806 and that its *libranzas* could not be paid in poverty-stricken New Granada.[44] These objections were not seriously considered, however, for the crown's need was great. In any event, only one more such expedition was organized, the successful voyage of the Portuguese vessel *Nueva Aurora* from Oporto.[45] Worse, however, was to come.

By 1807, the Caja de Consolidación had found a new partner for its enterprises in New Granada. The British firm of Gordon-Murphy and Company was induced to extend its activities to Cartagena. It was already involved in *comercio neutral* elsewhere in the empire and dominated the "secret" trade between Jamaica and Veracruz. The enterprise, however, involved a most peculiar type of commercial venture. Indeed, cold cash seems to have been its only real objective, though some of the outbound vessels also carried a moderate amount of cotton. The stage was set by a royal order of July 15, 1807, warning the viceroy that he was to allow the agents of the firm to take out 900,000 pesos from Cartagena. Four voyages are known to have taken place under this license. All involved seemingly small Danish vessels sailing from St. Thomas in the Virgin Islands to Cartagena and back. They carried in coin, respectively, 15,000, 36,000, 35,000, and 26,305 pesos.[46] For two of the ships, cash was the only return cargo. Clearly an export-

43. See Letter 469, Santa Fe, September 19, 1806, AGI, IG, leg. 2470; Letters 586/1, 586/2, Santa Fe, AGI, IG, leg. 2471; Amar to Soler, Santa Fe, September 19, 1806, AGI, SF, leg. 653; Letter 438, Santa Fe, January 19, 1806, AGI, SF, leg. 956; Manuel Sixto Espinosa to Soler, Madrid, September 23, 1805, AGI, Ultramar, leg. 839; Bills of Lading of the *William and Albert* and the *Juana Adriana,* AGI, Ultramar, leg. 840.

44. Francisco de Viana to the Ministry of Finance, Extract of Letter, August 23, 1807, AGI, SF, leg. 960.

45. See Letter 468, Santa Fe, AGI, IG, leg. 2470; and Letter 586/3, Santa Fe, AGI, IG, leg. 2471.

46. Royal Order, July 15, 1807, AGI, IG, leg. 2472; Letter 17/1, Santa Fe, AGI, IG, leg. 2471; Letters 17/2, 8/1, Santa Fe, AGI, IG, leg. 2472; Letter 18/2, Santa Fe, AGI, Ultramar, 742.

oriented economy's needs for transport no longer figured in Madrid's trade plans for Cartagena.

In conclusion, official trade policy with Cartagena in the reign of Charles IV was little less than disastrous. Neither *comercio libre* nor *comercio libre de negros* managed to stimulate the transformation of the local economy in the desired direction. On the contrary, the latter seems to have made the problem of illicit trade marginally graver. The official trade statistics offer little that could lead one to conclude that crown objectives were being realized. On the other hand, foreign domination of the New Granadan market does not seem to have increased either.

After 1793, however, the situation deteriorated considerably. The Guarda Costas were ineffective against contraband, and the Real Armada could not guarantee the port against blockade. Nor were the crown's belated contingency plans at all effective. The *comercio neutral* of 1797 and that of 1801 were too transient to have much of an impact in relatively distant Cartagena. As for the renewed neutral trade proclaimed in 1804, it had only slightly more significance. The expeditions sent from Hamburg and Oporto were of appreciable magnitude and did have the extraction of tropical products as an objective, but very few such sailings occurred. And the Gordon-Murphy enterprise resembled more the call of a bills collector than the expedition of a merchant.

Spanish trade policy for Cartagena in the closing years of the colonial period was a resounding failure. It offers mute evidence that the economy of the Caribbean zone of New Granada was one on the Antillean coast that was still not fully integrated into the world-market economy. Its ties to the Atlantic world were forged with the specie of the interior, not with its own production. Struggle as the Bourbons might against that reality, they achieved relatively little compared to such success stories as Cuba and the Río de la Plata.

Part Two

Commercial and Economic Overviews

LANCE R. GRAHN

Chapter 5

An Irresoluble Dilemma: Smuggling in New Granada, 1713–1763

This essay examines the problematical nature of illicit commerce in three Caribbean provinces of New Granada—Riohacha, Santa Marta, and Cartagena. Contraband trade serviced markets throughout the Spanish-American empire, but smuggling was especially intense along the northern coast of New Granada. As a result, imperial administrators confronted several crucial dilemmas as they sought to manage the wealth of this colony. By strict Spanish standards, smuggling was both illegal and immoral, but at the same time, it complemented legal trade in New Granada and supplied coastal residents with necessary commodities. It cost the treasuries of New Granada millions of pesos in lost tax revenue in the eighteenth century and millions more in political and military expenditures to stop it; yet treasury revenues from the sale and taxation of captured contraband rivaled those from licit commerce, which was taxed at the same rates, and provided steady income for the provincial treasuries. Smuggling also highlighted deficiencies—economic, political, and military—of Spanish rule in each of these three provinces and weakened the fabric of empire there. Nonetheless, illicit commerce vivified the economies of these three provinces and permitted the overlying Spanish political structure to remain in place.

Context

In 1741, John Campbell wrote in his *Concise History of the Spanish America* that "there is nothing more common than to hear Spain compared to a sieve, which, whatever it receives, is never the fuller. How common soever the comparison may be, most certainly it is a very true one." Campbell correctly recognized that the profits from the Spanish-American trade—"the principal foundation of the conservation of the [king's] dominions and of the wealth of [his] vassals"—that did not stay in the New World generally passed through the hands of Spaniards and into the coffers of foreigners.[1]

In the seventeenth century, the production of Spanish textiles and agricultural products failed to keep pace with the mounting American demand and with European competition, thus contributing to the American dependence on foreign products. Meanwhile, the principal rivals of Spain—the Netherlands, England, and France—established footholds in Curaçao, Jamaica, and Española, respectively, giving them excellent bases from which to challenge Spanish domination of the Caribbean and to expand their trade into Spanish-American markets. Faced with declining remittances of American silver and with rebellion in Catalonia and the Netherlands, the Spanish crown burdened its citizens in Castile and its Atlantic trade with higher taxes. After the War of the Spanish Succession, the Spanish merchant marine and navy had reached their nadir and increased foreign competitiveness in Caribbean commerce. And, in the early eighteenth century, Cádiz merchants deliberately restricted the export of legal trade goods to America to boost the prices they fetched in colonial markets.[2]

1. John Campbell, *A Concise History of the Spanish America* (London, 1972), 290–91; Royal Cedula, San Lorenzo, September 20, 1720, in Pedro González de Salcedo (ed.), *Tratado jurídico político del contra-bando* (Madrid, 1729), 370.

2. Herman J. Muller, "British Business and Spanish America, 1700–1800," *Mid-America*, XXXIX (1957), 11; Richard Pares, *War and Trade in the West Indies, 1739–1763* (Oxford, 1936), 5; Troy S. Floyd, *The Anglo-Spanish Struggle for Mosquitia* (Albuquerque, 1967), 26; Campbell, *Concise History*, 291–306; Floyd, *Mosquitia*, 26–27, 70–71; Jaime Vicens Vives, *Approaches to the History of Spain* (2nd ed., Berkeley, 1970), 106; Roland D.

In Spain, these interrelated factors diverted money into foreign accounts; in America, they fomented illegal commerce. The metropolis could not adequately supply its colonies, so an alternative informal economy met the remaining need for imports. Moreover, contraband goods were usually cheaper and of better quality than legal trade items.[3] American contrabandists and foreign merchants, then, built up a substantial trade throughout the Spanish colonies that, though illicit, was useful, profitable, and necessary.

This was particularly true in New Granada, where illegal commerce developed more than in any other American kingdom. In the early eighteenth century, the king's advisors estimated that fully one-half of all illicit trade by value in the Spanish Caribbean—perhaps six million pesos' worth annually—passed through New Granada. Even foreign diplomats considered New Granada, and the provinces of Riohacha, Santa Marta, and Cartagena in particular, to be among the most important regions in the empire for tapping the wealth of Spanish America.[4] The array of contraband goods regularly introduced along the Caribbean coast of New Granada testify to the abundance of illegal foreign goods found there: clothing, textiles of all sorts, foodstuffs and spices, oil and wines, manufactures, slaves, and other items, such as wax, playing cards, and naval stores. In return, New Granadan traders offered local products, including gold, cacao, pearls, livestock, and hides, that lacked sufficient legal outlet.[5]

Hussey, "Antecedents of the Spanish Monopolistic Overseas Trading Companies (1624–1728)," *HAHR,* IX (1929), 5–6; J. H. Elliott, *Imperial Spain, 1469–1716* (New York, 1966), 317–53.

3. Anonymous, Madrid, January, 1706, AGI, IG, leg. 2046A.

4. José Patiño to Andrés de Pez, Cádiz, April 14, 1722, AGI, SF, leg. 374; Ambrosio Daubenton [to Manuel García de Bustamente], Madrid, September 10, 1705, AGI, IG, leg. 2046A; Dionisio de Alsedo y Herrera, "Descripción de la extensión, situación, y distancias de las costas occidentales de la América," Madrid, September 30, 1761, AGI, Libros Manuscritos, 26; Margaret Anne Fisher, "The Role of the Spanish American Inheritance in European Diplomacy, 1659–1713" (Ph.D. dissertation, University of Washington, 1972), 121–22.

5. These observations are based on the accounts found in the AGI, Seville, and the AHNC, of more than 750 contraband cargos captured in Riohacha, Santa Marta, and Cartagena provinces between 1713 and 1763. See Lance R. Grahn, "Contraband, Commerce, and Society in New Granada, 1713–1763" (Ph.D. dissertation, Duke University, 1985).

The situation and condition of the Riohacha, Santa Marta, and Cartagena provinces especially facilitated illegal commerce. Each was easily reached from Jamaica and Curaçao, the principal bases for smugglers trading in New Granada. The long coastlines of the provinces provided traffickers with many coves and beaches where they could safely conduct their business. Equally important, foreign and domestic contrabandists often found provincial officials there willing to ignore, if not abet, their illegal practices. The Caribbean coast of New Granada also fronted a substantial market of over one million potential consumers.[6] Yet, constrained by the structural deficiencies of the American trade, legitimate Spanish shippers virtually ignored Riohacha and Santa Marta in the early eighteenth century and failed to meet the needs of Cartagena.[7]

Riohacha, Santa Marta, and Cartagena also provided smugglers with unique advantages that attracted their business. For example, weak Spanish defenses and a sparse Spanish population in Riohacha beckoned illegal traders to the province. The proximity of the ports of Santa Marta province to the Magdalena River delta and the hydrography of the area that connected the coast and river made it a suitable region for smuggling operations. The hub of Spanish defenses and the entrepôt of legal trade in the southern Caribbean, Cartagena de Indias was a major urban market whose bustle attracted smugglers. The gold and emeralds of highland mines and colonial revenues destined for Madrid passed through the port, and merchants from as far away as Popayán and Quito came there to purchase goods for retail in their home districts.

Other provincial distinctions, however, attracted contraband in each of the three areas. In Riohacha, inlets and anchorages were controlled by clans of unpacified Guajiro Indians who detested most Spaniards but who willingly traded with foreigners. Espe-

6. "Padrón general del Virreynato del Nuevo Reyno de Granada . . . 1776," in Miguel Urrutia M. and Mario Arrubia (eds.), *Compendio de estadísticas históricas de Colombia* (Bogotá, 1970), 19.

7. Only four galleon fleets sailed to New Granada in the eighteenth century (in 1721, 1723, 1730, and 1737), and between 1713 and 1763, only sixty-one registered ships left Cádiz bound for New Granada. "Libro de la razón de los navíos de registros . . . , Cádiz, 1701–25," AGI, Contratación, leg. 2901, libro 1; "Relación de los navíos de guerra y marchantes, registros, avisos, y otras embarcaciones . . . , Cádiz, 1717–43," AGI, Contratación, 2902B; "Libro donde se relacionan todas las armadas y navíos sueltos que se despachen a la América . . . , Cádiz, 1730–82," AGI, Consulados, libro 358.

cially in Santa Marta province, smugglers found governors who readily connived with them. Like Riohacha and Santa Marta, Cartagena depended on foreign supplies, but its dependence was relatively more important because the Cartagena coast guard—the keystone of contraband defense in the province—required Jamaican reexports of flour to stay in service. New Granadan, Mexican, and Spanish growers and merchants could not furnish the city with sufficient and affordable wheat flour, so Cartagena authorities turned to foreign suppliers, who covered illicit imports into the city.

Riohacha

In the early eighteenth century, Riohacha province was a frontier region. A hostile environment that perplexed Spanish colonists distinguished it, and equally hostile Indians, whom Spanish soldiers never defeated, dominated it. But to smugglers, these same conditions made Riohacha a place of profitable investment. Consequently, Guajiro Indians, Spanish outlaws, foreign and highland merchants, and impoverished residents developed a booming illegal business that supported the provincial economy. Smugglers in Riohacha dealt largely in small consignments of textiles, livestock, and slaves, but the combined value of these exceeded three million pesos per year.[8]

The statistics of Riohacha contraband support this high estimate and indicate that the volume of illegal trade through the province was far higher than generally supposed (see Table 1). Nearly one-third of the prizes seized in Riohachan waters each had values greater than the average annual value of legal trade through the port of Riohacha, even though contraband vessels almost never had full holds when captured. Furthermore, in 1734 and 1737, for example, smugglers landed contraband in Riohacha possibly worth 250,000 and 350,000 pesos, respectively.[9] Signifi-

8. Patiño to Pez, Cádiz, April 14, 1722, AGI, SF, leg. 374; Blas de Lezo to the Marqués de Torrenueva, Cartagena, May 4, 1738, AGI, SF, leg 1093; Juan de Vera y Fajardo to the king, Santa Marta, January 31, 1737, AGI, SF, leg. 1288; Lezo to José de Quintana, Cartagena, March 8, 1740, AGI, SF, leg. 1093; William Paul McGreevey, *An Economic History of Colombia, 1845–1930* (Cambridge, 1971), 30.

9. Sightings of a total of twenty-five vessels in Riohachan waters were reported in

TABLE 1
New Granadan Coastal Prizes, 1713–1763:
Frequency by Year

Year	Riohacha	Santa Marta	Cartagena
1713	1	0	0
1715	1	0	3
1716	0	0	4
1717	1	0	0
1719	1	0	1
1720	4	1	1
1721	8	0	1
1722	5	0	1
1723	5	0	3
1725	2	0	1
1727	0	0	2
1728	0	1	1
1729	0	0	2
1731	4	1	1
1732	0	0	0
1734	3	1	0
1735	1	1	0
1736	1	2	0
1737	0	1	4
1740	1	2	0
1742	2	0	0
1743	5	0	0
1744	2	0	0
1745	0	0	1
1746	1	0	2
1747	0	0	1
1748	4	1	2
1750	1	0	3
1751	0	0	3
1752	2	3	0
1753	2	0	2
1754	2	0	2
1755	0	0	2
1756	0	0	5
1757	0	0	1
1759	0	0	5
1761	0	0	6
1763	0	2	0
1764	0	1	0
Totals	59	17	60

SOURCE: Lance R. Grahn, "Contraband, Commerce, and Society in New Granada, 1713–1763" (Ph.D. dissertation, Duke University, 1985), 212–21, 278–84, 367–74.

cantly, the activity of one trafficker who operated in Riohacha province in the 1710s, a Seville merchant named Salvador de Mora, bore out those values. Riohachan authorities reckoned that his business alone brought in goods worth approximately 400,000 pesos annually.[10]

The effects of Riohacha contraband on highland markets in Santa Fe, Popayán, and Quito also reflected its high volume. More important to supplying highland consumers than contraband through Santa Marta and Cartagena, illegal goods from Riohacha led the way in saturating New Granadan markets. Such imports forced legitimate merchants in Santa Fe and Popayán to lower their prices 25 percent and more just to compete with contrabandists. They also drove the prices of textiles and merchandise in the Andes below those for the same items in the port of Cartagena.[11]

More than any other single group in Riohacha, the Guajiro Indians accounted for the strength and vitality of illicit trade in the province. Responding to the assaults of Spanish colonizers and culture, the Guajiros adopted a pastoral life-style and economy. They learned quickly the clerics' early lessons on animal husbandry and, starting with livestock that roamed the region in the sixteenth century, established fine herds of horses, mules, cattle, and goats. The Guajiros thereby fashioned for themselves a valuable economic resource that was mobile, renewable, independent of Spanish intervention, and marketable. The Guajiros supple-

---

1734, thirty-five in 1737. According to the testimony of a captured smuggler, José de Layesa (alias José Guayqueri), foreign smugglers had among themselves a gentleman's agreement that limited the value of contraband cargos aboard each smuggling vessel to one thousand pesos per crewman (Confesions of José Guayqueri, Santa Marta, July 6, 1735, AGI, SF, leg. 514, 1233). The figures, then, are based on reported sightings and captures of foreign vessels in Riohacha waters and on an average crew size of ten men. Because the estimates use only reported sightings and captures, they must be considered as conservative figures.

10. José Francisco de Herrera to Viceroy Jorge de Villalonga, Cartagena, August 20, 1720, AGI, SF, leg. 374.

11. Consulta, Council of the Indies, Madrid, November 20, 1736, AGI, SF, leg. 1094; José López Pintado to Patiño, San Ildefonso, September 15, 1734, AGI, SF, leg. 1093; Juan de Vera y Fajardo to the king, Santa Marta, February 14, 1735, AGI, SF, leg. 1233; Royal Cedula to the Viceroy Antonio de la Pedrosa y Guerrero, El Pardo, November 13, 1718, AGI, SF, leg. 286.

mented their herding with traditional weaving and by collecting and selling brazilwood, salt, and pearls.[12]

The Guajiros' relative numerical strength matched their commercial versatility. In the eighteenth century they outnumbered the Spanish residents of Riohacha by a ratio of at least forty to one, possibly even one hundred to one. Save for the port of Riohacha, then, they controlled the entire province. Hence, the Guajiros traded openly with foreign merchants, escorted contrabandists through Riohacha, and opposed Spanish troops stationed in the area to curtail smuggling.[13]

Flaws in the Spanish rule of Riohacha also contributed to Guajiro dominance by discouraging permanent Spanish settlement of the province. In the 1730s and 1740s, for example, Spanish authorities had fewer than thirty soldiers in Riohacha to deter smugglers and hostile Indians. That the provincial government seldom had the money to pay and supply the troops compounded the problem and in 1732 prompted them to rebel against the governor and desert their posts. Ten years later, the provincial treasury still empty, many of them turned to smuggling to support their families, probably accepting consignments of illegal goods and protecting smugglers.[14]

12. Johannes Wilbert, *Survivors of Eldorado: Four Indian Cultures of South America* (New York, 1972), 173–74; Omar González N., *Los Guajiros: Una cultura indo-hispana* (Caracas, 1973), 13; Miguel Acosta Saignes, "Algunos conceptos . . . sobre el problema indígena en Venezuela," in Manuel Matos Romero (ed.), *La Guajira: Su importancia* (Caracas, 1971), 32; Julian A. Weston, *The Cactus Eaters* (London, 1937), 86–87; [Segismundo del Real de Gandía], *Tribus que poblaron la costa y modo de civilizarlas: Conferencia dictada por el padre Segismundo del Real de Gandía en Santa Marta* (Bogotá, 1912), 35; [Real de Gandía], *Tribus que poblaron la costa,* 35–36; Francisco Silvestre, *Descripción del Reyno de Santa Fe de Bogotá, escrita en 1789* (Bogotá, 1950), 128; Antonio Julián, *La perla de América: Provincia de Santa Marta* (Bogotá, 1951), 36–37, 125–26, 220.

13. Silvestre, *Descripción del Reyno,* 60–62; Moreno y Escandón, "Estado del Virreinato," 583; Julián, *La perla de América,* 222; Vera to the king, Santa Marta, July 22, 1737, AGI, SF, leg. 1233; Pedro de Fidalgo to the king, Cartagena, June 4, 1739, AGI, SF, leg. 384; Corasa Carlos de Briones, Informe sobre la forma de contener el trato ilícito, Santa Marta, July 25, 1731, AGI, SF, leg. 1233; Confesión de Guayqueri, Santa Marta, July 6, 1735, AGI, SF, leg. 514, 1233; Vera to the king, Santa Marta, July 22, 1737, AGI, SF, leg. 1233; Alberto Luis de Acosta to Vera, Riohacha, May 18, 1737, AGI, SF, leg. 478.

14. Ernesto Restrepo Tirado, *Historia de la provincia de Santa Marta* (Bogotá, 1953), II, 136; G. Earl Sanders, "Counter-contraband in Spanish America: Handicaps of the Governors in the Indies," *Americas,* XXXIV (1977), 62–71; Restrepo Tirado, *Historia de la*

Civilian colonists in Riohacha were equally ill-supplied. Between 1713 and 1763 no registered ships left Cádiz bound for Riohacha, and only one landed at Santa Marta, the closest Spanish port, during that same period.[15] Other sources of legal trade were just as niggardly. Generally, import duties (the 10 percent *almojarifazgo* tax) deposited in the Riohacha treasury in the mid-eighteenth century seldom put the value of licit trade through the port in any given year at more than 2,500 pesos; over the twenty-year span, it averaged less than 1,700 pesos annually (see Table 2).[16] That represented yearly legal imports worth one-half peso per person. Even limiting the number of potential Riohacha consumers to the 350 Spanish clerics and colonists, the annual average value of legal imports per person rose to just five pesos, or the value of one piece of coarse linen cloth.[17] The residents of Riohacha, therefore, had no choice but to turn to smugglers for trade goods, which, in turn, facilitated the Guajiros' illegal trade.

Recognizing the reasons for contraband in Riohacha and its ill effect on colonial rule, Spanish authorities attempted to curb smuggling in the province, their many hindrances notwithstanding. Yet all of their efforts failed and depleted viceregal and provincial funds with no apparent economic reward. The primary in-

---

provincia de Santa Marta, II, 133–34; Marqués del Villar [José Alonso de Pizarro] to Antonio de Alcalá Galiano (governor of Riohacha), Santa Fe, February 12, 1751, AHNC, Virreyes, tomo 2, fols. 886–88; Consulta, Council of the Indies, Madrid, November 20, 1736, AGI, SF, leg. 1094; José de Andía y Rivero to the king, Santa Marta, June 28, 1732, Orden de Pedro José Mozo de la Torre, Riohacha, August 2, 1733, Orden de Mozo de la Torre, Riohacha, February 27, 1734, all in AGI, SF, leg. 1233.

15. "Libro de la razón de los navíos de registros . . . , Cádiz, 1701–25," AGI, Contratación, leg. 2901, libro 1; "Relación de los navíos de guerra y marchantes, registros, avisos, y otras embarcaciones . . . , Cádiz, 1727–43," AGI, Contratación, leg. 2902B; "Libro donde se relacionan todas las armadas y navíos sueltos que se despachen a la América, Cádiz, 1730–82," AGI, Consulados, libro 358.

16. In 1747, the value of legal trade reached 3,620 pesos; in 1750, 4,060 pesos; in 1757, 4,520 pesos; and in 1760, 3,040 pesos. In 1745, 1748, and 1749, however, no entry under port taxes (*almojarifazgos* of 10 and 15 percent) is recorded. Relaciones juradas de la Caja de Real Hacienda de Riohacha (hereinafter cited as Caja de Riohacha), 1743–60, AGI, Contaduría, leg. 1567; Cajas de Riohacha, 1761–65, AGI, SF, leg. 1288.

17. The Inventory, Valuation, and Disposition of the *Dragón* (AGI, SF, leg. 374) lists the appraised value of several types of cloth found in its captured cargo, among which was striped coarse linen cloth (*lienzo listado de olanda*) valued at five pesos per piece.

TABLE 2
Riohacha Treasury, 1745–1764: Revenues (Annual Average by Quinquennium)

Quinquennium	Almo 10[a] (pesos)	Almo 17[b] (pesos)	Comisos[c] (pesos)	Net Caja[d] (pesos)	Pct 1[e] (%)	Pct 2[f] (%)
1745–1749	81	168	547	2,629	13.0	3.9
1750–1754	223	365	1,037	4,463	23.9	8.7
1755–1759	234	489	1,074	6,112	16.7	8.2
1760–1764	136	223	782	4,131	15.9	4.8
Totals	3,364	6,288	17,201	86,675		

SOURCES: Relaciones juradas de la Caja de Real Hacienda de Riohacha, 1743–60, AGI, Contaduría, leg. 1567; Relaciones juradas de la Caja de Real Hacienda de Riohacha, 1761–65, AGI, SF, leg. 1288.
NOTE: The figures in this table represent annual averages by quinquennium, rounded to the nearest peso.
[a] Almo 10 = *Almojarifazgo* of 10 percent.
[b] Almo 17 = Combined *almojarifazgos* of 17 percent.
[c] Comisos = Revenues derived from *comisos* (contraband seizures).
[d] Net Caja = Total net revenue of the treasury.
[e] Pct 1 = Revenues derived from *comisos* as a percentage of the total net revenue (Comisos/Net Caja).
[f] Pct 2 = Total *almojarifazgos* as a percentage of a total net revenue (Almo 17/Net Caja).

stigators of illegal trade in Riohacha, the Guajiro Indians, were the major target of Spanish contraband control measures. Capuchin, Jesuit, and Franciscan missionaries attempted for nearly three hundred years to convert them, but without success.[18] Viceroys José Alonso Pizarro (1749–1753), José Solís Folch de Cardona (1753–1761), Manuel Guirior (1773–1776), and Manuel Antonio Flórez (1776–1782) tried to pacify the Guajiros and block their foreign trade by establishing new Spanish villages in the province, but the settlements were soon destroyed or abandoned. The Spanish army did not pacify the Guajiros either, despite large offensives in 1718, 1760, and 1771. In the end, Viceroy Pedro Mendinueta (1797–1803) concluded that because neither force nor gentleness had subdued the Guajiros and "because they [were] full of vices from free

18. Fray Andrés de Oliva to the Procurador General de la Religión de Capuchinos, Maracaibo, June 10, 1730, BNM, SM, MS 9728, fol. 2; W. Clarke Douglas, "Patterns of Indian Warfare in the Province of Santa Marta" (Ph.D. dissertation, University of Wisconsin, 1974), 22, 140; José Manuel Groot, *Historia eclesiástica y civil de Nueva Granada* (Bogotá, 1953–56), II, 133; Julián, *La perla de América,* 9, 220; Gregorio Arcila Robledo, *Las misiones franciscanas en Colombia* (Bogotá, 1950), 168–69. On the persistence of Guajiro intransigence as late as 1930, see Weston, *Cactus Eaters,* 44.

commercial intercourse with foreigners," the best that the Spanish government in New Granada could do was coexist with them.[19]

Ironically, the Riohacha treasury largely depended on the contraband trade. Legal trade through the port of Riohacha produced almost 6,300 pesos in combined *almojarifazgo* revenues between 1745 and 1764, but contraband seizures produced 17,200 pesos, or 270 percent more than legal trade, at the same tax rates as levied against licit imports. Similarly, taxes on legal commerce generally produced 4 or 8 percent of the total annual income, whereas deposits derived from the sale and taxation of captured contraband commonly represented 15 percent or more of the annual gross revenue of the Riohacha treasury (see Table 2).

Santa Marta

Substantial illegal trade also passed through the province of Santa Marta, though not to the extent found in Riohacha or Cartagena. Conservative estimates based on ship sightings and captures place the annual value of contraband imports in Santa Marta in the early eighteenth century at thirty thousand pesos (see Table 1). Nonetheless, that was seven times more than the average annual value of legal trade through the port (405 pesos) as measured by the 10 percent *almojarifazgo* duty (see Table 3). As in Riohacha, poor military defenses, troublesome Indians, and scanty legal trade contributed to illegal commerce and official fiscal damage in the province. But more important to smuggling in Santa Marta was another defect of Spanish colonial rule: the corrupt, inefficient rule of individual governors who diverted royal income into private accounts, wasted scarce public funds on private vendettas, and participated directly in illicit trade.

In 1718, Philip V declared that much of the smuggling along the coasts of New Granada resulted from the "neglect by tribunals

19. Kuethe, "The Pacification Campaign," 476–79; Kuethe, *Military Reform and Society,* 136, 149–50; Antonio de Alcácer, *Las misiones capuchinas en el Nuevo Reino de Granada, hoy Colombia (1648–1820)* (Puente Común, Cundinamarca, 1959), 218–19; Julián, *La perla de América,* 277–78; Silvestre, *Descripción del Reyno,* 61; Douglas, "Patterns of Indian Warfare," 130, 132, 138; Manuel Guirior, "Relación del estado del Nuevo Reino de Granada . . . 1776," in Posada and Ibáñez (eds.), *Relaciones de mando,* 177–78; Kuethe, "Pacification Campaign," 471–73; Pedro Mendinueta, "Relación del estado del Nuevo Reino de Granada . . . 1803," in Pasado and Ibáñez (eds.), *Relaciones de mando,* 559.

TABLE 3
Santa Marta Treasury, 1705–1759: Revenues
(Annual Average by Quinquennium)

Quinquennium	Almo 10[a] (pesos)	Almo 17[b] (pesos)	Comisos[c] (pesos)	Net Caja[d] (pesos)	Pct 1[e] (%)	Pct 2[f] (%)	Pct 3[g] (%)
1705–1709	67	94	992	5,721	15.6	1.0	1.5
1710–1714	893	992	3,056	9,906	13.9	6.2	7.3
1715–1719	17	243	93	3,846	2.3	0.4	5.3
1720–1724	251	605	328	4,422	7.3	4.9	12.3
1725–1729	625	1,245	2,262	9,900	22.8	5.6	12.0
1730–1734	722	1,516	1,265	11,603	9.5	7.2	15.2
1735–1739	493	1,041	1,784	8,056	19.7	5.7	12.3
1740–1744	78	285	2,285	13,231	8.5	0.5	2.4
1745–1749	164	548	709	25,536	3.5	0.8	2.4
1750–1754	1,126	2,684	6,502	48,825	11.6	2.3	5.7
1755–1759	19	237	345	19,671	1.8	0.1	1.4
Totals	22,277	47,455	99,108	803,581			

SOURCE: Relaciones juradas de la Caja de Real Hacienda de Santa Marta, 1705–59, AGI, Contaduría, legs. 1518–20, 1521A, 1521B, and 1521C.
NOTE: The figures in this table represent annual averages by quinquennium, rounded to the nearest peso.
[a] Almo 10 = *Almojarifazgo* of 10 percent.
[b] Almo 17 = Combined *almojarifazgos* of 17 percent.
[c] Comisos = Revenues derived from *comisos.*
[d] Net Caja = Total net revenue of the treasury.
[e] Pct 1 = Revenues derived from *comisos* as a percentage of the total net revenue (Comisos/Net Caja).
[f] Pct 2 = Revenues derived from the *almojarifazgo* of 10 percent as a percentage of the total net revenue (Almo 10/Net Caja).
[g] Pct 3 = Revenues derived from the combined *almojarifazgos* of 17 percent as a percentage of the total net revenue (Almo 17/Net Caja).

and by my ministers."[20] The king's judgment was substantiated three years later by the first viceroy of New Granada, Jorge de Villalonga (1719–1724), himself an active smuggler in Cartagena province.[21] Noting a discrepancy between the account books of the Santa Marta treasury and reports of the intermittent payment of military wages, he ordered an audit of Santa Marta records. The

20. Royal Cedula to Viceroy Antonio de la Pedrosa y Guerrero, El Pardo, November 13, 1718, AGI, SF, leg. 286.

21. See, for example, José de Herrera to the king, Cartagena, August 20, 1720, and Faustino Fajardo y Manuel de Cuesta to the king, Cartagena, June 4, 1721, both in AGI, SF, leg. 374.

investigators found that the governor of Santa Marta, Juan Beltrán de Caicedo (1718–1726), had embezzled funds designated for the salaries of soldiers. With the aid of presidio officers, Caicedo filled billets with nonexistent men or with local artisans and then pocketed the budgeted wages. The governor's scheme seriously undermined provincial defenses against foreign commerce because the destitute soldiers often offered their services to smugglers to secure a wage.[22]

Governor Caicedo's replacement proved no better. Manuel López Pintado, who commanded the galleon fleet of 1730 to New Granada and then stayed on for three years to command the Cartagena coast guard, charged that José de Andía y Rivero (1726–1733) had scandalously wrecked contraband control in Santa Marta. In the eighteenth century New Granadan officials relied on squads of soldiers posted in the province at places such as Concha on the coast and Chiriguaná in the south to deter contraband trade through the province. Andía replaced those infantrymen with his own lackeys, who protected his smuggling interests. Significantly, the Riohacha town council, which answered to the Santa Marta governor, corroborated the testimony of López Pintado. It too accused Andía of illicit trafficking and of using "insidious methods" to frustrate its attempts to prove his complicity.[23]

An incident in 1733 illustrates Andía's involvement. Early that year, Blas Antonio Niño, who was on detached duty from Cartagena, captured nine contraband-laden canoes and four contrabandists at the Ciénaga Grande of Santa Marta. The Cartagena authorities subsequently tried, convicted, and executed one of the smugglers, a resident of Cartagena named Pablo Santiago. The other three traffickers all hailed from Santa Marta province, so Governor Andía heard their cases. Implicating himself in the crime, Andía colluded with the treasury officials of Tamalameque to declare the contraband to be legal merchandise. Then, to the horror of Cartagena officials, he simply dropped all charges against the three.[24]

22. Jorge Villalonga to the king, Santa Fe, March 4, 1721, AGI, SF, leg. 286; Jose García de Luna to the king, Cartagena, October 12, 1722, AGI, SF, leg. 374.

23. Manuel López Pintado to Patiño, Aranjuez, May 10, 1734, AGI, SF, leg. 1093; Council of the Indies (De Oficio), Madrid, May 4, 1737, AGI, SF, leg. 1094.

24. Antonio Salas, Sebastián de Iglesias, and Ignacio Ibáñez to the king, Cartagena, September 20, 1733 (two letters), AGI, SF, leg. 478.

Such malfeasance in office, López Pintado later declared, had rooted contraband so deeply in the economy of Santa Marta that only the removal of the governor and his henchmen could excise it. The evidence against Andía similarly persuaded the Council of the Indies. In 1733, the councilors seconded the admiral's call and sacked the governor.[25]

The removal of Andía still did not check smuggling in Santa Marta. In fact, his replacement, Juan de Vera y Fajardo (1733–1743), created an even greater furor in the province. Although he had performed well enough as the governor of Margarita to warrant promotion, in Santa Marta Vera deeply embroiled himself in illegal commerce. As demonstrated in a 1735 criminal case, he abetted smuggling through the Santa Marta and Riohacha provinces. During the proceedings against a contrabandist known to be guilty, the governor perjured himself and, in fact, "sheltered, protected, [and] openly defended" the accused. Moreover, Vera cornered the salt market in Santa Marta and gained control of both the production and distribution of salt. He then charged exorbitant prices in his province and sold salt to foreign traders in Riohacha.[26]

In the end, the Council of the Indies concluded from the litigation and other reports that "the great disorder and abuse of continual illicit commerce" in Santa Marta province persisted because of a "manifest tolerance and complicity of the governors and their lieutenants." The council concluded that the only way to return the attention of provincial authorities to the control of smuggling was once again to replace the Santa Marta governor.[27]

Contraband in Santa Marta represented a significant loss to

25. López Pintado to Patiño, Cádiz, November 1, 1735, AGI, SF, leg. 1093; Council of the Indies (De Oficio), Madrid, May 4, 1737, AGI, SF, leg. 1094.

26. Vera to the king, Santa Marta, July 22, 1735, AGI, SF, leg. 1233; Salas to the king, Cartagena, September 4, 1735, AGI, SF, leg. 478; Vera to the king, Santa Marta, January 31, 1737, July 22, 1737, both in AGI, SF, leg. 1233; Consulta, Council of the Indies, Madrid, November 20, 1736, AGI, SF, leg. 1094; Salas to the king, Cartagena, September 10, 1735, AGI, SF, leg. 478.

27. Consulta, Council of the Indies, Madrid, May 4, 1737, AGI, SF, leg. 1094. It is interesting to note that these opinions of the council contradict the results of Vera's *residencia,* which reflected a clean service record. Residencia of Vera, AHN, Sección de Consejos, Consejo de Indias, leg. 20494 (año 1743); Sentence of Vera, Santa Marta, September 24, 1743, AGI, SF, leg. 1233.

TABLE 4
Santa Marta Treasury, 1705–1759: Expenditures
(Annual Average by Quinquennium)

Quinquennium	Infantry[a] (pesos)	Cbnd Def[b] (pesos)	Defense[c] (pesos)	Net Exp[d] (pesos)	Pct 1[e] (%)	Pct 2[f] (%)
1705–1709	17,939	0	18,623	26,454	75.6	96.4
1710–1714	12,260	0	12,654	19,393	63.1	97.2
1715–1719	8,624	0	8,870	15,191	60.1	97.4
1720–1724	9,154	0	9,742	17,818	57.3	94.5
1725–1729	12,452	0	13,276	21,755	63.3	93.7
1730–1734	21,154	0	22,116	36,444	61.5	95.9
1735–1739	26,528	0	27,305	40,793	65.9	96.6
1740–1744	31,534	369	34,667	50,100	72.6[g]	91.1[g]
1745–1749	34,542	26	35,239	40,389	71.6[h]	98.0[h]
1750–1754	30,555	76	31,754	46,869	69.0	96.3
1755–1759	23,208	0	23,208	44,267	49.5	100.0
Totals	1,139,747	2,353	1,187,271	1,789,411		

SOURCE: See Table 3.
NOTE: The figures in this table represent annual averages by quinquennium, rounded to the nearest peso.
[a]Infantry = Salaries paid to soldiers of the Santa Marta presidio, including the anticontraband guards.
[b]Cbnd Def = Extraordinary expenditures specifically for contraband defense.
[c]Defense = Total net expenditures on military defense of Santa Marta.
[d]Net Exp = Total net expenditures of the treasury.
[e]Pct 1 = Total defense expenditures as a percentage of the total net expenditures (Defense/Net Exp).
[f]Pct 2 = Salaries paid to soldiers as a percentage of the total net expenditures (Infantry/Net Exp).
[g]Excludes 1742.
[h]Excludes 1747.

the treasury in uncollected taxes and in expenditures on contraband defense, which returned to the treasury less than one peso for every twelve spent (see Table 4). But perhaps most galling of all to royal officials in Santa Fe and Madrid was the loss represented by the salaries of the royal officials of Santa Marta. Compared to the yearly average wages of the presidio infantry (20,730 pesos), they were relatively small, averaging about 4,000 pesos annually (Table 4). Nevertheless, that money was spent largely to ensure respect for authority and obedience to the law. Instead, it supported officials who openly betrayed their trust.[28]

28. Relaciones juradas de la Caja de Real Hacienda de Santa Marta, 1705–59, AGI, Contaduria, legs. 1518–20, 1521A, 1521B, and 1521C.

At the same time, official complicity in Santa Marta contraband demonstrated the weakness of the imperial structure in that region. The governors of Santa Marta were bound to oppose illegal trade, but participation in smuggling was one of the few, if only perquisites they enjoyed. A minor province characterized by economic underdevelopment, Indian unrest, chronic fiscal problems, fear of foreign invasions, and uncomfortable weather, Santa Marta was an inhospitable place of employment. Furthermore, the Council of the Indies and other royal advisors also bore some responsibility for the corruption of Santa Marta politics. They did not confront its root causes, but hoped in vain that a strong, honest governor would ultimately emerge to overcome the political and economic defects of Spanish rule in Santa Marta.

Cartagena

Cartagena de Indias was the political, economic, and military center of Cartagena province and the entire Caribbean coast of New Granada, but it was first a maritime city. As a result, Spanish authorities gave high priority to a naval strategy to combat smuggling between the mouth of the Magdalena River and Portobelo. Significantly, the Cartagena coast guard also illustrated the dilemmas of contraband defense better than any other embodiment of Spanish commercial policy in the province.

As with the infantrymen in Riohacha, the ability of the coast guard to function properly suffered from a lack of logistical support that even exemplary leadership could not overcome. The highly respected Lieutenant General Blas de Lezo had scarcely arrived in Cartagena with two coast guard ships in 1737 when he urgently requested reinforcements from Spain. The volume of smuggling through the port overwhelmed his forces; smugglers, he said, were so numerous in and around Cartagena that they had virtually blockaded the city. To substantiate his report, Lezo estimated—probably correctly—that New Granadan merchants, miners, and soldiers were illegally exporting three-fourths of the viceroyalty's gold production, worth about 1,250,000 silver pesos per year, through Cartagena province.[29]

29. "Libro donde se relacionan todas las armadas y navíos sueltos de registro que se despachen a la América . . . , Cádiz, 1730–82," AGI, Consulados, libro 358; General Blas

Lezo enlarged his coast guard squadron as war with England approached over the next three years, but he never achieved his targeted strength. The maintenance costs of his six ships were nonetheless considerable; in fact, they surpassed what any single group or body in New Granada could afford. In early 1740, for example, Lezo spent in just three months a subsidy of 150,000 pesos from Lima that was to have lasted an entire year. He then turned to the Cartagena merchant guild for additional support. Its directors loaned him another 100,000 pesos, which he spent within six months. In April and May, 1741, the expense of coast guard defense rose dramatically when Admiral Edward Vernon's forces attacked Cartagena. Lezo lost all six of his warships and died of wounds suffered while directing the defense of the port. Though finally repelled, Vernon's blow so devastated Spanish forces in Cartagena that coast guard vessels did not again patrol Cartagena waters until 1752.[30]

Equally debilitating to the coast guard was the inability of Spanish authorities to furnish the crews with food. Although flour shortages were endemic in Cartagena in the first half of the eighteenth century, they became so acute for the coast guard that they threatened to halt naval operations. In 1729 and 1763, respectively, Commander Gabriel de Mendinueta and Viceroy Pedro Messía de la Cerda (1761–1773) told metropolitan officials that they could

---

de Lezo to Torrenueva, Cartagena, March 21, 1737, AGI, SF, leg. 1093; Lezo to Torrenueva, Cartagena, May 8, 1737, AGI, SF, leg. 1093; Fidalgo to the king, Cartagena, May 8, 1737, AGI, SF, leg. 384; Lezo to Torrenueva, Cartagena, March 28, 1737, AGI, SF, leg. 1093; William Sharp, *Slavery on the Spanish Frontier: The Colombian Chocó, 1680–1810* (Norman, Okla., 1976), 73, 186–87; Ann Twinam, *Miners, Merchants, and Farmers in Colonial Colombia* (Austin, 1982), 28; McGreevey, *An Economic History of Colombia*, 28.

30. Inés Restrepo de García, "El ataque a Cartagena de 1741: Una lucha de mercados," *BHA*, LXIV (1977), 612; Auto of Miguel Laso de la Vega y Porras, Pedro Bernardo de Peralta y Córdoba, and José Ortiz de Escobar, Cartagena, April 20, 1740, AGI, Consulados, libro 767; Póliza, Cartagena, April 20, 1740, Viceroy Sebastián Eslava to the deputies of the commerce of Spain, Cartagena, October 30, 1740, Junta del Comercio to Eslava, Cartagena, November 9, 1740, all in AGI, Consulados, libro 767; Eslava to Quintana, Cartagena, May 9, 1741, in Cristóbal Bermúdez Plata, *Narración de la defensa de Cartagena de Indias contra el ataque de los ingleses en 1741* (Seville, 1912), 18–20, 39; Juan Manuel Zapatero, *La guerra del Caribe en el siglo XVIII* (San Juan, 1964), 33–62; Carlos Restrepo Canal, "El sitio de Cartagena por el Almirante Vernon," *BHA*, XXVIII (1941), 456; Enrique Marco Dorta, *Cartagena de Indias: Puerto y plaza fuerte* (Bogotá, 1960), 213–19; Royal Order to the Marqués de Villar, Madrid, July 29, 1752, AGI, SF, leg. 1094.

not put their ships out to sea because they had no rations. Messía de la Cerda even suggested that the sailors be paid one silver real instead of receiving their daily allotment of hardtack. In 1740, as Cartagena prepared for war, scant supplies of flour and other foodstuffs turned naval reinforcements into more of an encumbrance than a relief. As Viceroy Sebastián Eslava (1740–1748) explained, the arrival of the squadron of Rodrigo de Torres put the city "in dire straits and in the greatest distress because, in order to provide it food for three months, it was necessary to give it all . . . the food supplies of the ships and garrison [of Cartagena]."[31]

Flour shortages also hurt the coast guard and the entire city by inflating the price. Because flour production in the central New Granadan highlands did not yield enough to furnish the port consistently and because transportation costs reflected the tortuous four-month journey from Tunja to the coast, flour prices were at times 2,000 percent higher on the coast than in the highlands.[32]

Local provisioning of the Cartagena squadron also suffered from the carelessness and limitations of officials in Santa Fe. For example, despite growing rumors of a British invasion in the spring of 1740, ministers of the Audiencia of Santa Fe did not renew their contract with a merchant from the capital to supply Blas de Lezo's ships with highland flour. Other times, problems entirely out of their control thwarted their efforts to obtain flour from Spain and Mexico.[33]

The high price and scarcity of Spanish flour forced coast guard officers and civilian authorities in Cartagena to turn to alternative supplies, particularly reexports of Anglo-American flour.

31. Gabriel de Mendinueta to Patiño, Cartagena, February 26, 1729, AGI, SF, leg. 1093; Pedro Messía de la Cerda to Julián de Arriaga, Cartagena, January 22, 1763, AGI, SF, leg. 1094; Eslava to the Marqués de Villarias, Cartagena, March 31, 1741, in Bermúdez Plata, *Narración*, 33.

32. Enrique Marco Dorta, "Ganadería y abastecimiento en Cartagena de Indias (1766)," *Revista de Indias*, XXX (1970), 475; Juan de Santa Gertrudis, *Maravilla de la naturaleza* (Bogotá, 1956), I, 256; María Angeles Eugenio Martínez, "La competencia inglesa en el comercio del Nuevo Reino con Cartagena," *Temas Americanistas*, II (1983), 14.

33. Lezo to Quintana, Cartagena, March 28, 1740, AGI, SF, leg. 1093; Dorta, "Ganadería," 475; Restrepo de García, "El ataque a Cartagena," 614; Rodrigo de Torres y Morales to Quintana, Cartagena, October 26, 1740, AGI, SF, leg. 1093; Arriaga to the Marqués de la Ensenada, Cádiz, December 31, 1752, Messía de la Cerda to Arriaga, Cartagena, January 22, 1763, both in AGI, SF, leg. 1094.

Significantly, this flour trade became so mutually beneficial to the people and merchants in Cartagena and Kingston that neither depredations nor war seriously disrupted it. Only five months before Philip V declared war on Great Britain on November 28, 1739, officials of the Cartagena coast guard contracted with Jamaican merchants for foodstuffs and other supplies. In fact, it was an English frigate loaded with flour for the Cartagena squadron that first brought news to Cartagena of impending hostilities in the Caribbean. Furthermore, the local beneficiaries of this Jamaican connection considered the trade so essential to their well-being that they plotted on at least one occasion to prevent implementation of laws requiring that only domestic flour be consumed.[34]

The War of Jenkins' Ear (1739–1748) exacerbated the precarious position of Cartagena. The king's call to arms prohibited all trade with English subjects, forbade the admission of any English vessel into Spanish-American ports, and prescribed the death penalty for those who disregarded these regulations. The threat of execution had little effect, however. In 1742 a Jamaican factor reported that reexports of North American flour to the Spanish Main were so great that flour prices on the island remained high, despite the continual arrival of large shipments from Pennsylvania. Even in the early 1760s, when New Granadan flour became more plentiful, fell in price, and became competitive with Jamaican supplies, coast guard officers continued to rely on Anglo-American suppliers.[35]

Cartagena officials obtained flour from Jamaica in several

34. Mendinueta to Patiño, Cartagena, February 26, 1729, AGI, SF, leg. 1093; Pedro de Hordenaña to Ensenada, Cartagena, March 28, 1753, AGI, SF, leg. 1094; Antonio de Arévalo to the king, Cartagena, December 9, 1766, in Dorta, "Ganadería," 475; Sir Nicholas Lawes, governor of Jamaica, to Council of Trade and Plantations [Jamaica, 1719], in Great Britain, Public Record Office, *Calendar of State Papers, Colonial Series, 1719–1720* (London, n.d.), 277–79; Arthur L. Jensen, *The Maritime Commerce of Colonial Philadelphia* (Madison, 1963), 51; Lezo to Quintana, Cartagena, September 28, 1739, Lezo to Torrenueva, Cartagena, April 22 and June 24, 1739, all in AGI, SF, leg. 1093; José de Solis Folch de Cardona, "Relacion del Virreinato de Santa Fe . . . 1760," in Posada and Ibáñez (eds.), *Relaciones de mando,* 85.

35. Royal Cedula, Buen Retiro, November 28, 1739, Duke University, William R. Perkins Library, Manuscript Department, Sobre Ynglater Collection in Duque de Montemar Papers; Pedro Messía de la Cerda, "Relación del estado del Virreinato de Santa Fe . . . 1772," in Posada and Ibáñez (eds.), *Relaciones de mando,* 109–10.

legal ways. The port received flour as part of the slave *asiento* granted to the British monarchy under the 1713 Treaty of Utrecht. This contract, subsequently transferred to the South Sea Company, allowed the company to import at first one barrel and later two barrels of flour per imported slave into Spanish-American ports, in addition to the five hundred tons of cargo allowed the company's register ship. Secondly, local authorities contracted with Jamaican merchants for flour. In 1729, for example, Mendinueta arranged for Christopher Galvein, who two years earlier had stocked the galleons with comestibles and equipment before their return to Spain, to furnish the coast guard with flour, meat, and other items. Mendinueta's successor as commanding officer to the coast guard, Domingo Justiniani, similarly contracted with another Jamaican merchant, John Paris, for his flour. Subsequent commanders generally continued this practice, most often hiring the firm of George Fryer. Cartagena officials also tapped Jamaican flour supplies through private Spanish contractors, such as José Ruiz de Noriega, who monopolized the Jamaica-to-Cartagena flour trade in the 1740s.[36]

But the Cartagena coast guard acquired foreign flours through illegal trade as well. The coast guard's commission to deter smuggling notwithstanding, its reliance on Jamaican supplies provided easy and tempting cover for illicit introductions.[37] It was rare, therefore, that flour importers brought into Cartagena only those goods allowed and only in the amounts permitted. And because the coast guard, local merchants, and port officers all had a stake in the Jamaican trade, seizures of Jamaican flour were equally rare. So, English merchants often introduced more flour than was con-

36. Antonio Caballero y Góngora, "Relación del Nuevo Reino de Granada . . . 1789," in Posada and Ibáñez (eds.), *Relaciones de mando,* 739; Eugenio Martínez, "La competencia inglesa," 12; Restrepo García, "El ataque a Cartagena de 1741," 607; Mendinueta to Patiño, Cartagena, February 26, 1729, and December 18, 1731, Auto of Governor Salas, Cartagena, December 18, 1731, all in AGI, SF, leg. 1093; Diego Tabares, José Crespo Ortiz, and Rafael de Escobar to Arriaga, Cartagena, February 28, 1759, AGI, SF, leg. 1012; Eugenio Martínez, "La competencia inglesa," 13.

37. Solís, "Relación," in Posada and Ibáñez (eds.), *Relaciones de mando,* 85; Messía de la Cerda, "Relación," in Posada and Ibáñez (eds.), *Relaciones de mando,* 109; Guirior, "Relación," in Posada and Ibáñez (eds.), *Relaciones de mando,* 141–43; Viceroy Manuel Antonio Flórez to José de Gálvez, [Santa Fe], November 15, 1777, AGI, SF, leg. 1095; Viceroy Francisco Gil y Lemos to the king, Cartagena, January 30, 1789, AGI, SF, leg. 573.

tractually set and shipped other goods, such as clothing and textiles, inside flour barrels.

One of the few such cases that inspectors uncovered illuminates this aspect of illegal trade. In December, 1731, the Jamaican captain John Paris and his brother, Alexander, entered Cartagena with a license to import 1,200 barrels of flour for the coast guard squadron of Domingo Justiniani. They carried, however, 155 barrels of flour, 71 kegs of lard, and 27 kegs of rum in excess of their limit. The port officials of Cartagena declared the extra cargo to be contraband and prepared for its public auction. A local merchant established the price of the flour at 14.5 pesos per barrel, about 15 percent higher than contract prices; the lard at 8 pesos per keg; and the rum at 6.25 pesos per keg. The keenly competitive bidding quickly pushed the sale price to 25 percent over valuation plus 15 pesos. Clearly, flour was a valuable and coveted commodity in the city.[38]

Individual coast guard sailors also trafficked in contraband. In 1730, for example, Antonio López Márquez, the commissioner of Justiniani's squadron, strong-armed a Cartagena gatekeeper to let pass seven crates of illegal lace and silk stockings that he had stolen from the cargo of an English prize. Three years later, smuggling by naval officers and sailors was so commonplace that Governor Antonio Salas set up an inspection station "within gunshot of the walls of the city" to better monitor boat traffic in the harbor.[39] Paradoxically, the Spanish forces most responsible for contraband defense in Cartagena used their access to the port and their dependence on foreign trade to augment their wages and supplies with illicit profits and goods.

The dependence of the coast guard on Jamaican exports of flour revealed both the lack of Spanish and American resources to equip the naval vessels stationed at Cartagena and the ability of contrabandists to protect their trade. It also evidenced the need of Cartagena authorities to use effectively the money on hand for

38. Testimonio . . . sobre la entrada . . . del paquebot *La Sara* y la balandra *El Diamante* de la isla de Jamaica . . . , Cartagena, January 10–February 18, 1732, AGI, SF, leg. 477.

39. Auto of Governor Salas, Cartagena, March 19, 1730, Antonio López Márquez to Salas, Cartagena, March 22, 1730, Inventario, [Cartagena], March 28, 1730, all in AGI, Consulados, libro 786; Salas to the king, Cartagena, October 17, 1733, AGI, SF, leg. 1093.

TABLE 5
Cartagena Treasury, 1715–1764: Revenues (Annual Average by Quinquennium)

Quinquennium	Comisos[a] (pesos)	Prizes[b] (pesos)	Net Cbnd[c] (pesos)	Net Caja[d] (pesos)	Pct 1[e] (%)	Pct 2[f] (%)
1715–1719	15,461	205	39,062	77,327	21.6	48.0
1720–1724	4,317	24	4,986	53,995	11.6	13.2
1725–1729	5,657	3,000	8,826	73,051	11.4	19.6
1730–1734[g]	17,726	0	18,001	53,140	32.3	32.8
1735–1739	14,224	0	20,384	70,795	21.5	28.0
1740–1744	90,387	1,645	92,422	228,719	34.7	35.6
1745–1749	14,668	273	14,940	110,428	13.7	14.0
1750–1754	8,832	214	9,046	166,465	5.1	5.2
1755–1759	136	2,944	3,081	126,452	0.1	2.0
1760–1764	5,056	242	5,298	326,713	1.9	2.1
Totals	864,592	42,739	1,062,228	6,381,836		

SOURCE: Relaciones juradas de la Caja de Real Hacienda de Cartagena de Indias, 1715–64, AGI, Contaduría, legs. 1426–27, 1428A, 1428B, 1429; AGI, SF, leg. 1097.

NOTE: The figures in this table represent annual averages by quinquennium, rounded to the nearest peso.

[a]Comisos = Revenues derived from *comisos*.

[b]Prizes = Revenues derived from naval prizes.

[c]Net Cbnd = Total revenues from all seizures of contraband.

[d]Net Caja = Total net revenues of the treasury.

[e]Pct 1 = Revenues derived from *comisos* as a percentage of total net revenue (Comisos/Net).

[f]Pct 2 = Total revenues derived from all seizures of contraband as a percentage of total net revenue (Net Cbnd/Net).

[g]Excludes 1732.

coast guard support. The operating budget of the squadron usually exceeded appropriations, and prizes paid only a small fraction of the costs of the coast guard. In fact, naval prizes generated slightly less than 43,000 pesos in treasury revenues between 1715 and 1764, or about 0.5 percent of the estimated operational expenses of the coast guard squadron over the same period (see Table 5).[40] Therefore, the overseers of the coast guard bought the best product available for the best price possible, regardless of its origin or its seller's nationality.

40. On the basis of an annual budget of 225,000 pesos, the total operational cost of the coast guard from 1715 through 1764 was 8,325,000 pesos. That does not include 1742–1752, when there was no squadron. The following sources were used to determine the estimated yearly Cartagena coast guard budget: Presupuesto del caudal que se considere preciso

The Cartagena coast guard reflected the tension between Spanish policy and American economic and political realities. Publicly, Spanish officials pronounced their commitment to curbing illegal commerce in Cartagena with coast guard cruises. During the first half of the eighteenth century, the navy attempted to meet that challenge, if only intermittently; on the average, the coast guard captured one smuggling vessel each year (Table 1). Occasionally, the seizures were spectacular, such as Gabriel Mendinueta's single 1729 prize worth over 213,000 pesos and two of Domingo Justiniani's prizes that exceeded 100,000 pesos in value.[41] But, over the course of 1713–1763, the squadrons produced a net monetary loss of more than eight million pesos. To a large degree, their dependence on foreign supplies precluded their efficacy, and because of logistical problems and greed, sailors and naval officers even participated in the illicit trade through Cartagena.

Conclusion

The control of contraband in northern New Granada was a paradox of Spanish imperialism, a dilemma that could not be solved. Spanish tradition, law, and mercantilist principles demanded that Spain combat smuggling in its colonies and keep control of Caribbean commerce in Spanish hands; to refuse that command would be to surrender any claim of imperial hegemony in the circum-Caribbean. Therefore, the financial losses incurred by contraband defenses, though substantial, were necessary from a political perspective. Yet, at the same time, illegal trade in Riohacha, Santa Marta, and Cartagena provinces was too profitable and too necessary to stop completely.

Specific structural forces in each of the regions—Guajiro

---

cada mes . . . , Cartagena, February 26, 1753, AGI, SF, leg. 1094; Presupuesto del caudal que se necesita anualmente . . . , Cartagena, April 9, 1777, AGI, SF, leg. 1095; Viceroy Pedro Mendinueta to Francisco de Saavedra, Santa Fe, May 19, 1798, AHNC, Real Hacienda, Libros de Cuentas, no. 2915, fols. 177–78; Ruth Bourne, *Queen Anne's Navy in the West Indies* (New Haven, 1939), 284–85.

41. Testimonio de los autos obrados sobre la presa *La Señora Sara,* fragata holandesa . . . , Cartagena, 1729, AGI, Consulados, libro 494; Testimonio . . . de las presas echas por el capitán de navío Don Domingo Justiniani, Cartagena, May 12, 1732, AGI, Consulados, libro 787.

domination in Riohacha, official corruption in Santa Marta, and dependence on Anglo-American wheat flour in Cartagena—determined local smuggling patterns, demonstrating the complexity of illicit commerce in New Granada. Overlaid by weaknesses common to all Spanish-American trade, this provincial uniqueness required Spanish policymakers to think simultaneously in local, regional, and imperial terms, a difficult task at which they seldom succeeded. One eighteenth-century Spanish economist summarized the problem as follows: "It appears to me that the extermination of illicit commerce will require all the constancy of Hercules and will be a victory more difficult than his defeat of the Hydra because contraband trade is a monster with as many heads as there are merchants in foreign colonies [and consumers in Spanish colonies], and it is more deeply rooted and more fecund than weeds among the Spanish population, which, by habit, made it customary. Then, [smuggling] became the very nature of things."[42]

42. Informe, Pedro Garaicochea, Cádiz, November 4, 1764, AGI, IG, leg. 2046A.

JOHN R. FISHER

Chapter 6

The Effects of *Comercio Libre* on the Economies of New Granada and Peru: A Comparison

This essay arises from a general research project on free trade and its effects upon the economies of Spain and Spanish America. The project was designed to assess the consequences of the free trade legislation of 1778–1789 for commercial relations between Spain and America in the last quarter of the eighteenth century. The overall aim of the project was to reconstruct the volume, composition, and geographical distribution of Spanish exports to America and imports into Spain from America during 1778–1796 on the basis of official data, consisting primarily of the registers of individual ships.

Although the general findings of the project have now been published in monographic form, a direct comparison of the impact of free trade upon the viceroyalties of New Granada and Peru has not yet been attempted.[1] Clearly, the regional significance of free trade can be comprehended only within a global context. This essay therefore first summarizes the overall effects of free trade on

1. John Robert Fisher, *Commercial Relations Between Spain and Spanish America in the Era of Free Trade, 1778–1796* (Liverpool, 1985).

Spanish exports to America, then surveys the general American response to free trade, and closes with a specific consideration of the New Granadan and Peruvian experiences.

Free trade led to a massive increase in the value of exports from Spain to America after 1778; the average value during 1782–1796 was 400 percent higher than in the base year. Moreover, the share of Spanish products in this export trade rose from 38 percent in 1778 to an average of 52 percent in 1782–1796. In terms of their share of trade, Spanish producers were most favored in 1794, when they achieved 61 percent, though the volume of trade in that year was low, primarily because of the war between Spain and France, which also deprived Spanish merchants of French goods for reexport.

Despite the impossibility of precisely measuring the relative importance of Spanish manufactures and agricultural goods in overall exports, a large body of evidence suggests that agricultural producers were able to take much greater advantage than industrialists of the wider opportunities free trade offered in the American market. The commercial reforms thus failed to alter significantly the structure of the peninsular economy. The decision in 1778 to break the virtual monopoly of trade enjoyed by Cádiz did enable some ports (notably Barcelona, Málaga, Santander, and La Coruña) to develop commercial links with America of considerable importance for their respective hinterlands. Cádiz, however, succeeded in retaining no less than 76.4 percent of all exports to America during 1778–1796. An examination of the destinations of vessels leaving Cádiz for America between 1785 and 1796, or, in other words, of some three-quarters of the total Spanish exports in terms of value, confirmed that the circum-Caribbean region as a whole was by far Spain's most important market. It consumed 67 percent of the exports of Cádiz, and Veracruz alone accounted for 35.5 percent. Venezuela, which accounted for 10.1 percent, was the second most important market within the region after Veracruz, though New Granada, with 8.2 percent, supplied almost entirely through Cartagena, was not far behind. Honduras, which received goods worth an average of 15 million reales a year, was as important a destination as Cuba. Exports to the Río de la Plata and the Pacific coast of South America together make up the remaining 32.4 percent of Cádiz exports.

TABLE 1
Destinations of Cádiz Exports, 1785–1796

Destination[a]	Value (reales)	Percentage of Total
Veracruz	1,028,824,237	35.5
Caribbean Islands[b]	202,313,395	7.0
Venezuela	293,174,733	10.1
New Granada	238,000,726	8.2
Rio de la Plata[c]	312,304,568	10.8
Pacific coast[d]	626,728,927	21.6
Honduras	180,305,560	6.2
Campeche	14,111,096	0.5
Others[e]	3,289,044	0.1
Total	2,899,052,466	

SOURCE: John Robert Fisher, *Commercial Relations Between Spain and Spanish America in the Era of Free Trade, 1778–1796* (Liverpool, 1985), 55.
[a]Some imprecision is inevitable, for sometimes, though not frequently, ships were registered for a series of destinations that cut across the areas identified in this table (*e.g.*, Havana, Veracruz, and Campeche). In these cases, they have been credited to the area first named in the register. Values shown represent official (1778) values of goods rather than current values.
[b]The vast majority of ships were registered for Havana.
[c]The vast majority of ships were registered for Montevideo.
[d]The majority of ships were registered for Callao, but some for less precise destinations (Puertos de Mar del Sur; Callao y Manila, Callao y Arica; Valparaíso, Arica y Lima; etc.) without a breakdown of cargoes between ports. A precise distribution between Chile, Peru, and other areas therefore cannot be provided.
[e]New Orleans, Florida, San Blas, and California.

Table 1 provides confirmation of the oft-repeated assertion that after 1778 the Río de la Plata, formerly an imperial backwater, emerged as an important market, slightly more valuable for Cádiz than was Venezuela. On average it received goods worth 26 million reales (1.3 million pesos) a year at 1778 values, the average being boosted by particularly large shipments in 1785–1786. The Pacific market, by contrast, absorbed goods with an average annual value of 52 million reales (2.6 million pesos) at 1778 values. It is not possible, unfortunately, to calculate the distribution of these goods among Valparaíso, Arica, Callao, and Guayaquil, for, though nearly all the registers name Callao as the single destination, a few link it with the others without providing details of the proportions of cargoes intended for each port. It is quite clear, however, that the Pacific market as a whole, within which silver-producing Peru was by far the most important area, was more important for the merchants of Cádiz in this period than were the Río de la Plata and Venezuela markets put together; New Granada, too, though less important than these two expanding regions, continued to serve as an important market for Spanish exports. Peru was served by a handful of large ships carrying very valuable cargoes, whereas Buenos Aires and Montevideo attracted larger numbers of small vessels, often carrying relatively unimportant cargoes. In 1791, for example, sixteen ships left Cádiz for the Río de la Plata with goods worth 22 million reales (1778 values), whereas only five ships left for Callao with cargoes worth 80 million reales, and a sixth took goods worth 13 million reales to Callao, Valparaíso, Arica, and Guayaquil. The pattern was similar in 1792, when eighteen ships supplied the Río de la Plata with goods worth 22 million reales, while five ships supplied Callao with cargoes worth 49 million reales, and a sixth took another 14 million reales worth to Callao, Valparaíso, Arica, and Guayaquil. The destinations specified in the registers of the ships that sailed for America from Cádiz imperfectly reflect the relative importance to Spanish exporters of regional markets in America, partly because, as has been noted, that port's trade, though dominant, handled only three-quarters of the total exports from Spain and partly because initial destinations were often not final destinations for European products. Havana, for example, served not only as the funnel for supplying the Cuban market, but as an entrepôt for the entire Gulf of Mexico; Buenos Aires, too, was often the port of first destination for merchandise ultimately destined for Chile or the southern provinces of Peru. Goods shipped to Callao, by contrast, were, in view of the costs involved in transport, likely to be consumed in Peru and Upper Peru rather than transferred to the Río de la Plata or the interior of New Granada; similarly, most of those shipped to Cartagena were consumed in New Granada (Table 2 shows the chronological distribution of this trade). In the light of this latter consideration, the evidence in Table 1 relating to the importance of the Pacific market is sufficient to undermine the persistent myth that free trade destroyed the commercial importance of Lima. This point is reinforced by a consideration of the

TABLE 2
Exports from Cádiz to New Granada and the Pacific Coast, 1785–1796

Year	New Granada (reales)	Pacific (reales)
1785	25,114,951	130,186,556
1786	27,265,953	37,841,327
1787	27,547,813	12,469,204
1788	31,737,205	34,778,152
1789	22,185,542	73,510,754
1790	14,081,980	19,483,170
1791	18,732,681	92,955,573
1792	23,618,723	63,240,796
1793	20,049,040	42,913,310
1794	3,686,321	18,478,227
1795	10,701,355	55,601,976
1796	13,279,162	45,269,882
Totals	238,000,726	626,728,927

SOURCE: See Table 1.

Spanish-American response to the introduction of free trade, which centers around four general issues: first, the volume of American exports to Spain in 1778–1796, as measured by the registered values of cargoes landed in Spain; second, the distribution of these imports between the fourteen Spanish ports that received ships from America during this period; third, the composition of imports in terms of commodities; and fourth, the relative importance of distinct regions in America as suppliers of the commodities shipped to Spain. Again, the basic sources employed are ships' registers, over four thousand of which have been located.[2]

The overall impact of free trade upon imports into Spain from America was even more dramatic than for exports. During 1782–1796, the average value of imports was more than ten times greater than that of 1778; an overwhelming 84 percent of them came into Cádiz, and 4 percent into Barcelona. A breakdown of the commodities imported by these two ports confirms the success of free trade in promoting the exploitation of formerly neglected

2. For a detailed explanation of the nature and availability of these registers, see the discussion of sources and methods in Fisher, *Commercial Relations,* 20–44.

natural resources—tobacco, cacao, sugar, cochineal, indigo, hides, and other agricultural products—which now accounted for 44 percent of the total. These continued to be overshadowed, nevertheless, by precious metals, which made up the remaining 56 percent. One quarter of the treasure imports consisted of crown revenues, the bulk of which were remitted during the latter part of the period, when a strenuous effort was made to increase the profits of empire. New Spain remitted 36 percent of all American products imported into Spain. The Caribbean islands, led by Cuba, were in second place with 23 percent, followed by Peru with 14 percent, the Río de la Plata with 12 percent, and Venezuela with 10 percent. The viceroyalty of New Granada was a long way down the list with a mere 3 percent.

One obstacle to aggregating data on American exports to Spain by region is that many vessels arrived from combinations of ports in different regions. For example, 28 ships arrived from Cartagena-Havana and 2 from Cartagena–Santiago de Cuba, compared with 186 from Cartagena alone; similarly 5 arrived from Santa Marta and 1 from Santa Marta-Havana. Of the 72 arrivals from the Pacific, 52 listed Callao as the single port of departure, but the other 14 listed it in association with one or more additional ports. Unfortunately, the registers of these ships from combinations of ports do not differentiate between the cargoes loaded in each. For the regional breakdown, their cargoes have been attributed to the first-named ports, which means that the share of trade enjoyed by Cartagena, for example, is overstated somewhat, mainly at the expense of Havana. A third more general point to be borne in mind is that information on the ports of origin of the products shipped to Spain may in many cases reflect only the final stages of complex inter-American economic relationships. Virtually every ship from Callao, for example, included silver and cacao in its cargo. It is legitimate to assume that the silver was produced in Peru, but the ships' registers as such offer no clues to the processes whereby the cacao reached Callao from Guayaquil.

As the sources of 13.8 percent and 3.2 percent respectively of all goods imported into Spain from America in 1782–1796 (see Table 3), the viceroyalties of New Granada and Peru were relatively less conspicuous as exporters than as importers. One explanation for this, at least in the case of Peru, is that imported goods

TABLE 3
Imports into Spain from New Granada and the Pacific Coast, 1782–1796

Year	New Granada	Pacific
1782	4,329,082	—
1783	1,247,936	6,666,543
1784	2,358,717	25,534,221
1785	25,383,458	340,737,416
1786	20,145,096	167,643,693
1787	21,753,650	119,514,522
1788	51,367,904	123,569,850
1789	54,684,157	107,328,009
1790	41,186,607	97,568,480
1791	52,692,634	124,479,837
1792	32,004,087	98,302,866
1793	32,537,773	110,440,481
1794	17,474,213	102,449,145
1795	3,447,250	119,854,584
1796	27,119,843	143,345,709
Totals	387,732,407	1,687,435,356
Percentage of all imports	3.2	13.8

SOURCE: This table is derived from Fisher, *Commercial Relations,* 117–20, which provides a series of tables showing the regional origins of imports into Spanish ports.

tended to be brought by sea to Callao, whereas some of the silver to pay for them was exported to Spain via the Río de la Plata. The analysis of the commodities that made up each viceroyalty's share of exports is confined to those imported into Cádiz and Barcelona. In the case of Peru, the omission of other ports has a negligible effect, for 99.7 percent of Pacific imports were brought into Cádiz alone (see Table 4); in the case of New Granada, as Table 5 shows, other Spanish ports enjoyed a slightly higher share of its trade, 2.3 percent of the imports, but most were brought into Cádiz (88.1 percent) and Barcelona (9.7 percent).

A breakdown by commodities of imports into Barcelona and Cádiz, from New Granada and the Pacific ports, summarized in Table 6, contains, perhaps, no real surprises, but it is useful to have existing assumptions about the composition of exports verified by

TABLE 4
Imports into Spain from the Pacific Coast, 1782–1796

Year	Ships	Cádiz	Santander[a]	Totals
1782	—	—	—	—
1783	2	6,666,543	—	6,666,543
1784	5	25,534,221	—	25,534,221
1785	7	340,737,416	—	340,737,416
1786	6	167,643,693	—	167,643,693
1787	6	119,514,522	—	119,514,522
1788	5	123,569,850	—	123,569,850
1789	4	107,328,009	—	107,328,009
1790	2	97,568,480	—	97,568,480
1791	6	124,479,837	—	124,479,837
1792	3	98,302,866	—	98,302,866
1793	7	109,241,100	1,199,381	110,440,481
1794	8	99,164,784	3,284,361	102,449,145
1795	4	119,854,584	—	119,854,584
1796	7	143,345,709	—	143,345,709
Totals	72	1,682,951,614	4,483,742	1,687,435,356
Percentage of the total		99.7	0.3	
Percentage of all imports into Spain, 1782–1796				13.8

SOURCE: See Table 3.
[a]During this period Santander was the only port other than Cádiz to receive imports from the Pacific Coast.

reliable data. In each of the two regions, private shipments of precious metals, usually minted and consisting mainly of silver in the case of Peru but more of gold in New Granada, dominated exports to Spain. The percentages were identical, though the greater export of royal treasure from Peru (8.5 percent versus 2.5 percent) gave the senior viceroyalty a greater overall dependence on precious metals, particularly in the 1790s when the hard-pressed crown was attempting to obtain large remissions of funds from America. In terms of actual totals rather than percentages, Peru's export of precious metals in 1782–1796 averaged 89 million reales (4.4 million pesos) a year, compared with New Granada's much more modest 18 million reales (900,000 pesos). In addition to silver, Peru consistently exported large quantities of cacao (11.4 percent of exports, worth an average 13 million reales a year), most of which was obtained from Guayaquil in exchange for silver and imported manufactures, and *cascarilla,* or Jesuit bark (6.9 percent; average annual value 8 million reales). Given that these commodities—precious metals, cacao, and *cascarilla*—accounted for 96.8 percent of all exports, it follows that other commodities (mainly copper, vicuña wool, and cotton) were relatively insignificant, though of considerable local importance in the areas where they were produced. The range of exports other than precious metals from New Granada was wider and more evenly balanced. Cotton was of considerable importance (7.1 percent; average annual value 1.8 million reales), as was tobacco (5.2 percent; annual average 1.4 million reales). Cacao exports accounted for 4.4 percent (annual average 1.1 million reales), *cascarilla* for 3.8 percent (annual average 949,000 reales), and sugar 2.4 percent (annual average 618,000 reales).

TABLE 5
Imports into Spain from Cartagena/Santa Marta, 1782–1796

Year	Ships	Cádiz	Barcelona	Other Ports	Totals
1782	2	3,589,008	740,074	—	4,329,082
1783	2	1,247,936	—	—	1,247,936
1784	2	2,358,717	—	—	2,358,717
1785	11	24,022,607	1,360,851	—	25,383,458
1786	14	18,562,290	1,582,806	—	20,145,096
1787	14	19,692,101	1,649,211	412,338	21,753,650
1788	14	50,151,542	1,216,362	—	51,367,904
1789	26	48,401,368	4,284,098	1,998,691	54,684,157
1790	22	34,567,943	6,054,029	564,635	41,186,607
1791	26	44,011,038	8,513,636	167,960	52,692,634
1792	20	25,456,754	5,145,816	1,401,517	32,004,087
1793	19	27,788,389	4,382,026	367,358	32,537,773
1794	26	15,161,497	1,610,665	702,051	17,474,213
1795	6	1,966,931	885,966	594,353	3,447,250
1796	17	24,555,393	—	2,564,450	27,119,843
Totals	221	341,533,514	37,425,540	8,773,353	387,732,407
Percentage of the total		88.1	9.7	2.3	
Percentage of all imports into Spain, 1782–1796					3.2

SOURCE: See Table 3.

Dyewood and hides accounted for considerably less, 1.3 percent and 1.0 percent, respectively. The exportation of all of these natural and agricultural products increased substantially in the late 1780s and in most cases remained substantial in the 1790s, despite the dislocation caused by the Franco-Spanish war of 1793–1795. In the case of Peru, the expansion in nonmineral exports in the 1780s, a product of the attempts of the intendants to promote agricultural growth, was not sustained beyond 1790, though the expansion of silver production more than compensated for this relative decline. In general terms the Pacific region, centered around the viceroyalty of Peru, was much more important to Spain as both a market and a source of precious metals and raw materials; its registered exports to Spain were more than four times those of New Granada. The question that other researchers will hopefully answer is, to what extent was this apparent economic and commercial gulf between the two regions a product of the diversion of New Granadan resources into commercial channels outside of the framework of the official free trade system? In Peru it seems that contraband was of little importance during 1778–1796 because Spanish merchants were clearly able to supply the market abundantly with European manufactures, often at prices lower than those of earlier periods. One would be surprised, however, if the deep-rooted custom of trading with contrabandists in the New Granada region of Portobelo, Cartagena, and Santa Marta diminished to the same extent. It seems possible, therefore, that New Granada's relative commercial insignificance, particularly as an exporter, reflected not only its actual underdevelopment but also a continuing diversion of resources into illegal trade.

We now turn to Peru and the issue of whether free trade after 1778 promoted commercial growth and agricultural and mining development at the cost of destroying domestic industry. In New Granada, although the *obrajes* of Quito were undoubtedly adversely affected by free trade, the industrial decline had begun much earlier, partly as a reflection of internal factors, including major epidemics and high mortality in the centers of textile production in the 1690s, a series of major earthquakes, and a rise in the price of dyes. External factors included the gradual increase in foreign competition that began in 1700 as a result of both contra-

TABLE 6
New Granadan and Peruvian Commodities Imported into Barcelona and Cádiz, 1782–1796

	New Granada		Peru[a]	
Commodities	Value (reales)	Percentage	Value (reales)	Percentage
Gold and silver (private)	265,455,743	70.0	1,184,873,029	70.0
Gold and silver (crown)	9,361,173	2.5	143,325,532	8.5
Cacao	16,624,906	4.4	191,037,318	11.4
Cascarilla	14,237,645	3.8	116,123,610	6.9
Cotton	27,016,020	7.1	722,660	0.04
Tobacco	19,869,552	5.2	—	—
Sugar	9,272,896	2.4	1,576,030	0.09
Copper	11,252	—	30,963,696	1.8
Dyewood	5,084,941	1.3	4,560	—
Hides	3,626,819	1.0	1,181,802	0.07
Indigo	2,716,377	0.7	1,253,129	0.07
Other goods	5,681,730	1.5	11,890,248	0.7
Totals	378,959,054		1,682,951,614	

SOURCE: See Table 3.
[a]Guayaquil is included here as a Peruvian port.

band and the introduction of register ships to the Pacific, and the restructuring of trade routes after the Portobelo fairs were abandoned. One scholar has also suggested that the growing European demand after 1778 for cacao, and official attempts to promote the mining industry, led the mercantile capitalists of Quito and other New Granadan cities to withdraw their investments from the risky textile industry in favor of agricultural and mining enterprises.[3]

The truncated viceroyalty of Peru and its port of Callao inevitably suffered from the expansion of Spanish trade with the Río de la Plata, despite the fact that its nominal monopoly of South American trade had in reality ceased decades earlier. However, the gloomy prophecy of the Consulado of Lima in 1779 that free trade with the Río de la Plata and with Pacific ports other than Callao (Valparaíso, Concepción, Arica, and Guayaquil) would reduce the

3. Javier Ortiz de la Tabla, "El obraje colonial ecuatoriano: Aproximación a su estudio," *Revista de Indias*, CXLIX–CL (1977), 534.

volume of Lima's trade to little more than a third of its pre-1778 level was not borne out.[4] For Peru, little direct evidence exists of a causal relationship between the introduction of free trade and the growth of the mining industry in the late colonial period. The Lima capitalists, unlike their Mexican counterparts, showed little inclination for long-term investment in silver production, though they were closely involved in the industry, sometimes as owners of pits and more commonly as providers of short-term credit and supplies to local silver merchants (*aviadores*). There is clear evidence, however, of a dynamic relationship between the increase in silver production at Cerro de Pasco and the transmission there from Lima of imported European goods: as mining expanded, Peruvian regional economies benefited from increased demand for the cloth of Huamanga, the *coca* of Huanuco, the sugar and aguardiente of Jauja and Huaylas, the aguardiente of Ica, and the chilies of Chiquián. By far the greatest beneficiary, however, was Lima, whose exports to Cerro de Pasco quadrupled from 101,000 to 417,000 pesos between 1786 and 1795. In 1795 imports from Spain accounted for 49 percent of the merchandise dispatched to the mining center by merchants in the viceregal capital.[5] The same pattern emerges from an analysis of trade with Hualgayoc, the second mining center of Peru in the late colonial period. Although its development benefited the general agricultural economy of the province of Cajamarca, which had few alternative outlets for its products, it was the importing sector that profited the most: Ignacio de Lequanda's 1794 description of the province reports that imports into Cajamarca rose from a value of 50,000 pesos in 1768–1769 to 226,000 pesos in 1788, and that 74 percent (168,000 pesos) of the latter figure represented imported European goods.[6] The mining sector was thus a major consumer of the large volume of manufactured goods imported into Peru from Spain (between

4. Consulado of Lima to Viceroy Manuél Guirior, Lima, February 10, 1779, Archivo General del Ministerio de Relaciones Exteriores, Lima, Sección Colonial, libro 2-2.

5. J. R. Fisher, "Miners, Silver Merchants and Capitalists in Late Colonial Peru," *Ibero-Amerikanisches Archiv*, n.s., II (1976), 257–68. On the basis of more extensive use of *alcabala* accounts, Magdalena Chocano reached similar conclusions and reported that 82 percent of Cerro de Pasco's supplies reached it via Lima. Magdalena Chocano, *Comercio en Cerro de Pasco a fines de la época colonial* (Lima, 1982), 18–19.

6. Fisher, *Commercial Relations*, 79.

1785 and 1796 Peru absorbed 21.6 percent of all exports from Cádiz to America). It was also the source of the commodity, silver, that enabled the viceroyalty, with a 13.8 percent share of American exports to Cádiz and Barcelona in 1782–1796, to retain its position as Spain's most important trading partner in South America.

Peruvian commentators were divided in the 1780s and 1790s over the question of whether the introduction of free trade in 1778 had detrimentally affected the viceregal economy. The Consulado of Lima had no doubt that the repercussions had been disastrous: it complained bitterly in 1787 of a saturated market and the drain of circulating capital and demanded a complete ban upon trade between Buenos Aires and Peru, and a two-year moratorium on imports through the viceroyalty's own ports.[7] The superintendent, Jorge de Escobedo, sympathized with these demands—unlike Viceroy Teodoro de Croix, who was indifferent to local decline as long as imperial commerce as a whole expanded. Escobedo agreed that with the opening of Buenos Aires, European goods could be supplied more cheaply to the southern provinces of Peru overland from the Plate than by the Pacific route. Influential contributors to the *Mercurio Peruano,* however, believed that the fundamental grievance of the consulado was that the loss of its monopoly had reduced the easy profits of the merchants who dominated it, whereas smaller firms, willing to work for reduced margins, had expanded trade as a whole. Moreover, despite initial difficulties caused by the loss of Upper Peru, by 1790 trade between the two viceroyalties was still balanced in Peru's favor by 1,170,190 pesos, thus providing the viceroyalty with a net balance on all intercolonial trade of 725,190 pesos, without taking into account the invisible earnings of 400,000 pesos a year of shipowners and muleteers.

Some evidence suggests that in Peru, as in other viceroyalties, the profits of this vigorous local trade began to be diverted in the 1780s from established merchants to recent peninsular immigrants, particularly after 1784 when an organization of Spanish craft guilds that exported textiles, jewelry, and other products to America, the Cinco Gremios Mayores of Madrid, established an office in Arequipa and, two years later, one in Lima itself. The

7. Fisher, *Government and Society,* 130–34.

Arequipa merchants complained bitterly in 1790 that they were being ruined by the excessive imports of European manufactures for sale at lower prices than local merchants could offer; by 1796 the Arequipa representatives of the Cinco Gremios had expanded their business to such an extent that they were also taking over the distribution of local products—sugar, wines, brandy, and grains—to the still vigorous market in Upper Peru.[8] The net result was that local production was stimulated, and the market for Spanish merchandise expanded, but at the expense of those creole interests unwilling to adapt to the new, more competitive environment.

Throughout Peru, the greater availability and lower prices of imported manufactures in the 1780s stimulated commercial activity—the number of retail shops in Lima grew by a third, for example—and the production of foodstuffs for the increasingly affluent urban middle and lower classes. But what of the impact of free trade upon domestic industry? The consulado again was quite convinced that after 1778 the supply of manufactures through Buenos Aires had not only drastically reduced the Upper Peruvian market for Peruvian cloth, but had also undermined it within Lower Peru by encouraging a tendency for agricultural exports from Arequipa and Cuzco to be paid for in part with European textiles, which were cheaper and of better quality than those produced by local *obrajes*.[9] There is no doubt, in fact, that the consulado's basic observation was accurate: the traditional *obrajes* of the Cuzco region, producing woolen cloth for local consumption and for export to Upper Peru, did, indeed, decline in the last quarter of the eighteenth century, though in 1790 textiles still accounted for 60 percent of the exports to the Río de la Plata (and sugar from Abancay for a further 16 percent).[10] It is also clear that competition from imports was a significant factor in this decline. Internal factors, however, were probably of greater significance. These included the destruction of *obrajes* during the Túpac Amaru

8. Kendall W. Brown, *Bourbons and Brandy: Imperial Reform in Eighteenth-Century Arequipa* (Albuquerque, 1986), 168.

9. Fisher, *Government and Society,* 135.

10. See Maximiliano Moscoso, "Apuntes para la historia de la industria textil en el Cusco colonial," *Revista universitaria* (Cuzco), LI–LII (1962–1963), 67–94; Magnus Mörner, *Notas sobre el comercio y los comerciantes del Cusco desde fines de la colonia hasta 1930* (Lima, 1979), 7.

rising, a change in patterns of commercial activity as Peruvian capitalists shifted their attention from Upper Peru to the expanding mining zones of the center and north of the viceroyalty, and the abolition of the *repartimiento* system. A further factor that has received less attention than it deserves is that in Peru, as in other parts of Spanish America, the old-style *obraje,* the large establishment with two hundred to three hundred workers, tended to decline not only when faced with competition from imports, but also when smaller local establishments, *chorrillos,* began producing cheaper cloth for an expanding popular market. Ignacio de Castro's description of Cuzco, written in 1788, made precisely this point with his observation that the province's *obrajes* were idle "because of the indescribable multiplication of *chorrillos,* which are small establishments for producing baize cloths of inferior quality to those of the *obrajes,* but which satisfy at lower cost the majority of those who wear these textiles."[11]

It is possible, in this context, to suggest that, although the traditional textile industry declined, partly because of the introduction of free trade, other forms of production expanded in response to general economic and commercial growth. This interpretation is borne out by a recent study of textile production in the neighboring province of Huamanga.[12] There the *obrajes* underwent a period of crisis in the early 1780s, less because of the effects of free trade than as a result of a disruption of the supply of wool from the Collao during the Túpac Amaru rebellion provoked by both insurgency and by the simultaneous drought, which, by making pasture unavailable, prevented muleteers from undertaking their normal business. The *obraje* administrators obtained alternative supplies of wool from central Peru—mainly from Jauja—but its inferior quality caused production problems. These difficulties were compounded by the abolition of the *repartimiento* in 1780 because until that year, 40–50 percent of the cloth produced in Huamanga had been supplied to corregidores for distribution to Indian communities. The flood of imported textiles into Upper Peru certainly had repercussions for the Huamanga *obrajes,* but it

11. Fernando Silva Santisteban, *Los obrajes en el Virreinato del Perú* (Lima, 1964), 151–52; Ignacio de Castro, *Relación del Cuzco,* ed. C. D. Valcárcel (Lima, 1978), 60.

12. Miriam Salas de Coloma, "Los obrajes de Huamanga en la economía centro-sur peruana a fines del siglo XVIII," *Revista del Archivo General de la Nación,* VII (1984), 119–46.

was just one factor among many, partly because their products were destined for the working masses of the mines who normally received their wages partly in cloth. Imported cloth, even in the 1780s, was sold at "prices beyond the reach of the Indian worker." The principal competition in the Upper Peruvian market came, therefore, not from European manufacturers, but from "the cloth of the *chorrillos* and of domestic manufacture," which undercut the already cheap *obraje* cloth. However, the Huamanga *obrajes* survived the shrinkage of the Upper Peruvian market by seeking and finding new outlets for their cloth, both within the Sierra, where indigenous participants in local fairs apparently had the cash to make substantial purchases (possibly because the abolition of the *repartimiento* allowed them to retain their surplus for personal consumption), and in Lima itself, where the deregulation of trade allowed freer access to the urban market.

Even the province of Arequipa, which was not a traditional cloth producer, experienced a modest boom in textile production in the late colonial period, again for the poorer end of the market and in this case for cotton rather than woolen cloth. The province was a producer, and indeed an exporter, of raw cotton, which was increasingly in demand in Upper Peru, where cotton-cloth production grew even more substantially in Cochabamba during this period. By 1790 the city of Arequipa had a factory with 68 looms that produced 125,000 *varas* a year of *tocuyo,* a coarse, canvaslike cloth used by the lower classes for underclothes. There was also considerable local production of cotton gloves, handkerchiefs, scarves, and stockings, and considerable importation of woolen cloth from the Sierra for dyeing and selling in local markets. The intendant of Arequipa, Antonio Alvarez, commented in 1792 in his description of the province that all of these activities had increased during the previous ten years because imported European goods remained too expensive for the poorer classes, whose increasing demand for clothing motivated the producers to "double their looms" to meet it. In Arequipa, therefore, as in Puebla and Cochabamba, the cotton industry grew in the late colonial period, despite the influx of foreign textiles, because the latter were still too expensive for popular consumption. The woolen industry of Querétaro (New Spain) also survived, it seems, though it did so by partially shifting to smaller-scale production, as did that of Huamanga, which benefited from the increased purchasing power of the indigenous population in the late colonial period.[13]

The more traditional production of finer cloth for the urban market had been dying in Quito long before 1778, though free trade probably finished it off, partly because capitalists turned to more dynamic agricultural investment. In the province of Cuzco, too, the woolen industry declined, though it did survive on a reduced basis until, like other areas, it was fully exposed to the effects of genuine free trade after independence. The hiatus between the era of Hispanic "free trade" in 1778–1796 and the genuine free trade of the post-independence era was a period of contradictory trends when American industry first developed more quickly in response to the sudden reduction in the supply of manufactures through normal channels in 1797, but subsequently suffered from the increased supply of European manufactures through contraband and neutral channels. On balance, however, American industry gained more from the economic and commercial expansion generated by free trade during 1778–1796 than it lost from the influx of European manufactures. There was never any doubt that agricultural and mining exports multiplied many times during the same period, to the satisfaction of the crown and creole producers alike. The only disadvantages of this process for Americans were, first, that the pace of expansion was limited by the continuing exclusion of non-Spaniards from international trade, and second, that those enterprising Spanish merchants who migrated to America on the tide of the commercial growth that did occur were more privileged and more successful businessmen than their American counterparts.

13. "Memoria legalizada de la Visita que . . . hizo a la Provincia de Arequipa su Gobernador Intendente, Don Antonio Alvarez y Jiménez," March 1, 1793, in V. M. Barriga (ed.), *Memorias para la historia de Arequipa* (Arequipa, 1941), I, 57–58; John C. Super, "Querétaro Obrajes: Industry and Society in Provincial Mexico, 1600–1810," *HAHR*, LVI (1976), 197–216.

MAURICE P. BRUNGARDT

Chapter 7

The Economy of Colombia in the Late Colonial and Early National Periods

Colombia's tropical location and three-cordillera Andean overlay support one of the world's most complex and diverse ecosystems. On the eve of its independence from Spain, this geographical marvel was administered from Santa Fe de Bogotá as part of the viceroyalty of New Granada (1739). The viceroyalty included Panama, Venezuela, and Ecuador also, but separate audiencias at Caracas (1786) and Quito (1563), a captaincy-general at Caracas, and Panama's distance left Santa Fe with only nominal suzerainty over those far-away lands. Even within the area that would become modern Colombia, a tradition of loose control prevailed right up to the end of the colonial period. In other parts of the Spanish Empire the Bourbons aggressively attacked similar lax and casual bureaucratic habits of the late Hapsburg period by moving towards greater administrative efficiency and rationality. But in Colombia attempts at mining, military, and administrative reforms either failed, were delayed, or were never implemented. Tax reform in the late 1770s without brokered agreements with local and regional elites provoked the Comunero Rebellion of 1781, which in turn further postponed reform.

Colombia's geographical complexity—including an extreme diversity of climates, topographies, resources, and populations—contributed significantly to the Bourbons' inability to create appropriate administrative formulae for managing imperial affairs there. Each Colombian region and subregion had its corresponding elite, and historically their consent was essential in the conduct of regional affairs. Describing this localism and its roots and integrating it into the larger context of Colombian history has been a special challenge to scholars. Many worlds have existed within Colombia. The archetype of Colombia's local communities was immortalized in Gabriel García Márquez' *Cien años de soledad* (1967), but historians have had their problems in synthesizing the many Macondos into one Colombia.

For the colonial and early national periods, the annual tithe auctions are admirably suited to reducing the elusive Colombian reality to a common denominator. They homogenize the separate, distinct, and unique Macondos into comparable units for analysis. The tithe was an annual percentage tax on all agrarian production. As a percentage of agricultural production, it is a useful instrument for measuring, in relative rather than absolute terms, agricultural production. In the preindustrial period, statistics were not collected to answer modern economic questions. Nevertheless, the tithes can be used as a crude index of gross domestic production, at least in the agrarian sphere, the source of most of the production in preindustrial Colombia, and are the single most important device for answering modern economic questions about the colonial period.

This study uses the tithe auctions to organize, structure, and frame the regional components of the economy of Colombia on the eve of independence. The regions addressed include all of present-day Colombia except for Pasto in the extreme south; Barbacoas, Buenaventura, and part of modern Chocó on the Pacific coast; the small area of Ocaña between the northern part of the Eastern Cordillera and the Caribbean coast; the island chain of San Andrés; and the entire Caribbean coast, including Cartagena,

Mompós, Barranquilla, Santa Marta, and Riohacha. According to the 1835 census, the part excluded contained a population of 360,348, or 22.1 percent of the 1,627,729 inhabitants.[1] The 1,267,381, or 77.9 percent, remaining included the Llanos, Valleys of Cúcuta, Santander, Eastern Cordillera, Upper Magdalena River Valley, Central and Western Cordilleras, Cauca Valley, part of Chocó, and Antioquia. In other words, except for the coast, all of the major regions of Colombia are surveyed, ordered, and ranked according to their agrarian production as reflected in the tithe auctions. All tithe auctions are from the year 1808 except for those from some tithe *juzgados* (districts) in Antioquia (Antioquia, Marinilla, Medellín, Rionegro, and Santa Rosa de Osos), which are from 1810.[2]

Individual tithe districts are placed in appropriate regional groupings. For example, the Llanos of Casanare and Meta included four tithe *juzgados:* Morcote, Pore, Santiago de Atalayas, and San Martín. This allows the isolation, comparison, and measurement of their relative importance. Measuring the tithe production share of each region allows a certain order and rank to be assigned, and in conjunction with other information, this ordering can lead to useful conclusions about the roles and functions of the regions in the larger economy.

Population data provide an invaluable parameter that throws into high relief many of the important conclusions to be gained from regional and district tithe production totals. Unfortunately, the 1835 census is the earliest taken in Colombia that permits a reconstruction of data according to categories paralleling those of the tithes. For such a reconstruction, population counts must ap-

1. All population figures from the 1835 census were elaborated from a microfilm copy held by the author that was made of the original census in the Archivo Histórico Nacional de Colombia. The census is reproduced in Miguel Urrutia M. and Mario Arrubla (eds.), *Compendio de estadísticas históricas de Colombia* (Bogotá, 1970), 20–24, but only on a province-by-province basis. A canton-by-canton count, much less a parish-by-parish enumeration, is not reproduced in this source. To match tithe auction amounts with population counts for the same area, one must go back to the original census and put together the population figures on a parish-by-parish basis so that they match the geographic coverage of the tithe *juzgados* (districts).

2. See the Appendix for tithe auction totals, sources, and a listing of the places that belonged to each tithe *juzgado.*

COLOMBIAN TITHE DISTRICTS IN THE
EARLY NINETEENTH CENTURY
Cartagena
Caribbean Sea
CUCUTA
Rio Cauca
SANTANDER
ANTIOQUIA
LLANOS
Medellín
WESTERN SLOPE
CHOCÓ
Tunja
Pacific Ocean
EASTERN
CORDILLERA
CAUCA VALLEY
Bogotá
Ibagué
Cali
Rio Magdalena
Neiva
UPPER MAGDALENA
RIVER VALLEY
Popayán
Pasto
0
100
Miles

pear parish by parish and cover all of Colombia, a condition the colonial and 1825 censuses do not meet. The 1835 census allows the creation of per capita ratios of tithe production as well as population density ratios for each tithe *juzgado* and region. Per capita ratios are fundamental for answering questions about the agrarian economy.

Population and agrarian production are much more strongly correlated in preindustrial societies than in more advanced ones. Most people in preindustrial societies are engaged in agricultural pursuits, and in a particular society they possess more or less the same technology. Where the same quality of land is available to all and everything else is equal, agrarian output is essentially a function of numbers. Although Colombia's tithe production was not an exact reflection of agrarian output, since tithes were farmed out and bid on in monetary units rather than in kind, tithe production and population were strongly correlated. For example, if a region had 30 percent of the population of Colombia, it also should have had 30 percent of the tithe production. Any deviation from this correlation indicates that all other factors were not equal and may lead to the establishment of the conditions responsible for the deviation. Comparing population and tithe production is one of the chief methods of isolating distinctive regional characteristics and patterns that differentiate a region from its neighbor.

Calculating the ratios between land surface areas and tithe production is another useful procedure.[3] The production of more tithes per land unit in a region was usually due to (1) the kind of agricultural commodity raised—crops required more labor but less land than livestock; (2) the availability of labor—regions with hotter climates, like the Llanos and the Upper Magdalena River Valley, lacked the manpower of colder regions and often compensated by concentrating on labor-saving commodities like cattle; (3) intensive or extensive exploitation of the land—population densities or specific crops necessitated radically different ways of using the land; (4) the land's fertility—the Valley of Sogamoso, for example, had far richer soil than its neighbor Tunja.

3. All surface measurements for *juzgados* were obtained by taking the areas of present-day *municipios* and grouping them by the *juzgado* they would have belonged to in 1808 and 1810. All surface areas are taken from Colombia, Departamento Administrativo Nacional de Estadística, *División político-administrativa de Colombia* (6th ed.; Bogotá, 1967).

Regional Components of Colombia's Economy

Llanos: Morcote, Pore, Santiago de Atalayas, and San Martín

The Llanos of Casanare and Meta depended primarily on the large number of wild cattle and horses that roamed these vast plains. The rise of this pastoral economy was directly related to the missionary work of the Jesuits and other religious orders in the seventeenth and eighteenth centuries.[4] At 0.93 pesos per person, the Llanos had the highest per capita tithe yield of any region in Colombia (see Appendix). Two features distinguished the Llanos from other regions—the limited population and the extensive exploitation of the land. The Llanos supported far fewer people than any other region of Colombia (0.18 inhabitants per km^2). Given its sparse human resources, an economically profitable exploitation of its vast tracts of land required an agricultural activity that demanded only small outlays of capital and labor. As a result, the economy of the Llanos came to depend primarily on the many wild cattle and horses that roamed its expansive plains. This extensive use of the land satisfied the region's very special labor requirements. Its low population density and its wild herds gave the Llanos the highest per capita tithe output of any region of Colombia.

An analysis of each tithe *juzgado* of the Llanos on an individual basis only confirms the general observations already made about the Llanos as a whole. Per capita tithe output was highest in the districts of Pore (1.47 pesos) and Santiago de Atalayas (1.13 pesos), the *juzgados* most dedicated to extensive ranching. Morcote's lower tithe yield resulted from its higher population density and its more intensive utilization of the land. Its economy was more sedentary and depended more on cropping, especially of cotton, than on ranching. It was also not a true part of the Llanos, being more on the eastern slope of the Eastern Cordillera rather than on the great plains. San Martín's yield (0.72 pesos) was lower than that of Pore or Santiago de Atalayas because the missionary effort was weaker there, and the new society it created was less organized and less capable of exploiting the wild herds. San Martín

4. For the most complete account, see Jane M. Rausch, *A Tropical Plains Frontier: The Llanos of Colombia, 1531–1831* (Albuquerque, 1984).

also suffered from geographic isolation; unlike the Llanos of Casanare it did not border the populous regions of Boyacá, and although it was closer to Santa Fe, travelers found the routes to the north in Casanare more convenient.

In the larger economy of Colombia, the Llanos on a volume basis had a relatively minor impact, supplying only 4.5 percent of the tithe production, but this was far out of proportion to its 1.4 percent of the population.

Valleys of Cúcuta

The Valleys of Cúcuta are at the juncture of the Eastern Cordillera where one branch extending northward forms the western rim of the Lake Maracaibo basin and the other curves northeastward into Venezuela. This region developed into an important cacao-producing region in the eighteenth century as an offshoot of the Venezuelan cacao boom around which the Caracas Company financed the greater part of its development. The Valleys of Cúcuta had the second highest per capita tithe ratio of any region in Colombia (0.63 pesos). This elevated ratio reflected the profits made by exporting cacao, primarily to Veracruz in New Spain. Such profits led to the establishment of some of the largest slave plantations in Colombia.[5]

The low population density of 7.94 inhabitants per square kilometer was a natural accompaniment of the hot and disease-ridden climate of this region, though its density was much higher than in other *tierra caliente* zones like the Llanos or the Upper Magdalena River Valley. Its higher density resulted from the intensive labor requirements of the cacao culture, which were much greater than those of the extensive livestock-raising activities of the Llanos and the Upper Magdalena River Valley.

In the larger economy of Colombia, the Valleys of Cúcuta on a volume basis played a minor role, supplying only 2.7 percent of the tithes, but the region had only 1.3 percent of the population.

5. Eduardo Arcila Farías, *Comercio entre Venezuela y México en los siglos xvi y xvii* (México, 1950), 310–11; Germán Colmenares, *Las haciendas de los Jesuítas en el Nuevo Reino de Granada, siglo XVIII* (Bogotá, 1969), 79, 103, 134, 137–38.

Western Slope of the Eastern Cordillera: Vélez, Muzo, La Palma, Guaduas, and Tocaima

Extending north to south along the Western Slope of the Eastern Cordillera were the tithe *juzgados* of Vélez, Muzo, La Palma, Guaduas, and Tocaima. These districts encompassed a transitional region lying between the hot, debilitating, and sparsely populated lowlands of the Upper Magdalena River Valley and the cold but healthful and densely populated uplands of the fertile *sabanas* and valleys of the Eastern Cordillera. The Western Slope itself was a series of broken escarpments deeply indented with swift streams and densely wooded ravines and gorges; it was frequently interspersed with small valleys and pockets of cultivable land.

Except for the Chocó, per capita tithe production for the Western Slope was by far the lowest (0.21 pesos) for any region in Colombia. Much of the Western Slope's land was rocky, mountainous terrain so steep as to be difficult to exploit, and though the population density for this area initially appears low (10.74 inhabitants per km^2), compared with Santander (17.39 inhabitants per km^2), or the highlands of the Eastern Cordillera (13.67 inhabitants per km^2), the apparently low density masks a high concentration of people in a few fertile valleys. Through the years many people spilled out of the valleys and over the Western Slope on ever more marginal lands. This produced the significantly lower tithe yields.

In the larger economy of Colombia, the Western Slope on a volume basis played a major role, supplying 10.4 percent of the tithes, but it needed 14.2 percent of the population to achieve this production. The region was the major supplier of sugar, aguardiente, tobacco, and other tropical products to the highlands of the Eastern Cordillera. In fact, the size and weight of the Eastern Cordillera, where 39.8 percent of the population resided, drew the Western Slope into its orbit and molded its economic function and role.

Santander: Girón, Mogotes, San Gil, and Socorro

Santander contained the tithe *juzgados* of Girón, Mogotes, San Gil, and Socorro, and occupied the principal part of the present-day department of Santander. The most distinguishing feature of the economy of Santander was its artisan trade, which supplied many of the clothes, shoes, and hats worn by the masses of Colombia until as late as the 1850s.[6] Although artisan activity was not actually a part of the agrarian economy, the cotton, henequen, and fibers raised to supply the spinners, weavers, cobblers, and hatters were. More important, however, was that the well-being of the agrarian sector depended on the performance of the artisan. Much of the money made in the industrial trades went to buy foodstuffs to sustain those artisans living in town and supplement the diet of those in the countryside.

What distinguished Santander from other regions was the extent of this trade, which occupied thousands of men, women, and children in gainful employment and which entered commercial channels as far west as the Pacific province of Chocó, as far south as Neiva, as far north as Cartagena and Santa Marta, and as far east as Venezuela.[7] The income gained by the artisans accounted for the strength of the region's agrarian economy and the density of its population compared with other regions. Its per capita tithe production was significantly higher (0.38 pesos) than the average for Colombia as a whole (0.30 pesos), yet Santander had the highest population density (17.39 inhabitants per km^2) of any region in Colombia. Ordinarily, a greater concentration of population tended to lower per capita tithe figures as more and more marginal land was brought into production. In the case of Santander, its flourishing artisan trade with the rest of Colombia strongly affected the value of its agrarian production.

Santander played a major role in the economy of Colombia, as evidenced by its production of 13.4 percent of the tithes with 10.6 percent of the population. The region specialized in the manufacture of handicrafts. The dynamics of its specialization simply allowed Santander a higher return on its division of labor than that achieved in other regions whose economies lacked the complexity of Santander's and its more highly organized patterns of production.

The region's specialization in textiles, for example, had carried it far beyond supplying just its own internal needs. It clothed

6. José Joaquín García, *Crónicas de Bucaramanga* (Bucaramanga, 1944), 62–65, 85–86; Manuel Ancízar, *Peregrinación de alpha* (Bogotá, 1970), I, 147–59.

7. Pedro Fermín de Vargas, *Pensamientos políticos y memorias sobre la población del Nuevo Reino de Granada* (Bogotá, 1953), 31, 50, 86.

the masses of Colombia as well as the campesinos of Antioquia and the slaves in distant Chocó. Producing for much of the country brought it significant revenue that was not available in other regions, and that additional income had a multiplier effect on the agrarian sector of the economy. The manufacturing sector was sufficiently developed and complex enough to sustain a large group of artisans who did not farm or who at least did not produce enough for their own subsistence by farming. As a result, the agrarian sector produced more than what was needed for its own existence, and the extra production went to sustain the artisans in the industrial sector. The region's premier position as a fashioner of handicrafts allowed its agrarian and industrial sectors important economies as a result of the greater division of labor, and these savings, along with the additional income from goods sold in other regions, permitted it a higher standard of living. At least that is what Santander's higher per capita tithe ratios suggest for the agrarian sector of the economy.

Eastern Cordillera: Bosa, Funza, Zipaquirá, Chocontá, Leiva, Tenza, Tunja, Sogamoso, Santa Rosa de Viterbo, Soatá, Málaga, and Pamplona

The Eastern Cordillera encompassed 39.8 percent of the population and produced 40.0 percent of the tithes. In terms of size and weight, the region tended to bend and mold the economic patterns and functions of all of the other regions of Colombia. It alone had twelve tithe districts. Extending diagonally from southwest to northeast were the tithe *juzgados* of Bosa, Funza, Zipaquirá, and Chocontá in the present-day department of Cundinamarca; Leiva, Tenza, Tunja, Sogamoso, Santa Rosa de Viterbo—now curving back on a more northerly course—and Soatá in Boyacá; Málaga in the northeast corner of Santander; and Pamplona in Norte de Santander.

As a general rule the Eastern Cordillera possessed a *tierra fría* climate with an average temperature of 45 to 65 degrees and an altitude ranging from 6,500 to 10,000 feet. Above this stretched the treeless, windswept, and uncultivable *páramos* as far as the snow line that began at about 15,000 feet. Inhabitants in the *tierra fría* zone of the Eastern Cordillera grew a wide variety of agricultural crops like wheat, barley, corn, potatoes, beans, onions, garlic, cabbage, turnips, peaches, and apples, and raised all kinds of livestock like cattle, horses, mules, pigs, sheep, goats, and chickens.

In spite of its *tierra fría* reputation, the Eastern Cordillera did possess semitropical zones in the valleys on the eastern slope. Most of these valleys belonged to upland *juzgados,* as was the case with Cáqueza (Bosa), Gachetá (Chocontá), and Miraflores (Tunja), though Tenza constituted an entire tithe district itself. These valleys produced the same commodities in their lower elevations as the semitropical Western Slope and, like that region, also specialized in the production of sugar.

Within the Eastern Cordillera was a wide diversity of population and tithe ratios. Bosa's low population density (5.89 inhabitants per km^2), even with Santa Fe (11.28 per km^2), resulted from having within its boundaries the backbone of the eastern trunk of the Andes with its craggy heights and rugged promontories that thrust east and south of Santa Fe. Its tithe ratio without the capital (0.33 pesos per inhabitant) was a good one and about equal to that of Chocontá (0.35 pesos) and Zipaquirá (0.32 pesos), two of the three other *tierra fría juzgados* of Cundinamarca. Population density varied substantially, however, between Chocontá (13.63 per km^2) and Zipaquirá (19.96 per km^2). The rich Sabana de Ubaté included in the Zipaquirá district increased the density there, whereas *páramo* land and towns on the steeply inclined eastern slope lowered Chocontá's density.

Funza, the last *tierra fría juzgado* in Cundinamarca, included most of the fertile Sabana de Bogotá and is especially interesting in view of its reputation as a zone of latifundia and extensive stock-raising haciendas. It serves as a useful contrast to the intensive agriculture practiced in the other highland *juzgados*. As expected, it produced the highest per capita tithe average (0.59 pesos) of any *tierra fría* district of Colombia and rivaled those ratios produced by the extensive stock-raising areas of the Llanos, though it did not achieve the extraordinary return of the Pore *juzgado* (1.47 pesos). On the other hand, it sustained a population 140 times greater than the stock-producing *juzgado* of the Llanos. As Le Moyne observed, one-fourth to one-third of the Sabana was given over to crop production as a way of striking some sort of balance between the two activities.[8] The Sabana obviously could have supported a substantially larger number of people, and much of its higher per capita tithe ratio derived from the labor-saving ranching operations practiced there. The colonial elite preferred to use these lands to fatten livestock destined for Santa Fe.

The most surprising aspect of the *juzgados* of the Eastern Cordillera in Boyacá was the extreme population density of Tenza (30.27 inhabitants per km^2), which surpassed densities in all of the other districts of Colombia. The Valley of Tenza lay on the eastern slope of the Eastern Cordillera and was a semitropical sugar-producing zone in its middle and lower elevations. Slope land tended to be inferior to the flatter and colder highlands, and this factor along with the district's labor-intensive society probably accounted for its low per capita tithe output (0.18 pesos), which nevertheless compared favorably with *juzgados* of the Western Slope. Today the valley is a zone of extreme minifundia. Its relatively high population density in 1835 suggests that the minute division of land was already a well-established phenomenon by the beginning of the nineteenth century. More intriguing still is the fact that in the colonial period the decline in Indian population from the sixteenth to the seventeenth century as well as the miscegenation process occurred at a much faster rate in this valley than in highland areas of Boyacá.[9]

Leiva had the second highest population density (19.19 per km^2) and the third lowest tithe yield (0.26 pesos) of any *juzgado* in the Eastern Cordillera. Curiously, Leiva was not founded until 1572 and then not by encomenderos but by "various laborers . . . who had left Spain with the intention of colonizing."[10] Perhaps the colonists were more equitable in their initial distribution of the land than the encomenderos would have been, and the fairer division accounted for the higher population density. However, the labor-intensive situation probably was responsible for Leiva's lower per capita returns.

8. A[uguste]. Le Moyne, *Viajes y estancias en América del Sur, La Nueva Granada, Santiago de Cuba, Jamaica y El Istmo de Panamá* (Bogotá, 1945), 157.

9. Germán Colmenares, *La provincia de Tunja en el Nuevo Reino de Granada: Ensayo de historia social (1539–1800)* (Bogotá, 1970), 60, 88.

10. *Ibid.*, 159.

Santa Rosa de Viterbo, Tunja, and Málaga had similar tithe ratios (0.28, 0.30, and 0.29 pesos) and population densities (17.99, 17.53, and 16.83 per km^2). Sogamoso's higher tithe output (0.42 pesos) reflected the greater fertility of its valley, one of the richest in the Eastern Cordillera.

The extremely low population density (3.88 per km^2) of Pamplona resulted from its straddling a particularly mountainous area of the Eastern Cordillera. Much of the land was either cold and windswept *páramos* or had precipitous drops that inhibited habitation. Small valleys of cultivable land, however, were nestled in the mountains at Pamplona, Labateca, Silos, Chitagá, and Cucutilla. Pamplona's tithe yield (0.40 pesos per inhabitant) was well above average.

Upper Magdalena River Valley: Honda, Mariquita, Ibagué, Purificación, Neiva, and Timaná

As the Central and Eastern Cordillera thrust and jut upward on their northerly course through Colombia, they wall off on the west and east the scooped-out trough of the Upper Magdalena River Valley containing the present-day departments of Tolima and Huila. On the eve of independence this region held, from north to south, the six tithe districts of Honda, Mariquita, Ibagué, Purificación, Neiva, and Timaná.

On a regional basis the Upper Magdalena River Valley achieved an almost perfect balance between agrarian production and population if everything else was equal: 9.1 percent of the population produced 9.2 percent of the tithes.

The region's principal agrarian product was livestock, and cattle drives were made not only to the highlands of the Eastern Cordillera but also over the Central Cordillera to Popayán and points beyond.[11] The Upper Magdalena River Valley was especially suited for extensive ranching operations on account of its low population, small number of Indians, difficult climate, and wide-open spaces. The region's highest per capita tithe production was achieved by Purificación (0.38 pesos), the *juzgado* with the most important livestock haciendas and ranching operations.

11. Vicente de Oviedo, *Cualidades y riquezas del Nuevo Reino de Granada,* ed. Augusto Cuervo (Bogotá, 1930), 240.

Except for the Llanos (0.18 per km^2) and Chocó (1.35 per km^2) the Upper Magdalena River Valley had the lowest population density (2.50 per km^2) of any region. For a major stock-raising area, per capita tithe ratios (0.30 pesos) were much lower than those (0.93 pesos) provided by the Llanos. But the valley's population density was more than thirteen times greater than that of the Llanos, and as a result, the labor-saving yields of livestock haciendas were not so plainly evident in the Upper Magdalena River Valley.

Antioquia: Antioquia, Cáceres, Marinilla, Medellín, Rionegro, and Santa Rosa de Osos

In the northern Central Cordillera lay the highlands and valleys of Antioquia. The long- and well-publicized reputation of the *antioqueños* as Colombia's leading entrepreneurs makes this region of special interest. On the eve of independence Antioquia had the six tithe *juzgados* of Antioquia, Cáceres, Marinilla, Medellín, Rionegro, and Santa Rosa de Osos.

Antioquia offers several intriguing patterns. First, compared to other regions, population densities were low (3.85 and 6.45 inhabitants per km^2), even with the marginal *juzgado* of Cáceres factored out. Since much of Antioquia was rough and mountainous terrain, the low density may have masked a high concentration of people in a few fertile valleys. However, its population density was much lower than that of Santander (17.39 inhabitants per km^2), a region in many ways similar to Antioquia, and that of the Western Slope (10.74 inhabitants per km^2), where the terrain was even more broken than Antioquia's. That the *antioqueño* population has long been said to increase at a rate well above that of the rest of the country[12] may indicate that *antioqueños* have had more possibilities open to them than their regional counterparts.

Per capita tithe yields were also much less (0.25 pesos) than for most other regions. This was consistent, however, with the commentary of colonial observers who noted "the high cost and scarcity of foodstuffs" in Antioquia. The region produced only 10.3 percent of the tithes with 12.5 percent of the population.

12. James J. Parsons, *Antioqueño Colonization in Western Colombia* (2nd ed.; Berkeley, 1968), 102.

Antioqueños paid for some of these agrarian imports with the precious metals they mined. One writer noticed, for example, how *antioqueños* "carried on [such] a well-developed commerce" in textiles from Santander that "many of them resided in [Bogotá]" in order to buy the goods with the gold "sent to them from [Antioquia]." *Antioqueños* annually spent 200,000 pesos in Santa Fe "on products from Socorro [Santander]."[13]

Cauca Valley: Buga, Cali, Popayán, and Almaguer

The Cauca Valley was between the Western and Central Cordillera, and on the eve of independence encompassed, from north to south, the four tithe districts of Buga, Cali, Popayán, and Almaguer. Notwithstanding their fertility, Buga and Cali did not have outstanding per capita tithe yields (0.31 pesos). Equally interesting was their low population density of 3.08 inhabitants per square kilometer. From Cali to Popayán, the Cauca Valley begins to narrow and rises considerably. Almaguer drains into the Río Patía rather than the Cauca, but Almaguer was easier to reach from Popayán than from Pasto. The lands of Popayán and Almaguer were not as rich as those of Buga and Cali, and this was reflected in their significantly lower per capita tithe ratios (0.21 pesos). The people of the Cauca Valley annually spent 300,000 pesos on *santandereano* merchandise acquired by merchants in Santa Fe.[14] Like Antioquia, Cauca Valley purchased some of its agrarian supplies from outside.

Chocó

The hot and debilitating gold-producing region of Chocó lay between the Pacific and the Western Cordillera. It had a low population density (1.35 inhabitants per km^2) and very low per capita tithe yields (0.16 pesos), suggesting that much of its agrarian supplies came from the outside, either from over the Cordillera or from the contraband trade coming from the coast and up the rivers. In terms of the larger economy of Colombia, Chocó was unimportant, producing less than 1 percent of the tithes.

13. Guillermo Wills, *Observaciones sobre el comercio de la Nueva Granada, con un apéndice relativo al de Bogotá* (1831; rpr. Bogotá, 1952), 43, 71.

14. *Ibid.*, 71.

In terms of significant statistical patterns on the eve of independence, Colombia divided into two great parts—a western and eastern section. Western Colombia included Chocó, Cauca Valley, and Antioquia, and had 23.6 percent of the population but only 19.7 percent of the tithe production. Eastern Colombia formed the greater bulk of the whole and had 76.4 percent of the population and 80.3 percent of the tithe production. For the agrarian sector the net transfer passed from east to west in return for the precious metals of western Colombia. This exchange represented a fundamental relationship that framed many activities at the beginning of the republic, but this pattern changed somewhat during the nineteenth century. Even in the colonial period, many *antioqueños* exercised control over this transfer in their role as merchants. By the nineteenth century, many *antioqueño* entrepreneurs had established offices in Santa Fe.[15] How this relationship between east and west changed in the course of the nineteenth century is an *antioqueño* story.

Economic Impact of the Wars of Independence

Such was the configuration of the Colombian economy on the eve of independence. The wars of liberation changed much of the old order, exacerbated structural problems, speeded up trends, and forced a realignment of power among various regions and subregions. Given the nature of the war, some areas suffered more than others. Particularly vulnerable were strategic locations. The coastal cities of Cartagena, Mompós, and Santa Marta were devastated time and time again. Control of them was essential, because the easy movement of men and materiel by sea could radically change the nature of the war at any moment. In addition, each city instinctively sensed that the war was a time of realignment and that only one would emerge from the struggle as the dominant Colombian port. This is why they fought, often as patriot against patriot. Each wanted to dominate. The end result was a self-inflicted misery that left each checkmated as the possible victor. This condition endured far into the nineteenth century and set the stage for the rise of Barranquilla and Buenaventura as the dominant Colombian ports.

15. Twinam, *Miners, Merchants, and Farmers,* 149.

Natural invasion routes and corridors were another important focal point in the struggle, and as areas shifted back and forth from one group to another—not always a royalist-patriot exchange, as the Patria Boba period demonstrated—they suffered repeated losses. Occupying and invading forces repeatedly pillaged the Valleys of Cúcuta; corridors rising from the Llanos into the Eastern Cordillera such as the valleys of Cáqueza, Gachetá, Miraflores, and Tenza; and the narrow Cauca Valley. For example, the Valleys of Cúcuta, which straddled the traditional overland route between Colombia and Venezuela, were repeatedly under siege. Whenever one side had control over Colombia or Venezuela but not over both, the valleys became the key access route, along with the Llanos, through which the aggressor would pour his army for a push over the Eastern Cordillera into the heart of Colombia or for a thrust along the Sierra Nevada de Mérida with options for attack on the Venezuelan coast, the Llanos, or Caracas. The Valleys of Cúcuta changed hands ten times during the Wars of Independence.[16]

Certain kinds of agrarian activities attracted the depredations of military forces more than others. Large livestock operations of the opposition elite were the military's preferred objects of forced requisitions. Moving soldiers and supplies required horses and mules. The easiest way to transport food was to drive cattle. If royalists and patriots frequently lacked the political capacities to provision their armies, their soldiers were adept at forcibly taking what they needed. Elite landowners of the opposing side suffered proportionally more, especially those with large livestock operations. A case in point was the task the Congress of the Confederation of New Granada gave Simón Bolívar in Tunja in November, 1814, to force Bogotá into the federal union. On his march to the capital in December, part of his army bivouacked near Sesquilé and Suesca at an inn called El Moralito in the tithe *juzgado* of Chocontá. In the area was the hacienda of Achuria of the Spaniard Ignacio Hernández de Alba. Those "troops of Bolívar" who continued on their way to the capital "sacked the hacienda, carrying off cattle, horses, and sheep," and those that stayed in the area "supplied themselves daily with cattle and sheep of the hacienda,

16. Restrepo, *Historia de la revolución,* I, 223, 271, 303–306, 314, 380, 391, II, 44, III, 212–13; Camilo Riaño, *La campaña libertadora de 1819* (Bogotá, 1969), 170–74.

eating, selling, and giving away meat, suet, and internal organs as they pleased . . . dissipating with prodigality" the resources of the hacienda. To passers-by, they sold a fourth of a cow for three-fourths of a peso.[17]

Slaves were also a target during the Wars of Independence. Early in the campaign such leaders as Antonio Nariño and Bolívar recruited them as canon fodder for their armies. A standard tactic of Bolívar was to compel all slave owners to contribute one of every three slaves; these slaves in turn were to be given their freedom after two years of military service.[18] As a result, slave operations, whether in the agrarian or mining sector, were grievously wounded by the end of the Wars of Independence and doomed to wither away as a functioning part of the Colombian economy.

Nineteenth-Century Evolution of the Colombian Economy

A survey of the Colombian economy at the end of the Wars of Independence reveals important changes. The Llanos were destroyed as a functioning contributor. The mission structure was irreparably damaged. The Indians had been carried off, much like the slaves in other areas. The livestock haciendas had been put out of commission. Banditry and disorder prevailed. In Venezuela leaders of the *llaneros* dominated the political system intermittently throughout much of the nineteenth century. But this did not happen in Colombia. Demographically and geographically the Colombian Llanos were smaller and less important than their Venezuelan counterpart. In addition, in Colombia the Andes were higher and more difficult to breach than in Venezuela. The Llanos were never again important in Colombia after the Wars of Independence.

Another region decimated was the Valleys of Cúcuta. The cacao plantations had disappeared. There were virtually no slaves left. After the Wars of Independence, cacao-plantation production was made passé by the necessity for a large initial capital investment to buy land, cacao trees, and slaves; build a complex irrigation system; and then wait six to eight years before the first tree

17. Restrepo, *Historia de la revolucion,* I, 372; AHNC, Anexo, Diezmos, tomo 35, fol. 603v.

18. AHNC, República, Secretaría de Guerra y Marina, tomo 1540, fols. 385r–387v.

bore fruit. Few had the required capital, and fewer still were willing to risk it given the vagaries of the early republican period.

The Western Slope of the Eastern Cordillera survived the Wars of Independence in its advantageous position between the densely populated Eastern Cordillera and the outside world. Opposite the Eastern Cordillera from the Llanos, the Western Slope suffered less from marauding armies. It continued to send its tropical products to its highland consumers. Guaduas especially blossomed in the republican era as it became the main transportation route between the Magdalena River and Bogotá.

Santander also came out of the wars less damaged than other regions. Located away from the coast and the Llanos and with no narrow corridors through which massing armies would pass, it emerged with its artisan structure intact. As the nineteenth century unfolded, it came to be considered one of the most prosperous regions in Colombia. It, along with Antioquia, had become one of the new regional powers in the country. Santander became strongly identified with Colombian liberalism, and along with the Eastern Cordillera states of Cundinamarca and Boyacá, it forced its radical liberalism on the rest of the country in the period immediately following 1867. But black clouds had already appeared on the horizon. Patterns of trade changed and gradually curved outward toward the coast, shattering the old internal economic order on which *santandereano* artisan production rested. Foreign textiles began to undercut *santandereano* textiles in price in the late 1820s, even in the heart of the *santandereano* region, where three stores in Bucaramanga specializing in the sale of foreign textiles were already present by 1835.[19] Boxed in without easy access to the outside world via the Magdalena River or via the Zulia River–Lake Maracaibo route and isolated from other Colombian regions beyond the Eastern Cordillera, its position of power and strength gradually eroded. In time Antioquia replaced it as the most important new regional power.

The Eastern Cordillera came out of the wars with significant losses in the areas of large landed estates, like the Sabana de Bogotá and Sogamoso, and the areas close to Cúcuta, such as Pamplona and Málaga, both of which straddled invasion routes from

19. Wills, *Observaciones sobre el comercio,* 45; García, *Crónicas de Bucaramanga,* 86.

Venezuela and from the Llanos. But in spite of these problem areas, the Eastern Cordillera would continue to exercise a dominant role in the Colombian economy through the present day. Above all else, it had a third of the population of Colombia at the beginning of the national period, even with Panama counted in the total. By its sheer weight and size, it bent and molded the economic patterns and functions of the other Colombian regions. Secondly, at the apex of everything was Bogotá, the economic, bureaucratic, political, and religious center of the country. Although its mountain fastness and its location at the southeastern edge of Colombia's population cluster did not allow it to impose itself on the other regions as did a Mexico City or a Buenos Aires, it continued to function as Colombia's capital.

The middle and upper reaches of the Magdalena River valley also did not overly suffer from invading armies. This area was well positioned at the beginning of the republican period to take advantage of its location between the Eastern and Central Cordilleras. Honda did well as trade up and down the Magdalena River increased in importance. It was the most important river port in the hinterland and served as a clearinghouse for goods and passengers coming upriver and going overland to Antioquia, Popayán, Bogotá, and points beyond, or for those leaving the interior and heading downriver for the coast. Although not ports, Ibagué and Mariquita functioned in much the same way and were necessary areas of passage for many travelers moving between the two cordilleras. Purificación survived with its large livestock operations intact and was able to supply the densely populated Eastern Cordillera. Neiva and Timaná in the upper reaches of the Magdalena River valley were more bottled up and isolated.

An interesting long-term trend was growing in the west with the rise of Antioquia and the decline of the upper Cauca Valley and Popayán. Buga, Cali, and Popayán suffered greatly as a result of the Wars of Independence. Popayán changed hands repeatedly in the course of the wars because it was a strategic swing point in western Colombia much like Cúcuta was in the east between Colombia and Venezuela. Moving south from Popayán opened the door to Pasto and Quito, and moving north down the Cauca Valley exposed Antioquia as a potential prize. The end result of this location was to make Popayán and the narrowing stretch of the

Cauca Valley extending from Cali through Buga, Cartago, and Anserma a graveyard after they were looted and pillaged time and time again. Adding to the misery of the region was its heavy investment in slaves. The slave-worked mines and sugar plantations of the Popayán elite were especially vulnerable to the destruction. Many of these slaves were carried off by the invading armies of both sides. After the Wars of Independence, the elite from Popayán clung to the old order, but this was essentially a rear-guard action that delayed the structural realignment within the Cauca Valley as well as within the larger area of western Colombia. Cali eventually emerged as the premier regional city in southern Colombia as it gradually expanded and consolidated its power as a result of its proximity to the Pacific port of Buenaventura and its growing importance as the shortest distance between a port and the Colombian interior.

But the more dramatic story was the growth of Antioquia. Its development as the foremost regional power in Colombia outside the Eastern Cordillera resulted from several factors. First, it escaped the cruder aspects of the wars and was spared the extensive destruction wreaked on the Caribbean ports and Popayán. Second, gold gave it a stimulus other regions did not have. By the end of the colonial period it was already producing more gold than any other region, and by the second half of the nineteenth century this would be as much as 70 percent of Colombia's total production.[20] At a time when Colombians complained about a lack of cash and credit, much of which had disappeared in the orgy of wartime consumption, *antioqueños* used their access to precious metals to great advantage. Other factors were also crucial. Antioquia, like Popayán, had important slave-mining operations in the colonial period. But when political leaders like Nariño tried to gain popular support by offering slaves their freedom if they joined his army, *antioqueño* political leaders were astute enough to move towards gradual abolition. Antioquia appeared to have a more diverse labor force, and so had more than enough free labor to replace the slaves. These political leaders also generally tended to keep Antioquia out of the various civil wars that plagued Colombia in the

20. James William Park, *Rafael Núñez and the Politics of Colombian Regionalism, 1863–1886* (Baton Rouge, 1985), 60–61.

nineteenth century. Finally, Antioquia's location favored its continued growth as a regional power. Because it was closer to the Caribbean coast and had easier access to the Magdalena River than most other regions, it was easier for more and more *antioqueños* to become traders and merchants. Interregional trade increased as they exchanged their gold for foreign merchandise and provisions.

APPENDIX

Population, Land Area, Tithe Auctions, Ratios, and Percentages of Regions and *Juzgados* of Colombia

Region, *Juzgado*	Population (1835)	Land Area (km^2)	Density (persons/(km^2)	Tithe Auctions (pesos)	Percentage of Population	Percentage of Tithes	Per Capita Tithe Output (pesos)
Llanos							
Morcote	6,687	3,997	1.67	2,422	00.5	00.6	0.36
Pore	6,423	59,609	0.11	9,466	00.5	02.5	1.47
Santiago de Atalayas	3,513	8,277	0.42	3,973	00.3	01.1	1.13
San Martín	1,625	30,868	0.05	1,174	00.1	00.3	0.72
Regional totals	18,248	102,751	0.18	17,035	01.4	04.5	0.93
Valleys of Cúcuta							
Cúcuta	8,001			3,720	00.6	01.0	0.46
Salazar	8,271			6,538	00.7	01.7	0.79
Regional totals	16,272	2,048	7.94	10,258	01.3	02.7	0.63
Western Slope							
Guaduas	24,588	2,023	12.15	4,891	01.9	01.3	0.20
La Palma	16,802	2,590	6.48	3,237	01.3	00.9	0.19
Muzo	7,800	1,956	3.98	2,402	00.6	00.6	0.31
Tocaima	59,348	5,155	11.51	14,385	04.7	03.8	0.24
Vélez	72,004	5,083	14.16	14,439	05.7	03.8	0.20
Regional totals	180,542	16,807	10.74	39,355	14.2	10.4	0.21
Santander							
Girón	25,113	1,909	13.16	9,150	02.0	02.4	0.36
Mogotes	11,349	1,086	10.45	3,768	00.9	01.0	0.33
San Gil	51,258	2,035	25.19	20,175	04.0	05.4	0.39
Socorro	46,132	2,665	17.31	17,451	03.6	04.6	0.37
Regional totals	133,852	7,695	17.39	50,545	10.6	13.4	0.38

Eastern Cordillera							
Bosa	82,548	7,321	11.28	14,644	06.5	03.9	0.18
(without Bogotá)	(43,106)		(5.89)		(03.4)		(0.33)
Chocontá	41,498	3,045	13.63	14,594	03.3	03.9	0.35
Funza	18,238	1,155	15.79	10,800	01.4	02.9	0.59
Leiva	34,620	1,732	19.99	8,859	02.7	02.3	0.26
Málaga	35,255	2,912	16.83	10,532	02.8	02.8	0.29
Pamplona	23,172	5,979	3.88	9,341	01.8	02.5	0.40
Santa Rosa de Viterbo	33,594	1,868	17.99	9,440	02.7	02.5	0.28
Soatá	48,573	3,375	14.99	16,828	03.8	04.5	0.34
Sogamoso	21,019	1,249	16.83	8,830	01.7	02.3	0.42
Tenza	37,017	1,223	30.27	6,781	02.9	01.8	0.18
Tunja	81,713	4,663	17.53	25,073	06.4	06.6	0.30
Zipaquirá	47,215	2,365	19.96	15,159	03.7	04.0	0.32
Regional totals	504,462	36,887	13.67	150,881	39.8	40.0	0.30
Upper Magdalena River valley							
Honda	4,204	3,732	1.13	516	00.3	00.1	0.12
Ibagué	10,707	3,253	3.29	1,406	00.8	00.4	0.13
Mariquita	8,127	2,820	2.88	1,588	00.6	00.4	0.19
Neiva	28,549	12,270	2.33	8,385	02.2	02.2	0.29
Purificación	33,745	13,150	2.57	13,107	02.7	03.5	0.38
Timaná	30,182	11,024	2.74	9,786	02.4	02.6	0.32
Regional totals	115,514	46,249	2.50	34,788	09.1	09.2	0.30
Eastern Colombia	968,890	212,437	4.56	302,861	76.4	80.3	0.31
Antioquia							
Antioquia	30,812	5,171	5.96	6,309	02.4	01.8	0.20
Marinilla	13,485	3,760	3.59	2,614	01.1	00.7	0.19
Medellín	46,108	5,026	9.17	14,489	03.6	03.8	0.31
Rionegro	43,378	4,407	9.84	8,927	03.4	02.4	0.21
Santa Rosa de Osos	19,223	5,345	3.60	4,330	01.5	01.1	0.23
(Subtotal)	(153,006)	(23,709)	(6.45)	(36,668)	(12.1)	(09.7)	(0.24)
Cáceres	5,011	17,283	0.28	2,268	00.4	00.6	0.45

APPENDIX (*continued*)

Region, *Juzgado*	Population (1835)	Land Area (km^2)	Density (persons/(km^2)	Tithe Auctions (pesos)	Percentage of Population	Percentage of Tithes	Per Capita Tithe Output (pesos)
Regional totals	158,017	40,992	3.85	38,937	12.5	10.3	0.25
Cauca Valley							
Buga + Cali	71,044	23,043	3.08	21,690	05.6	05.8	0.31
Popayán + Almaguer	48,236	14,935	3.23	10,227	03.8	02.7	0.21
Regional totals	119,280	37,978	3.14	31,917	09.4	08.5	0.26
Chocó	21,194	15,697	1.35	3,343	01.7	00.9	0.16
Western Colombia	298,491	94,667	3.15	74,197	23.6	19.7	0.25
Colombia	1,267,381	307,104	4.13	377,058	100.0	100.0	0.30

SOURCES: See footnotes 1 and 3 for population and land area figures. Tithe auctions are found in AHNC, Anexo, Diezmos, tomo 26, fols. 142r–177v; Archivo Central del Cauca (Popayán), signatura 7061; and Archivo Histórico de Antioquia (Medellín), tomo 709, documento 11340. All tithe auctions are for the year 1808 except those from the *juzgados* of Antioquia, Marinilla, Medellín, Rionegro, and Santa Rosa de Osos, which are from 1810.

APPENDIX (Continued)

Places Belonging to Regions and Juzgados *of Colombia*

LLANOS

Juzgado of Morcote in 1808. The following eight places appear: Cravo, Labranzagrande, Manare, Morcote, Paya, Pisava, Támara, and Ten. The right to collect tithes in 1808 in these eight places was auctioned off individually. The total for these eight auctions—2,422 pesos of 8 reales—is entered under the *juzgado* of Morcote in column 5 of the Appendix table. Similar auctions were carried out for each place listed under the individual *juzgados*. See the Appendix table for the archival sources for the tithe auctions and lists of places under each *juzgado*.

Juzgado of Pore in 1808. The following sixteen places appear: Aguativa, Arauca, Betoyes, Caviona, Cuiloto, Chire, Guacacia, Guanapalo, Macaguane, Macuco, Nunchía, Pore, Patute, San Salvador, Tame, and Trinidad.

Juzgado of Santiago de Atalayas in 1808. The following ten places appear: Barroblanco, Casimena, Chámeza, Hato de Marimare, San Nicolás de Buenavista, San Pedro, Santiago de Atalayas, Surimena, Taguaná, and Zapatosa.

Juzgado of San Martín in 1808. The following four places appear: Apiay (Cumaral), Medina, San Juan, and San Martín.

VALLEYS OF CÚCUTA

Juzgado of Cúcuta in 1808. The following two places appear: Rosario and Cúcuta.

Juzgado of Salazar in 1808. The following three places appear: Salazar, San Cayetano, and Santiago.

WESTERN SLOPE

Juzgado of Guaduas in 1808. The following nine places appear: Chaguaní, Guaduas, Nimaima, Nocaima, Quebradanegra, Sasaima, La Vega, Vergara, and Villeta.

Juzgado of La Palma in 1808. The following seven places appear: Caparrapí, Murca, La Palma, La Peña, Terama, Topaipí, and Yacopí.

Juzgado of Muzo in 1808. The following six places appear: Coper, Itocó, Maripí, Muzo, Paime, and Pauna.

Juzgado of Tocaima in 1808. The following seventeen places appear: Ambalema, Anolaima, Bituima, Coello, El Colegio, Espinal, Guataquí, Guayabal de Síquima, La Mesa, Melgar, Pulí, Piedras, San Juan de Rioseco, Santa Rosa, Simones, Tocaima, and Venadillo.

Juzgado of Vélez in 1808. The following fifteen places appear: Aguada, Chipatá, Chitaraque, Guadalupe, Guavatá, Güepsa, Jesús María, Moniquirá, Pare, La Paz, Puente Real, San Benito, Santa Ana, Suaita, and Vélez.

SANTANDER

Juzgado of Girón in 1808. The following six places appear: Bucaramanga, Cañaverales, Girón, Pedral, Piedecuesta, and Rionegro.

Juzgado of Mogotes in 1808. The following three places appear: Mogotes, Onzaga, and Petaquero.

Juzgado of San Gil in 1808. The following ten places appear: Aratoca, Barichara, Cepitá, Curití, Guane, Pinchote, Robada (Galán), San Gil, Valle de San José, and Zapatoca.

Juzgado of Socorro in 1808. The following eleven places appear: Charalá, Chima, Cincelada, Confines (Culatas), Encino, Ocamonte, Oiba, Páramo, Riachuelo, Simacota, and Socorro.

EASTERN CORDILLERA

Juzgado of Bosa in 1808. The following thirty-four places appear: Bosa, Bosa, Cáqueza, Cáqueza, La Catedral, Chipaque, Chipaque, Choachí, Choachí, Cunday, Fómeque, Fómeque, Fosca, Fosca, Fusagasugá, Las Nieves, Pasca, Santa Bárbara, San Victorino, Soacha, Soacha, Suba, Suba, Ciénaga y Tena, Tibacuy, Tibacuy, Ubaque, Ubaque, Une, Une, Usaquén, Usme, Usme, and Sutagaos. Tithe accounts for Bosa from earlier years show that when a place is entered twice, such as Bosa or Choachí, one is for "Bosa de Españoles" and the other is for "Bosa de Indios."

Juzgado of Chocontá in 1808. The following nineteen places appear: Chipasaque, Chipasaque, Chocontá, Chocontá, Gachetá, Gachetá, Guasca, Guasca, Guatavita, Guatavita, Machetá, Machetá, Manta, Sesquilé, Sesquilé, Suesca, Suesca, Tibirita, and Tibirita.

Juzgado of Funza in 1808. The following seventeen places appear: Bojacá, Bojacá, Facatativá, Facatativá, Fontibón, Fontibón, Funza, Funza, Engativá, Engativá, Serrezuela, Serrezuela, Subachoque, Tenjo, Tenjo, Zipacón, and Zipacón.

Juzgado of Leiva in 1808. The following twelve places appear: Chiquinquirá, Chiquizá, Gachantivá, Guachetá, Leiva, Lenguazaque, Monquirá, Ráquira, Saboyá, Suta (Sutamarchán), Sáchica, and Tinjacá.

Juzgado of Málaga in 1808. The following thirteen places appear: Capitanejo, Carcasí, Concepción, Enciso, Guaca, Macaravita, Málaga, Molagavita, San Andrés, San Miguel, Servitá (Cerrito), Servitá, and Tequia (San José de Miranda).

Juzgado of Pamplona in 1808. The following eleven places appear: Arboledas, Bochalema, Cácota (de Velasco), Cucutilla, Chinacota, Chopó (Pamplonita), Labateca, Matanza, Silos, Suratá, and Toledo.

Juzgado of Santa Rosa de Viterbo in 1808. The following fourteen places appear: Betéitiva, Busbanzá, Cerinza, Cerinza, Corrales, Duitama, Gámeza, Mongua, Santa Rosa de Viterbo, Socotá, Socha, Tasco, Tópaga, and Tutasá.

Juzgado of Soatá in 1808. The following fifteen places appear: Boavita, La Capilla, El Cocuy, El Cocuy, Cheva (Jericó), Chiscas, Chita, Guacamayas, Guacamayas, Güicán, Salina, Sátiva, Sátiva, Soatá, and La Uvita.

Juzgado of Sogamoso in 1808. The following nine places appear: Cuítiva, Firavitoba, Iza, Monguí, Nobsa, Pueblo Viejo, Sogamoso, Tibasosa, and Tota.

Juzgado of Tenza in 1808. The following eleven places appear: Capilla, Garagoa, Guateque, Guateque, Macanal, Pachavita, Somondoco, Sutatenza, Sutatenza, Teguas, and Tenza.

Juzgado of Tunja in 1808. The following twenty-nine places appear: Boyacá, Cómbita, Cucaita, Chiribí, Chivatá, Gámbita, Hato Viejo, Miraflores, Motavita, Las Nieves, Oicatá, Paipa, Pesca, Ramiriquí, Samacá, Santa Bárbara, Santiago, Siachoque, Sora, Soracá, Sotaquirá, Tibaná, Toca, Tuta, Turmequé, Umbita, Ventaquemada, Viracachá, and Zetaquirá.

Juzgado of Zipaquirá in 1808. The following thirty-five places appear: Cajicá, Cajicá, Cogua, Cogua, Cota, Cota, Cucunubá, Cucunubá, Chía, Chía, Fúquene, Fúquene, Gachancipá, Gachancipá, Nemocón, Nemocón, Pacho, Pacho, Simijaca, Simijaca, Sopó, Sopó, Susa, Susa, Sutatausa (Sutapelado), Sutatausa (Sutapelado), Tabio, Tabio, Tausa, Tocancipá, Ubaté, Ubaté, Zipaquirá, and Zipaquirá.

UPPER MAGDALENA RIVER VALLEY

Juzgado of Honda in 1808. The following four places appear: Guarumo, Honda, Nare, and Rioseco.

Juzgado of Ibagué in 1808. The following three places appear: Esmeralda (Payandé), Ibagué, Miraflores (Rovira).

Juzgado of Mariquita in 1808. The following five places appear: Bocaneme, Guayabal, Mariquita, Peladeros, Lajas y Santa Ana (Falan).

Juzgado of Neiva in 1808. The following thirteen places appear: Aipe, Caguán, Carniserías, Guagua (Palermo), Hobo, Iquira, Nátaga, Neiva, Otas, Retiro (Teruel), San Antonio, Villavieja (Nepomuc), and Yaguará.

Juzgado of Purificación in 1808. The following eleven places appear: Alpujarra, Ataco, Coyaima, Chaparral, Dolores, Guamo, Nataima, Prado, Purificación, San Luis, and Valle de San Juan.

Juzgado of Timaná in 1808. The following fourteen places appear: Avirama, Garzón, Gigante, Inzá, La Plata, Pital, San Agustín, San Antonio de Abajo, San Antonio del Alto, Suaza (y Pueblo de Naranjo), Tagua, Tálaga, Timaná, and Toboyma.

ANTIOQUIA

Juzgado of Antioquia in 1810. The following ten places appear: Antioquia, Anzá, Buriticá, Cañasgordas, Sabanalarga, Sacahojas, (El Valle de) San Andrés (de Cauca), San Jerónimo, Sopetrán, and Urrao.

Juzgado of Marinilla in 1810. The following four places appear: Carmen (de Viboral), Marinilla, Peñol, and San Carlos.

Juzgado of Medellín in 1810. The following nine places appear: Amagá, Barbosa, Copacabana, Envigado, Hato Viejo, La Estrella, Medellín, San Cristóbal, and Santo Domingo.

Juzgado of Rionegro in 1810. The following six places appear: Arma, Concepción, Rionegro, San Vicente, Santa Bárbara, and Sonsón.

Juzgado of Santa Rosa de Osos in 1810. The following five places appear: (La) Carolina (del Príncipe), San Antonio del Infante, San Luis de Góngora, San Pedro, and Santa Rosa de Osos.

Juzgado of Cáceres in 1808. The following six places appear: Cáceres, Cancan, Remedios, San Bartolomé, Yolombó, and Zaragoza.

CAUCA VALLEY

Juzgado of Buga and Cali in 1808. The following thirty-two places appear: Amaime á Amaimito, Ansermanuevo, Ansermaviejo, Buga, Cali, Calima, Cartago, Cerillos, Dagua, El Salado, Guacarí de Amaimito á Sabaletas, Guavitas á Sonso, (La) Honda al Naranjo, Iurmangui, La Paila de Bugalagrande á la Quebrada de Murillo, Llano Grande de Bolo al Sanjón de Romero, (La) Montaña, Murillo á la Honda, Quebralomo, Raposo, Río Frío, Roldanillo, Sabaletas á Guavitas, San Juan, San Pedro á Tuluá, Sanjón de Romero á Amaime, Santa Ana (ó Naranjo), (La Vega de) Supía, Toro, Tuluá, Tuluá á la Quebrada Honda, and Yumbo.

Juzgado of Popayán and Almaguer in 1808. The following twenty-three places appear: Almaguer, Caloto, Candelaria, El Tambo, El Trapiche, Frisoles, Gelima, Guambía, Jambaló, Jamundí, La Vega de San Lorenzo, Mercaderes, Paniquitá, Patía, Popayán, Puracé, Quinamayo, San Antonio, San Pablo, Toribío, Timbío, Tulumito, and Tunía (Piendamó).

CHOCÓ

Juzgado of Chocó in 1808. The following eleven places appear: Bebará, Chamí, El Cajón, Lloró, Murrí, Noanamá, Nóvita, Quibdó, Sipí, Tadó de Españoles, and Tadó de Indios.

Part Three

Resistance and Rebellion

ANTHONY MCFARLANE

Chapter 8

The Rebellion of the *Barrios*: Urban Insurrection in Bourbon Quito

In 1765, the city of Quito saw one of the longest, largest, and most formidable urban insurrections to take place in eighteenth-century Spanish America. Throughout that year, the city was affected by a conflict that touched virtually every level of its society, shook the foundations of government, and eventually required a military expedition fully to restore royal authority. It was not the only challenge to government authority to occur in the Audiencia of Quito during the eighteenth century: other incidents of civil disorder of varying proportions and potency occurred mainly among the large Indian population of the Ecuadorean highlands.[1] But in terms of its scale, duration, and the directness of the challenge that it presented to colonial government, the insurrection of the capital city was without precedent or parallel. The Quito rebellion was, moreover, a significant episode in the history of late colonial Spanish America, for it was the first of the major insurrections provoked by the Caroline reforms of the later eighteenth century and

1. See Segundo Moreno Yañez, *Sublevaciones indígenas en la Audiencia de Quito, desde comienzos del siglo XVIII hasta finales de la colonia* (Bonn, 1976).

one that, in some respects, prefigured the later rebellions of the Comuneros in New Granada and Túpac Amaru in Peru.

Yet, like much else in the history of Ecuador, the Quito rebellion has attracted relatively little attention from historians. In Ecuadorean historiography—where it has become known as the "rebellion of the *barrios*" and is regarded as an early avatar of independence—the events of 1765 have never been fully reconstructed, and analysis of their significance has been confined within a national framework.[2] The only recent work has been that of Joseph Pérez, a French historian. Drawing on the rich and previously unused documentation in the Archivo de Indias, Pérez provided both a more detailed account of the rebellion and a broader interpretation of its significance, linking it to the other major rebellions of the later eighteenth century.[3]

There is, however, considerable scope for enhancing and revising our view of Quito's "rebellion of the *barrios*." First, the nature of its causes has yet to be adequately explored. A view commonly taken at the time, and one that has been echoed by historians since, was that the city's poverty, brought on by economic decline, goaded its people to react fiercely to the threat of more taxation. This explanation is, however, inadequate in two respects. It fails to show why changes in the excise brought such a powerful and widespread rejection in 1765, when previous changes—such as the introduction of the aguardiente *estanco* years earlier—had been made without evoking a similar response. It also fails to explain why the reforms provoked such widespread antagonism, ranging across a social spectrum that reached from the urban patriciate to the plebeians of the city's popular *barrios*.

Another aspect of the rebellion that deserves reexamination concerns the political culture within which it emerged and developed. Although identifying economic discontents and material interests is a necessary condition for explaining the rebellion, it is

2. The earliest history of the rebellion appeared in 1789, in Juan de Velasco's *Historia del Reino de Quito* (Quito, 1971), I, 136–149; another account is given in the classic nineteenth-century history of Federico González Suárez, *Historia general de la República del Ecuador* (Quito, 1970), I, 1126–39. A more recent account is found in Carlos de la Torre Reyes, *La revolución de Quito del 10 de 1809* (Quito, 1961), 147–54.

3. Joseph Pérez, *Los movimientos precursores de la emancipación en Hispanoamérica* (Madrid, 1977), 46–63.

not sufficient. Economic grievances and social resentments were not new to Quito: the interaction of other elements was required to channel them into sustained insurrection against the colonial government. An element hitherto absent from analysis of the rebellion is ideology. What were the ideas, beliefs, and attitudes by which the rebels understood and justified their actions? Can we detect any coherent ideology behind their behavior, and if so, where did it come from? How did ideas and aims vary between social groups, and how did they emerge and develop during the course of the rebellion?

Like any large-scale rebellion, that of Quito was based on a mobilization of elements of the lower classes. And yet the popular dimension of the rebellion has been virtually ignored. To the official mind, searching for scapegoats, only one explanation seemed possible: a hidden agency existed behind the popular uprising, composed of creole conspirators who sought to manipulate mob violence when they failed to achieve their political objectives by peaceful means. But though this judgment has appealed to historians of the Quito rebellion, it is far from adequate. It simply reflects the contemporary social prejudice that the plebeians of Quito were an ignorant and manipulable mass, stirred by spontaneous passions and without independent ideas or organization. Reexamining this position requires a closer focus on the people of the *barrios,* their behavior, and their goals and, thus, on the values and beliefs that shaped their actions.

What, then, stood at the heart of the Quito rebellion, and what was its significance? Did it present a precocious challenge to Spanish sovereignty, or were its aims more limited? Was it one movement, in which an entire community stood together to defend its interests against new taxation, or was it several expressing social conflicts within the community? What held it together, and what, ultimately, did it achieve? To examine these issues, this essay will draw on contemporary accounts of the rebellion to reconstruct its history and, by blending a narrative of its development with an analysis of its content, seek to throw some fresh light on its character and comparative significance.[4]

4. The main source of data on the rebellion is the collection of correspondence relating to the events of 1764–1766 compiled by the viceroy of New Granada's secretary, which constitutes a kind of official "history" of the rebellion. It is found in AGI, Quito, leg.

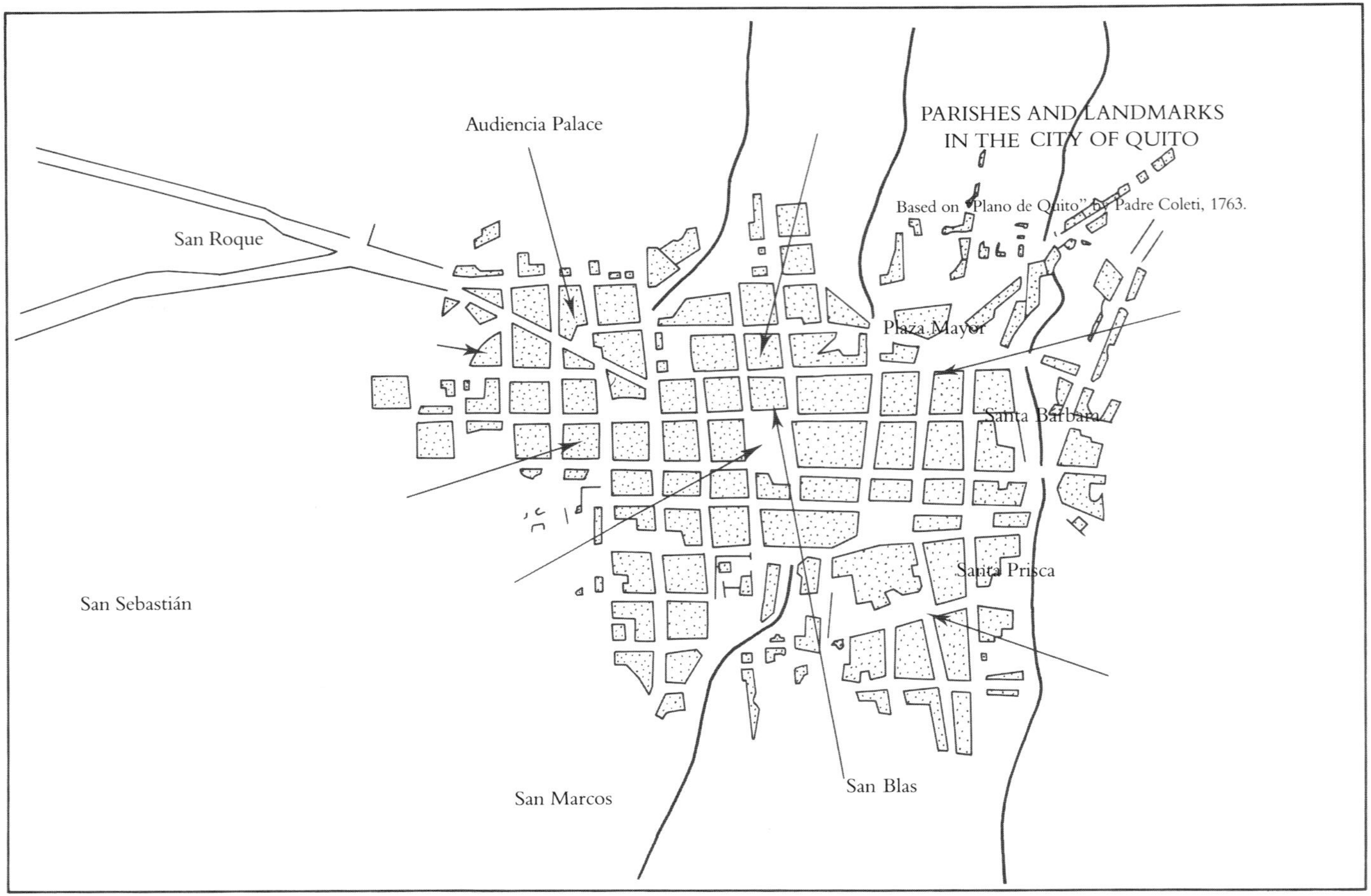
PARISHES AND LANDMARKS
IN THE CITY OF QUITO
Based on "Plano de Quito" by Padre Coleti, 1763.
Audiencia Palace
San Roque
Plaza Mayor
Santa Bárbara
Santa Prisca
San Sebastián
San Marcos
San Blas

Patrician Politics: The Conflict of Words

The outbreak of violent action that was to mark the beginning of rebellion in Quito occurred on May 22, 1765, when a crowd of rioters stormed and ransacked the royal sales tax administration and aguardiente distillery. The rioters' targets reflect the immediate cause of the disturbance: the efforts of Viceroy Pedro Messía de la Cerda to reform Quito's excise administration.

Since the reestablishment of the viceroyalty of New Granada in 1739, the Audiencia of Quito had come under the fiscal and military jurisdiction of the viceroys in Santa Fe, and as a result, Quito was exposed to the process of administrative revision and reform that was affecting New Granada itself. And in Quito as elsewhere, the viceroy's main concern was with increasing the revenues available to meet rising expenditures. Indeed, in the field of crown finance, Quito was an area of special interest for the viceroys, since its revenues provided the subsidies vital for maintaining the military establishment of Cartagena, New Granada's principal port and bastion for coastal defense. The reassessment of Quito's fiscal organization began during the 1750s, when Viceroy Solís investigated irregularities in Quito's treasury and made a preliminary, apparently unsuccessful effort to remedy them.[5] After his successor, Pedro Messía de la Cerda took office in 1760, however, the reform of the Quito treasury was to begin in earnest.

On investigating the fiscal affairs of Quito, Messía de la Cerda discovered that much of its revenue was kept by the tax-farmers who collected it, in a fiscal administration already undermined by widespread and habitual tax evasion.[6] The aguardiente monopoly and the *alcabalas* collected in the city of Quito seemed to show particularly obvious signs of mismanagement, since they yielded only a third of the revenues generated by their counterparts in Santa Fe, a city of comparable size. Hence, apparently acting on his own initiative rather than on direct instructions from Spain, Viceroy Messía de la Cerda ordered that both the state

---

398–399. The numbers of the documents cited here conform to the numbers given in the original index; the folio numbers conform to the modern foliation.

5. Posada and Ibáñez (eds.), *Relaciones de mando,* 80–81.

6. *Ibid.,* 99.

monopoly of aguardiente sales and the *alcabala* tax in the city and its province be removed from the administration of private tax-farmers and passed into direct management by royal officials.[7] To carry out this task, the viceroy appointed Juan Díaz de Herrera, a peninsular Spaniard who had successfully operated a similar administration in Santa Fe. Díaz de Herrera was ordered to go first to the city of Popayán and put its *estanco* and *alcabala* administrations under direct crown management and then, having carried out this task, to move on to Quito, there to repeat the exercise. This, in the viceroy's view, was to be an important step toward improving royal revenues in Quito, a source of income that had assumed a new importance as viceregal government sought to sustain and expand military expenditure.[8]

It was, however, easier to plan reform than to implement it. When Díaz de Herrera set about his work in Quito, he met with stiff opposition. Any change in taxation was likely to be a delicate and difficult matter for, as one contemporary was later to comment, "there is no American who does not reject any novelty whatsoever in the management of taxation."[9] And the viceroy's reforms in Quito touched two particularly sensitive and potentially controversial areas of taxation. Both the aguardiente monopoly and the *alcabala* affected large sectors of the city's population, including producers, traders, and consumers alike. Thus both were fiscal areas in which change had repercussions that crossed class lines. But, if reforms in these areas were generally disliked, each of them encountered the greatest opposition among different social groups. The proposed reorganization of the *estanco* appears to have excited antagonism primarily among the hacendados who produced the sugar from which aguardiente was distilled, while the *alcabala* reform provoked the most intense hostility among the small householders and traders of the city's popular *barrios*. As we

7. AGI, Quito, leg. 398, no. 1, fols. 32–35. The viceroy's order was not officially approved by the crown until more than a year after it was issued. Julián de Arriaga to Viceroy Messía de la Cerda, Aranjuez, June 5, 1765, AHNC, Impuestos Varios (Cartas), tomo 17, fol. 21.

8. Letter of Messía de la Cerda, Santa Fe, October 10, 1765, AGI, Quito, leg. 398, no. 149.

9. Joseph de Cistué to Messía de la Cerda, Quito, April 1, 1766, AHNC, Historia, tomo 3, fols. 33–34.

shall see, this difference helps to explain both how peaceful protest, originating in patrician political circles, was transformed into rebellion, and how, once launched, the rebellion was able to merge disparate groups in a common endeavor.

The Mobilization of the Elites

Of the two elements of fiscal reform, the reorganization of the aguardiente monopoly provoked the first wave of opposition and led to a confrontation between Quito's urban patriciate and colonial government. This was not surprising, as the monopoly had already aroused dissension and discord long before the viceroy's reform. In 1752, the cabildo had sought to have it extinguished, on the grounds that, with the transfer of its revenues from public works to the treasury, it would further drain circulating currency from an already impoverished province. When this attempt to end the monopoly failed, dispute shifted to the question of who should control it. Indeed, in March, 1764, at the very time that the viceroy decided on reform, a quarrel over control of the monopoly administration was already in progress, generating conflict within the Quito patriciate. Two men—one acting for the cabildo and the other in his own personal capacity—claimed that the recent leasing of the *estanco* administration had been fraudulently organized and was contrary to both the public interest and the interests of the hacendados who produced sugarcane. The cabildo's representative alleged that the successful contractor, Don Melchor de Rivadeneira, was an impoverished lawyer whose bid was simply a front for other interests, probably those of the town of Ibarra, whose hacendados wanted to take over supplying the *estanco* in Quito, to the great detriment of Quito's landowners. The other complainant also alleged a conspiracy to take control of the *estanco,* but argued that Rivadeneira was the creature of the fiscal José de Cistué and his ally, the previous contractor, Don Antonio de la Sala. It seems that Sala, backed by Cistué and the *oidor* Félix de Llano, sought to prevent the monopoly from passing into new hands.[10] Whatever

10. Cabildo of Quito to Messía de la Cerda, Quito, September 7, 1752, AHNC, Impuestos Varios (Cartas), tomo 23, fols. 754–56; Joseph Gómez Lasso de la Vega to Messía de la Cerda, Quito, March 5, 1764, Pedro Guerrero y Otañon to Messía de la Cerda, Quito, March 8, 1764, both in AHNC, Impuestos Varios (Cartas), tomo 22, fols. 761–64, 769; Francisco de Borja to the crown, Quito, January 24, 1767, AGI, Quito, leg. 399, no. 423.

the truth of the matter, the aguardiente monopoly and its management clearly already stood high on the local political agenda and were capable of generating friction both between the Quito patriciate and government, and within the ranks of each.

As soon as Díaz de Herrera arrived in Quito in late October, 1764, to begin reorganizing the city's excise taxes, he encountered stirrings of creole dissent. This was first publicly expressed within the cabildo of Quito, the political instrument of the creole patriciate and a body that had long played a part in conflicts between peninsular and American factions in the city.[11] At the end of October, the regidor Luis de la Cuesta complained to the viceroy that Francisco de Borja was arousing opposition to the projected reform, on the "affected pretext that it would be harmful to the common interest."[12] He also called for Borja's expulsion from the cabildo, on the grounds that his recent co-optation to it contravened municipal law. Borja was, however, to remain an active and very effective member of the cabildo, and in the months that followed, he stood at the center of a vigorous campaign against the viceroy's reform, seeking by various methods to delay and ultimately to prevent its implementation.[13]

Borja's recruitment to the cabildo signals the start of the first phase of *quiteño* resistance, during which the urban elites formed an alliance to reverse the reforms through a coordinated political campaign. Borja—who had been brought into the cabildo as a substitute for his father-in-law, the *alférez real* Juan de Chiriboga—was to act as the representative and spokesman for an important section of the creole patriciate. Through his family ties, Borja formed part of a network of rich and noble families that dominated Quito's economy and society. His connections included some of the most illustrious and aristocratic names in the city, such as the Marquises of Villa Orellana, of Villarocha, of Lices, and of

11. For general comments on the city's politics from the 1730s until the 1760s, see González Suárez, *Historia general,* V, chaps. 3, 4.

12. Luis de la Cuesta to Messía de la Cerda, Quito, October 29, 1764, AGI, Quito, leg. 398, no. 6, fols. 61–62.

13. Borja sought to delay the establishment of a royal aguardiente distillery on the grounds that it would interfere with the public water supply. He also persuaded the audiencia that the corregidor of Quito should not participate in the cabildo's deliberations on the new policy because he was personally prejudiced. Juan Díaz de Herrera to Messía de la Cerda, Quito, December 8, 1764, AGI, Quito, leg. 398, no. 12, fols. 85–92.

Solanda, all members of a creole oligarchy that had built its fortunes on the ownership of great estates and, in some cases, investments in textile workshops and hat manufactories.[14] Furthermore, his interest in the aguardiente economy was very direct, as his father-in-law was one of the largest producers of sugarcane in the region.[15] Thus, while he posed as the spokesman for the *común*, or community, of Quito, Borja was the mouthpiece for both a family with a strong interest in the aguardiente economy and an aristocratic landowning elite of which he was a prominent member.

As opposition took shape in the secular ranks of the urban patriciate, it also spread to the ecclesiastical wing. On November 14, 1764, the prelates of the city's clerical establishment petitioned the municipal council to convene a *cabildo abierto* to discuss the proposed reform. For the cabildo, this move by the leaders of the clergy must have been doubly reassuring. Not only did it signal the allegiance of an influential section of city society, but it also enabled the cabildo to present its case as a matter of public, rather than purely private, interest. The petition was accordingly welcomed by the cabildo, whose *procurador general* duly passed it to the audiencia for a decision. The tribunal responded favorably and, on November 22, named the time, place, and membership for a *cabildo abierto*.[16] The stage was thus set for creole opposition to move into a new arena, away from the relatively narrow institutional base afforded by the city council, into the wider setting of a more general congress that purported to represent the interests of the whole community.

Why, when the proposal for a *cabildo abierto* seemed to strengthen the cabildo's challenge to the viceroy's policy, did the audiencia agree to permit it? The *fiscal,* José de Cistué, advised the

14. For some data on Borja's social connections and their positions in the local economy, see Javier Ortiz de la Tabla, "Panorama económico y social del corregimiento de Quito (1768–1775)," *Revista de Indias,* CXLV–CXLVI (1976), 83–98.

15. In a "Memoria de los individuos, en Hacendados, quienes se han prorrateado de su libre voluntad por las quadras de caña dulce que tienen en sus haciendas de trapiches en donde se fabrican aguardientes de caña que se expende en esta ciudad y sus cinco leguas," drawn up in August, 1752, Juan de Chiriboga appears as the second largest producer, after the Jesuits, with 150 quadras devoted to the production of sugarcane. AHNC, Impuestos Varios (Cartas), tomo 22, fols. 372–75.

16. "Testimonio del ocurso hecho por las Religiones y Commun del Vecindario de la Ciudad de Quito . . . ," AGI, Quito, leg. 398, no. 148, fols. 601, 605–606.

audiencia that, provided that it was presided over by an *oidor* who would support the viceroy's policy, a *cabildo abierto* should be permitted. If they refused, he argued, they would not only convey the misleading impression that the viceroy was seeking to impose new taxes, but would also be ignoring precedent and denying the *quiteños* the "facilities for defense permitted by divine and human law in representation to superiors."[17] Clearly, then, there was a case in both law and politics for allowing open discussion of the viceroy's plans. It is unlikely, however, that the audiencia was swayed by these considerations alone; other factors also affected its judgment.

For a number of reasons, the audiencia had little cause to welcome the viceroy's reformist initiative. Indeed, there was at least as much scope for conflict as for cooperation between the viceroy and the *oidores* of Quito. Composed of four *oidores* (one of whom acted as president) and a *fiscal,* the audiencia also included one supernumerary *oidor* in 1764–1765 and had a majority of creole judges.[18] Of the six serving ministers, four were Americans: Luis de Santa Cruz, Gregorio Ignacio Hurtado de Mendoza, and Félix de Llano were all from Lima, while Juan Romualdo Navarro was from Quito itself. All had initially purchased their positions as supernumeraries, and all—except Félix de Llano—had served in Quito for long periods, ranging from fifteen to nineteen years. The two peninsular Spaniards were Manuel Rubio de Arévalo and José de Cistué, respectively the most senior and the junior members of the audiencia. Rubio de Arévalo was an established member of Quito's patrician society, having spent his entire career in the city, and as senior *oidor,* he had also been its acting president since the death of the Marqués de Selva Alegre in 1761. He had first been appointed in 1720 and, though suspended and heavily fined for professional misconduct in 1747, Rubio de Arévalo had remained in Quito and had been granted a dispensation to hold property there.[19] The other peninsular Spaniard, José de Cistué,

17. *Ibid.,* fol. 604.

18. Information on the audiencia members is from Mark A. Burkholder and D. S. Chandler, *From Impotence to Authority: The Spanish Crown and the American Audiencias* (Columbia, 1977), 219–21.

19. González Suárez, *Historia general,* II, 1054–57.

had spent less time in Quito, but after serving seven years as *fiscal,* he was also well established in the city's social and political life.

Thus, all but one member of the audiencia, Félix de Llano, had served for long periods in Quito and were very familiar with, if not sympathetic to, the preoccupations and interests of the local patriciate. For this reason, the viceroy in Santa Fe did not regard these ministers as reliable instruments for implementing his policy innovations. Indeed, he was later to blame them for the breakdown of order in Quito, because the *oidores'* overriding aim was "to promote their private interests and to avoid displeasing the *vecindario* because of the friendships and relationships they have with its distinguished individuals."[20] Messía de la Cerda did not consult them about his new policy, nor adequately inform them of the manner in which they were to proceed. Instead, he made his decision in consultation with the Tribunal de Cuentas in Santa Fe and gave the power to implement it to his commissioner, Juan Díaz de Herrera. Díaz de Herrera was responsible directly to the viceroy, and he, in turn, did not display any great respect for the audiencia, nor make an effort to engage the *oidores'* support. Indeed, he described the audiencia as a major obstruction to the process of reform and identified two of its ministers as his main enemies.

One of these was the *oidor* Félix de Llano who, having been appointed *juez conservador* of the new *estanco* administration, struggled to be relieved of the post and regaled the viceroy with arguments against the reform. The reform, he asserted, would not only be damaging to the hacendados of the area, it would also threaten public order by provoking disorder among the students, friars, and plebeians of the city, already notorious for their turbulent dispositions.[21] Llano's companion in opposition to the reform was the *fiscal,* José de Cistué. According to Díaz de Herrera, these men prevailed upon the audiencia to obstruct *alcabala* reform because they feared that more rigorous collection would uncover

20. Messía de la Cerda to Arriaga, Santa Fe, July 5, 1765, AGI, Quito, leg. 398, no. 59, fol. 358.

21. Félix de Llano to Messía de la Cerda, Quito, November 20, 1764, AGI, Quito, leg. 398, nos. 8–9. Llano's fears of an uprising were not necessarily exaggerated: he had only recently returned from Riobamba, where his efforts to enumerate the Indian population had sparked a local rebellion. See Moreno Yañez, *Sublevaciones indigenas,* 42–107.

the "interests that the *fiscal* and Llano (who are those that direct and dominate the others) manage by means of *cajeros,* servants, household members, and followers," as well as the smuggling of prohibited goods from Lima. Díaz was less specific in his condemnation of the other judges, though no less dismissive. They were, he told the viceroy, arrogant and conceited men, anxious for flattery and unable to tolerate contrary opinions.[22]

Such allegations do not mean that the ministers of the audiencia were disloyal to the crown: supplementing a salary with earnings from local business interests was not unusual among colonial officials, and it was also common for audiencia judges to form strong local ties during long periods of office in a particular capital.

In this case, however, the existence of such private interests and local ties had important repercussions because it impeded the progress of reform and opened up divisions in the highest ranks of colonial government. Whereas the viceroy and his administrator were determined to push ahead with reform, the judges of the audiencia put up obstacles, apparently in the hope that, by slowing reform, they might eventually stop it. At the very least, as Díaz de Herrera observed, the audiencia's tactics gave the creole opposition led by Borja time to organize a strong resistance.[23] And, at most, it provided that opposition with the encouragement of knowing that they had allies within the upper tiers of government. Certainly their equivocations on the issues confronting them helped to create an atmosphere of division and indecision at the apex of government, which, in turn, undermined authority and thus widened the political path that was ultimately to lead to open rebellion.

It was against this background that the main currents of opposition converged in the *cabildo abierto* of December 7, 1764. Under the chairmanship of the senior *oidor,* Manuel Rubio de Arévalo, this meeting convoked deputies to speak on behalf of all sections of the community. The *protector de indios* was to speak for the Indian community, deputies from the ecclesiastical cabildo were to represent the secular clergy, various prelates were to speak

22. Díaz de Herrera to Messía de la Cerda, Quito, January 18 and February 2, 1765, AGI, Quito, leg. 398, nos. 21, 24.

23. Díaz de Herrera to Messía de la Cerda, Quito, December 8, 1765, AGI, Quito, leg. 398, no. 12.

for the monastic orders, and members of the cabildo, together with deputies for agricultural and commercial interests, were to present the opinions of civil society. When the *cabildo abierto* took place, it was brief, restrained, and contained little that was spontaneous or improvised. The meeting consisted of a succession of short speeches from clerics denouncing the evils of aguardiente drinking, especially among the Indians, and pronouncing support for the petition previously presented to the meeting by Francisco de Borja. Their recommendation and the decision of the meeting were unanimous. They called for an end to the *estanco* and agreed that a representative should be dispatched to intervene with the viceroy and sent to Spain if necessary.[24]

Since Francisco de Borja, with his strong connections to the landowning elite, played a central part in organizing and orchestrating the *cabildo abierto,* and given that this meeting concentrated on the issue of the aguardiente monopoly, the hacendados involved with sugar production were apparently the driving force behind opposition to the viceroy's plans. It would be a mistake, however, to regard the developing protest as simply the defense of a narrow, elite economic interest, camouflaged as an issue of public concern. Other sectors of city society were also involved because of their connections, direct and indirect, with the aguardiente economy. These included the small traders—the *tenderos* and the *pulperos*—and the monasteries; both distilled and sold aguardiente.[25] Indeed, according to the *oidor* Llano, the city was filled with bootleggers, as virtually everyone was involved in distilling aguardiente "without exception of person, class, or estate, including even monasteries and leading families." Consumers of aguardiente might also have regarded stricter regulation of distilling and distribution with suspicion, since restriction threatened to

24. Díaz de Herrera also reported that it had been agreed that the hacendados and *vecinos* of the province of Quito should raise six thousand to eight thousand pesos by *pro rata* contributions to send Francisco de Borja to Spain to present their case at court. Díaz de Herrera to Messía de la Cerda, Quito, December 13, 1764, AGI, Quito, leg. 398, no. 16. See, too, no. 35, fols. 205–15.

25. According to Díaz de Herrera, the monasteries regularly contravened the *estanco* regulations, but could not easily be controlled because aguardiente was distilled in the cloisters, where guards could not enter, and often taken out by women. Díaz de Herrera to Messía de la Cerda, Quito, December 8, 1764, AGI, Quito, leg. 398, no. 10.

increase prices. And, as the main group of consumers was, according to a contemporary, the "craftsmen, Indians, and mestizos of all the trades," they represented a potentially formidable source of dissent.[26] Thus, the proposed reform of the monopoly was itself enough to prompt a broad spectrum of opposition, spanning the city's social classes. In early December the publication of pasquinades in the city's *barrios* warned of clandestine efforts to mobilize this opposition.[27] Initially, however, members of the city's creole elite, led by Francisco de Borja, took the initiative, and the opposition concentrated on negotiation rather than intimidation. For the moment, the opposition met in the *cabildo abierto* rather than on the streets.

Elite Economic Grievances

Behind the objections set forth during the meeting of the *cabildo abierto* lay a series of petitions from the different groups represented, and in these, rather than in the peremptory verbal statements made at the meeting, the main arguments against the reform were rehearsed. Each group representative advanced a detailed account of the group's objections to the reform, in written submissions supposedly based on prior canvassing of opinion. The careful attention to detail in the submissions reflects a degree of political sophistication and an expectation that reasoned argument would produce results. Rather than simply make sweeping objections, they were at pains to show why the new measures were not only damaging to the economic interests and welfare of their groups, but were also unworkable and counterproductive to the very royal purposes that they were supposed to serve. There was, moreover, one common theme running through all the presentations: the problems of the economy of the Audiencia of Quito in general and the poverty and misery of the inhabitants of the city of Quito in particular.

26. Llano to Messía de la Cerda, Quito, November 20, 1764, AGI, Quito, leg. 398, no. 8, fol. 67; Lasso de la Vega to Messía de la Cerda, Quito, March 5, 1764, AHNC, Impuestos Varios (Cartas), tomo 22, fol. 760.

27. Díaz de Herrera to Messía de la Cerda, Quito, December 8, 1764, AGI, Quito, leg. 398, no. 12. These threats were serious enough for Díaz to ask for a guard to protect him and for the audiencia to initiate an investigation. See Díaz de Herrera to Messía de la Cerda, Quito, December 8, 1764, and Audiencia of Quito to Messía de la Cerda, December 13, 1764, AGI, Quito, leg. 398, nos. 11, 17.

The first petition submitted to the *cabildo abierto* was that of Francisco de Borja, the spokesman designated for the *vecindad,* or the *común.* Drawn up and circulated before the *cabildo abierto,* Borja's petition was evidently intended to serve as a manifesto, deliberately if discreetly designed to rally all sections of elite opinion against the viceroy's plans.[28] Directed against the aguardiente monopoly, it was clearly concerned primarily with defending the threatened interests of the urban elites.

In his presentation, Borja sought first to impugn the legitimacy of the viceroy's intention to bring the aguardiente monopoly under direct crown administration. He recalled that the monopoly had been introduced as a purely temporary measure, to cover the costs of rebuilding the audiencia palace, and that it had outlived this purpose. Thus, Borja argued, though the monopoly was not new, its reorganization was tantamount to imposing a new tax on the city, since it aimed to increase net revenues. This assault on the legality of the viceroy's policy was buttressed by an attack on its morality. The monopoly, Borja asserted, was indefensible in law because, by encouraging the spread of drunkenness, with its attendant vices, it promoted sin and scandal. It would also be counterproductive to royal interests because of its impact on the local society and economy. Heavy drinking among the Indians increased their mortality and thereby damaged royal revenues from tribute. The monopoly would also damage the province's agriculture because it was ill-adapted to the conditions of local sugar production and threatened to reduce the price paid for sugar products. Finally, Borja pleaded the poverty of the province, stating that the depression of the textile trade caused by competition from European imports in Peruvian markets had deprived its people of their sole reliable source of income.

The other petitions presented to the *cabildo abierto* echoed the themes of Borja and supported his contentions without reserve. The economic arguments were taken up by the representatives of civil society, who testified to the province's economic depression and outlined their own particular difficulties. The *vecinos* of Latacunga opposed reform of the *alcabala* and *estanco* on the grounds that it would impose intolerable burdens on an economy where

28. Francisco de Borja, Informe por el vecindario, November 28, 1764, AGI, Quito, leg. 398, fols. 215–25.

agriculture had been afflicted by volcanic eruptions and earthquakes (the most recent near Quito and been in 1757) and where many *obrajes* had been ruined by competition from imported English cloth.[29] The landowners and sugar producers argued that the aguardiente monopoly would send agriculture into a spiral of decline that would ruin all who depended on the land for their living and even affect the dead, since damage to agriculture would undermine the chantries devoted to prayer for departed souls. The merchants of Quito joined this chorus, arguing that the reorganization of taxes would aggravate the already chronic shortage of specie that resulted from the decline of Quito's textile exports to Peru.[30]

Borja's denunciation of social and spiritual corruption, on the other hand, provided an appropriate theme for the clergy. The leaders of the city's ecclesiastical establishment detailed the pathology of aguardiente, warned that drink led to damnation, and duly called for the aguardiente monopoly to be suppressed in the interests of public health, both physical and moral.[31] Despite their denunciation of drink, however, the clergy called for suppression of the state monopoly, not for a ban on private production, much less consumption, of aguardiente. Clearly more was at stake than the sturdy values of temperance. Although they did not admit it, the clergy had a strong material interest in sugar and aguardiente production, both as owners and holders of mortgages on haciendas, and as distributors and consumers of aguardiente.[32]

29. Informe de los vecinos de Tacunga, AGI, Quito, leg. 398, fols. 230–33. Of the two signatures on this document, one was that of the Marqués de Maenza who, it should be noted, had been involved in the recent successful bid for the aguardiente monopoly as a guarantor for Melchor de Rivadeneyra. See AHNC, Impuestos Varios (Cartas), tomo 22, fol. 769.

30. Informe de los hacendados, Informe de los trapicheros, Informe del comercio, all in AGI, Quito, leg. 398, fols. 233–44.

31. Informes de la Compañía de Jesus, Fray Jacinto de la Cruz, and Rector del Colegio Imperial de San Buenaventura, AGI, Quito, leg. 398, fols. 244–47.

32. In 1752, the Jesuits had headed the list of landholders contributing on the basis of their acreage under sugar production; the convents of San Agustín and la Merced were also among the leading contributors. See AHNC, Impuestos Varios (Cartas), tomo 22, fols. 372–75. In the same year, the cabildo said that the haciendas of Quito were "so burdened with mortgages that their owners are in reality no more than mayordomos for the mortgagors." *Ibid.*, tomo 23, fol. 754. For further comment on clerical involvement in the agrarian and urban economy of Quito, see Jorge Juan and Antonio de Ulloa, *Discourse and Political Reflections on the Kingdom of Peru*, ed. John J. TePaske (Norman, Okla., 1978), 306–307.

Thus, under the leadership of Francisco de Borja, a united front was formed in Quito to oppose reform, composed of all the leading sectors of its society, enjoying the sympathy of some members of the audiencia, and claiming to speak for the whole community. Clearly, behind the rhetoric about public interest, there was some special pleading by patrician and clerical economic interests. Long sheltered from efficient taxation, these interests, together with those that profited from the private administration of the excise taxes, were naturally opposed to any fiscal innovation that threatened to interfere with their business. But their pleas of poverty cannot simply be dismissed as specious rhetoric. Resentment at fiscal reorganization was undoubtedly sharpened by the experience of economic decline, associated primarily with the problems of the textile industry.

This decline had begun many years before, with demographic crisis in Quito during the 1690s.[33] But the industry's problems had grown worse during the eighteenth century, as it was increasingly affected by competition from Spanish and foreign contraband imports. This competition had intensified around midcentury, causing the number and output of its *obrajes* to fall considerably.[34] This recent contraction stemmed from changes in commercial policy that, by opening Cape Horn, permitted direct maritime contact between Peru and Spain and thereby made it more difficult for Quito textiles to compete in Peruvian markets. Furthermore, the problems caused by the redirection of transatlantic trade were particularly acute at the very time that the viceroy was pursuing his reforms. For, having been severely disrupted by war in 1762 and 1763, Spanish transatlantic commerce in-

33. After a major demographic crisis in the 1690s, the Quito textile industry had entered a phase of decline from which it never fully emerged. See John Leddy Phelan, *The Kingdom of Quito in the Seventeenth Century: Bureaucratic Politics in the Spanish Empire* (Madison, 1967), 66–71.

34. Robson B. Tyrer, "The Demographic and Economic History of the Audiencia of Quito: Indian Population and the Textile Industry, 1600–1800" (Ph.D. dissertation, University of California, Berkeley, 1976), 184–341. For a classic contemporary statement concerning the problems facing Quito around midcentury, see "Razón que cerca del Estado y Governación Política y Militar de las Provincias, Villas y Lugares que contiene la Jurisdicción de la Real Audiencia de Quito da . . . el Marqués de Selva Alegre" (1754), in *Arbitraje de límites entre Perú y el Ecuador: Documentos anexos al alegato del Perú* (Madrid, 1905), I, 138–69.

creased sharply in 1764 and 1765 to restock markets depleted by war.[35] Thus, in the years before the rebellion, prospects for the Quito economy looked especially bleak, and *quiteños* could attribute this decline to recent modifications in crown policy. Under such conditions, fiscal innovations that threatened to increase the real burden of taxation heaped insult upon injury. Indeed, in such depressing economic circumstances, the *quiteños* were looking to the crown for policies that would provide economic relief rather than fiscal rigor. And, if they had good cause to criticize crown economic policy, such criticism interacted with, and was reinforced by, a set of political ideas that helped both to inspire and to shape resistance to reform.

Political Issues and Constitutional Conflict

In opposing reform, the *quiteño* elites evidently sought to protect their economic interests. But the means by which they did so, the arguments they deployed, and the alliance they formed suggest that their campaign also involved political issues. Their conflict with the viceroy was precipitated by fiscal reform, but it was not simply about reorganization of the aguardiente monopoly. As they mobilized in defense of their economic interests, the creole patriciate of Quito also drew on a set of political ideas that, though not set out in any systematic formulation, clearly influenced their attitudes toward reform and justified their campaign of resistance.

From the start of this campaign, the *quiteño* patriciate claimed a right to participate in government as the representative of the community as a whole. To exercise this claim, the creole leadership called for the convocation of a *cabildo abierto,* an institution that, by its very nature, embodied notions of urban autonomy and corporate representation.[36] Like its Spanish medieval predecessors, Quito's *cabildo abierto* reflected the belief that the community should be allowed to represent its interests directly to the crown and thereby share in the deliberations of government when they touched on matters of pressing local concern. By setting itself to

35. See Antonio García Baquero, *Cádiz y el Atlántico (1717–1778)* (Seville, 1976), II, 173.

36. For a general account of the *cabildo abierto,* see John Preston Moore, *The Cabildo in Peru under the Hapsburgs* (Durham, N.C., 1954), 125–35.

deliberate on "the public good, on justice, on the Christian and natural law, applying itself to find the means of invigorating the life of a moribund republic," the *cabildo abierto* in Quito appealed to a concept of government by negotiation and implicitly rejected the arbitrary exercise of royal power.[37] It also claimed to represent the whole community, invoking the concepts of the *común,* the *bien común,* or the *bien público.* And, to fortify this claim, the *cabildo abierto* rested on a representative principle, derived from the medieval practice of representing the estates or orders of a society through delegates chosen from their most distinguished members, duly adjusted to accord with colonial circumstances.[38] Thus, while the clergy, the hacendados, and the merchants were represented by leading members of each group, the delegate for the Indians was the *protector de indios.* The mestizos and the common people in general were also represented indirectly through the patrician Francisco de Borja, who was deputed to speak for the *común.* Last but not least, the *cabildo abierto* included the leading member of royal government in the city: it was both convoked and moderated by the president of the audiencia.

If, as an institution, the *cabildo abierto* implicitly embodied a traditional view of government—that leading members of the community might represent the "public good" in order to influence royal policy—that view was advanced explicitly in the arguments raised against reform. These sought to identify the limits of governmental power in various ways. First, in attacking the aguardiente monopoly, Francisco de Borja claimed that the king's ministers should suspend any royal order that might, under certain conditions, lead to sin or scandal.[39] The notion that laws that encouraged offenses against morality were indefensible was unexceptionable enough. More interesting is the suggestion it implicitly contains, namely, that the local authorities had a responsibility to change royal orders in accord with local circumstances.

This line of reasoning was most clearly adduced by the *procurador* of the Quito cabildo, Lasso de la Vega. He contended that laws had to be clearly promulgated if they were to command obe-

37. "El cabildo secular . . . ," AGI, Quito, leg. 398, no. 35. fols. 248–49.

38. On Spanish medieval practice, see José Antonio Maravall, *Las comunidades de Castilla: Una primera revolución moderna* (2nd ed.; Madrid, 1979), 117–18.

39. "El cabildo secular . . . ," AGI, Quito, leg. 398, no. 35, fol. 220.

dience. Thus, he not only sought to defend refusal to comply with the new excise arrangements on the grounds that they had not been explained to the public, but by stating that the government had to explain its measures, he also implied that it must justify them to its citizens. Finally, he advanced the argument that when formulating policy the crown should consider local practices and customs. Calling attention to the differences between Santa Fe and Quito "in styles, manners and customs," as well as in physical and climatic environment, Lasso de la Vega argued that a law that was beneficial in the viceregal capital might be harmful in Quito. Indeed, he elevated the customs of the province of Quito to the level of established laws or entrenched privileges, likening them to the *fueros* of the Basques and Aragonese, the *ordenanzas* of Peru, and the municipal laws of the Indies.[40]

This was not an unorthodox reading of the law. A senior *oidor* of the Quito audiencia, Luis de Santa Cruz, also stated it with great clarity to support his opposition to viceregal reform. Early in 1765, Santa Cruz refused to publish the proclamation announcing the reform of the *alcabala* administration, arguing that it was essential to modify these plans in accord with "the circumstances in which we find ourselves and the deplorable state of this province."[41] He also claimed that local officials like himself were better acquainted with the province and the customs of its inhabitants, and that their advice should be heeded to ensure that policy was suitable to local conditions. No law, he asserted, was universally applicable: even in the same country, there were laws that could not be applied in all cases, at least not without risk of perpetrating injustice and promoting disorder. On these premises, *oidor* Santa Cruz raised several specific objections to the viceroy's project. He pointed to the problems of taxing landowners without regard for their ability to pay, to the problem of levying taxes on ecclesiastical property, and to the threat of violent reactions from a plebeian society renowned for its insolent manners.

The significance of these statements deserves emphasis. Behind these practical points lay an organizing notion of what consti-

40. "Informe del señor procurador," AGI, Quito, leg. 398, no. 35, fols. 227–28.

41. Luis de Santa Cruz to Messía de la Cerda, Quito, February 1, 1765, AGI, Quito, leg. 398, no. 22.

tuted good and just government. Appealing to the authority of the seventeenth-century jurist Juan de Solórzano, to all the most celebrated political theorists (*regnícolas*) who had interpreted the public law of the Spanish kingdoms, to the ancient laws of the Siete Partidas, and to Canon Law, Santa Cruz concluded that the law had to be adapted to the needs of specific societies and to the customs and welfare of their peoples. Thus, like the petitioners for the *cabildo abierto,* the *oidor* appealed to a traditional theory of the state that monarch and subject were joined by mutual obligations and that the monarch's interests were identified with the preservation and prosperity of his subjects.

The conflict over fiscal reform in Quito, then, had an important political dimension embracing constitutional claims whereby leading members of the local social and political hierarchy asserted the right to consultation in the decisions of royal government and called for local approval of new taxation. In this sense, the dispute in Quito was a striking example of that "indigenous tradition of no taxation without bureaucratic representation" that John Phelan found at the heart of a later rebellion in the viceroyalty, that of the Comuneros of New Granada in 1781. Like the Comunero leadership nearly two decades later, the *quiteño* patriciate drew on an ideological tradition fed by the concepts and conventions of Hispanic political theory in the Golden Age, rather than by the new ideological currents emanating from the European Enlightenment.[42] For the creole elites, the viceroy's fiscal reform not only threatened their economic interests, it also challenged their right to negotiation and consultation within the colonial bureaucracy. And such opposition was not confined to the creoles; it also included the political establishment of the colony, the judges of the audiencia, who saw their own authority and role as power brokers being threatened by the viceroy's intervention and who accordingly tried to defend their traditional autonomy. This was not a defiance of the crown's authority; it was rather an attempt to use and defend an existing system of government, inherited from Hapsburg practice, against Bourbon innovation. Only when this aim was frustrated, by a viceroy determined to pursue his plans, was negotiation superseded by rebellion.

42. Phelan, *The People and the King,* 35, 79–88.

Plebeian Insurrection: The Conflict of Arms

Initially, it seemed that negotiation would bear fruit as the petitions of the *cabildo abierto* were passed on to Santa Fe for the viceroy's consideration. But, unknown to the *quiteños,* Viceroy Messía de la Cerda never had any intention of abandoning his scheme. By February, 1765, he had already decided to take a hard line. If necessary, he was ready to enforce obedience to his orders, and he called upon the metropolitan government to provide for a contingent of two hundred troops to be drawn from the cities of Quito, Cuenca, and Guayaquil. As for the deliberations of the *cabildo abierto* and the arguments of the Quito *oidores,* the viceroy refused to take them seriously. There was a lapse of five months before he announced his opinion, and when he did so, he gave short shrift to the arguments emanating from Quito. He scornfully dismissed the proposal that the aguardiente monopoly be abolished, observing that pious condemnation of the evils of alcohol was a flimsy cover for unwillingness to pay taxes. The subsidiary proposal—that Quito might send a representative to put its case in Madrid—was conceded, though not without a snub. The cabildo's favorite candidate, Francisco de Borja, was specifically debarred from holding this commission.[43]

When the viceroy made his pronouncement, he was probably persuaded that the opposition in Quito had weakened. Certainly there were some signs that it had slackened after the flurry of antireform activity in late November and early December of the previous year, when Díaz de Herrera had been threatened with violence and the clergy and the audiencia had hindered his efforts to prepare the new excise administration.[44] In the new year, opposition seems to have receded, as the audiencia temporized by placing petty procedural difficulties in Díaz de Herrera's way and the patriciate awaited the viceroy's response to the *cabildo abierto.*[45] In the early months of 1765, the first steps toward the new administration

43. Messía de la Cerda to Arriaga, Santa Fe, February 1, 1765, and "El cabildo secular . . . ," both in AGI, Quito, leg. 398, no. 23, no. 35, fols. 265–67.

44. Díaz de Herrera to Messía de la Cerda, Santa Fe, December 8 and 9, 1764, documents these antireformist activities. AGI, Quito, leg. 398, nos. 10–14.

45. Díaz de Herrera to Messía de la Cerda, Quito, January 18, 1765, AGI, Quito, leg. 398, nos. 20, 24.

went ahead until, on March 1, Díaz de Herrera opened the aguardiente monopoly and its distillery.

At first, sales were slow; rumors circulated that the aguardiente was adulterated, and the audiencia still refused to cooperate with its administrator. However, presented with this *fait accompli,* opposition seems to have faltered. Early in May, *oidor* Juan Romualdo Navarro replaced Félix de Llano as *juez conservador* of the aguardiente monopoly, thus removing a leading opponent from the workings of its administration. In mid-May, Díaz de Herrera confidently reported that the new arrangements were working smoothly, with cooperation from prominent hacendados and no signs of the predicted popular uprising. Quito had no stomach for rebellion.[46] As soon as he proceeded to reform the administration of the sales tax, however, he was proved wrong.

The Entry of the Plebe

On May 22, 1765, the long-anticipated popular reaction against the viceroy's reform finally began. The protests of the elites, expressed through petitions and meetings, were now superseded by direct and forceful action. After failing to achieve their goals by peaceful persuasion, the Quito patricians now found allies among the plebeians who joined in the riot that triggered the first phase of Quito's rebellion.

While Quito's elites opposed the aguardiente monopoly, plebeian antagonism was triggered by reform of the sales tax administration. After his success with installing the aguardiente administration, Díaz de Herrera had moved to reform the *alcabala* and almost immediately aroused popular anger. On May 15, he set up a new machinery for assessing and collecting the sales tax; on May 20, he published a proclamation outlining the penalties for evasion; on May 21, his subordinates registered all plots of land in the parish of San Roque for tax purposes and began the same task in the parish of San Sebastián. They imposed a tax of four pesos per *solar,* in spite of protests that these lands were inadequate even for domestic uses. The tax collectors also began to enforce *alcabala*

46. Llano to Messía de la Cerda, Quito, March 4, 1765, Díaz de Herrera to Viceroy, March 22, 1765, Llano to Messía de la Cerda, Quito, May 3, 1765, Díaz de Herrera to Messía de la Cerda, Quito, May 12, 1765, all in AGI, Quito, leg. 398, nos. 26–27, 29, 33.

payment in areas previously exempt. They demanded that clerics pay taxes on foodstuffs that the latter regarded as alms and gifts. The Indians who came to the city market were also forced to pay tax on small quantities of salt, vegetables, peppers, eggs, and other provisions, and their goods were confiscated if they did not pay. Popular remonstration with the tax collectors evoked an unsympathetic response and threats to erect a gibbet in each parish to deal with complaints. Such official intransigence no doubt encouraged the circulation of wild rumors among the populace during these days before the riot. It was said that plans existed to impose high land taxes, tribute on children in the womb, and taxes on the river stones used by washerwomen, and to create government monopolies on salt, tobacco, potatoes, sugar, and maize.[47]

The circulation of such rumors suggests that the reform of the sales tax evoked strong feelings among several lower-class groups and created a fertile recruiting ground for riot. The assessment of small plots of land for tax was first carried out in the *barrios* of San Roque and San Sebastián, predominantly plebeian parishes that housed concentrations of mestizo artisans and Indian weavers and that were to play a leading role in the rebellion.[48] For such people, new taxation was bound to be a potent source of disaffection. More rigorous collection of taxes on sales would affect the products of their workshops and their plots of land and thus aggravate the problems already present in a city where the main industry was in decline. It would likewise have antagonized the petty traders, mestizo and Indian, who ran small liquor stores and retailed foodstuffs in city markets.

The authorities were ill-prepared when the riot broke out on the night of May 22.[49] Although the city had a population of about thirty thousand, Quito, like most colonial cities, lacked any strong

47. For an account of events leading up to the riot, see the anonymous "Relación sumaria de las dos sublevaciones de la Pleve de Quito," *Boletín de la Academia Nacional de Historia* (Quito), XV (1937), 103. Also, Domingo de Araujo to Messía de la Cerda, Quito, July 13, 1765, AGI, Quito, leg. 398, no. 65.

48. Information on the social composition of these *barrios* is from A. M. Minchom, "Urban Popular Society in Colonial Quito, c. 1700–1800" (Ph.D. dissertation, University of Liverpool, 1984), 220–21, 236.

49. The following reconstruction of the May 22 riot is based on several firsthand accounts, all sent to the viceroy within days of the riot. First, from the audiencia tribunal, Quito, AGI, Quito, leg. 398, no. 39, fols. 281–88; second, from *oidor* Hurtado de Men-

policing apparatus. A regular army garrison was a feature of urban society still mainly confined to ports on strategic coastlines, and for public order government relied on the usual municipal officials and the support of the white citizenry. When the riot began, it was soon apparent that the government was without such support and, accordingly, virtually defenseless.

The riot began at about eight in the evening, when the concerted ringing of parish bells sounded the alarm in the *barrios* of San Blas, San Sebastián, and San Roque and brought their people into darkened streets. The riot focused on the plazuela de Santa Bárbara, where crowds from the *barrios* converged to concentrate around an attack on the royal excise office and aguardiente distillery. Faced with this tumult, the audiencia, together with the corregidor and *alguacil mayor* of Quito, sought to restore order with the only means at their disposal. They sent a small force of about two dozen men to confront the rioters, gathered arms for the defense of the Plaza Mayor, and appealed to the *vecinos* for support, calling on them to take up arms and to illuminate the streets by lighting their doorways, windows, and balconies. However, none of these measures produced the desired effect. The *vecinos* failed to cooperate, while the rioters proved uncontrollable. The patrols led by *oidor* Hurtado de Mendoza and by the *fiscal* Cistué were showered with stones and forced to retreat. Both men reported that they gave orders to fire on the crowd, but were disregarded and deserted by their men. *Oidor* Romualdo Navarro, accompanied by the Conde de Selva Florida, tried to parley with the rioters, but these overtures were rejected, and they, like the other ministers, were forced to retreat to the audiencia palace.[50]

Having failed to quell the riot with a show of force, the audiencia called on the leaders of Quito's religious communities to deal with the rioters. Jesuit intermediaries were sent to the Plaza de Santa Bárbara, and though they were too late to prevent the rioters from breaking into the excise office, spilling its stores of aguar-

doza, *ibid.*, no. 38, fols. 276–80; third, from the corregidor of Quito, *ibid.*, no. 40, fols. 289–94; fourth, from the prelates of the religious communities, *ibid.*, no. 36, fols. 269–71; and fifth, from the bishop of Quito, *ibid.*, no. 37, fols. 272–75.

50. Biblioteca Nacional de Colombia, Libros Raros y Curiosos, Fondo Quijano Otero, MS 179, no. 5; Gregorio Ignacio Hurtado de Mendoza to Messía de la Cerda, Quito, May 24, 1765, AGI, Quito, leg. 398, no. 38; AGI, Quito, leg. 398, no. 67, fols. 426–31.

diente in the streets, and destroying its contents, including the sales-tax records, they did eventually succeed in establishing a dialogue with the crowd. In their efforts to restore order, and presumably in response to the demands of the rioters, the clerics promised that a general pardon would be granted if the crowd dispersed. The crowd then insisted that *oidor* Romualdo Navarro and the Conde de Selva Florida should publicly ratify this promise. Navarro duly appeared before the rioting crowd, which he estimated at around eight thousand men, armed with lances, sticks, stones, and other weapons, and promised them a pardon in the king's name. Finally, the crowd dispersed in the early hours of the morning, after warning Navarro and his companions that failure to honor the promised pardon would cost them their property and their lives.[51]

The end of the riot and the promise of pardon did not immediately restore public order. Having failed to impose its authority by force, the audiencia had now to submit to a humiliating process of negotiation with a turbulent populace, in an atmosphere charged with excitement, fear, and suspicion. The destruction of the excise office, begun on the night of the riot, continued on the following day until it had been completely demolished, stone by stone. Although this demolition was later attributed to the Indians, in order to acquit the people of the *barrios* of any accusation of wanton vandalism, this act clearly had great symbolic importance for the rioters and signaled popular determination to see an end to the new administration. At the same time, the city's parishes remained in such an agitated state that the audiencia feared another uprising, this time in confederation with the largely Indian villages of the city's hinterland.[52]

To forestall further disturbances, the leaders of the religious communities, together with the bishop of Quito, toured the parishes to reassure the populace that neither the king nor the viceroy wished to harm common interests. But the *barrios* remained distrustful and demanded that the clerics persuade the audiencia to give solemn and official assurances that the new fiscal plans would be abandoned and a general pardon extended to all the rioters. The

51. AGI, Quito, leg. 398, no. 67, fol. 429.

52. Domingo de Araujo to Messía de la Cerda, Quito, July 13, 1765, AGI, Quito, leg. 398, no. 65; AGI, Quito, leg. 398, no. 34, fols. 281–88.

audiencia was reluctant to meet these terms, but agreed to publish an *auto de perdón*. This was initially couched in vague and ambiguous terms, as the audiencia tried to win time while leaving the way open for later punishment of the rioters.[53] This failed to deceive the rebels, who pressured the *oidores* to make real concessions. It was agreed that the bishop should go to the *barrio* of San Roque—described as the most populous of the city's parishes—and talk with the rioters. After preaching a sermon of peace and reconciliation, the bishop conferred with the assembled people and relayed their message to the audiencia. This called for a great general public meeting in the city's main square, the Plaza Mayor, where they would declare their loyalty to the king in return for clear ratification of the general pardon and of the abolition of the new fiscal administration.

To meet this demand, the judges of the audiencia assembled in the courtyard of their palace, together with an armed escort and flanked by artillery primed to fire. In their presence, the bishop went forward with *oidor* Romualdo Navarro to confront the "multitude of people" congregated in the square. They announced a general pardon and suspended the aguardiente monopoly and the new *alcabala* administration. When told that this decision needed viceregal confirmation, the crowd was distinctly displeased. After Romualdo Navarro insisted that the audiencia had gone to the limits of its power, however, the assembled people dispersed and returned to their homes.[54] An uneasy calm now settled on the city.

The Crowd and Its Composition

Clearly, the riot was an important escalation of the dispute over reform. It opened a new phase in the protest against the viceroy's fiscal reforms, in which patrician negotiation gave way to popular action and new actors had entered the political arena.

The numbers involved in the riot cannot be accurately gauged. Because contemporary estimates vary from a credible three to four thousand to an improbable sixteen to eighteen thousand, they indicate only that the crowds were impressively large. The social

53. Bishop of Quito to Messía de la Cerda, Quito, May 24, 1765, Audiencia of Quito to Messía de la Cerda, Quito, May 24, 1765, both in AGI, Quito, leg. 398, nos. 37, 34.

54. Bishop of Quito to Messía de la Cerda, Quito, May 24, 1765, AGI, Quito, leg. 398, no. 37. This is the only account of this meeting.

identity of the rioters is also difficult to determine because contemporary descriptions are vague, and we have no trial records to provide even a sample of those who took part. In describing the rioters, contemporaries refer to the "plebeians" or to the "people of the *barrios*," but as these terms are not clearly defined, the composition of the crowds remains rather blurred.

Contemporary commentators agreed that the riot was the work of more than one social group. The audiencia stated that "the conspiracy was general among all classes and orders." The corregidor of Quito, Manuel Sánchez Osorio, was equally convinced that leading citizens were responsible for the riot. He not only denounced Francisco de Borja and other cabildo members for stirring up popular feeling with their campaign against the monopoly, but he also alleged that "people of the better sort" must have been implicated in the riot, as the rabble was incapable of such organized action.[55] Contemporary references to a secret investigation of the riot, conducted by *oidor* Hurtado de Mendoza, also suggest that prominent members of *quiteño* society had been involved in the riot, though, as no action was ever taken against any such individual, such allegations remained unproven.[56]

Whatever its leadership, the main body of the rioting crowd was drawn from various segments of the city's population. The riot started in the slaughterhouse district, and according to Juan de Velasco, it was started by a group of some sixty butchers. When they attacked the excise house, they were then joined by some three to four thousand people from other *barrios*.[57] The "plebeians" who rioted were also joined by Indians who, on the following day,

55. Audiencia to Messía de la Cerda, Quito, May 24, 1765, Manuel Sanchez Osorio y Pareja to Messía de la Cerda, Quito, May 26, 1765, both in AGI, Quito, leg. 398, nos. 34, 35.

56. Hurtado recorded sending the results of this secret investigation to the viceroy in August, 1765, and said that it included the testimonies of eighty-one witnesses, from "all classes and hierarchies." Hurtado de Mendoza to Messía de la Cerda, Quito, September 30, 1765, AHNC, Milicias y Marina, tomo 123, fols. 138–39. Unfortunately, this document is not included among the papers directly related to the rebellion, and though there are other references to it, it has not been found. The references suggest that it was sent on to the viceroy in Santa Fe and subsequently to the Consejo de Indias, but despite a search in the correspondence of the Audiencia of Quito, the viceroy of New Granada, and the Consejo de Indias found in the archives of Santa Fe, Seville, and Madrid, these papers have not been traced.

57. Velasco, *Historia del Reino de Quito,* I, 144.

dismantled the excise building and carried away its materials. The riot itself, however, seems to have been mainly the work of "plebeians," so called because they were mestizos and poor whites rather than Indians.[58]

The riot was not, then, simply the work of a disorganized rabble drawn from the lowest ranks of city society. While a *lumpenproletariat* of transient workers, vagabonds, and beggars may have been drawn into the riot, its driving force came from the artisans, small tradesmen, and shopkeepers who were the bedrock of the city's business.[59] These were the people who felt most threatened by the viceroy's projected reforms, particularly that of the sales tax, since they promised to place new burdens on the most common forms of exchange. And, because they were associated in guilds and confraternities, and in daily contact through their economic activities, such groups had an organizational basis that could be mobilized for political ends when necessary.

The plebeians who rioted must also have been aware that they enjoyed widespread sympathy among the city's population. Certainly the behavior of *quiteños* during the riot indicates a broad basis of support for the rioters' objectives. During the riot, few complied with the audiencia's orders to illuminate the streets by lighting their houses, and from a white population of several thousand, only about twenty prominent *vecinos* rallied to the audiencia's call for aid. This indifference persisted after the riot. Although measures were taken to raise militia companies in the days after the riot, militiamen failed to stay at their posts, while merchants and traders evaded enlistment by closing up their shops and going into hiding, showing a disloyal attitude, which, the audiencia averred, was shared by the clergy and many private citizens.[60] However, though officials were eager to show that the elite were involved in the riot, their presumption that the plebeians were simply the instruments of a conspiracy within the creole "nobility" should not

58. Domingo de Araujo, who was later appointed counsel for the *barrios* of San Roque, San Blas, and San Sebastián, referred to "mestizos and criollo plebeians," whom he distinguished from the Indians who dismantled the excise building. AGI, Quito, leg. 398, no. 65, fol. 412.

59. For a description of the social groups of Quito, see Jorge Juan and Antonio de Ulloa, *A Voyage to South America,* ed. and trans. John Adams (New York, 1964), 135–46.

60. AGI, Quito, leg. 398, no. 42, fols. 297–305.

be taken at face value. The plebeians were not simply the manipulable instrument of upper-class cliques. They were instead part of an alliance between social groups, and though they may have been influenced by patrician patronage, they had their own grievances and objectives. These were reflected in both the timing of the first riot and the subsequent movement toward rebellion when patrician objectives were overtaken by other issues and demands.

How these different social groups were brought together is not entirely clear. The role attributed to the city's butchers in promoting the riot suggests that petty tradesmen were the vital intermediary group who mobilized and led a popular tumult that joined the patrician campaign against the aguardiente monopoly. Certainly the parish of Santa Bárbara—where the butchers had their shops and where the riot took place—had a greater social mixture than the more popular and more mestizo *barrios* of San Roque and San Sebastián and was accordingly more open to creole political influence.

It is also possible that plebeian defiance of the authorities was legitimized, even promoted, by sections of the clergy, particularly the regular clergy, who enjoyed close relations with lay society. When the audiencia referred to the participation of all classes in the riot, it did not exclude the clergy, and there were strong suspicions that clerics, particularly from the monastic houses, were involved. As we have seen, elements of Quito's large clerical population had strong motives for disliking the aguardiente monopoly reform, and their leaders had actively opposed the viceroy's reform, disguising their material interest by appeal to moral considerations. Indeed, on the very day of the riot, the bishop issued orders to the abbesses of Quito's convents stating that under no circumstances should they participate in the now illegal private trade in aguardiente. And the secular clergy, led by the bishop of Quito, were also involved in a conflict with the government due to the efforts to the *fiscal* José de Cistué to curb clerical exploitation of the Indians.[61]

We have no direct reports on the role of the parish clergy or the monasteries in the popular uprising. But both, and particularly

61. Bishop of Quito to Messía de la Cerda, Santa Fe, May 22, 1765, AGI, Quito, leg. 398, no. 34; Messía de la Cerda to Arriaga, Quito, April 9, 1767, AGI, Quito, leg. 399, no. 419.

the monasteries, had abundant opportunities for spreading dissent to a wider population. Juan and Ulloa's account of the Quito clergy suggests that the regulars, particularly the Franciscans, were intimately involved in the city's social and political life. Not only did the monks have an essentially secular lifestyle, often living outside their monasteries, maintaining mistresses, and fathering children, but they were also organizers of the *fandangos* that brought them together with lay men and women in dissolute drinking parties. Such social contact was paralleled by the overlap of civil and ecclesiastical politics. It was common, Juan and Ulloa observed, for disputes between clerical factions—often between Europeans and Americans—to spread outwards into the lay population, arousing and dividing it into competing groups and creating discord. Indeed, there was a major instance of such discord in 1747–1748, when the plebeians of the *barrio* of San Roque mobilized behind a Franciscan faction in a protracted series of popular disturbances, the most serious to occur in eighteenth-century Quito before those of 1765.[62] Thus, given the interest of monastic houses in both the production and sale of aguardiente and their close links with different social groups in Quito, the regular clergy had both a purpose for encouraging opposition to reform and a position from which they might link different social groups in a common movement.

The timing of the May riot certainly strengthens speculation about clerical involvement, facilitated by an overlap of secular and ecclesiastical activity. For it fell within the period of preparation for the great festival of Corpus Christi, a time when the urban confraternities came together to organize and celebrate a major ritual event under the auspices of the clergy.[63] In the days after the riot, popular preparation for this festival (which occurred on June 5 in 1765) could have provided an associational structure for extending and continuing the political organization of the populace in opposition to the authorities. The organization behind the May riot clearly did not dissolve with the suspension of the reformed aguardiente monopoly and *alcabala* administrations. The riot had released emotions that were difficult to control, and the

62. Juan and Ulloa, *Discourse and Political Reflections,* 283–86, 294–98; Minchom, "Urban Popular Society," 340–46.

63. On this festival, see Minchom, "Urban Popular Society," 145–49.

popular *barrios* remained in a volatile state. In the words of a contemporary observer, "The heat of victory gave off a smoke that filled their eyes and blinded them to the enormity of their crime."[64]

Repercussions of the Riot

Recognizing the instability of the situation and aware of its isolation, the audiencia proceeded cautiously in the weeks following the riot. After issuing the general pardon, it suspended all the usual demonstrations of government authority in the city. Street patrols were canceled, the new excise was inoperative, and Díaz de Herrera and his subordinates remained in hiding.[65] Such caution was dictated by circumstances, for the *barrios* were still restive and threatening. On May 26, there was a commotion in the *barrio* of San Blas; this was followed by a general mobilization of all the *barrios* on May 29, when threats to stone or burn down the houses of officials were averted only by the intervention of clerics on both that and the following day. One of those threatened was *oidor* Hurtado de Mendoza, whose efforts to conduct an inquiry into the riot met with intimidation of witnesses and threats to raze his house.[66]

This did not mean that order had broken down completely in Quito. On the contrary, the *barrios* called for the resumption of patrols to deal with petty crime and were quite prepared to countenance the arrest of common criminals. This respect for the law was reflected in an incident in the parish of San Blas. When an *alcalde* arrested a local criminal, his brother, seeking to take advantage of the unstable political conditions, sounded the tocsin and called up a tumult in the *barrio*. The parishes of San Sebastián and San Roque, however, offered to come to the magistrate's aid, and when the people of San Blas discovered why the tocsin had

64. "Relación sumaria," 104.

65. Díaz de Herrera sought sanctuary in a Franciscan convent, where he remained until June 21, when he finally left the city under cover of darkness with an armed escort provided by the Marqués de Villa Orellana and returned to Bogotá. Díaz de Herrera to Messía de la Cerda, Popayán, July 22, 1765, AHNC, Milicias y Marina, tomo 123, fols. 88–93.

66. Biblioteca Nacional de Colombia, Libros Raros y Curiosos, Fondo Quijano Otero, MS 179, no. 5; Hurtado de Mendoza to Messía de la Cerda, Quito, July 4, 1765, AGI, Quito, leg. 398, fol. 341.

been sounded, they not only restored order but also handed over the individual who had sounded the alarm.[67] The *barrios* were, then, ready to maintain order and capable of doing so in an organized manner.

A consensus against common criminality did not extend, however, to government treatment of rioters as criminals. The rapidity with which the *barrios* assembled to the sound of the alarm indicates that they remained on their guard, ready to oppose any reprisal against the rioters of May 22 or other unwanted interference. Other incidents also mirrored this state of popular agitation. On June 8, pasquinades calling for the expulsion of peninsular Spaniards appeared in the city, followed by demands on June 14 for a proclamation announcing this expulsion. On June 18, a crowd from San Blas careered through the streets to demonstrate in front of the bishop's palace, demanding a parish priest of their choice and refusing to disperse until the bishop acceded. On June 19, to the sound of bells and fireworks, San Blas rose again and launched an abortive attack on the jail to try to release a prisoner recently taken into custody. This was prevented by *oidor* Romualdo Navarro, who defended the jail with a heavily armed patrol and, after several hours of confrontation, forced the rioters to disband without achieving their object.[68]

The increasingly agitated state of the *barrios* in mid-June suggests an incipient radicalization of the movement born in protest at fiscal reform. For, with the weakness of government revealed by the May riot, new issues were drawn in, and anti-Spanish feelings were starting to surface. But the troubles of June must also be seen in the context of the city's social and religious calendar, for the disturbances of mid-June occurred during the approach of a major festival, St. John's Day, on June 24. An important date in both the secular and ecclesiastical calendar and a time when the Indians paid a half-yearly installment of tribute, St. John's Day was associated with a period of celebration that, under normal circumstances, would have called for more intensive policing in the city. In the

67. "Relación sumaria," 104.

68. Biblioteca Nacional de Colombia, Libros Raros y Curiosos, Fondo Quijano Otero, MS 179, no. 5; AHNC, Milicias y Marina, tomo 125, fols. 93–95; AGI, Quito, leg. 398, no. 67, fol. 43.

aftermath of the May riot, however, any official show of force risked a strong response from *barrios* that had already shown their suspicion that policing would bring reprisals for the May riot. Thus, when on the night of June 23 the corregidor of Quito conducted a patrol through the parishes of San Roque and San Sebastián, his behavior stimulated further agitation. The patrol rounded up dozens of prisoners and took them to the city jail, where fines were levied and whippings administered.[69] At least one of those whipped by the corregidor was a creole, which seems to have aroused considerable anger and to have fueled the suspicion that the authorities were planning retribution for the May riot. The people of the *barrios* now began to mobilize once more, aided no doubt by the occasion of the festival. On St. John's night itself, rioting again broke out in a major recrudescence of urban disorder. With it went all hopes for a gradual restoration of royal authority, and Quito now entered a more serious phase of rebellion.

The "Noche de San Juan"

The first signs of renewed rebelliousness appeared on the morning of June 24, when pasquinades posted in San Roque called for a union of all the *barrios* against the corregidor of Quito and threatened to burn down his house. Throughout the day, rumors of a popular uprising swept through the city, facilitated no doubt by the drinking and carousing of a public holiday. In the late afternoon, the president of the audiencia was warned of this danger, but was told by representatives from the *barrios* of San Roque and San Sebastián that such fears were exaggerated. He took no action until some hours later, when the corregidor arrived in alarm to inform him that about three hundred men from San Sebastián were moving to join forces with those of San Roque. Rubio de Arévalo ordered a cannon shot to be fired, as a prearranged signal for citizens to rally to the defense of the city. About a hundred men, including all the available peninsular Spaniards resident in Quito and many prominent creoles, assembled at the audiencia palace. However, deciding that the tumult was no more than a rowdy affray

69. Unless otherwise indicated, this account of events leading up to the June 24, 1765, riot is based on the report made by the audiencia president. Manuel Rubio de Arévalo to Messía de la Cerda, Quito, July 11, 1765, AGI, Quito, leg. 398, no. 62, fols. 391–400.

like those of preceding nights, the majority decided to return to their homes.[70]

Had the matter been left there, nothing further might have happened. But among those who remained was an aggressive group of peninsular Spaniards, led by the corregidor Sánchez Osorio, who insisted that a patrol should be sent out into the city. The *oidores* Romualdo Navarro, Santa Cruz, and Hurtado de Mendoza argued against this, sensibly seeking to avoid confrontation. But the corregidor insisted that there was a riot in the *barrio* of San Sebastián and prevailed upon the audiencia president to dispatch an armed patrol to contain it. Thus, at about ten o'clock on St. John's night, the corregidor led his Spanish friends and allies to sally out toward San Sebastián. En route, they attempted to make some arrests and, when they encountered resistance, opened fire on a crowd, killing two of its members. From this moment, events moved towards a swift and violent climax.[71]

After fighting with the crowd, the patrol was forced to retreat, and it headed for the protection of the audiencia palace. Now popular anti-Spanish feeling, already apparent before this riot, came into the open. The rioters first turned their attention to the house of Angel Izquierdo, a Cádiz merchant reputed to have been one of those who had fired on the crowd. When Izquierdo learned of the danger to his home, he rushed a group of some fifteen men and a mortar to defend his family and property. After a protracted fight with several hundred rioters who had seized his house, Izquierdo and his party were driven back by weight of numbers, losing their mortar in the process and leaving the crowd to ransack the house, destroying Izquierdo's belongings, but allowing his wife and child to escape unharmed.[72]

70. This was reported by Fernando de Echandía, a peninsular Spaniard who was personally involved in these events. "Relación del nuevo tumulto popular acaecido en la Ciudad de Quito," AHNC, Milicias y Marina, tomo 123, fols. 93–95.

71. This reconstruction of the riot and events that followed is based on several sources: the report of the audiencia (AGI, Quito, leg. 398, no. 52, fols. 324–35); that of Domingo de Araujo (AGI, Quito, leg. 398, no. 65, fols. 409–17); and the anonymous "Relación sumaria," 105–109. Where other sources provide additional detail, they are cited separately.

72. A graphic personal account of the riot and the attack on Izquierdo's house, including the ordeal of his wife, was given by Izquierdo himself. It is reprinted in "Noticia de

By now, the main scene of battle had moved to the Plaza Mayor and centered on the palace of the audiencia and its small guard of officials, soldiers, and volunteers, most of whom were peninsular Spaniards. The rioters launched determined attacks on the audiencia palace, dividing their forces in separate actions against its two entrances. The audiencia later estimated that this attack involved ten thousand men, armed not only with sticks and stones, but with lances, swords, and some firearms. This figure was doubtless exaggerated, as the defeated audiencia had every reason to overestimate the forces it had confronted. Nonetheless, all contemporary reports indicate that the mobs were very large and far outnumbered the forces seeking to restrain them. Their attacks continued from around eleven o'clock at night until four o'clock in the morning, and left many dead among the rebels and several wounded among the besieged defending force.[73] Near dawn, various bands renewed the assault and killed two of the defenders before retreating among their own dead and wounded. By now, the rebel force had swelled still more; groups of rebels were spread all over the city, and reinforcements continued to arrive from the neighboring country villages.

The day after the "noche de San Juan," the fighting slowed. But the rising was not yet over, and its consequences had yet fully to be felt. The small force of 150 defenders in the audiencia palace had managed to fend off repeated attacks, but exhausted by its efforts and facing overwhelming numbers, it could not sustain its position. Attempts were made to negotiate with the rebels, using clerical intermediaries. The bishop and other leading ecclesiastics went to the *barrios* of San Roque, San Sebastián, and San Blas, where they sought to persuade some "more rational" plebeians to mollify the fury of mobs that "moved by depraved designs . . . ,

---

los movimientos de Quito en el año de 1765," *Museo Histórico* (Quito), III, no. 9 (1951), 37–54.

73. Eyewitness accounts of the fighting were given by soldiers who testified to the leading role of the *alcalde* Mariano Monteserín in the defense of the palace. These are reprinted in "Sublevación de Quito por la Aduana y los Estancos," *Museo Histórico* (Quito), II, no. 7 (1950), 25–37, III, no. 8 (1951), 16, 31. Domingo de Araujo reported that between three and five hundred persons among the "gente miserable" were killed without the death of a single European. The two whites killed were both creoles. AGI, Quito, leg. 398, no. 65, fol. 417.

wanted to make the whole city the spoil of their ambition."[74] But efforts at peacemaking failed. By the close of the day, the audiencia was told that more than five hundred Indians had joined the ranks of the rebels in San Blas, that the entrances and aqueducts of the city were occupied and food and water supplies therefore blocked, and that another great rising was being organized in the *barrios*. Deciding that their position was hopeless, the officials and their allies went into hiding, seeking sanctuary in churches, monasteries, and convents, and placing the royal treasury funds in the care of the Jesuits. At nightfall, crowds advanced again into the city center and, meeting no opposition, celebrated their victory.

The St. John's night riot was, in one sense, simply an extension of the protest expressed in the first riot in May. Because it stemmed from the official efforts to reimpose the social discipline that had been broken in the May riot, it rekindled earlier antagonisms toward government. When the corregidor's patrol provoked a street incident, the people of the *barrios*—still on their guard against reprisals for the earlier tumult—were quick to respond. But this second riot was also qualitatively different, for now the rioters were no longer just protesting against fiscal reform. The June riot was a more spontaneous and more violent outburst, born in different circumstances and with different aims. The corregidor's draconian methods of reasserting his authority confirmed rumors that the Europeans planned to punish a *plebe* that they despised and fueled popular animosity towards Europeans.[75] Furthermore, while the occasion of a public festival provided a rationale for resuming strong policing in the streets, such a festival also provided a cultural context for expressing popular antagonism towards authority.[76] In such an atmosphere of public suspicion and excitement, the corregidor's tactics had the opposite of

74. AGI, Quito, leg. 398, no. 52, fol. 327.

75. Domingo de Araujo argued that the riot would not have occurred if it had not been for the behavior of the "European faction." He explained that the Europeans, who despised American Spaniards in Quito, and even more the plebeian mestizos and creoles, persuaded the corregidor to punish the rioters, using the street patrol as a pretext for violent retribution against the *barrios* for their pride and ardor. AGI, Quito, leg. 398, no. 65, fol. 412.

76. St. John's Day was a *día de precepto*, a holiday when attendance at Mass was obligatory. See "Notas historicas. Fiestas que se celebran en Quito a fines del siglo XVIII," *Boletín de la Academia Nacional de Historia* (Quito), VII (1923), no. 19, 262–66. As no contemporary description of the festival in the city of Quito itself is available, it is not clear

the intended effect. Far from dampening disorder, they provoked an incident that sparked a great riot and brought disaster on the government.

Directed initially against the members of the patrol involved in the street clash, popular retaliation grew into a more general attack on the bastions of authority. As the European Spaniards, who had attacked the crowd in the name of authority and justice, sought refuge behind the shield of government, so the crowds, attacking the Spaniards in search of their own retributory justice, were drawn into an assault on government itself. Thus Quito's second great riot was not only more violent than the first, it was also anti-European and antigovernment and, born in the popular *barrios* themselves, laced with the enmity of the poor towards the wealthy. When the riot subsided, the damage done was not easily repaired. A major urban insurrection was under way, with a dynamic of its own, and it was to be some months before order was fully restored. For these reasons, the riot of the "noche de San Juan" had more serious implications than the riot of May 22 and marked a second, more radical phase in Quito's rebellion.

From Riot to Rebellion

After the riot, the balance of power in the city changed dramatically. Gangs attacked the property of some of the Spaniards who had gone into hiding, and the authorities were unable to intervene. The audiencia, defeated and destitute of authority, had no alternative but to negotiate. On the morning of June 26, the ministers convened a meeting with the bishop, only to have their weakness fully revealed. Soon after they arrived in the palace, a large crowd, estimated at more than two thousand people, surrounded the building and began to insult and threaten them. Francisco de Borja then appeared, together with two Jesuits, to mediate between the crowd and the ministers. The crowd demanded the surrender of firearms held in the royal stores. Eventually, a compromise was reached, after the *oidores* present had personally pleaded

what specific ritual activities it might have involved. In the provincial town of Otavalo, however, it was a major festival in which *barrios* competed, masks and disguises were used, and Indians engaged in dances and mock battles. See Pedro de Carvalho Neto, *Antología del folklore ecuatoriano, 1653–1963* (Quito, 1964), 168–74.

with the assembled people. It was agreed that clerics should conduct these arms to the Monastery of San Domingo and hold them there. Other concessions are also said to have been made, including the release of prisoners from jail, the exchange of prisoners taken by the crowds for those under sentence of death, and the removal of troops from the city.[77] But though the priests were allowed to carry off some small arms, the crowd soon broke its side of the bargain and carried off the cannons to the *barrios*.

The situation now became still more confused and volatile. Several observers reported that many Indians from the surrounding villages started to move into the city and that even more were assembled in the neighboring Valley of Anaquito. *Oidor* Hurtado, who stated that more than three thousand Indians had entered the city on June 26, feared that they would also rebel, refusing to pay tribute and killing the whites. Although many Indians probably came into the city at this time—St. John's Day being both an important festival and the time for a half-yearly payment of tributes—whether any real threat existed that the disorders in Quito would encourage an Indian rebellion in its rural hinterland or lead to an alliance between urban plebeians and indigenous peasants is unclear. Talk of such a threat may have been no more than an attempt by the authorities and their allies to distract the Quito rebels. Certainly the audiencia tried to use fears of an Indian invasion and rebellion to bring the urban populace back to order. Using parish priests as intermediaries, it sought to manipulate ethnic divisions, playing on the mestizos' dislike of the Indians to persuade them that the Indians were a danger to all.[78] But this failed to win the *barrios* over, or to convince them to return stolen arms. Indeed, it was said that the cannons were used to fortify the main entrances to the city to keep the Indians at bay.[79]

After the violence and excitement had subsided, the implications of the June riot became clearer. The city was in the hands of

77. AHNC, Milicias y Marina, tomo 123, fols. 93–95; AGI, Quito, leg. 398, no. 62, fol. 396; "Relación sumaria," 110.

78. AGI, Quito, leg. 398, no. 55, fols. 340–45, no. 52, fol. 331.

79. Domingo de Araujo to Messía de la Cerda, Quito, July 13, 1765, AGI, Quito, leg. 398, no. 65. Araujo was the only observer to detail the response of the *barrios* to the threat of an Indian invasion; he also stated that Indians attacked various entrances of the city. However, no other evidence exists of such armed conflict between the Indian peasants and urban mestizos.

armed rebels who had effectively overturned the political hierarchy and who, because their power rested on the force of popular action, implicitly threatened the stability of the social order. But how serious was the challenge to the constituted political and social order? Was Spanish sovereignty in danger? Did the entry of the plebeians radicalize the rebellion or introduce any sense of incipient social revolution?

Fernando de Echandía, a peninsular who had been in Quito throughout the period of the riots and who stayed until July 2, took a very somber view of recent events. He reported that government had been completely subverted and replaced by the rule of the people. The people, he said, "have made themselves magistrates, ordering gibbets to be built in various places, dealing with disputes, giving freedom to slaves and freeing the Indians from tribute; and, what is more, swearing allegiance to a new king." It seems that they had attempted to persuade the creole aristocrat the Conde de Selva Florida to become their king, and though he emphatically refused, they went on to depose "all that bore resemblance to royal justice," replacing it with their own proclamations and laws, and showing disrespect even for the Holy Sacrament.[80]

This was almost certainly an exaggerated version of events in Quito. It was written by a man who had been among the Spaniards expelled from the city by the rebels, and who had every reason to view the rebellion in a dramatic light, colored by his personal experience of anti-Spanish feeling in the city. Nonetheless, other accounts also suggest that the anti-tax movement begun in May did take on a more subversive tone after the St. John's night riot as underlying social tensions came to the surface. Royal government had broken down, hostility toward Europeans had come into the open, and effective government had passed into the hands of local tribunes who enjoyed popular trust and acclaim. The audiencia, clinging to the tattered shreds of its dignity, could do no more than bend with the prevailing political winds. On June 27, it was forced to divorce itself from the cause of the European Span-

80. "Relación del nuevo Tumulto . . . ," AHNC, Milicias y Marina, tomo 123, fols. 93–95. Echandía was among the peninsulars expelled from Quito, and he sent his account of events in the city while in Pasto on July 11, en route to Popayán. It was sent to Pedro Agustín de Valencia in Popayán, who forwarded it to the viceroy.

iards and to order their expulsion from the city, within the term of a week.[81] It was also forced to accede to demands for another general pardon, this time for the insurrection that was still under way.

The only concession that the audiencia was able to obtain was that the expulsion order should not include those peninsulars who were married and permanently resident in the city. Otherwise, its surrender was complete. It was, moreover, conveyed in full public gaze on June 28, in an extraordinary ceremony in the Plaza Mayor, in front of the audiencia palace. A ceremonial bench was placed on its balcony, and the *oidores,* the dean of the cathedral chapter, the ecclesiastical cabildo, the prelates of the regular orders, some city councilors, and "vecinos nobles" were arraigned upon it, looking out over the four or five thousand people from the *barrios* who filled the main square. A singular spectacle then took place. The president of the audiencia called out "long live the king," bringing an enthusiastic response from the crowd. A speech from one of the ministers followed, pardoning the rebels before the bishop gave them absolution, which they received on their knees. Finally, the crowd dispersed peacefully, amidst a mood of reconciliation and with promises of future good behavior.[82]

This affirmation of loyalty to the crown did not, however, immediately restore order in Quito. For at least two months after the St. John's night riot, the authority of colonial government in Quito was essentially titular, and the audiencia lived in fear of further disturbances. In the immediate aftermath of the riot, anger focused on those who had fought the crowds and who were thought to oppose the *barrios. Oidor* Hurtado de Mendoza went into hiding, in fear of the mob, as did corregidor Sánchez Osorio, and the *alguacil mayor,* Antonio de Salas. The *fiscal* Cistué also took religious sanctuary before he fled the city in early July, seeking to escape to Santa Fe.[83] The nonresident peninsulars were also forced to leave, in accord with the agreement made between the rebels and the audiencia. Government now passed into the hands of men

81. "Relación sumaria," 111. A list of eighty-one peninsulars was drawn up, of whom twenty-five were liable for expulsion.

82. AGI, Quito, leg. 398, no. 68, fol. 434.

83. AGI, Quito, leg. 398, no. 54, fols. 336–37, no. 54, fol. 339; Cistué to Messía de la Cerda, Guanacas, September 9, 1765, AGI, Quito, leg. 398, no. 105, fol. 507.

acceptable to the *barrios*, who enjoyed an uneasy and conditional authority over the populace.

To restore its own authority, the audiencia turned to the creole patriciate and the religious communities, particularly the Jesuits. The audiencia chose prominent creoles acceptable to the *barrios* to act as "captains" or "deputies," giving them the right to police the city, and sent a Jesuit mission into the parishes of San Roque, San Sebastián, San Blas, and Santa Bárbara. By July 2, the captains of the *barrios* were in position, and organized by the Conde de Selva Florida, they were instrumental in persuading the *barrios* to return stolen arms to the officers of the crown. On July 3, president Rubio de Arévalo also reported on the captains' activity in the *barrios*, stating that their presence promised the possibility of negotiations and so gave reason for hope. Within a short time, this hope was fulfilled. On July 4, people from all the *barrios* convened once again in the Plaza Mayor, and amidst protestations of fidelity and repentance, they handed over the captured arms. The *oidores* were forced to restate the pardon they had granted, and the arms were then solemnly returned, amid much public clamor. Finally, as a symbol of the city's loyalty, the royal standard was raised on the balcony of the audiencia palace, to be kept illuminated for three days and nights.[84] Thus, in the aftermath of the St. John's night riot, an informal government emerged in the city as the audiencia was forced to rely upon creole notables to sustain royal authority.[85]

84. AGI, Quito, leg. 398, no. 62, fol. 399, no. 52, fol. 333, no. 53, fols. 336–38, no. 56, fols. 346–47, no. 57, fols. 348–49; Pedro Agustín de Valencia to Messía de la Cerda, Popayán, July 17, 1765, AHNC, Milicias y Marina, tomo 123, fol. 85; AGI, Quito, leg. 398, no. 58, fol. 350.

85. Audiencia to Messía de la Cerda, Quito, July 13, 1765, AGI, Quito, leg. 398, no. 64. In this letter the audiencia stated that these captains were "from the highest nobility" and that their purpose was to serve "as interlocutors and emissaries" with the "vulgo" so that the latter might communicate its ideas. Those appointed were the Conde de Selva Florida (for the *barrio* de San Roque), Don Nicholas Calixto de Alarcon (for San Sebastián), Don Mariano Perez de Ubillas (for San Blas), Don Joseph Lasso de la Vega (for Santa Bárbara), and Don Manuel González and Don Francisco de Borja (for San Marcos). Two priests (Don Ramón Yepes and Don Ramón Monteserin González) were also involved in negotiation with the *barrios*. The two *alcaldes ordinarios*, together with some of the regidores of the cabildo, also played a part in government, but the corregidor Sánchez Osorio remained in hiding.

This "aristocratic government," as it was called by audiencia president Rubio de Arévalo, was the only effective force in the city for the remainder of the year. The audiencia was generally powerless, unable to do much more than tolerate popular demands while secretly encouraging the creole patriciate's efforts to restrain such demands. Despite the audiencia's initial optimism after the ceremony of July 4, the rebellion was still far from finished. The people of the *barrios* continued to assert themselves, amidst official fears that open insurrection might flare up again in the city and that rebellion might spread to the provinces. Reports emanating from the city throughout August testify to these anxieties and the continuing problems facing the audiencia. At the beginning of the month, treasury officials reported that they were having great difficulty in collecting taxes. Not only had revenues from the *alcabala* declined considerably within the city, but, due to the threat of violent rejection, they were unable to find tax-farmers for the rural hinterland and had been forced to suspend *alcabala* collection there. Toward the end of the month, the audiencia reported that the city was quiet, partly as a result of an epidemic that had affected most homes. It confirmed the earlier report of a virtual breakdown in the taxation system, however, stating that the Quito plebeians had sent many emissaries out to the Indian villages, inciting them to refuse tribute, and that, in consequence, collecting taxes in the area of Quito, Latacunga, and Ambato was difficult and risky.[86]

Plebeian rebelliousness was, then, expressed mainly by refusal to pay taxes or to tolerate assertions of authority by European Spaniards and showed few signs of seeking fundamental changes in the political and social order. There were, however, some signs that an incoherent lower-class radicalism had found some space to develop in the aftermath of the June riot, for reluctance to pay taxes was not the only sign of continuing popular insubordination. The informal government headed by the creole captains also found it difficult to overcome popular disregard for other aspects of the law, and it seems that popular resentments were being openly expressed through delinquency and disobedience.

86. Salvador Sanchez Pareja and Juan Antonio Abel de Blas to Messía de la Cerda, Quito, August 3, 1765, Audiencia to Messía de la Cerda, Quito, August 25, 1765, both in AGI, Quito, leg. 398, no. 92, fols. 480–81, no. 99, fols. 495–96.

The captains reported a great increase in crime after the June riot, which, as magistrates, they tried to combat by creating district militias to maintain day and night patrols. This, however, was not welcomed by the plebeians, who, having "thrown off the yoke of Justice and broken the reins of Obedience," threatened the lives and property of the captains and challenged their decisions as magistrates. That the resentments of the poor underpinned this defiance is reflected in the comment of the *barrio* captains that it was difficult to convince all the plebeians "that being poor was not a safe-conduct for crimes, nor a passport for excesses."[87] Such popular inversion of the official version of justice was no doubt helped by the takeover of minor posts in municipal government by plebeian leaders and the recognition that all such positions were "at the behest of the *barrios*."[88] Moreover, these *barrio* leaders sought to control the movement of Europeans in and out of the city, claiming the right to give licenses to peninsular merchants for specified periods, limited to the time necessary for their business. Differences over how Europeans should be treated were beginning to divide the rebels, however. In mid-September, Francisco de Borja and other leading captains of the *barrios* had to order all the "delegates and leading citizens of all the *barrios*" to help transfer the corregidor from the convent of San Francisco to the cabildo because his life was being threatened.[89]

If plebeian autonomy within Quito was a major worry for the audiencia, its anxiety was aggravated by the fear that the city's example would be imitated in the provinces, spreading rebellion throughout the highlands. At the end of May and in early June, there were riots against the aguardiente monopoly and *alcabalas* in Ibarra, Otavalo, and Cuenca, all of them imitating the action taken by Quito's *barrios*. Such action naturally aroused fears of a general rebellion in the provinces, and to avert this danger, the audiencia instructed all corregidores and other provincial officials to proceed with special caution, to avoid recourse to arms unless life and

87. Diputados de los barrios to Messía de la Cerda, Quito, September 19, 1765, AGI, Quito, leg. 398, no. 106, fols. 519–22.

88. Letter, Guanacas, AGI, Quito, leg. 398, no. 105, fol. 509. In this letter, *fiscal* Cistué referred to mestizo leaders; his list of leaders includes several Indian names.

89. *Ibid.*, fol. 511; Phelipe Baquero, Quito, September 19, 1765, AGI, Quito, leg. 398, no. 110.

property were endangered, and to suspend the aguardiente monopoly, if necessary to preserve order.[90]

This conciliatory policy seems to have worked well, although, as the riots of Quito developed into rebellion, fears of a more general insurrection were not easily dispelled. Information gathered by the *fiscal* Cistué suggests that there were still some reasons for apprehension later in the year. In mid-September, he reported that in Riobamba popular solidarity with the Quito *barrios* had led to attacks on a tax official exiled there from Quito; unrest had also spread into ecclesiastical politics when the convocation of the Franciscan chapter led to a popular riot in favor of a candidate related to the parish priest of San Blas in Quito. The town of Ibarra was said to have risen against European Spaniards, refusing them entry, while popular antagonism towards the aguardiente monopoly was creating insecurity in Cuenca.[91] Thus, by mid-September, there were still grounds for official concern about the situation, not only in the capital city, but also in the provinces.

The Restoration of Royal Government

In any event, insurrection in Quito did not spread to other areas of the audiencia to become a great regional rebellion. Apart from the early imitative rioting in provincial towns, the Quito rebellion remained confined to its urban precinct and did not spread serious disorder, even in the surrounding rural hinterland of the "five leagues." The Indian villagers of this zone around Quito did not strike up an alliance with the urban plebeians, and rather than uniting the poor of town and countryside against the social groups that dominated them, the rebellion remained one of community rather than class.

The reasons for the rebellion's truncated development may be explained by two factors. First, there seems to have been limited potential for solidarity between urban plebeians and Indian peasants. This was partly because many, if not most, plebeians were mestizos, who would have considered themselves both different from and superior to the Indian peasantry. Equally, the city's Indian population did not necessarily identify with the native people

90. AHNC, Impuestos Varios (Cartas), tomo 22, fols. 94, 99, 723–25, 100.
91. AHNC, Impuestos Varios (Cartas), tomo 22, fols. 513–14.

of the rural hinterland. While some were no doubt recent migrants who retained close contacts with nearby rural areas, others were long-established members of the city population, absorbed into its economy and society as artisans and tradesmen and without any close contact or sympathy with the rural population. That there were tensions between town and country was attested by the efforts of the audiencia to exploit urban fears of an Indian invasion of the city as a means of controlling the rebellion and encouraging the rebels back to order and by the report that Indian peasants were kept out of the city by the people of the *barrios*.

The potential for developing radical political ideas among the Quito *plebe* was limited by the nature of local political culture. The plebeians of Quito, when joined in collective action, behaved like the classic urban mob in contemporary Europe. Indeed, the Quito crowd seems to fit well with the definition E. J. Hobsbawm has given to the *city mob*. Like the European city mob, the crowd in Quito was a "movement of all classes of the urban poor for the achievement of economic or political change by direct action—that is by riot or rebellion—but as a movement which was as yet inspired by no specific ideology; or, if it found expression for its aspirations at all, in terms of traditionalism and conservatism."[92] However, as Hobsbawm has explained, for such a movement to be pre-political does not mean that it is without ideas about politics. Typically, by its direct action, the urban mob makes a claim to participate in politics, tends to be directed against the wealthy and powerful, and tends to be hostile to foreigners.

These were precisely the characteristics of the crowd in Quito. By rioting, it made forceful, extralegal representation of its opposition to tax reform; by attacking official buildings, government officers, and wealthy Spaniards, it directed its antagonism against targets that symbolized the abuse of power and the inequity of the social order; finally, by focusing on peninsular Spaniards, the rioters combined animosity toward the wealthy with that xenophobia so characteristic of urban crowds. As we have seen, however, the rebels were also eager to avoid any suggestion of disloyalty to the crown and, indeed, sought to legitimize their rebellion

92. E. J. Hobsbawm, *Primitive Rebels: Studies in Archaic Forms of Social Movement in the 19th and 20th Centuries* (Manchester, 1958), 108–205, 110.

by protestations of loyalty to the king and demands for royal pardons. Moreover, although Quito's plebeians expressed their political ideas in direct action by asserting their right to voice their views to the king over the heads of his ministers and their resistance to new taxation, their behavior after the St. John's night riot shows that they did not trespass beyond the boundaries of a traditional political culture, founded on deference to the existing social and political hierarchy. The appointment of *barrio* captains, chosen by the audiencia from among the creole elite reflects this plebeian deference toward the traditional social order and customary methods of government. For, in accepting creole notables as their captains, the Quito plebeians showed their acceptance of the normal methods of municipal government, whereby men were selected according to their rank and wealth. Nor was popular preference for local men in government and rejection of rule by outsiders in any real sense a radical departure from the axioms of the existing political culture. Conflicts between creole and peninsular factions had long been a major theme in the politics of the city, and popular involvement in such factional politics does not imply any protonationalist rejection of colonial rule. It was, perhaps, more akin to the "municipal patriotism" that Hobsbawm found to be common among the city mobs in Europe.

Another major factor that helped to limit the development of the rebellion was the conciliatory stance taken by those members of the audiencia who remained after the June riot and the growing willingness of leading creoles to cooperate in the restoration of normal government in the months that followed. After the defeat inflicted on the authorities and their peninsular allies on the "noche de San Juan," the audiencia had little choice but to conciliate, since it could not call on any military force to impose its will on the rebels. But, by formally conceding an end to fiscal reform, offering general pardons to the rioters and rebels, and expelling the European Spaniards whom the *quiteños* had identified as their enemies, the audiencia succeeded in lowering tension and reestablishing the legitimacy and authority of government. This was, nevertheless, a slow process, and the cooperation of leading creoles was vital to its success. The reports of the creole captains show why this cooperation was forthcoming: now that they no longer needed popular violence to oppose the reforms and as popular indiscipline grew, they became alarmed by popular lawlessness and anxious to reconstruct the old order.

Faced with a wave of crime against property, with disrespect for their own persons and property, and with popular questioning of their decisions as magistrates, they sought to check the rebellion before it threatened their own privileged position. This they did by organizing militia companies in the main districts of the city and by taking advantage of divisions within the populace. Thus, in seeking to repress those challenges that still arose from the ranks of the *plebe,* the captains allied themselves with those plebeians whom they considered "more rational, more obedient, and more committed to the obligations of vassallage," and persuaded them that, if necessary, they should expel "the ungovernable and the vagabonds." Furthermore, to pacify the populace, the creoles did not rely simply on persuasion by argument, nor on appeals to deference. When Nicolas Calixto de Alarcón asked for permission to retire from his task as a *barrio* captain, he argued that he had not only exhausted himself in the effort of restoring government, but had spent much of his wealth in the presents and bribes needed to win popular support.[93]

These efforts by the creole patriciate, working with the audiencia, gradually bore fruit. In mid-September, the viceroy officially ratified the general pardon announced by the audiencia in early July, and this seems to have marked a turning point in the rebellion. Apart from some minor tumults, popular restiveness began to subside. By the beginning of October, the president reported that the city was stable and showed signs of submission to authority. Nonetheless, his optimism was still tempered by misgivings, for much remained to be done. Hundreds of illegal stills were operating in the city, turning out aguardiente at low prices, while an official agreement suspended the collection of revenues from the farmers of the aguardiente monopoly in Quito and its jurisdiction for fear that any effort to operate the monopoly would lead to renewed disturbances. Rubio de Arévalo also testified to the continuing weakness of royal government, stating that it was

93. Bishop of Quito to Messía de la Cerda, Quito, September 19, 1765, Nicolas Calixto de Alarcon to Messía de la Cerda, Quito, September 19, 1765, AGI, Quito, leg. 398, no. 108, fol. 521, no. 109, fols. 530–31.

unable to influence appointments to minor posts in municipal government, which had consequently fallen into the hands of "criminals." Nor was he entirely confident of the future. Like the *fiscal* Cistué, who continued to send alarmist reports to the viceroy from his exile, Rubio de Arévalo lamented the erosion of deference and the decay of social discipline. The *plebe,* he said, had triumphed, it had chosen its tribunes, and it would rise again whenever it was challenged.[94]

In fact, any renewal of confrontation was avoided. Beginning in December, when Rubio de Arévalo retired and was replaced as interim president by *oidor* Santa Cruz, the audiencia gradually restored its authority. This was partly because the rebels had achieved their objectives: the new excise had been suspended, a pardon had been ratified, and so long as they were not provoked by any show of force or retribution, they had nothing left to fight for. The restoration of the audiencia was also assisted by the diplomacy of its new president, Santa Cruz, who sought to co-opt, and cooperate with, the *barrios.* Thus, when disturbances threatened at the end of December, he called the delegates of the *barrios* to his house and negotiated with them; when there was a conflict in the election of *alcaldes* in January 1766, he resolved the problem by electing two extra *alcaldes;* and when the corregidor refused to cooperate with Francisco de Borja, Santa Cruz not only ordered him to do so, but also showed his confidence in the creole Borja by placing him in command of the presidential guard, thereby converting an erstwhile opponent of government into its principal defender. Furthermore, to stiffen creole commitment to the pacification of Quito, Santa Cruz prevented the departure of leading citizens, on pain of confiscation of their property, and encouraged the return of those who had left, arguing that their presence contributed to containing "the pride of the mob."[95]

With cooperation within the patriciate, between the creole elite and members of the government, the city slowly returned to

94. Rubío de Arévalo to Messía de la Cerda, Quito, October 2, 1765, AHNC, Milicias y Marina, tomo 123, fols. 155–56.

95. Santa Cruz to Messía de la Cerda, Quito, December 29, 1765, AGI, Quito, leg. 398, no. 212, fols. 893–94; Messía de la Cerda to corregidor Sánchez Osorio, Quito, February 13, 1766, Santa Cruz to Messía de la Cerda, Quito, May 17, 1766, Messía de la Cerda to Santa Cruz, Quito, March 5, 1766, all in AGI, Quito, leg. 399, no. 247, fol. 73, no. 339, fols. 215–16, no. 279, fols. 214–16.

normality. It seems that, after the June riot had infused the anti-tax movement with dangerous popular animosities toward Europeans and colonial government, the urban patriciate chose to side with the audiencia in order to bring the people back under control. Gradually, under the careful supervision of select members of the creole elite and the audiencia, the popular parishes were brought to heel, a process no doubt helped by lax collection of sales taxes and the removal of controls on the manufacture and sale of aguardiente.

By the early months of 1766, the lingering symptoms of disaffection and fear of rebellion gradually faded. In early March, an Indian rebellion in nearby Latacunga was rapidly suppressed without repercussion in Quito. At the end of March, Quito received news that a military expedition was being sent to the city, something that had previously been a closely guarded secret. According to the exiled *fiscal* Cistué, this news brought a sharp change in attitudes, spreading apprehension and encouraging the "nobles" to shift blame for the rebellion onto the leaders of the *barrios*. It certainly appears that the creole patriciate was anxious to bring an end to the long period of disturbances. In early May, Francisco de Borja reported to the viceroy that the city was quietly awaiting the arrival of troops, and he raised no objection to the sending of the military expedition.[96]

Other reports indicate, however, that a groundswell of opposition still existed among the lower classes. At the end of May, a Spaniard in Quito pointed to the danger that another uprising would be induced by popular rumors that the arrival of troops would lead to mass executions and the imposition of heavy tributes on the mestizos. However, the creole patriciate, working with the audiencia, retained its grip on the city. On September 1, 1766, the troops entered the city and were warmly received by its inhabitants.[97] Command of the city was now transferred to the military commander, Pedro Zelaya, who, though he emphasized recon-

96. Santa Cruz to Messía de la Cerda, Quito, May 17, 1766, AHNC, Juicios criminales, tomo 129, fols. 848–53; Messía de la Cerda to the governor of Guayaquil, Santa Fe, May 22, 1766, AGI, Quito, leg. 399, no. 283, fol. 263; Cistué to Messía de la Cerda, April 29, 1766, AHNC, Milicias y Marina, tomo 123, fol. 114; Francisco de Borja to Messía de la Cerda, May 2, 1766, AGI, Quito, leg. 399, no. 323, fol. 194.

97. Cistué to Messía de la Cerda, Pujili, May 29, 1766, AHNC, Milicias y Marina, tomo 126, fols. 258–60; Phelipe Baquero, September 2, 1766, AGI, Quito, leg. 399, no. 397, fols. 363–66.

ciliation rather than retribution, took the precaution of forming a battalion of Europeans to prevent any further plebeian insults to authority.[98] After a respectable interval, the audiencia was purged of all surviving ministers associated with the debacle of 1765, pending an investigation into the events of that year.[99] And, on February 14, 1767, the aguardiente monopoly, source of so much discord, was restored without opposition from any quarter.[100] Quito, now occupied by a garrison, had been brought firmly back under Bourbon control.

Conclusions

In his brilliant analysis of rebellion in a sixteenth-century French town, Emmanuel Le Roy Ladurie has proposed two paradigms for classifying urban revolts, and though they pertain to a quite different historical context, they offer a useful starting point for some closing comments on the Quito insurrection of 1765. The first—the "Ibn Khaldun paradigm"—approaches urban violence as a function of rivalries between families or clans and their clienteles. The second—the "Karl Marx paradigm"—sees it as a class struggle, rooted in the conflicts of social groups with contradictory economic interests.[101] Although the Quito case cannot be accommodated within either of these models, analysis in their terms offers a useful concluding perspective.

The Ibn Khaldun paradigm is useful because it draws attention to a common feature of urban political life in colonial Spanish America and its role in generating local political conflict, namely, the rivalries and enmities of leading families, often expressed in conflicts over municipal and bureaucratic office, in judicial disputes over property, and in other conflicts over local resources. Of

98. Audiencia to Arriaga, Quito, October 12, 1766, AGI, Quito, leg. 399, no. 404. A company of volunteer cavalry, made up of European residents in Quito, was established in November, 1766. AGI, Quito, leg. 399, no. 416.

99. Real orden, January 1767, AGI, Quito, leg. 269. By this order, all the ministers of the audiencia, except Santa Cruz, were suspended while the rebellion was investigated and three new *oidores* were appointed.

100. Pedro de Zelaya to Arriaga, Quito, April 3, 1767, AGI, Quito, leg. 399, no. 418, fol. 481.

101. Emmanuel Le Roy Ladurie, *Carnival in Romans: A People's Uprising at Romans, 1579–1580* (Harmondsworth, Middlesex, England, 1981), 269.

course, in America such conflicts had an additional edge: they tended to form along the social lines dividing American and European Spaniards. Although the history of the city of Quito remains to be written, the evidence available suggests that it was at least as prone to such divisions as any comparable city and that rivalries between creole and peninsular factions were intense. But, in the Quito case, the Ibn Khaldun paradigm must be adapted to its context if it is to be useful. In Quito, the conflict within the elite cannot be reduced to that of rival families or clans; it was much more complicated, drawing on disputes between clergy and government, between officials within government, between cabildo and corregidor, and between European and American Spaniards. Nor was this simply a conflict between creoles and peninsulars as rivals within the dominant social group. The conflict also had an important political dimension, since the creole patriciate and its allies were evidently moved by a determination to resist the encroachments of a reformist and centralizing monarchy.

The rebellion in Quito was, then, in part the expression of several overlapping disputes within the urban elite and government. Indeed, for the viceroys of New Granada and Peru, this was all it was. Viceroy Messía de la Cerda finally concluded that it had stemmed from the "seditious spirit of the principal citizens of that city," who had promoted hatred of taxes and Europeans, aided by the partiality of ministers in the audiencia and by conflict between the secular clergy and the government. Thus, he concurred with Viceroy Amat of Peru in attributing responsibility to the creole patriciate, whom they both saw as the "hidden hand" impelling and guiding an ignorant and disorganized populace for its own purposes.[102] This official view of the rebellion is, however, only partly correct, and historiographical interpretations based upon it need to be revised. For, though the creoles clearly colluded in the rebellion—if only by failing to defend royal government against attack—the patriciate was simply one element in a loose coalition of social and corporate groups drawn into a temporary alliance. If factional quarrels within the dominant groups played a part in preparing the ground for rebellion, the rebellion also expressed the

102. Messía de la Cerda to Arriaga, Santa Fe, April 9, 1767, AGI, Quito, leg. 399, no. 419, fol. 483; Viceroy Amat to Gregorio Hurtado, Lima, July 16, 1765, AHNC, Historia, tomo 3, fol. 24.

grievances of plebeian groups capable of organized collective action in defense of their own interests.

In this sense, the Marxian model of urban insurrection as a class struggle of artisans and city workers against merchants and nobles also has some relevance to Quito's rebellion. The rebellion was clearly not an undiluted class struggle dominated by a clash of social groups with opposing economic interests. But there can be little doubt that the political mobilization of the *plebe* owed much of its force to the strains imposed by recent economic dislocations. Economic decline did not, however, generate rebellion: if contemporary reports are to be believed, this had been slowly crippling the city for many years. Much more important was the experience of a recent sharp downturn, described by the merchants' delegate as a "profound depression," which had undermined exports, reduced trade in the city to the exchange of basic necessities, and caught merchants and traders in a chain of credit where none could hope for payment.[103] This economic squeeze brought class and ethnic tensions to the surface. The expulsion of peninsulars after the June riot was prompted by the desire to punish the Europeans for their behavior on St. John's night, but it also reflected a division along class lines in which plebeian artisans and tradesmen vented their anger on merchants. Europeans dominated Quito's trade, and thus, as the importers of the very textiles harmful to the city's economy (and possibly also because they stood at the head of the chains of credit that bound merchants to shopkeepers and shopkeepers to consumers), they could be identified as profiting from the city's economic decline. The possibility, then, exists that the Quito rebellion was tinged by conflict between artisans and merchants, though not in the conventional European sense of a struggle between groups involved in the production and distribution of the same product. The attack on merchants was, rather, a sign that the rebels attributed responsibility for their economic ills to Spanish government because of its changes in commercial policy and to Spanish merchants because they were not only identified with this policy, but also appeared to be profiting from it. Thus the revolt was not propelled by mere poverty, but given shape and direction by the identification of specific agents for Quito's social ills.

103. Informe del comercio, AGI, Quito, leg. 398, no. 35, fols. 237–38.

In its later stages, the rebellion showed more direct symptoms of a struggle between rich and poor as a wave of delinquency brought property under attack. But such activity remained on its fringes, and the rebellion cannot be regarded as a struggle between the upper and lower classes of urban society. Inevitably, in a society in which differences of ethnic status were at least as important as divisions defined by wealth and occupation, if not more so, conflicts of class gave way to conflicts rooted in differences of race. In this sense—and like most other rebellions in late colonial Spanish America—the Quito insurrection was the rebellion of a community rather than a class. In Quito, that community was an agglomeration of urban whites, mestizos, and Indians who, though they could unite briefly behind the common goal of resisting changes in taxation, could not find any lasting cohesion nor develop links that went beyond the urban community into its rural hinterland. With the European Spaniards to serve as scapegoats, with fears that the Indian peasants might enter and overwhelm the city, and with the moderating leadership of a creole patriciate anxious to retain its own privileges, there was little scope for popular resentments to build into an organized attack on the social order. Despite rumors of slave and Indian emancipation, plebeian discontents were channeled into retribution rather than revolution. Ultimately, the Quito rebellion remained a protest against a policy, not against the power from which policy emanated.

The rebellion did not put forward any written program nor any systematic account of the ideas that the participants might have held. This should not, however, disguise the ideological currents present in the rebellion nor shroud their importance. On the one hand, the arguments of the creole patriciate and its allies, both in the *cabildo abierto* and in supporting correspondence with the authorities, all allude to a belief in a kind of constitutionalism in the conduct of state business. It would be mistaken to dismiss the arguments concerning the need to recognize local needs, customs, and conventions as mere rhetoric, cynically employed to disguise selfish sectoral interests. Of course, the creole opponents of reform were concerned about protecting and defending their economic interests. But they did not need to disguise this, for they saw it as a right, facilitated and sanctioned by the traditional procedures of government, with their lengthy consultations, delayed deliberations, and tendency to respect the status quo. Thus, although the rebellion did not produce a manifesto, the letters and petitions of the leading opponents of reform reveal a patrician, primarily creole discourse concerning the distribution and exercise of power within the colonial state.

Another ideological dimension of the rebellion is found among the plebeians. This is much more difficult to identify and define because it was not articulated in any written form, nor, without prosecution of the rebels, can we even attempt to trace it among the testimonies of defendants and witnesses at trials. Nevertheless, as E. P. Thompson has suggested in another historical context, an unsophisticated and unsystematic ideology can be glimpsed in the behavior of rioting crowds.[104] Thompson found that the actions of the eighteenth-century English mob were underpinned by a sense of legitimacy—the belief that they were defending some rights or traditional customs—and that this was reflected in disciplined and directed action, governed by certain norms and geared toward certain goals.

The riots that provided the main expressions of plebeian participation in the Quito rebellion reveal such a notion of legitimacy. In the May riot, there were some references to the drunkenness and insolence of the mob, but beneath its disorderly surface, the riot displayed elements of structure and discipline. That there was some drunkenness is hardly surprising: the rioters' target housed a distillery and liquor store. But there was no indiscriminate violence or plunder. Damage was inflicted on the excise building, but in a manner that displayed a purposeful attitude. Its contents were destroyed, not simply stolen, and the systematic demolition of the excise building suggests a deliberate symbolic gesture rather than a disordered attack. Throughout the period of the riot, the crowd remained in the area of the excise office, and although the audiencia took precautions to defend the Plaza Mayor, the riot showed no signs of turning into a general assault on government. Nor was there any deliberate assault on the persons of officials: Díaz de Herrera and his subordinates were able to escape and take religious sanctuary, and none of the officials involved in trying to restrain

104. E. P. Thompson, "The Moral Economy of the English Crowd in the Eighteenth Century," *Past and Present*, no. 50 (1971).

the rioters reported any direct attack against them. Clearly, the rioters had what they regarded as legitimate goals, signaled by their choice of target and the restraint exercised in unleashing their anger on these targets. Furthermore, having directly vented its anger against the symbols of fiscal oppression, the crowd then emphasized its claim to legitimacy by seeking formal recognition for its rejection of reform by using clerical intermediaries to negotiate with the authorities. It then disbanded peacefully, once its demands were met.

The June riot was more violent, but displays similar elements of structure. Rallied by the bells of the *barrios'* parish churches, the rioters turned against the corregidor's patrol because it represented a form and style of government that, in the wake of the May riot, had lost its legitimacy. Indeed, the crowd was drawn into an attack on government because it was itself attacked, and though there was loss of life and property, the riot never became simply a destructive rampage by an infuriated and mindless mob. Moreover, though signs of growing indiscipline existed among the urban lower classes after the riots, especially in the weeks after the "noche de San Juan," not even the most prejudiced observers suggested that the city had been submerged by a tide of uncontrollable violence.

There were many facets of civil disorder and popular protest in late colonial Spanish America, among all ethnic groups and at different social levels. Most were, of course, at the lower ends of the social scale, among people of color, most of whom were poor. These included the rebellions of black slaves who took collective actions to improve their conditions or to secure their freedom; the many outbursts of agrarian communities against those that they perceived to be predators, whether tax collectors, abusive officials, or competing communities; and the riots of urban mobs, again usually against tax collectors or other officials. More rarely, relatively wealthy creoles actively promoted rebellion, as in the case of the Caracas rebellion of 1749–1752, in which creole landowners protested their economic subordination to a Spanish monopoly company. Occasionally, these protests might cluster together within a short time, to form a recognizable conjuncture of rebellion. Or, again on rare occasions, the disparate strands of rebellion might merge in time and space to produce great regional rebellions that blended the discontents of disparate groups, even different cultures, into prolonged upheavals that, as with the rebellions of Túpac Amaru in Peru or Hidalgo in Mexico, might become veritable civil wars.

Quito's rebellion of the *barrios* did not become a great regional social and political movement like those that were to occur in Peru and New Granada during the early 1780s. It has, indeed, been overshadowed by those great rebellions, especially by that of the southern Andes, where several overlapping revolts, mainly among the native peasantry, unleashed a conflict of unparalleled duration and violence. It was, nevertheless, a significant episode in the history of rebellion in colonial Spanish America. First, it was part of a conjuncture of rebellions that affected the southern regions of the viceroyalty of New Granada during the early 1760s and signaled the first widespread, if scattered, resistance to Bourbon fiscal reform among both urban and rural communities.[105] Thus, it stands as an important moment in a major regional conjuncture of resistance to the new phase of Bourbon reformism, associated with the government of Charles III, that started in the 1760s. By the same token, it also constitutes a striking episode in that wider, pancontinental movement of rebellion that developed during the final half century of colonial rule, a movement better known for its great regional exemplars in Peru and New Granada.

The Quito rebellion is also important because of its character as an urban movement. It was indeed the first in a series of urban uprisings that was to be directed against colonial government during the next half century of Bourbon rule. Uprisings such as those in the Socorro region of New Granada and in towns in different parts of Peru and Upper Peru in the early 1780s constituted important elements in the great conjunctures of rebellion that occurred in this period and contributed to the development of the larger, regional movements that challenged the crown's new policies. Urban popular protests were, moreover, to play an important role in politics again in 1810, when urban mobs were frequently to engage in the political struggles that gave rise to the first movements for colonial autonomy. Thus, as an urban insurrection, the rebel-

105. On this conjuncture of rebellion, see McFarlane, "Civil Disorders and Popular Protests," 22–27.

lion of the *barrios* in Quito draws our attention to the political practices and beliefs of those urban centers that played an essential role in shaping the colonies' political culture.

This tradition of urban revolt, which has tended to be submerged in analyses of larger rebellions or political movements, deserves much more attention from historians. Spanish-American towns, with their concentrations of population and more intense social stratification, were—like their contemporary North American counterparts—often more susceptible to economic change and had a more active political life than the small, scattered settlements of the countryside.[106] Often, perhaps invariably, this political life was confined to small oligarchies, with the inevitable tendency for politics to decline into mere factionalism. But, as the Quito rebellion shows, there were moments when conflict could open this narrow and exclusive political system, revealing divisions within the community and providing some scope for wider political participation and for changing political attitudes. Although these urban movements were less violently disruptive in their impact and less radical in their implications than the great peasant movements, such as those found among the Quechua and Aymara-speaking natives of the central and southern Andes, they are nevertheless important. For, born in towns and cities, they were at the heart of colonial culture, where the tensions generated by economic change, political centralization, and ethnic and social rivalries were concentrated and where, during the great crisis of imperial rule in the early nineteenth century, the final struggle between colonies and metropolis was to be played out.

106. These comments draw upon the excellent and suggestive discussion of the urban polity in North America found in Gary B. Nash, *The Urban Crucible: Social Change, Political Consciousness, and the Origins of the American Revolution* (Cambridge, Mass., 1979), 27–53.

DAVID CAHILL

Chapter 9

Taxonomy of a Colonial "Riot": The Arequipa Disturbances of 1780

There is a rich corpus of historical literature relating to riots, rebellions, and sundry disturbances in preindustrial Europe that focuses on the composition of the crowd, its political culture, and the capacity of the plebeian strata to organize themselves politically in defense of traditional rights and conditions and even to seek some increment in those very rights and conditions.[1] This approach—associated above all with the names of George Rudé, Edward

This essay is based on research in Spain in 1983 funded by the Institute of Latin American Studies of the University of Liverpool. Further research in Peru in 1984 was funded by the Economic and Social Research Council (UK). Reference number: G0023117.

1. Fundamental works within this genre are Hobsbawm, *Primitive Rebels;* Thompson, "Moral Economy of the English Crowd"; Michel Vovelle, "Le tournant des mentalités en France, 1750–1789: La sensibilité pré-revolutionaire," *Social History,* II (1977), 605–29; George Rudé, *The Crowd in History: A Study of Popular Disturbances in France and England, 1730–1848* (New York, 1964). For an important critique of Rudé's approach, see Robert J. Holton, "The Crowd in History: Some Problems of Theory and Method," *Social History,* III (1978), 219–33; and for a valuable perspective on the use of class as an organizing concept in preindustrial societies, see E. P. Thompson, "Eighteenth-Century English Society: Class Struggle without Class?" *Social History,* III (1978), 133–65.

Thompson, Eric Hobsbawm, and Michel Vovelle—has in the past decade been applied with notable success to the study of the North American Revolution, and its influence is evident in recent publications on Latin America by William Taylor, Scarlett O'Phelan Godoy, and Anthony McFarlane.[2] The approach consists essentially of the simple device of lending an ear to the testimonies of the numerous lower-class witnesses and defendants buried within the voluminous depositions generated in the wake of the incessant riots, rebellions, and protests that so characterized late colonial Spanish South America. Moreover, such history from below heeds not only what the plebeian strata had to say for themselves, but precisely *how* they expressed it; this historiographical current has thus absorbed the concern with *mentalité* and *sensibilité collective* preached for so long by Lucien Febvre and now such a prominent feature of French historical writing.

The incidence of political disaffection in late colonial Spanish South America allows historians concerned with these themes to investigate such questions on the basis of documentation possibly even richer than that surviving from a cognate timeframe in preindustrial Europe. Without even adverting to the plethora of localized disturbances in the Peruvian sierra at the time, one thinks especially of the almost infinite bureaucratic output stemming from the Túpac Amaru Rebellion, in which the crown permitted tax collectors, muleteers, itinerant peddlers, minor *caciques,* tributaries, artisans, and a whole grab bag of refugees the opportunity to set down at length not only what they had seen, heard, and experienced, but how they themselves interpreted such untoward phenomena.[3]

This essay, however, will treat but one of a series of political demonstrations that collectively have been viewed as a kind of vestibule to the uprisings of Túpac Amaru and Túpac Catari. It will focus on the eruption of political violence in the city of Arequipa

2. On the American Revolution, see, e.g., the essays in Alfred Young (ed.), *The American Revolution: Explorations in the History of American Radicalism* (De Kalb, Ill., 1976). On Latin America, see William B. Taylor, *Drinking, Homicide, and Rebellion in Colonial Mexican Villages* (Stanford, 1979); McFarlane, "Civil Disorders and Popular Protests"; and Scarlett O'Phelan Godoy, *Rebellions and Revolts in Eighteenth Century Peru and Upper Peru* (Cologne, 1985).

3. See O'Phelan Godoy, *Rebellions and Revolts,* for a full survey of localized disorders in the Peruvian sierra before the uprising of 1780.

in January, 1780, the best known and best documented of this constellation of antifiscal protests. These demonstrations—in Arequipa, Huaraz, Cerro de Pasco, La Paz, and Cochabamba, and some less spectacular disturbances in the Diocese of Trujillo, as well as an abortive conspiracy in Cuzco—have thus come to be seen as what one author has called the "prelude to the conflagration."[4] Others have stressed, rightly, that the protests were a response of local society to the fiscal reforms initiated by the visitor-general José Antonio de Areche and implemented in the viceroyalty from mid-1777 onwards.[5]

An assumption, though, pervades most such accounts that the riots were a natural, even mechanistic, response to Areche's reforms, much as if Peruvians shared with their North American analogues a belief in a putative right of "no taxation without representation." This essay will analyze the manner in which the new fiscal system was implemented and examine how and why increased taxation led to political violence. It will then address questions that have been left fallow or only partially treated in existing accounts: the level of popular versus elite participation in the protests; the extent to which the events were spontaneous or controlled—or, put another way, the degree to which the crowd was the instrument of patrician elements; the participation of rural inhabitants in what was an urban phenomenon; the degree to which the events constituted a transient fiscal protest or bore witness to a more durable popular ideology. An attempt will also be made to uncover a

4. Francisco A. Loayza, *Preliminares del incendio: documentos del año de 1776 a 1780 . . . anteriores y sobre la Revolución Libertadora que engendró y dio vida José Gabriel Túpak Amaru, en 1780* (Lima, 1947).

5. Surveys of this group of antifiscal protests can be found in Boleslao Lewín, *La rebelión de Túpac Amaru y los orígines de la Independencia de Hispanoamérica* (Buenos Aires, 1943), 131–89; Loayza, *Preliminares del incendio;* O'Phelan Godoy, *Rebellions and Revolts,* 162–207. Other works that treat this constellation of protests are Melchor de Paz, *Guerra separatista, rebeliones de Indios en Sur América: la sublevación de Túpac Amaru* (Lima, 1952); Palacio Atard, "Areche y Guirior"; César Espinoza Claudio and Jose Boza Monteverde, *Alcabalas y protesta popular: Cerro de Pasco, 1780* (Lima, 1981). On the Arequipa disturbances, see John F. Wibel, "The Evolution of a Regional Community within Spanish Empire and Peruvian Nation: Arequipa, 1780–1845" (Ph.D. dissertation, Stanford University, 1975), 16–52; Eusebio Quiroz *et al.*, "La rebelión de 1780 en Arequipa," in Carlos Urquizo Sossa (ed.), *La emancipación americana en Bolivia y Perú* (La Paz, 1976), III, 13–87; Alejandro Málaga Medina and Eusebio Quiroz Paz Soldán, "La Rebelión de Túpac Amaru en Arequipa," *Historia* (Arequipa), II (1983), 98–137.

structure within the apparently anarchic disturbances and to detect political fault lines in colonial society and the ways or mechanisms by which a colonial crowd could either mobilize itself or be mobilized politically.

The Fiscal System: Old and New

A lengthy report written soon after the four days of political violence in Arequipa (January 13–16, 1780) expresses the view that the new administrator of the customs house (*aduana*) in the city, Juan Bautista Pando, had commenced where he should have finished in implementing the new system, and that had he undertaken his task with more skill, he would eventually have achieved his goal.[6] This opinion was just one of many, of course, but it does indicate the radical difference between the old and new systems of customs. For the threat to *arequipeño* interests consisted not merely in a 2 percent increase in the *alcabala* (sales tax) as well as new imposts of 12.5 percent on aguardiente production (*nuevo impuesto*) and the fifth (*quinto*) on minted and worked silver and gold, but quite as much in the rigor with which the exercise was undertaken, its differential social impact, and, not least, the arrogant manner in which Pando and his lieutenant, Pedro de la Torre, whom he had brought with him from the Lima *aduana,* set about complying with their responsibilities. To comprehend the seriousness of the threat posed to *arequipeño* interests by the establishment of the *aduana,* however, we first need to assess the nature of the fiscal system in Arequipa before Pando's arrival in late 1779.

Alcabala had been charged at a rate of 2 percent from its inception in the viceroyalty in 1591 until 1772, when Viceroy Amat y Junient raised the excise to 4 percent. In spite of Areche's belief

6. "Relación de lo ocurrido en la ciudad de Arequipa del Perú con motivo del estavlecimiento de la Aduana. Enpadronamientos de Sambos, Cholos, y Mestissos para q. pagasen Trivuto, y principio de Sublevación de Indios," AGI, Lima, leg. 1052, cuaderno 4 (Compulsa de los Autos seguidos), fols. 295–300. The author of this account appears to have been an escribano, Joseph Patricio Chacón, identified as the brother of the *cacique de forasteros,* Nicolas Chacón. For this identification, see Informe de Ambrosio Cerdán, AGI, Lima, leg. 1052, fols. 63–64; and Juan Ramón Puente to Cerdán, December 5, 1780, AGI, Lima, leg. 1052, cuaderno 4, fols. 290–91. But see also Quiroz *et al.,* "La rebelión de 1780," in *La emancipación americana en Bolivia y Perú,* 56, n. 16, wherein the author is said to have been one Mateo Urbicain.

that customs officials had failed to implement the Amat reform in Arequipa, it is clear that *arequipeños* had been obliged to pay at a rate of 4 percent at least since 1775, well before the implementation of Areche's reforms, though this percentage had never been collected with the rigor that the visitor-general's appointee was to introduce in 1780.[7] Under the regulations Amat introduced in 1773, hacendados and merchants had been conceded a year of grace in which to make good the sales tax and, to judge from the surviving customs records, were accustomed to "rolling-over" their debts from one year to the next. It was Pando's express intention to do away with such practices instituted by the royal officials who had been responsible for *alcabala* collection and who, he alleged, had exercised their office "to acquire friends, establish a good name, and a fortune."[8]

A royal decree of July 6, 1776, had provided for a further increase in the sales tax from 4 percent to 6 percent, and Areche was sent to the viceroyalty to oversee, *inter alia,* the implementation of this measure. The new rate of 6 percent began to be charged in the Lima *aduana* in mid-1777, snaring among its earliest victims José Gabriel Túpac Amaru and his cousin Diego. In Arequipa, *alcabala* was collected at the rate of 6 percent at least from the end of 1778, and the new aguardiente excise had begun to be collected sometime in 1777.[9] That is to say, the new measures were implemented

7. See O'Phelan Godoy, *Rebellions and Revolts,* 161ff. on the early history of the *alcabala* in the viceroyalty, and 163 on Areche's belief.

8. The list of debtors is available in AGN, Aduanas, leg. 6, cuaderno 34 (Libro de Alcabalas for 1779). Among them are the corregidor of Arequipa, Balthasar de Sematnat, and his chief escribano, Pedro Josef Salazar, both of whom were suspected of fanning or provoking the initial protests against the establishment of the *aduana* in Arequipa. Another prominent debtor was Juan Flores del Campo, a prominent hacendado and de facto deputy corregidor of the adjoining province of Camaná, who in late 1779 quarreled with the new administrator of the *aduana* of Arequipa and in mid-1780 obstructed the progress of the garrison sent from Lima to quell the disturbances in Arequipa. AGI, Lima, leg. 1052, cuaderno 1, fols. 273–80; Wibel, "Evolution of a Regional Community," 23; Chacón, "Relación," AGI, Lima, leg. 1052, cuaderno 4, fol. 296. Pando's vigorous defense of his actions is in Juan Bautista Pando to Balthasar de Sematnat, January 12, 1780, Pando to Guirior, March 18, 1780, both in AGI, Lima, leg. 1052.

9. December 18, 1777, payment made in Cuzco on a *guía* issued in Lima, October 9, 1777, AGN, Aduanas, leg. 162, cuaderno 14 (1777); Libro de Alcabalas for 1779, AGN, Aduanas, leg. 6, cuaderno 34; Libro del derecho de nuevo impuesto, 1777, AGN, Aduanas, leg. 5, cuaderno 30.

in Arequipa at least a year before Pando established the customs house in that city; all collections were the responsibility of the royal officials of the provincial treasury, aided by minor functionaries who manned customs posts on the outskirts of the city. For this reason, the pasquinades that accompanied the political turmoil of January, 1780, leveled threats against those very officials and other lower-level functionaries. Nonetheless, when one looks at how *alcabala* was enforced before 1777, the wonder is that anything was collected at all. There was a profusion of exemptions from which muleteers, merchants, hacendados, *caciques,* corregidores, and assorted travelers could choose, with apparently little need actually to prove their rights to exemption. Excise collection appears to have relied upon something like an honor system.

The surviving customs invoices for Arequipa do not, unfortunately, record exemptions, but those for the Cuzco region record not only the exemption but its ostensible justification. A selection from the Cuzco invoices for 1774 reveals that exemptions from sales tax were granted for goods stated to be for the use of Indians; for goods destined for consumption on a hacienda; for goods emanating from a hacienda or textile workshop subject to the property tax (*encabezonamiento*); for goods to be used in a convent or monastery; for goods allegedly already charged at another customs post; for merchandise declared to be for first sale but that had not yet been transferred to its new owner; for goods declared to be for consumption in a house; for goods declared to belong to a corregidor; in the case of livestock, for a herd stated to be in transit from one part of the province to another; for goods claimed to be the produce of tribute payments to be marketed by or on behalf of a corregidor or *cacique;* for goods destined for the use or benefit of a church; and for goods declared to be the product of a chantry.[10] Quite clearly, custom as well as legal privilege had determined that distinct social categories were exempt from sales tax, while those who stood outside such privileged groups might choose from a phalanx of excuses or loopholes to avoid payment in full or in part. Failing that, there was always graft. Again, in Cuzco in 1780, two of those executed for their role in the abortive

10. Libro Boletero de la Administración del Cuzco, 1774, AGN, Aduanas, leg. 161, cuaderno 1, for the *guías de aduana.*

conspiracy of that year, Eugenio Cárdenas and the ringleader Lorenzo Farfán de los Godos, were employees of the *aduana*. The implementation of the new system threatened the livelihood of those who had cooperated in, and profited from, the informality of the old. Among the targets of the pasquinades in Arequipa in 1780 were two peninsulars employed by the *aduana*—a doorman and a lower-level official—as well as the *limeños* Pando and De la Torre.[11] In the anti-peninsular sentiments of the time is implicit the slogan "local jobs for local people."

From the first Pando vigorously defended his role in the establishment of the *aduana,* laying the blame for the disturbances on the corregidor of Arequipa, Balthasar de Sematnat, his commercial connections, and the treachery of the local patriciate, pointing out that the first pasquinade directed against its implementation had appeared even before the new *aduana* had begun to function.[12] In so doing, however, he unwittingly focused on his own personality and maladroit methods as causal factors in the disturbances. For several months prior to the establishment of the customs house, Pando had startled, angered, and finally instilled fear into all *arequipeños* who had anything at all to lose. In late 1779, he had commenced a visitation of neighboring valleys and the provinces of Camaná and Moquegua. Many witnesses attested that in those two provinces and the nearby Valley of Tiabaya he had publicly boasted that he would leave their denizens in their undergarments; in Tiabaya, seeing the inhabitants dressed with "considerable decency," he had exclaimed that he would yet see them clothed in the coarse cloth customarily worn by the urban and rural poor.[13]

Such arrogance seemed to find its echo in his very actions in those provinces, for in Camaná and Moquequa he took a detailed inventory of all haciendas, lands, houses, taverns, occupations, and shops and market stalls. It appeared that no one, not even a

11. The employees were Josef Avanalde and Josef Camborda, the former having been brought by Pando to Arequipa as *portero*. Avanalde's testimony is at AGI, Lima, leg. 1052, cuaderno 1, fol. 58ff.

12. The original pasquinades are incorporated in the autos of the case, found in AGI, Lima, leg. 1039, 1052. Many of them are reproduced in Lewín, *La rebelión de Túpac Amaru,* 131–89; and in Quiroz *et al.*, "La rebelión de 1780," in *La emancipación americana en Bolivia y Perú,* 37–55.

13. AGI, Lima, leg. 1052, cuaderno 1, fols. 29ff., cuaderno 4, fol. 116.

humble housewife, was to be exempt from some new form of taxation. Word of this of course filtered through to the city of Arequipa, where he began a similar inventory upon his arrival. It was believed, at any rate, that he intended a tax "on the wage of the poor artisans, bakeries, taverns, and street stalls."[14] Accordingly, sometime before dawn on December 31, 1779, the first pasquinade, threatening violence if the *aduana* was established, appeared on the doors of the cathedral, scarcely days before the inauguration.

That event encapsulated all of the fears of the *arequipeños,* and then some. If citizens had expected the new taxes to be implemented with rigor, they had not anticipated the notion of indirect taxation. Indians had always been exempt from *alcabala,* but now that custom—indeed, existing legal privilege under the 1773 regulations—was summarily revoked by Pando. This served as a provocation to *arequipeños* not because of any nascent *indigenista* spirit, but rather because the Indians of the sierra and the surrounding villages were the principal purveyors of foodstuffs, handicrafts, and fuel to the city. The custom was either for the Indians to bring their wares for marketing or to send them with small traders, or for the Indians of the city itself to set out each day to procure produce, which they would then sell upon their return. In this way the city was supplied daily with fresh produce. The opening of the *aduana* vitiated this mutually satisfactory marketing arrangement in several ways, abrogating "that right [of exemption for] the grains and seeds for supply sold in the markets and public places for the provisioning of the towns."[15] Indians were immediately charged sales tax on the goods that they brought to market and, at the same time, were subject to maltreatment by leading officials.

The almost instant effect of such treatment was that many, perhaps most, Indians ceased to bring their merchandise to market, and where they continued to do so, they sold it at inflated prices. The effect on the small retailers of the city was that they either could not obtain the provisions from which they earned their livelihood, or else they were forced to pay higher prices,

14. *Ibid.*, cuaderno 1, fols. 32ff., cuaderno 4, fols. 118, 125; Chacón, "Relación," AGI, Lima, leg. 1052, cuaderno 4, fol. 296r.

15. Informe of Ambrosio Cerdán, AGI, Lima, leg. 1052, fol. 16. See also fol. 6 for a list of the exemptions being abrogated by Pando.

which they perforce passed on to their customers. Overall, the principal result of the opening of the *aduana* was that when servants sallied forth from the houses at daybreak to purchase the daily provisions, there were none to be had. Even where foodstuffs had reached the market at an elevated price, they tended not to be available much before noon because of the habit of customs officials of detaining goods inside the *aduana* until that hour. Moreover, on Sundays and feast days none at all was available, as Pando had ruled that on such days the *aduana* was to be closed and no one permitted to bring goods into the city, travelers and muleteers being obliged to camp outside the city.[16] The entire population of the city, whether merchant or not, was thus immediately and deleteriously affected by the establishment of the *aduana* in Arequipa.

All social classes felt the arrogance of the new officials of the *aduana,* but the Indians bore the brunt of such high-handedness. When they claimed that they had never paid sales tax, Pedro de la Torre, said to be even less pleasant than Pando, treated them as fools. None of their goods, be they foodstuffs, cloth, fuel, or carpets, passed muster, and where they lacked the wherewithal to pay, as they usually did in that only partly monetarized local economy, their goods were impounded. Moreover, they, in common with other travelers, were obliged to remove their hats and spurs upon entering the customs house. Torre's racial contempt reached such a pitch that on one occasion he set about a group of Indians who were passing through the *aduana.* When a long-time employee of the *aduana* reminded Torre that *alcabala* was not charged on the merchandise of the Indians, the latter flew into a rage and began to charge the Indians with even more rigor. In the two attacks on the customs house on the nights of January 13 and 14, the only official to be injured was Torre, who received a lance through his face, and for some time was thought to be on the brink of death.[17]

As with the Indians, the mestizos, *cholos,* and other castes were likewise the victims of such imperious treatment. Perhaps more crucial, however, for subsequent developments was the rigor to

16. AGI, Lima, leg. 1052, cuaderno 1, fols. 29, 53ff., 58–67.

17. "Les trataban mal de razones," AGI, Lima, leg. 1052, cuaderno 1, fol. 66; AGI, Lima, leg. 1052, cuaderno 1, fols. 54ff.; Chacón, "Relación," AGI, Lima, leg. 1052, cuaderno 4, fol. 296v; AGI, Lima, leg. 1052, cuaderno 1, fols. 28ff., 36–39, 54–58ff.

which hacendados, merchants, and other members of the patriciate found themselves subjected. There are numerous cases of such luminaries having to pay the excise on goods for which they had previously been exempt, but a few examples will suffice. Pando's survey of haciendas had been undertaken "without reserving the fruits nor even the alfalfa that was grown among the vines" of those lands devoted to viticulture, the staple of the local economy. The hacendado Raimundo O'Phelan complained of having been charged excise on wine produced by his vineyard in the Vitor Valley when he was already contributing *encabezonamiento* to the royal coffers for the property. Most hacendados appear to have believed that this property tax was paid in lieu of *alcabala,* a reflection of the relatively liberal interpretation of the regulations under the previous fiscal regime. Another hacendado from Tiabaya was obliged to pay the impost on a load of firewood that he admitted was for marketing in the city, but at such a rate that his profit margin would all but disappear. This same complainant also had to pay excise on a "gift" of avocado, this being the term used for small quantities, the word also reflecting the semantics of colonial tax avoidance.[18] Grains, too, appear to have been exempt from taxation hitherto, possibly because of the fiction that payment of the property tax freed all grain-growing haciendas from excise. The surviving customs records for the 1770s indicate, however, that many prominent hacendados were accustomed to paying the impost, so that such claims may well represent little more than frustrated hyperbole. Of equal annoyance for landowners were the refusal of Pando to allow them the twelve months of grace that the regulation of 1773 permitted them and the probability that, for the first time, their word as to value, volume, and weight of merchandise was distrusted and goods would be measured and weighed.[19] It was significant that, in the wake of the "riots," the corregidor held a meeting with prominent hacendados to patch over differ-

18. Chacón, "Relación," AGI, Lima, leg. 1052, cuaderno 4, fol. 295v; AGI, Lima, leg. 1052, cuaderno 1, fol. 43; Pando to Sematnat, January 12, 1780, AGI, Lima, leg. 1052, cuaderno 1; AGI, Lima, leg. 1052, cuaderno 1, fols. 67ff.

19. This seems implicit in the new measures. The insistence of the administrator of the *aduana* of La Paz on weighing and measuring all merchandise helped provoke the disturbances in that city. See Scarlett O'Phelan Godoy, "Las reformas fiscales borbónicas y su impacto en la sociedad colonial del Bajo y el Alto Perú," *Historia y cultura,* XVI (1983), 124.

ences and, it is likely, to obviate any conflicting testimonies in the face of forthcoming investigations.[20]

The new aguardiente excise was just as damaging to the interests of this social group because Arequipa was the leading wine producer in the viceroyalty and the major exporter of wines to Upper Peru.[21] This impost meant that wine producers were paying the property tax and a further 12.5 percent, a considerable erosion of their profit margin. The new tax had a wider impact in that it forced an increase in the prices in popular taverns throughout the province. An indication of the attitude of hacendados to the new excise charges was revealed by a peer of Domingo Benavides, one of the more prominent patrician landholders. Benavides, attested this witness, had suggested in high dudgeon that because "there were so many gravamens, the haciendas didn't give [profit], and that it was more worthwhile to revolt [*levantarse*]."[22] Benavides' son Diego was later to be identified by several witnesses as the leader of the attacks on the customs house on January 13–14, as indeed was the son of the mayordomo of Domingo Benavides' inn, where goods stolen from the corregidor's house on January 15 were also to be found.[23] The late colonial haciendas in Peru were characterized by heavy mortgage or lien burdens and high turnovers in ownership. Clearly, a key to the success of such an operation lay in minimizing the tax burden payable to the treasury, the adroit avoidance or limitation of which might well prove to be the difference between survival and bankruptcy, whatever the position of the owner in the social pecking order.

If the *alcabala* affected the urban poor and the peasantry quite as much, in relative terms, as it did hacendados and the more comfortable urban dwellers such as merchants, it was also the case that

20. "Los Testigos que se fueron llamados," AGI, Lima, leg. 1052, fols. 27ff.

21. See Marie Helmer, "Documents pour l'histoire economique de l'Amerique du Sud: Commerce et industrie au Pérou a fin du XVIIIme Siècle," *Revista de Indias,* X (1950), 519–26. On Arequipa's wine industry, see Keith A. Davies, *Landowners in Colonial Peru* (Austin, 1984).

22. AGI, Lima, leg. 1052, cuaderno 2, fol. 110.

23. "Relación del alboroto de Arequipa y sus acaesimientos en este presente año de 1780," Lorenzo Justo Rendón, AGI, Lima, leg. 1052, cuaderno 2, fol. 287. For the connection, see the notation of Ambrosio Cerdán at fol. 292. See also the Informe of Cerdán, AGI, Lima, leg. 1052, fols. 50, 66, 73, which remarks that the families of Domingo and Diego Benavides "are entwined with those of the most illustrious."

the extension of tribute liability to mestizos, *cholos,* and *zambiagos* embodied in Areche's circular order of November 16, 1779, might, in the worst of all cases, reach into the urban and rural patriciate, some of whose members conspicuously lacked *limpieza de sangre.* Here, again, our anonymous chronicler avers that those who came within the ambit of the new tribute regulations included "the plebeians of the city and rustics and even many who, being mestizos, etc., are considered patricians because their circumstances have elevated them."[24] Moreover, it is clear that this new tribute provision had been made immediately and widely public, with copies having been distributed to all the parish priests of the region.[25] Even more so than in the case of the sales tax, the tribute question was a matter of fear of future developments rather than resentment at anything yet implemented by the crown, though Sematnat had undertaken a census of the residents of Tiabaya in November, 1779, that had been abruptly canceled when social unrest there and in Cailloma became evident. Such attenuation was, of course, an abrogation of the corregidor's fiscal responsibilities.[26] The chronicler noted that the designation of "tributary" was heard with revulsion, but a lowered social status and the monetary contribution itself comprised only a portion of the burden that such a designation implied.

The ramifications and fears involved were expressed by a group of mestizos from Ica, to the north of the Diocese of Arequipa, in early 1780. Complaining of an unholy alliance between Areche's appointee there, Juan Bazo, and the priest Andrés Bravo, they noted that in Ica there were four parishes, three of which were Indian.[27] They attended the parish for *españoles,* and their concern was that as a result of another of Areche's decrees relating to tribute (that of June 10, 1779), they would be obliged to switch to an

24. Chacón, "Relación," AGI, Lima, leg. 1052, cuaderno 4, fol. 295r. The word translated as *patricians* appears as *nobles* in Spanish.

25. The Informe of Cerdán, AGI, Lima, leg. 1052, fol. 21, refers to the circular order of November 16, 1779, to all corregidors of the viceroyalty for a new *revista* of the tributary population.

26. "Relación," Lorenzo Rendón, AGI, Lima, leg. 1052, cuaderno 2, fol. 286r. See also Quiroz *et al.*, "La rebelión de 1780," in *La emancipación americana en Bolivia y Perú,* 37.

27. *Memorial* of Juan Gavino Valenzuela *et al.* to Areche, July 1, 1779, AGI, Lima, leg. 1039.

Indian parish. The consequence of this would be that as tributaries, they would henceforth be liable for *mita* and personal service (*pongueaje*) in the houses of the priest and corregidor and that they would also become victims of the forced sale of merchandise. They also dismissed the one ostensible benefit that their new status would permit them, that of freedom from the obligation for parochial fees, for they noted that for this purpose, the cura had devised his own system of racial classifications. To be categorized as a tributary thus signified not only an instant loss of social status but also a financial devastation and the possibility of forced-labor service. In Arequipa, however, the correlation between tributary status and financial loss was rather more blurred, as Sematnat had included in his *repartos* many mixed-race individuals.

The third impost that drew forth protests and pasquinades was the quint affecting primarily miners, traders in silver and gold, and the guild of silversmiths, though at a lower remove the customer was of course also affected.[28] Gold and silver were nonessential goods for the wider society, but not for the clergy and confraternities who were regular purchasers of silver vessels and silver and gold thread for the ongoing work of ornamentation and embellishment of the numerous churches and chapels in the diocese. The new measure implied a 20 percent increase in the cost of such devotional activities. Moreover, silver plate appears to have been, in the absence of savings banks in colonial life, an item in which the more comfortable sectors of society invested in order to safeguard their savings.[29] Two of the seven conspirators executed in Cuzco in 1780 were silversmiths and another two goldsmiths, one of whom was the mayordomo of a confraternity.[30] Several of the organizers of the political demonstrations of January 15–16 in

28. AGI, Lima, leg. 1052, cuaderno 4, fol. 46.

29. See, for an extreme example, "Autos de Notación e Inventario de los vienes . . . , del D. D. Martín de Zugasti y Foronda Cura Propio que fue de la Doct de Lampa," August 17, 1804, ADC, Real Audiencia, Ordinarias 51, cuaderno 5. He had accumulated well in excess of eight hundred *marcos de plata labrada* as part of his personal fortune.

30. Juan de Dios Palomino y Vera and Melchor Chacón y Becerra were silversmiths, and Asencio Vergara and Josef Gómez were the goldsmiths. Gómez was mayordomo of the *cofradía* of San Eloy; for this identification, see "Proceso seguido a los sediciosos de 1780," transcribed by Manuel Jesús Aparicio Vega, in *Revista del Archivo Histórico del Cuzco,* XII (1967), 217; but cf. O'Phelan Godoy, *Rebellions and Revolts,* 196, which identifies Melchor Chacón as the mayordomo of this *cofradía*.

Arequipa appear to have been members of the confraternity of San Antonio Abad, who had been unable, several days before the feast of their patron saint, to complete a chapel for the fiesta owing to lack of funds.[31]

The injection of Bourbon efficiency into excise collection in the Arequipa region thus affected not only those more conspicuously involved in the marketing of bulk foodstuffs, aguardiente, and cloth, but the lower strata of urban and rural society as well: Indians, artisans, petty merchants, and consumers, of whatever social provenance. Pando argued that Indians who had been charged the excise were in fact either overtly or covertly the factotums of hacendados, priests, merchants, and other interested parties who availed themselves of indigenous carriers precisely with a view to evading customs duties. There is even an allegation that hacendados used the royal postmaster to smuggle goods into the city markets.[32]

There was undoubtedly some truth in such allegations, yet it nevertheless remains clear that Pando's activities vitiated the commercialization of indigenous production in the region necessary to generate the cash with which Indians met the cost of tribute, *reparto,* indulgences, and parochial fees. A good deal of this commercialization of indigenous handicrafts and agricultural produce nevertheless appears to have taken place in the aftermath of the actual collection of tribute, its agents being the corregidores and *caciques.*

However, the rebarbative personalities of Pando and his henchmen have tended to obscure the fact that colonial officialdom's exploitation of Indian carriers and street traders had antedated the arrival in Arequipa of those fiscal adventurers. A city councilor testified that before Pando's arrival the lower orders had been "terrorized" by employees of the provincial treasury as they entered or left the city and forced to pay excise on whatever goods they carried with them, however trifling, which were impounded at will. There is, too, testimony that city councilors also made a tidy living from such extra-official practices, charging each street trader two reales for the privilege of setting out his or her goods

31. Testimony of Lorenzo de la Quintana, AGI, Lima, leg. 1052, cuaderno 4.

32. Wibel, "Evolution of a Regional Community," 25–26.

and four reales for each carcass sold to meet the city's provisioning requirements. So, too, the corregidor was said to receive four pesos from each tavern for the privilege of not being forcibly sold wine, in a region that was the major wine producer in the viceroyalty.[33] In the colonial period, exploitation usually begins at home.

Added to the effects of fiscal measures new and old, legal and illicit, the meticulousness of Pando's inventorying threatened some barely imagined new form of taxation on houses, occupations, shops, taverns, market stalls, haciendas, and even the street-corner sites from which local government officials already garnered bribes. All had lost something, directly or indirectly, as a result of the opening of the *aduana,* and all stood to lose more as Areche's underlings developed their fiscal rhythm. The proposal—indeed law, which the corregidor had as yet failed to implement—to widen the tribute net was calculated not only to reap the crown vast increases in revenue from this source but to enrage a large proportion of the existing nontributary population. How, indeed, could it be otherwise after some 250 years of miscegenation? Many might see generations of social climbing and economic consolidation evaporate when they found themselves, with the designation of "tributary," forced to meet biennial payments and *reparto,* as well as liability for personal service. If this constellation of gravamens represented the worst-case position, the designation itself constituted adequate offense in a racially and status-conscious society. A host of others, less socially prominent, were similarly affected by the measure: the urban masses, the artisans, the mayordomos and cowboys employed on the haciendas, and the smallholders, who played a vital role in local production but who appear only infrequently in the historical record. There was every reason in the world for everyone to join an insurrection.

The wide-ranging social impact of the new taxes constituted what may be called the structural cause of the civil disorder that was to follow. But there were, as there usually are, contingent factors that exacerbated the already highly charged political atmosphere in the city. Aside from the uncivil manner of the collection of the new imposts, such factors tended to center on the figure of the corregidor. Social unrest in Tiabaya and Cailloma had accom-

33. Informe of Cerdán, AGI, Lima, leg. 1052, fols. 46, 70.

panied his attempt to draw up new tribute lists, unrest that provided something of an overture to the establishment of the *aduana*. The officials of the provincial treasury had requested its erection, and in late 1779 considerable bad blood existed between these officials and the corregidor, though the precise reasons for this are lost to us.[34] In any case, Sematnat's own financial interests were not served by the opening of the *aduana,* and a rivalry was quickly established between the corregidor and Pando.

Sematnat seems to have chosen for himself the role of local hero, and indeed many saw him, or conveniently chose to cast him, in such a light, notwithstanding the general odium in which he was held in Arequipa.[35] Others, however, to judge from many among the pasquinades, accredited the corregidor as well as local treasury officials with being the joint authors of their misfortunes by bringing the *aduana* there in the first place. A flurry of pasquinades and reports of suspicious nocturnal movements in the city and suburbs induced Sematnat to call Pando to order, advancing the thesis that the administrator's activities constituted a threat to the peace of the realm. The latter's prompt response revealed his contempt for the self-serving corregidor, and a breach was thereby established, with both vying for preeminence: a conflict of jurisdiction rooted in irreconcilable personalities. This exchange of correspondence took place on January 12.[36] Pando's rejection of the corregidor's overtures became known at once, and the next night the first of the attacks on the customs house took place.

The Events

In his appeal to Pando, Sematnat had referred to "bands of masked persons" passing through the streets "at strange hours" of the night, on foot and on horseback. On the nights of January 5

34. "Relación," Lorenzo Rendón, AGI, Lima, leg. 1052, cuaderno 2, fol. 286r.

35. The Informe of Cerdán, AGI, Lima, leg. 1052, fol. 71, states that Sematnat was "hated almost generally" for his unpopular measures, for being a foreigner ("no siendo del País"), and for the malevolent clique that surrounded him. This general dislike of the corregidor also emerges from the testimonies that were not prepared and sworn before Sematnat.

36. Sematnat to Pando, January 12, 1780, Pando to Sematnat, January 12, 1780, both in AGI, Lima, leg. 1052, cuaderno 1.

and 8, the city guards reported such movements in various parts of the city. On January 10 there was a discernible increment in these bands, evidently calculated at this juncture more as a threat than as an intent. A cleric reported that at 1:30 A.M. on January 11 he saw some sixty horsemen "wearing ponchos and with white caps that almost covered their entire faces," riding in good formation.[37] After having thoroughly and intentionally frightened one of the customs officials living on the outskirts, they set out for the center of the city, riding slowly two by two, at an interval of a block between each pair. These demonstrations were obviously intended to drive home the message of the pasquinades, which were by now multiplying rapidly.

That message was not confined solely to the abolition of the *aduana,* as the activities of the nocturnal rangers might have suggested. One functionary reported that, before the outbreak of violence, many persons (whom he was unable or unwilling to identify) passing by his post had said that if the *cholos* and *zambos* were to be charged tribute, then "they have to revolt (*alzarse*)." Again, on the night of the tenth, the *cacique* of the villages of Chimba and Tiabaya, Colonel of Militias Esteban Condorpusa, was visited by two of those mysterious horsemen, now armed, who demanded details of the new tribute list that the corregidor and Condorpusa had undertaken the previous November. When the *cacique* denied that such a register existed, they riposted that they had been reliably informed that it did, and that not only *cholos* but *españoles* had been included. Both horsemen were *mulatos.* The message had, however, already been well taken by Sematnat, who had refrained from taking any further census and who now made concentrated efforts to deter Pando from his potentially destructive course. Yet on the thirteenth, in spite of such overtures, there was a disturbance (*alboroto*) at the *aduana* when a group of "peons" belonging to a client of the *aduana,* together with another group of *muchachos cholos y indios,* assailed an employee with sods of earth, accompanied by whistles, shouts, and general pandemonium; the protest was against Pedro de la Torre's ill-treatment of some Indian car-

37. AGI, Lima, leg. 1052, cuaderno 1; Testimonies of Pedro de Uria and Juan de Montoya, AGI, Lima, leg. 1052, cuaderno 1, fols. 25–31v; Testimony of Licenciado Luis Gallegos de la Cuba, AGI, Lima, leg. 1052, cuaderno 1.

riers.[38] The intransigence and arrogance of Pando and Torre thus served to ignite the steadily deteriorating political climate in the city. That night the *aduana* was attacked.

In view of Pando's refusal to heed the warnings and entreaties of an unlikely alliance that comprised the authors of the pasquinades, the masked horsemen, the corregidor, the town council and assorted patricians, no other recourse was left to *arequipeños*—at least in the short-term—but open violence. The attack on the thirteenth, however, should probably be regarded as a final warning, inasmuch as it was short and its damage was limited, consisting of a hammering on the doors of the customs house and a hurling of mud and stones against the building and its two guards. Nonetheless, the demonstrators numbered five hundred to six hundred, an indication of the popular base of the movement. This crowd retired, almost evaporated, in good order, apparently convinced, as one chronicler of the event asserted, that they had achieved by their actions either a complete abolition of the *aduana* or at least a diminution in the level and nature of the imposts henceforth to be charged.[39] The naïveté of that illusion became apparent the following day.

After reviewing the damage at dawn on the fourteenth, Sematnat called a *cabildo abierto* that demanded the lifting of all fiscal innovations, at least until representations could be made to Lima, and at the same time avowed to defend the *aduana* to the death.[40] A delegation accordingly met with Pando, who gave it to understand that he was in favor of such a course of action, but that very day he proceeded to collect the excise with even more temerity than hitherto, even forcing some interregional traders to pay the excise twice on the same item of merchandise. The reply of the

38. Testimony of Francisco Xavier Slaguero, AGI, Lima, leg. 1052, cuaderno 1, fols. 29–30v; Testimony of Coronel Estevan Condorpusa, with Auto of Sematnat of January 12, 1780, AGI, Lima, leg. 1052, cuaderno 1; AGI, Lima, leg. 1052, cuaderno 1, fols. 66ff.

39. AGI, Lima, leg. 1052, cuaderno 1, fols. 16–22, 25–32; "Relación," of Rendón, AGI, Lima, leg. 1052, cuaderno 2, fol. 284v; Chacón, "Relación," AGI, Lima, leg. 1052, cuaderno 4, fol. 297v.

40. Chacón, "Relación," AGI, Lima, leg. 1052, cuaderno 4, fol. 297v. See also AGI, Lima, leg. 1052, cuaderno 1, fols. 28ff., for the delegation to Pando following the *cabildo abierto*.

victims was swift. That night a horseman was seen to ride toward the *aduana,* whereupon, approaching his goal, he gave a whistle. This signal was immediately answered by a rocket fired from behind the nearby Convent of San Francisco, at which the block was filled with some 600 horsemen, riding, again, "in such good order." Several versions attest to an overall number of some three thousand participants in this protest, all of whom were armed after a fashion, with pistols, lances, sticks, and stones. This multitude destroyed and selectively looted the offices, stealing some three thousand pesos but leaving other sums untouched, and most notably refusing to violate the sanctity of the considerable merchandise that had earlier been interned in the *aduana.* As one commentator put it, "they had no mind to rob but rather to kill or terrorize the administrator."[41] Pando and other employees made good their escape by scuttling over a back fence and into hiding. The following day, Sematnat formally abolished the application of Areche's innovations in the region, permitting local hacendados to remove their merchandise from storage without even paying excise at the old rates. It had been a skilfully executed "riot," a resounding success. The matter should have rested there, at least until such time as recriminations from the authorities in Lima could reach the city.

The *alcabala, nuevo impuesto,* and the quint were not, however, the only targets of the demonstrators during the two nights of orderly rioting, for there had been shouts for a cessation to all tribute innovations as well. As dawn broke on the fifteenth, large crowds were found to have gathered in both the villages of Cayma and Yanahuara, each a short distance from the city, in support of pasquinades there posted. That in Cayma threatened the life of anyone who dared remove it, even if he were a priest.[42] While the corregidor issued a decree reaffirming the abolition of the *aduana,* a venerable Dominican famed for his virtue was dispatched from the city to disperse the menacing crowd in Cayma. He returned to the city without having achieved the slightest success; rather, he

41. Chacón, "Relación," AGI, Lima, leg. 1052, cuaderno 4, fol. 297; AGI, Lima, leg. 1052, cuaderno 1, *passim*; Chacón, "Relación," AGI, Lima, leg. 1052, cuaderno 4, fol. 297r.

42. Chacón, "Relación," AGI, Lima, leg. 1052, cuaderno 4, fol. 298v. The Cayma pasquinade is reproduced in Quiroz *et al.,* "La rebelión de 1780," in *La emancipación americana en Bolivia y Perú,* 51.

himself had been threatened.[43] The targets were now the corregidor, his henchmen and business associates, peninsulars and all outsiders generally, the patriciate, and, in the minds of some, all royal institutions.[44] The events of January 13–14 seem to have generated their own momentum and to have awakened class hatred in the lower orders. Several witnesses claimed that Diego Benavides had been the inspiration or leader of the attack of the fourteenth, while another witness, close to the action, had claimed that that of the thirteenth had been in certain measure spontaneous.[45] But no one was to associate Benavides or his ilk with subsequent events. The class antagonism, material aspirations, and even bloodlust awakened by those anterior events drew inspiration and encouragement from the circumstance that those attacks had demonstrated that the city was, in fact, defenseless.

The nights of the fifteenth and sixteenth bear witness to a spirit of iconoclasm loosed in the city. This is not to say that there were no clearly defined targets: on the fifteenth, the corregidor's house was attacked by a large crowd, and men were posted in the back gardens of adjoining houses to kill Sematnat as he fled.[46] He had, though, already done so in the early evening, when he took refuge in a monastery after being tipped off by a faint heart among the multitude. He had taken the precaution of removing his prized possessions, but left the rioters some sixty-seven crown rifles. His house was despoiled of its remaining contents and then set on fire, whence the crowd moved to the house of a prominent merchant, rumored to be the financier of the corregidor's commercial interests, whom they robbed of approximately thirty thousand pesos in money and cloth. Then it was on to the royal jail, the heavy doors of which were broken down, Bastille fashion, releasing the prisoners, who then joined forces with their liberators. By now it was nearing dawn, so the leader—at least he who wielded the trumpet that marshaled the throng—ordered everyone to disperse, con-

43. Chacón, "Relación," AGI, Lima, leg. 1052, cuaderno 4, fol. 298v.

44. This much may be distilled from the proliferating pasquinades, to which may be added the reports of the shouts of the crowd. See especially, AGI, Lima, leg. 1052, cuaderno 1, fols. 20ff., 36ff., 50ff.

45. *Ibid.*, fols. 34ff.

46. *Ibid.*, fols. 23ff., 26–34. See also "Relación," Rendón, AGI, Lima, leg. 1052, cuaderno 2, fol. 284r.

voking them for a further assault the following night on the provincial treasury and on the house and persons of prominent members both of the corregidor's inner circle and the urban patriciate generally.[47]

There now occurred a general exodus of families and their prized chattels to the convents and monasteries of the city, where, indeed, the corregidor had been the first to take refuge, despite his function as guarantor of law and order. The political demonstration directed against the establishment of the *aduana,* which in part at least had been organized by disaffected members of the elite, had clearly run out of control. On the sixteenth the corregidor convoked the numerous militia companies of the city and surrounding districts, infantry and cavalry, to protect life, limb, and loot from the attack they knew was to come. At this gathering Sematnat was able to confirm what all had suspected, that "the suspicion was vehemently against those persons who form the infantry and cavalry militias." The cavalry of Tiabaya made it publicly clear that not only would they not contribute to saving the corregidor's hide, but that they also intended to join the attack on him that very night. Their colonel was Mateo Cossío, a business associate of Sematnat, so they availed themselves of the existing crisis to demand a diminution in the *reparto* debts, normally collected by Cossío and Sematnat when the militia was paid. All the cavalry companies were said to be composed of mestizos and *cholos* of the city and environs. It was not surprising, then, that the corregidor and his dwindling band of supporters, mostly the patrician elements based in the city itself, felt that they could rely only on the infantry company of nobles and "some soldiers" chosen from the company of grenadiers.[48]

The attack came in three waves between 10:00 P.M. and 2:00 A.M., from the countryside, and comprised Indians, mes-

47. "Relación," Rendón, AGI, Lima, leg. 1052, cuaderno 2, fols. 284r–85; Chacón, "Relación," AGI, Lima, leg. 1052, cuaderno 4, fol. 298r; Informe of Cerdán, AGI, Lima, leg. 1052, fols. 8, 52; AGI, Lima, leg. 1052, cuaderno 1, fol. 23; Chacón, "Relación," AGI, Lima, leg. 1052, cuaderno 4, fol. 289; AGI, Lima, leg. 1052, cuaderno 1, fols. 26ff., 32ff., 50, 63.

48. Chacón, "Relación," AGI, Lima, leg. 1052, cuaderno 4, fol. 298v; Informe of Cerdán, AGI, Lima, leg. 1052, fols. 42, 71; AGI, Lima, leg. 1052, cuaderno 2, fols. 14–15; Chacón, "Relación," AGI, Lima, leg. 1052, cuaderno 4, fol. 300, 299.

tizos, and other castes armed with lances, sticks, and the classical weapon of Andean warfare, the sling. The main thrust was from the Pampa of Miraflores, but there was also a contingent from across the river, from the direction of Yanahuara, and many among the urban poor appear to have joined in the battle, for battle it was.[49] The first wave drove back the company of cavalry that constituted the first line of defense, almost to the center of the city, which was defended by only two companies and a handful of volunteers. Four other companies had been posted at various strategic points at the circumference of the city, but were conspicuously absent from the scene until after the invasion had been decisively repulsed. Significantly, the corregidor had left these companies without arms, and on the three days succeeding the invasion, Sematnat and other frightened whites thought fit to have the city guarded by only two companies, despite the expectation of a further assault. On the sixteenth, the occasion was saved by the company of nobles, who turned back the thrust with their superior firepower, with the assistance of non-militamen who had sallied forth to protect their families and the city itself from the revolting lower orders. After some four hours of fighting—much of it hand-to-hand—the third and final wave was dispersed. Having seized the initiative, the two patrician militia companies embarked on a policy of exemplary reprisals. That very night they set out on a punitive expedition and searched, looted, and burned the houses and huts of the Pampa of Miraflores and took prisoners in droves. Particular care was taken to destroy all of the *rancherías* belonging to *indios forasteros*. Five cadavers of luckless invaders were hung in the Plaza de Armas on the seventeenth as a preventative warning, and on the following day six prisoners went to the gallows.[50] Who were all these rioters and how had they been organized?

The Composition of the Crowd

If the attacks of the thirteenth and fourteenth were in certain measure distinct in character from those of the succeeding two days, there does appear to have been some continuity of personnel,

49. Accounts of the fighting are in Chacón, "Relación," AGI, Lima, leg. 1052, cuaderno 4. See especially the testimonies at fols. 254ff.

50. *Ibid.*, fols. 299–300; "Relación," Rendón, AGI, Lima, leg. 1052, cuaderno 2, fols. 285–86, 285r.

though a change of leadership is evident, perhaps a seizing of the baton from the erstwhile organizers by some involved as participants during the first two days. The events of the first phase appear to have been organized, at least in part, by disaffected patricians, to judge by the presence of Diego Benavides, but also by militiamen, who continued to involve themselves during the final two days.[51] In the first phase, the presence of the militia appears to be attested by reports of large groups of well-disciplined horsemen riding in good formation. Their involvement on the fifteenth is similarly suggested by a report that when the corregidor's house was sacked, the surrounding streets were guarded by armed horsemen.[52] On the sixteenth the Tiabaya militia, encouraged by its officers, publicly boasted that they would join the attack on the city that night, an intention underscored by the fact that the city was then defended by no more than two companies and a handful of volunteers.

One chronicler of the events asserted that the bulk of the militia of the province was composed of mestizos and other castes. This explains the attitude of the Tiabaya militiamen, for they also protested against their heavy *reparto* debts. It also helps to explain the action of the corregidor, who, on the eve of the violence, entrusted police powers not only to city magistrates but also to the *cacique* Condorpusa and men of his confidence, though not, apparently in his capacity as a militia colonel.[53] Another report had it that, on the night of the sixteenth, the Tiabaya company had allied with Indians and castes of the Pampa.[54] On that night, lower-class creoles and a group of mestizo riders had incited the inhabitants of the Pampa to attack the city and avail themselves of the wealth of the patriciate.[55] The militia, comprising as it did such racial categories, was to be subject to the new tribute regulations in the same manner that it was already victim of *reparto*.

51. For the involvement of the militia, see especially Chacón, "Relación," AGI, Lima, leg. 1052, cuaderno 4, fols. 289–300.

52. AGI, Lima, leg. 1052, cuaderno 1, fols. 32ff.

53. Chacón, "Relación," AGI, Lima, leg. 1052, cuaderno 4, fol. 300; AGI, Lima, leg. 1052, cuaderno 2, fols. 47ff., cuaderno 1, fols. 1–2.

54. On the Tiabaya militia, see "Relación," Rendón, AGI, Lima, leg. 1052, cuaderno 2, fol. 285v; Chacón, "Relación," AGI, Lima, leg. 1052, cuaderno 4, fols. 298–300; AGI, Lima, leg. 1052, cuaderno 1, fols. 43ff., cuaderno 4, *passim*.

55. AGI, Lima, leg. 1052, cuaderno 4, fols. 254ff.

All of the *plebe* of the city and countryside were identified at various times by many witnesses; the racial composition of this designation included "cholos, mestizos, sambos, negros e indios." Of the crowd of the fifteenth, several witnesses distinguished the prominent role of women—"varias tropillas de muchachas, cholas, indias, y mestizas"; or another—"muchachittos, muchachittas, cholos, mestizos." There is here some accent on youth, reports that prompted the corregidor to issue a circular asking citizens if they really knew where their adolescent children were after lights out. Again on the fifteenth, in the assault on the house of the corregidor were identified "cholitos and cholitas" as well as mounted rustics.[56] Responsibility for the disturbances was never really established, as the crown, in issuing a general pardon, was apparently willing to let the matter rest.

Nevertheless, some evidence of the ringleaders exists, especially regarding the events of the second phase of the disturbances. Domingo and Diego Benavides, father and son, appear to have been the principal organizers of the demonstrations of the thirteenth and fourteenth; the latter was the street leader, and the former was reported to have made insurrectionary suggestions before the disturbances. More incriminating was the disclosure that an inn owned by Domingo Benavides had been the point of reunion for the participants on the fourteenth, that the signal rocket had been fired from the same inn, that the son of its mayordomo had been identified among the rioters, and that booty from the sacking of the *aduana* had been discovered in the very same locale.[57]

We are on firmer ground regarding the leaders of the fifteenth and sixteenth since a virtual cascade of names was revealed during the investigations. All of those inculpated appear to have been residents of the Pampa of Miraflores on the edge of the city: Pedro and José Alarcón; their brother-in-law Antonio Figueroa; a tenant farmer, Lorenzo Cornejo; the "lieutenant of the Pampa," Tadeo Mantilla; an anonymous "collector" of the Pampa; three tailors, two of whom were mulattoes; another mulatto, "Pechito"; a stone-

56. Chacón, "Relación," AGI, Lima, leg. 1052, cuaderno 4, fol. 298r; AGI, Lima, leg. 1052, cuaderno 4, fols. 87ff., cuaderno 1, fols. 81–82, cuaderno 4, fols. 63ff., cuaderno 1, fols. 26ff., 32ff.

57. "Relación," Rendón, AGI, Lima, leg. 1052, cuaderno 2, fol. 287; Informe of Cerdán, AGI, Lima, leg. 1052, fols. 50, 66, 73.

mason (*cantero*); the innkeeper Antonio Sanabria; and a "rich Indian," Huamán Vilca. Most of these participants appear to have been members of a confraternity; the sixteenth was the eve of the feast day of the patron of the Pampa of Miraflores, San Antonio Abad, and one witness testified that insurrectionary talk had started several days before the disturbances at a reunion at which the group was attempting to complete a chapel for the feast. Lacking the necessary funds, Pedro Alarcón had inveighed against the "shoeless paupers" who had come to Arequipa to enrich themselves from the "blood of the poor." He wanted to proclaim "kill the corregidor and all *chapetones*" and rob them so as to provide the "money and alms" that were necessary to complete the chapel.[58] At a time when the Bourbons were moving to control the confraternities, then, we appear to have an *arequipeño* confraternity doubling as a revolutionary cell.

The undisputed leader of this group—possibly mayordomo of the confraternity or other informal religious association—was Pedro Alarcón, identified by several witnesses as the convoker of the crowds on January 15–16. Alarcón appears to have been an acknowledged community leader of the less-than-genteel society of the Pampa, bearing the honorific title "little king of the Pampa." He appears to have been, notwithstanding his protestations of poverty to his fellow religious devotees, a man of substance. He was said to have financed one of Sematnat's *repartos,* and was held to have paid the corregidor eleven thousand pesos for his freedom when slated as the organizer of the disturbances. Other participants had similar connections to officialdom. Mantilla, the "lieutenant" of the Pampa, may have been the corregidor's subaltern there, but in any case probably possessed some police powers. The anonymous "collector" of the Pampa was in all likelihood either a tribute collector or a collector of *reparto* debts, either way an employee of the corregidor. Two witnesses alleged that another employee of Sematnat, José Diaz, had convoked them to attack the *aduana* on January 14.[59] This is not necessarily to say, however, that the

58. Testimony of Lorenzo de la Quintana, AGI, Lima, leg. 1052, cuaderno 4; "Relación," Rendón, AGI, Lima, leg. 1052, cuaderno 2, fols. 285–87; Testimony of Quintana, AGI, Lima, leg. 1052, cuaderno 4.

59. Informe of Cerdán, AGI, Lima, leg. 1052, fol. 28; "Relación," Rendón, AGI, Lima, leg. 1052, cuaderno 2, fol. 286; Informe of Cerdán, AGI, Lima, leg. 1052, fol. 67.

corregidor was a prime mover of the disturbances—which then slipped from his control—for we know that several of the employees of the corregidor of Tinta became close allies of Túpac Amaru after the outbreak of rebellion in November 1780.

Among the organizers of January 15–16, the "rich Indian" Huamán Vilca merits our attention. In 1781, the *cacique* of Yanahuara, Ambrosio Quispe Cabana, attested that one Fernando Huamán Vilca, described as a butcher of the Pampa, was, according to "all the Indian butchers" of the Pampa, one of the troop leaders of Túpac Amaru. In January, 1780, Huamán Vilca fled the Pampa in the face of the avenging militia. He was never captured, as his "woman," described as a "nun," was alleged to have paid the corregidor some four thousand pesos to leave things well alone; the Huamán Vilca of 1781, however, is associated with a female butcher. However, of the six prisoners hanged on the eighteenth of January, three were butchers of the Pampa, two of them Indians and the other a mestizo. More generally, residents of lower-class boarding houses in the city itself were discovered to be in possession of goods stolen from the corregidor's house, as were Sanabria and Huamán Vilca. The Indians who invaded the city on the sixteenth were said to have comprised a confederation of those of the city parish of Santa Marta together with those of the villages of Cayma, Yanahuara, Chiguata, and "other nearby parishes."[60]

The authors of the pasquinades were variously identified as a young seminarian, Pablo Zárate, who fled to Cuzco after he had been apprehended, evidently fearful that all the pasquinades would be attributed to his hand; Lorenzo Rendón, an occasional errand boy and informer of the corregidor, said to have "some knowledge of poetry . . . having no other means, with which to gain his living"; an unnamed friar who was held to be perpetually inebriated; and the escribano and *éminence grise* of Sematnat, Pedro José Salazar, and his army of scriveners.[61] Some witnesses even testified that on one occasion a pasquinade, not yet public, dropped from

60. Málaga Medina and Quiroz Paz Soldán, "La Rebelión de Túpac Amaru," 113; "Relación," Rendón, AGI, Lima, leg. 1052, cuaderno 2, fols. 285–86; AGI, Lima, leg. 1052, cuaderno 4, fols. 254ff.; "Relación," Rendón, AGI, Lima, leg. 1052, cuaderno 2, fols. 285–86; Chacón, "Relación," AGI, Lima, leg. 1052, cuaderno 4, fol. 299r.

61. "Relación," Rendón, AGI, Lima, leg. 1052, cuaderno 2, fols. 286–87; Informe of Cerdán, AGI, Lima, leg. 1052, fols. 25–27.

the corregidor's pocket, though this was after the four nights of rioting. As to Sematnat and Salazar, the theory offered was that they continued to foment trouble so as to assure the arrival of a battalion from Lima for their own protection and to prevent the possibility of a reestablishment of the *aduana,* which competed with their own financial interests.

Apart from the Indians, mestizos, and other castes, then, there were present an urban underclass of artisans, minor officials, those who lived in rental accommodations, and nonelite men of substance, such as Alarcón, Sanabria, and Huamán, who were prominent in the organization of the demonstrators of January 15–16. These men were able to take leading roles because, apart from the immediate issues of the day, a subterranean class antagonism existed, which they themselves shared, due to the arrogance of the customs officials, the hatred of outsiders, and the crippling financial impositions of the corregidor and his cronies, all of which flowed into the fear that such exactions would become insupportable with the coming of a more comprehensive tribute system and the range of new taxes that Pando had seemed about to implement.

The new aguardiente excise had affected not only innkeepers but their lower-class customers as well by raising prices, and there is also the report that the corregidor received a tax or bribe from innkeepers for the privilege of not being forcibly sold aguardiente. This helps to explain Sanabria's involvement in the events of the second phase. The Alarcóns, Sanabria, and Huamán all lived on the Pampa, and all appear to have been community leaders there. These instigators had been presented with the opportunity of the sixteenth being not only the sabbath but also the eve of the feast of the patron-saint of the Pampa, San Antonio Abad; that is to say, there was widespread drunkenness among its residents—the "profane" side to Andean religion—a phenomenon that is often an overture to Indian riots or uprisings in the colonial period.

Finally, an intriguing note on *agents provocateurs.* At the outset of the Túpac Amaru rebellion, a nephew of José Gabriel, Simón Noguera, was hanged by the corregidor of Lampa.[62] Shortly before his death, the nephew confessed or bragged to his jailer that

62. Informe of Cerdán, AGI, Lima, leg. 1052, fol. 37.

he and his illustrious uncle had been in Arequipa at the outbreak of the violence, which the Inca had actually fomented. The records of the customs invoices that would enable us to test for the presence of Túpac Amaru in Arequipa at that date are not extant, presumably having been destroyed in the attack on the customs house on January 14.

Ideology and Political Culture

We are afforded entry to the political consciousness of this racially mixed crowd—or, best to say, crowds—by way of both the import of the pasquinades and the shouts and slogans of the crowd as it went about its business. The pasquinades are our best source, but are fraught with interpretive difficulties. Although some prose versions exist, on the whole they belong to the free verse tradition known as *décimas,* which survived well into the twentieth century in Peru as a form of literary expression and, indeed, even now are not entirely extinct. Now, *décimas* ranged from elegant, witty verse to jaunty doggerel and plain graffiti. It is tempting to divide pasquinades on the grounds of literary quality, with the more unpolished being held to represent the popular mentality. Within the corregidor's immediate circle, however, it was believed that at least one of the early pasquinades posted in the city "was of no rustic despite its style being disguised."[63] Even where such a pamphlet did indeed derive from a lower-class group or individual, chances were that it had been composed by someone of a higher social rank, thereby probably distorting, if not the message itself, then the form and idiom in which it was expressed. In distinguishing popular ideology, form is often of more moment than the precise message, which is often ephemeral. In the wake of the disturbances, three prisoners were sent to Lima; one of these was Lorenzo Rendón, who, as something of a poet, appears to have earned his living composing rhymes, *décimas,* and probably prosaic correspondence for those either functionally illiterate or not blessed with similar literary prowess. These problems of interpretation are difficult to resolve, but are probably best dealt with by correlating the reports of the shouts and slogans of the crowd with the pas-

63. AGI, Lima, leg. 1052, cuaderno 5, fol. 17.

quinades themselves. Occasionally, too, the geographical location of a pasquinade may be a guide to its popular origins; for example, the pasquinade that appeared in the village of Cayma was more likely to have been an expression of lower-class sentiment than one posted on the doors of San Francisco or the cathedral, simply because of differences in the respective social compositions of Cayma and the city.

In distinguishing the popular elements of this verse, it is helpful to keep in mind George Rudé's distinction between "inherent" and "derived" ideology. To simplify his equation somewhat, the former may be said to consist of that learned by "direct experience, oral tradition or folk-memory," whereas the latter is acquired from without, from books, sermons, or "more structured" systems of political and religious ideas.[64] A qualification of this distinction is that, over time, some derived ideas become so grafted onto the popular consciousness that they become transmuted into "inherent ideology." This notional qualification appears to fit the Spanish-American case rather well, wherein the ideas of popular sovereignty first expressed in late medieval–early modern juridical treatises filtered into the popular consciousness, possibly because such ideas corresponded precisely to innate popular sentiment concerning the common weal.[65] Thus the rejection of "bad government" with its fiction that a benign monarch is surrounded by "bad ministers" is a common denominator of popular protests across Europe from Britain and France to Russia, and from late medieval times to the early industrial age.

It is never really quite clear what is subsumed under the rubric of "bad government" in the popular consciousness, and it is frankly not any use adverting to Spanish juridical tracts to ascertain this content, for original formulations become mediated through the existing popular consciousness and may be tempered by cultural and even geographical variants until they acquire a new content in the process. The concept obviously refers to an acceptable ambit and level of authority and its exercise, beyond which limits such authority becomes excessive. This excess describes physical violence, for example, corporal punishment either gra-

64. George Rudé, *Ideology and Popular Protest* (London, 1980), 27–38.

65. Some treatment of these ideas is to be found in Phelan, *The People and the King.*

tuitous or meted out without due process; arrogance in the exercise of office—a certain fraternal spirit seems to have been expected from functionaries; and, most of all, graft and corruption in the exercise of office, with the emphasis on the lining of pockets at the expense of the lower orders. There is or was a widely shared view among historians that the use of such terms as "corruption" in the Spanish-American context is anachronistic and eurocentric because such practices were so vital to the livelihoods of so many; they oiled, in fact, the colonial economy and the whole machinery of government. This position conveniently overlooks the circumstance that colonial Americans of all social classes knew only too well what comprised corruption, which they denounced frequently. The following slogan, uttered on the night of January 15, neatly captures all of these components of the precept of "bad government": "die these thieving dogs, they and not the king are the cause of our woes." The four elements are here: corruption expressed as thievery, bad officials, the exculpation of the monarch, and, implicitly here, the parish-pump xenophobia, directed against peninsulars and all other outsiders (in this case the *limeño* customs officials). The mutinous Tiabaya militiamen's chanting of "long live the king and death to bad government" on the afternoon of January 15, however, has a ritualistic, even legalistic dimension; one of their officers told them to chant clearly, so that later they could not be accused of *lèse-majesté*.[66]

Other elements of popular political culture were also present. In the popular consciousness ran a historical drama, a kind of "El Cid" of the masses, which vested distant peoples with a heroism so much more potent than their own, forgetting their own dislike and distrust of those from without. Thus, as individuals drew inspiration from their favorite saint or martyr in the churches, chapels, and confraternities of the towns and countryside, so too they derived inspiration from a more heroic age. In Arequipa in 1780, such a moral force was to be found in the valiant deeds of the *quiteños* of 1765 and the *cochabambinos* of 1731; a half-century is a long time in international affairs, even in the eighteenth century. A kind of pan-imperial affinity was even present as *arequipeños* drew

66. AGI, Lima, leg. 1052, cuaderno 1, fol. 20, fols. 43ff.

comfort from the Madrid riots of 1766. This historical consciousness was not confined to *arequipeños,* but is found in Cuzco, Cerro de Pasco, and other sites of popular disturbances at this time, whose protesters, like the *arequipeños* themselves, were to join the ranks of the heroic. It was not, however, just the event itself that was remembered, but details, apocryphal or not. Thus Lorenzo Farfán de los Godos told his coconspirators in Cuzco in 1780 that in Quito in 1765 four men had turned the city around in a day and night, had appointed captains, as well as a recruiting sergeant who went to all the taverns posing as an imbecile so as to avoid suspicion. There is history, and there is historical romance.[67]

There is, too, an invocation of patron saints to help or guide a people in their political ventures. Santo Domingo is invoked twice; San Francisco once; Jesus, Mary, and Joseph are called on individually and collectively; and even Santiago is called upon, though in which of his manifestations is not clear.[68] One pasquinade asks the Virgin Mary for "divine grace" to achieve the popular "designs," while another, even more remarkable, asks Jesus to intercede with God the Father for "license" to behead the corregidor and his henchmen. This is popular religion with a vengeance. No real reason exists to doubt that such invocations were sincere; before the establishment of the *aduana,* there were reports of what sound like apocalyptic expectations in the city. A public argument between the corregidor and the officials of the provincial treasury, whose grounds for contention are lost to us, gave rise to wild rumors in the city that various of the convents and monasteries would have to "be extinguished" and that "much blood had to run."[69]

It is important to clarify also that the familiar exculpation of the king and the laying of blame on his ministers was not merely formulaic, not a mere epiphenomenon, but bore witness to a belief deeply held at least among some members of the community.

67. Informe of Cerdán, AGI, Lima, leg. 1052, fol. 12; "Proceso seguido a los sediciosos de 1780," 227, 230.

68. AGI, Lima, leg. 1052, cuaderno 4, fols. 101–102. See also the pasquinades collected in Quiroz *et al.,* "La rebelión de 1780," 37, 51.

69. Quiroz *et al.,* "La rebelión de 1780," p. 37; "Relación," Rendón, AGI, Lima, leg. 1052, cuaderno 2, fol. 286r.

After a night of frenetic destruction on the fifteenth, when the suggestion was made that the demonstrators sack the provincial treasury, many among their number rejected the proposal on the grounds that the money therein belonged to the king. That same night, another witness of the events cautioned a group of *cholos* not to proceed to the sacking of the provincial treasury because if they did they would find themselves in trouble with the law—this, after a night of devastation. Clearly, to some among the citizens, there were legitimate and illegitimate targets of the public ire. Perhaps the key to understanding the concept of *mal gobierno* is to understand the popular notion of kingship, an understanding that we entirely lack; what is required is a study along the lines of Marc Bloch's of the thaumaturgical or numinous powers that a king was believed to possess in early modern France and England.[70] Essentially, however, the notion is defensive, a conduit for expressing political grievances without harming the fabric of the polity, that is to say, without harming the monarch.

The concept was not, though, a closed system of political reference. Among the authors of the pasquinades, some rejected the monarch as well, perceiving, rightly, that the king himself was in great measure responsible for what ailed *arequipeños* that year. What, then, did they propose to do about it? In fact, they scratched around for alternatives, suggesting either an alliance with Great Britain—whose king, in contrast to Spain's Charles III, "loves his vassals"—or the coronation of an Inca. The Inca nominated was a certain Casimiro, also called Casimiro III in one pasquinade (to provide a witty counterpoint to Charles III), "to whom we swear as king." This personage was identified as an Indian noble of either the Huaraz or Tarma; quite how he came to be known and nominated by *arequipeños* is not entirely clear, especially when the nearby Cuzco, Puno, and Charcas regions were awash with indigenous nobility. However, the "rich Indian" of the Pampa, Huamán Vilca, was alleged to have been in contact with "Indians of Tarma and Jauja." The sales tax records of this time also provide us with the name of Casimiro Condorpusa, possibly a relative of Colonel Esteban Condorpusa, and, if so, an Indian noble. The pasquinade

70. AGI, Lima, leg. 1052, cuaderno 1, fols. 32ff., 50; Marc Bloch, *The Royal Touch: Sacred Monarchy and Scrofula in England and France,* trans. J. E. Anderson (London, 1973).

of Cayma mentioned both Inca and Inglaterra in the same breath, while another in the city was said to refer to the possibility of rule by "a confederation of the Indians of Cuzco."[71]

George Rudé argued on the basis of European evidence that "inherent" ideology is not in itself sufficient for the transmutation of rebellion into revolution, that it requires crucial "derived" ideas that would allow a people to transcend their condition. This argument, obviously inspired by the Marxist concept of "false consciousness," appears to fit the European case very well, but it is manifest that the idea of an Inca state cannot be said to be derived in the case of Peru. What is evident is that in Arequipa in 1780 there were glimmers of a search for a political alternative to the colonial state, however rudimentary these might have been. For a larger scheme to have emerged in Peru probably would have depended as much on the fragile communications of the epoch as it did on the need for a derived ideology. It is now clear that, at least at some point in his rebellion, if not perhaps at the beginning, José Gabriel Túpac Amaru conceived the reimposition of an autocratic Inca state. But for this to take root among creole elites was perhaps another matter. Perhaps to Rudé's hypothesis we need to add the word "successfully." Peru's only clear-cut separatist movement during the colonial period was that of 1814, which fused Incaic symbolism with the derived ideas of Hispanic liberalism.

The defensiveness of the political stance of most of the rioters in Arequipa in 1780 is evident from their frequent shouts that they only "wanted" to pay the old rate of excise, but no other pension. But what is to be made of the many threats and imprecations against not only the officials of the *aduana* but also against the corregidor, his cohorts, and all those families "of honor and affluence"? E. P. Thompson suspected that the incidence of such rebellious phrases in eighteenth-century England was "usually . . . to chill the blood of the rich with their theatrical effect."[72] Something of the kind is probably in evidence here, but it nevertheless re-

71. Lewín, *La rebelión de Túpac Amaru,* 156, 159; Informe of Cerdán, AGI, Lima, leg. 1052, fol. 3; Chacón, "Relación," AGI, Lima, leg. 1052, cuaderno 4, fol. 296; "Relación," Rendón, AGI, Lima, leg. 1052, cuaderno 2, fol. 286; Málaga Medina and Quiroz Paz Soldán, "La Rebelión de Túpac Amaru," 113; AGN, Aduanas, leg. 6, cuaderno 34, fol. 130; AGI, Lima, leg. 1052, cuaderno 4, fol. 168.

72. Thompson, "The Moral Economy of the English Crowd," 126.

mains true that blood was spilled and that an ambush was prepared behind the corregidor's house to kill him when the main body of rioters flushed him out from the front. The first two days of rioting also appear to have activated a class envy, even class and racial hatred, which then made possible the final two days of calculated assault, two days that threatened the whole fabric of the polity in that provincial city.

In spite of the threats to the town worthies, the events of January 1780 came to be a source of much pride to *arequipeños,* perhaps the germ of that rebellious spirit for which the city came to be renowned in republican Peru. Its children are our guide to this spirit. One of the crown investigators of the disturbances reported that, by 1781, the children of the city had developed a popular game based on the assault on the *aduana.* Two children seated themselves on chairs acting out the roles of Pando and Torre, while others brought them parcels, representing merchandise subject to the excise. At a signal, another crowd of children would rush the two seated figures and beat them to a symbolic death, all the while chanting the slogans that their elders and betters had shouted during the actual attack on the *aduana* of January 14, 1780.[73]

The political disturbances in Arequipa of January 13–16, 1780, were made possible in the first instance by the uncanny manner in which the fiscal reforms of *alcabala,* tribute, *nuevo impuesto,* and the quint managed to detrimentally affect all classes in the city as well as the surrounding countryside, an effect exacerbated by the arrogance of the *aduana* officials. The temporary cross-class alliance thus generated provided a springboard from which the underclasses of the city and countryside were able to protest that most-hated of imposts, the *reparto,* which affected not only the Indians, the conventional victims, but mestizos and other castes as well. If the events of the thirteenth and fourteenth were to some degree directed or inspired by aggrieved members of the patriciate, those of the succeeding two days of violence signified the traditional elite's loss of control over both the city and the surrounding countryside. From that moment, the rioters, who had had at

73. Informe of Cerdán, AGI, Lima, leg. 1052, pp. 72–73.

least the blessing of those patricians who wished to see the *aduana* banished once and for all from the region, perceived that the city was undefended. That it was undefended was due to the folly and avarice of the corregidor, who had included mestizos and castes in his forced distributions, precisely those racial categories that constituted the bulk of the militia of the region. On the sixteenth, the city was defended by two companies of patrician militiamen, now fearful for their families and wealth, and fearful, too, of the designs the lower orders had on their very own white skins. Had they remained solid with the bulk of their brother militiamen, the city would surely have fallen.

The events certainly represent much less than an attempt at revolution, but surely, too, something more than a mere antifiscal protest. The attacks of the fifteenth and sixteenth bore witness to considerable class antagonism, a notion of class expressed in its most simple terms between those who have and those who have not. We have the confessions of the five Indians and one mestizo who were executed on January 18 for their part in the attack on the city on January 16. They testified that mestizo horsemen had convoked them to rob the provincial treasury of the undefended city, to "go from poor to rich" by "giving war" to the city and "those of" the city.

There is here, though, something more than class antagonism. All of these prisoners were from the Pampa of Miraflores, as indeed were those who convoked and directed them. An antagonism existed between the city and the countryside, especially between the city and the curious society of the Pampa, where *indios forasteros* had made their home and where the community leaders were wealthy traders and storekeepers whose lack of breeding and gentility, their relative rusticity, precluded their acceptance among the racially conscious patriciate of the city. The bitter Pedro Alarcón epitomized this socially marginalized subclass. He and his companions, in convoking the poor denizens of the Pampa to the assault, relied on lust for gain and class antagonism to win their recruits, rather than on any more overt political terms. Nevertheless, this latter aspect must remain open to some doubt, inasmuch as there is testimony that the attacks of the sixteenth were in part an expression of a confederation of the Indian parishes of the surrounding countryside, and the attack clearly came not only from the Pampa, but from other directions as well.[74]

The attacks of the thirteenth and fourteenth were organized around the companies of militia, judging from the considerable numbers of well-disciplined horsemen and, indeed, from the sheer numbers of armed assailants. The militia also appears to have involved itself on the final two nights, though with less solidarity than hitherto. At least on the first two nights, the crowd probably included peons and other employees of haciendas, drafted especially for the event. The network of haciendas and the distribution of the militia companies provide the two obvious means of communication and recruitment of large numbers of individuals acting in concert. The taverns represent a third possible network: the presence of Sanabria among the organizers of the fifteenth and sixteenth and the use of Domingo Benavides' inn as a staging point for the attack of the fourteenth suggest that this network was used to conscript a crowd. In 1777 and early 1780, the taverns of Cuzco were so used in an attempt to spread sedition and recruit aggrieved citizens.

The alienation of the militia through its liability for *reparto* and possibly tribute provides one explanation of why the traditional means of social order had ceased to function, but it is evident that the social control exercised by the clergy had also broken down. The clergy was, of course, also deleteriously affected by the fiscal innovations, but on the two occasions when the crown sought their intervention, the rioters peremptorily rebuffed it. On January 15, the confraternities of the convents and monasteries were on the streets with their rosaries in response to a plea from the corregidor; when they attempted to soothe and disperse the rioters, they were abruptly told to get out of the way. Moreover, when a Dominican famed for his virtue held aloft the image of Jesus in this attempt to pacify the multitude, the crowd responded by firing rifles and hurling stones at the sacred image. That same Dominican friar was sent to Cayma to disperse a gathering, but, not only were his entreaties ignored, he himself was personally threatened.[75] In Uru-

74. The accounts of the prisoners taken on January 16 are at AGI, Lima, leg. 1052, cuaderno 4, fols. 254ff.

75. Chacón, "Relación," AGI, Lima, leg. 1052, cuaderno 4, fol. 298; Informe of José Plácido de Barverena, January 18, 1780, AGI, Lima, leg. 1052.

bamba in 1777, the bishop of Cuzco similarly sought to quell a revolt by holding aloft the sacred host; he, too, was stoned and later died from his wounds. In the Andes, profound religious sentiment often exists with equally profound anti-clericalism, yet attacks on an effigy of Jesus and on the sacred host point to a drastic cessation of normality.

Yet, overall, the movement had its own momentum. When the lower-class rioters perceived that the city was undefended, class and perhaps even racial hatreds repressed in quotidian life flared to the surface. The events in Arequipa in January, 1780, demonstrated all too clearly that Spanish power in the Americas rested on fragile foundations that, if challenged by a cross-class alliance, might easily crumble. That cross-class alliance was vitiated not only by racial fear and distrust, but also by a yawning gap between the material conditions of life of the rich few and the many poor.

BRIAN R. HAMNETT

Chapter 10

Popular Insurrection and Royalist Reaction: Colombian Regions, 1810–1823

Sources of conflict within New Granada's provinces during the Wars of Independence have received remarkably little attention. Similarly, the question of popular participation has usually receded before the customary emphasis on the leading creole protagonists and their more developed ideological formation. Overridingly important is the extent to which provincial rebellions after 1810 reflected or extenuated existing social tensions. Anthony McFarlane, in his recent examination of the local roots of popular discontent in eighteenth-century New Granada, argues that protest and rebellion were not motivated by any preconceived ideology and usually had scant repercussions beyond their original areas. Yet, at the same time, they constituted authentic evidence of a popular challenge to the existing powers, often beyond simply fiscal protest. The viceroyalty, moreover, contained an estimated 70,000 slaves and 140,000 free blacks in 1800. The Cauca Valley was the center of a slavocracy that dominated western New Granada well into the nineteenth century. Michael Taussig points to the reappearance of slave rebellions and flights in the late eighteenth century "as a major social factor alongside the growing restlessness of free blacks and a general wave of discontent in the colony as a whole." This regional discontent was especially intense in the valley, where "plots were uncovered for regional revolts, some of which included alliances with Indians, and there is a suggestion that secret black societies or slave cabildos, common enough along the Caribbean coast, even existed in some of the Cauca Valley haciendas." The most striking protest in late colonial New Granada was the Comunero movement of 1780–1781, which went beyond fiscal grievances. The extent and initial impact of the Comunero revolt derived from the ability of the regional elites in Socorro to draw together, at least for a short time, a broad spectrum of popular support. This multiclass alliance rocked the colonial authorities in Santa Fe.[1] A similar type of alliance, though consisting of different social groups, accounted for the early impact of the Túpac Amaru rebellion in Peru in November, 1780.[2] Neither of these two movements brought about the political emancipation of their participants. Nevertheless, the experience of the 1780s provided important guidelines for the independence movements of the 1810s because it demonstrated the efficacy of cross-class alliances and the potential of popular-class recruitment by the dissident elites.[3] Where the elites did not learn this lesson, as in the case of the Venezuelan planters, who sought to transform Spanish abolutism into a slave owners' oligarchy, the popular reaction was decisive. It led to the collapse of the first and second Venezuelan republics in April, 1812, and August, 1814, respectively.[4]

In New Granada, the political fragmentation following the

1. Anthony McFarlane, "Riot and Rebellion in Colonial Spanish America," *Latin American Research Review,* XVII (1982), 212–21; McFarlane, "Civil Disorders and Popular Protests"; Leslie B. Rout, Jr., *The African Experience in Spanish America, 1502 to the Present Day* (Cambridge, 1976), 95, 134, 236–49; Michael Taussig, "The Evolution of Rural Wage Labour in the Cauca Valley of Colombia, 1700–1970," in K. Duncan and I. Rutledge (eds.), *Land and Labour in Latin America* (Cambridge, 1977), 397–434, 408; Phelan, *The People and the King.*

2. See Scarlett O'Phelan Godoy, "Elementos étnicos y de poder en el movimiento tupacamarista, 1780–81," *Nova Americana,* V (1982), 79–101.

3. See J. R. Fisher, "Royalism, Regionalism and Rebellion in Colonial Peru, 1808–1815," *HAHR,* LIX (1979), 232–57; and Fisher, "La rebelión de Túpac Amaru."

4. Germán Carrera Damas, *Boves: Aspectos socioeconómicos de la guerra de independencia* (Caracas, 1972); Miguel Izard, *El miedo a la revolución: La lucha por la libertad en Venezuela (1777–1830)* (Madrid, 1979).

creole revolution of July 20, 1810, in Santa Fe weakened central government, led to a series of interregional civil wars, and compromised the positions of hitherto predominant social groups. Political disarray may well have provided lower-class groups with a chance to redress long-standing grievances at the local level. Similarly, participation, even for a limited time, in a broader-ranging struggle, whether on the patriot or the royalist side, may have been seen as a means of social improvement for the community or upward mobility for the individual.

Colonial New Granada: A Case of Undergovernment

Allan Kuethe argues for the relatively minor impact of the Bourbon reforms in New Granada (see Chapter 1). In contrast to New Spain and Peru, the structure of royal administration remained largely unchanged; the intendant system was never introduced; mining reform proved to be a failure; and the disciplined militia system affected primarily the coastal zone. Neither military reforms nor a *visita* took place in the 1760s before the reforming impulse in metropolitan government circles slowed down again between 1766 and 1776. When the *visita* of New Granada finally took place in the later 1770s, fiscal reform, that is, in reality, new tax impositions, preceded both consensus building around the principle of administrative rationalization and commercial reforms that could redound to the benefit of the creole elites. In consequence, fiscal innovations provoked violent responses and polarized colonial opinion across social groups in opposition to government policy. Kuethe concludes that delay of general reform set the stage for Spain's political catastrophes in the 1810s. Spanish colonial government in New Granada had long demonstrated a striking incapacity to mobilize the territory's fiscal potential and to control revenue from commerce. Failure to halt the contraband trade led to relatively scant revenues from commerce and mining. This in the long run denied the viceregal government the opportunity to finance reform.

Contraband had a long history in New Granada. The Bourbon government had inadvertently compounded the problem by creating a state tobacco monopoly, established in stages between 1766 and 1778. The aim was not primarily to encourage exportation but to raise revenue for the crown at a time of pressing imperial defense requirements. Controversial from the start and a contributory factor to the rebellion of 1781, the monopoly confined growing to only four areas, Girón and Zapatoca in Socorro, Ambalema in the Upper Magdalena zone, Pore and Numchia in the Llanos of Casanare, and the Llano Grande on the eastern side of the Cauca Valley. In many areas illegal cultivation continued. In the Cauca region, for instance, free black peasants began growing tobacco on the periphery of the Arboleda family's slave hacienda in the last quarter of the eighteenth century. Taussig describes these communities as "a type of internal 'republic' or state within the state, cut off from the rest of society except for the illegal cash and crop transfers of tobacco upon which so much of their autonomy depended." This zone on the Río Palo included a runaway slave *palenque*. In the external trade the principal destination for New Granada's contraband was British Jamaica.[5] Along the Caribbean coast gold and tropical produce were exchanged for manufactures. In this clandestine trade Riohacha occupied pride of place. The Río Atrato provided the outlet for gold from Chocó. The large haciendas of the Magdalena Valley, the principal means of access to the interior, were deeply involved in the contraband trade.

Mompós stood at the center of both legal and illegal commerce. Not even the customs house after 1720 nor the deputation of the Consulado of Cartagena after 1796 could halt the illicit trade through Mompós, which by the 1770s had already become one of New Granada's most important towns. In fact, from that time, the contrabandist and mercantile group consolidated its position in opposition to representatives of the official colonial power.[6] In the late colonial period, the Bourbon commercial reforms helped to stimulate the expansion of New Granada's trade, particularly in tropical produce.[7] This, however, did not signify any change in

5. Phelan, *The People and the King,* 18–23; Taussig, "Rural Wage Labour," 407–408.

6. Orlando Fals Borda, *Mompox y Loba: Historia doble de la costa* (Bogotá, 1980), I, 85A, 86A, 87A, 124B.

7. Anthony McFarlane, "El comercio exterior del Virreinato de la Nueva Granada: Conflictos en la política económica de los Borbones, 1783–1789," *ACHSC,* VI–VII, (1971–72), 78–81. McFarlane argues that although precious-metal exports reached a value of over two million pesos in 1787, commercial reform had a greater overall impact on agricultural produce than on mining.

the direction of trade away from the contraband sector. On the contrary, the Cartagena merchant José Ignacio de Pombo estimated the value of imports through the contraband trade to total as much as 3,000,000 pesos, a figure that contrasted with the value of licit trade at 2,562,812 pesos. The suspension of transatlantic trade from 1796 and the prevalence of contraband increased the rivalry between Cartagena and the interior and, in turn, weakened the Cartagena merchants' predominance in the overseas trade.[8] Fals Borda draws attention to the increasing tension between the Mompós contrabandists and the traditional slave-owning planter elite in the coastal zone concerning the question of control of the routes of trade. This conflict reached a climax when, on August 6, 1810, the merchant majority on the Mompós cabildo proclaimed independence from Spain and formed a merchant-controlled patriotic junta. The effort of this group to establish Mompós as a separate province led to civil war with Cartagena during the following year.[9]

The Wars of Independence exacerbated the problem of contraband, which had been endemic and beyond resolution during the colonial period. At the end of the eighteenth century, New Granada's annual gold production reached 3,060,000 pesos, and a considerable quantity, particularly from the placer deposits of the Chocó, which accounted for one-third of this total, went into the contraband trade, rather than the colonial exchequer.[10] Indeed, the food supply to the Chocó communities traveled precisely up the Río Atrato. A characteristic route in the Chocó contraband trade in gold was to Panama, with a further trade also to Guayaquil in the south. The lieutenant governor of Buga, in the center of the

8. Fals Borda, *Mompox y Loba,* I, 88B, 102A, 118A–20A; McFarlane, "Comerciantes y monopolio en la Nueva Granada," 64, 67–69.

9. Fals Borda, *Mompox y Loba,* I, 118A, 119A, 122A, 128A, 135A, 136A. Mompos had a reputation for unruliness as the center of construction for the *champanes* that carried trade and passengers from the coast to the interior. Most of the *bogas* who manned these craft, generally Negroes and *zambos,* lived in the town. See Charles Stuart Cochrane, *Journal of a Residence and Travels in Colombia* (London, 1825), I, 104–105. John P. Hamilton, *Travels Through the Interior Provinces of Colombia* (London, 1827), I, 74–75, considered the *bogas* "as drunken and dissipated a set of fellows as any under the sun."

10. Restrepo, *Minas de Colombia,* 76, 185. Popayán, Barbacoas, Iscuandé, and El Raposo produced 670,000 pesos in gold.

Cauca Valley, writing in the midst of the conflicts of the *patria boba* era, appealed for royalist authorities to take measures to stop the Panama and Guayaquil contraband trades with the Chocó.[11] A major problem continued to be the remote location of the gold-producing zones and the repeated failure of the colonial administration to remedy the situation. Recurrent conflict across the lines of commercial transit served to make matters worse during the 1810s. Barbacoas illustrated this dilemma. The small settlement lay on the Río de Telembí, which flowed into the Río de Patía, which in turn discharged into the ports of Iscuandé and Tumaco on the Pacific coast. Rich deposits of gold had made the region important in the previous two hundred years, and teams of Negro slaves of both sexes, comprising some four thousand individuals, worked them. White settlement always remained scant, and everything but maize and bananas had to be imported from Pasto on the backs of Indian carriers along the high mountainous paths. There was no road, only the Indians trails used since the pre-Colombian era. This remote but significant area was drawn into the conflicts in southern New Granada.[12]

As the Barbacoas case illustrated, gold needed a large labor force. The great families of Popayán, such as the Mosquera and Arboleda, rose to prosperity through their ownership of slave teams and their employment in the gold sector during the eighteenth century. Wealth from the Chocó and the Cauca zones passed into Popayán to sustain its elites. The important Cauca-region towns of Cali, Anserma, Buga, Toro, and Almaguer equally rose upon the gold trade and the slave-labor system. The Wars of Independence, however, tended to disperse the labor force and led in

11. Juan Sámano (governor of Popayán) to Toribio Montes, Popayán, November 6, 1813, ANHE, PQ, Vol. 483 (1813), doc. 27, fol. 27. The propensity of Guayaquil merchants (in a royalist-held city) for the contraband trade with the insurgents (in control of Quito until November, 1812) occasioned comment. Governor Juan Vasco y Pascual to Montes, Guayaquil, July 16, 1812, ANHE, PQ, Vol. 471 (1812), III, doc. 94, fols. 114–15v.

12. "Expediente sobre la apertura de la montaña de Barbacoas para el libre tránsito de los traficantes," ANHE, PQ, Vol. 564 (1818), VI, exp. 12,308, fols. 101–16; Procurador General Pedro Díaz del Castillo to Juan Ramírez (president of Quito), Barbacoas, February 18, 1818, *ibid.*, fols. 103–107. The object was to open trade to Panama, Cartagena, Popayán, Pasto, and Quito as an alternative to Guayaquil, where the Río Guayas flooded for six months of the year, and to the Magdalena route.

some instances to the decline of operations, as in the case of the Chachafruto mine in the Supía region.[13]

It is surprising that the Spanish colonial authorities managed to maintain their position in the Americas at all, in view of the small amount of policing available to them. The scant military establishment in New Granada was a further case in point. In 1799, the army in New Granada consisted solely of 3,576 regulars and 8,460 disciplined militia.[14] Evidently, so small an army, formed with the object of retaining political control of a widely dispersed territory, would be incapable of holding the entire viceroyalty in times of emergency. Such a situation gave insurgency movements the opportunity to establish themselves in remote areas and then extend their influence outward. Precisely because of this state of affairs, the Llanos of Casanare, the lowlands east of the cordillera of Cundinamarca and Boyacá, became a crucially important strategic zone. In itself it had always been rather tangential to the affairs of the viceroyalty, especially after the decline of its textile industries in the later eighteenth century. The official military presence in the Llanos had always been limited, since the central power remained distant and financially constrained through its incapacity to master the sources of revenue. According to Jane Loy, central government control in Casanare was weaker in 1810 than in 1780. This suggests that, were an insurgency to occur in that perennially troubled zone, the central government would lack the means of containing or extinguishing it. Loy argues that the Llanos in 1800–1810 were still experiencing the repercussions of the expulsion of the Jesuits from the missions and of the rebellion of the Comuneros in the cordillera zone. Furthermore, several Comunero rebels had sought refuge in the Llanos, and in some instances they were to take part in the insurgency of the 1810s.[15] The Llanos were in a state of turmoil well before the creoles made their bid for political supremacy in Santa Fe in July, 1810.

13. Restrepo, *Minas de Colombia,* 65–67, 70–73, 75, 79, 184; Germán Colmenares, *Historia económica y social de Colombia, 1537–1719* (Cali, 1973), 267, 285–87, 298–303.

14. Kuethe, *Military Reform and Society,* 210–11, 217–18.

15. Jane M. Loy, "Forgotten Comuneros: The 1781 Revolt in the Llanos of Casanare," *HAHR,* LXI (1981), 235–57. These features of the history of the Llanos recurred at several intervals, most notably during the *Violencia,* when a "guerrilla campesina" formed a

We have already remarked on the contraband trade along the river systems of the Caribbean lowlands. That region, too, was undergoverned in the late colonial period and like the Llanos, though for different reasons, would prove to be a zone of heavy fighting during the Wars of Independence. During the second half of the eighteenth century, the region between Mompós, Cartagena, and Santa Marta revealed little evidence of effective viceregal authority. The central power had made efforts to remedy this lax administrative control by grouping dispersed settlements into new towns during 1744–1770. A major reason for this policy was the need to safeguard the region between Mompós and the coast from the depredations of the Chimila Indians. Even so, unpacified Indians continued to threaten the routes of transit into the interior, including the Magdalena route itself.[16] The situation in this coastal zone was further complicated by the jurisdictional rivalry between the three cities, which continued throughout the Wars of Independence and into the following decades. Even though Santa Marta lacked the commercial importance of Cartagena, its strategic position between New Granada's revolutionary city-state and royalist-controlled Maracaibo guaranteed that possession of it would be bitterly contested in the 1810s. During the struggle for independence long-standing intraregional tensions resulted in armed conflicts. Similarly, the latent social tensions within these zones also rose to the surface to cause further complications. The conflicts within the city of Cartagena itself in 1810–1815 were a case in point. Hermes Tovar has perceptively commented that the Wars of Independence "represented in those early years of the revolutionary juntas and republics a checkboard of hidden vendettas."[17]

---

major aspect of the provincial response to the events of April 9, 1948, in Bogotá. The Llanos became one of the first nuclei of resistance: by the end of 1952, at least twenty thousand combatants had fought there and in the following year passed on to the offensive. See Gonzalo Sánchez and Donny Meertens, *Bandoleros, gamonales y campesinos: El caso de la violencia en Colombia* (Bogotá, 1983), 32–33, 38–40.

16. Fals Borda, *Mompox y Loba,* I, 106A–14B.

17. María Dolores González Luna, "La política de población y pacificación indígena en las poblaciones de Santa Marta y Cartagena (Nuevo Reino de Granada), 1750–1800," *Boletín americanista,* XX (1978), 87–118; Cochrane, *Journal,* I, 57–59; Tovar, "Guerras de opinión," 196.

Patria Boba

The social conflicts of Cartagena were real and of long duration. The revolution in Caracas in April, 1810, presented the city's aspiring dissident merchant and lawyer group with the opportunity to launch a swift bid for political control to make themselves independent of both metropolitan Spain and viceregal Santa Fe. Cartagena proclaimed itself an independent sovereign state on November 11, 1811. This action was central to the internal struggle in the city, described by Indalecio Liévano Aguirre as a social conflict between "el partido de los patricios" and "el partido revolucionario," which took power on November 11, 1811, with the support of "los estratos populares del puerto." With the fall of the "notables," power was transferred to Rodríguez Torices, who became president of the state of Cartagena. The city's military situation became critical during the next year with the collapse of the first Venezuelan republic in April, 1812, which enabled the royalists of Santa Marta and Panama to intensify their naval and land blockade. Already, the royalists of Santa Marta had fortified positions such as Tenerife and Chiriguana along the Magdalena River. The Cartagena revolutionaries were obliged to launch a campaign into this region and burned the towns in 1812.[18]

These royalist positions on the coast enabled Benito Pérez to reconstitute the viceroyalty of New Granada in the isthmus of Panama. However, the remoteness of Panama and the military expansion of Cartagena obliged the royalists briefly to abandon control of Santa Marta and the Ocaña district early in January, 1813, and repair from the Magdalena line into the safety of Maracaibo. Local resistance to the Cartagena patriots forced the revolutionaries out on March 6, 1813, and enabled the incoming viceroy, Francisco de Montalvo, to take up residence in Santa Marta in June and prepare for the reduction of the patriot positions. He described the city as prostrate and faced by a naval blockade from Cartagena and an attempt by land to cut off the food supply from Ciénaga

18. Indalecio Liévano Aguirre, *Los grandes conflictos sociales y económicos de nuestra historia* (7th ed.; Bogotá, 1978), II, 864–65, 879–86, 902–903; Eduardo Lemaitre, *Breve historia de Cartagena* (Cartagena, 1958), 91–138; T. Blossom, *Nariño: Hero of Colombian Independence* (Arizona, 1967), 92; Tovar, "Guerras de opinión," 192–93; Hamilton, *Travels*, I, 62.

Grande and the right bank of the Magdalena. This danger was not finally dispelled until royalist ships from Portobelo reopened the food supply in September and brought troops and émigré civil servants. Montalvo reunited all Santa Marta forces into a provincial battalion and began to plan for the refortification of the Magdalena line. Royalist naval action late in March, 1814, reopened Ciénaga Grande and forced the patriots to abandon the province and withdraw across the Magdalena. By June, 1814, the royalist cause was better placed than ever in the Caribbean zone—especially with the Quito royalist victories in southern New Granada in May, which led to the capture of Antonio Nariño, and with the impending collapse of the second Venezuelan republic.[19]

The social and economic impact of these military conflicts is not easy to quantify. The tithe revenues of the Santa Marta diocese fell from 25,000 to 9,000 pesos between 1810 and 1815. The loss of the city in 1813 made matters worse, and the royalist commanders, eager to find someone to blame, complained that the city council was incompetent and the Ciénaga Indians indifferent. The patriot campaign in that year led to the burning of towns along the Magdalena line and the dispersal of their inhabitants. The royalist retreat took the military conflict into the region of Valledupar as the patriots pressed towards Riohacha in 1814. Mompós, a revolutionary center, suffered greatly during the advance of the Spanish expeditionary force into the interior in 1815. General Francisco Tomás Morales, who commanded the Magdalena Valley section, ordered the execution of large numbers of rebel supporters after his entry into the town. Colonel Francisco Warletta persecuted prominent patriot families, obliging them to leave the town and abandon their estates. The population of Mompós before the revolution had been eighteen thousand; by the early 1820s, it had sunk to ten thousand. Santa Marta's population fell from eight thousand to three thousand during the war years. Since the city was a royalist position, the victorious patriots after 1821 drafted many of its leading citizens into the army. Furthermore, the neglected condition of the region enabled Indian tribes from the hinterland to

19. R. Blanco-Fombona (ed.), *Ultimos virreyes de Nueva Granada: Relación de mando del Virrey Francisco Montalvo y noticias del Virrey Sámano sobre la pérdida del reino (1813–1819)* (Madrid, 1918), 10–20, 25, 30–35, 45–48.

sweep into the city in January, 1823, under the command of a former Spanish governor, Pujol, operating possibly in conjunction with Morales, who retained control of Maracaibo, and occupy it for three weeks with disastrous consequences. Cartagena was besieged three times, including the 116-day siege by General Pablo Morillo's Spanish force, which lasted until the capitulation of the suffering city on December 6, 1815. Morillo entered to find a city of death and horror.[20]

Upon the collapse of the second Venezuelan republic, Bolívar fled to Cartagena and thence to Mompós (October, 1814). Inside the Caribbean city social and political tensions had escalated to the point that the notables, strengthened by the military defeats suffered by the popular regime, conspired to recover power therein. Internal conflict led to the withdrawal of Cartagena troops from the right bank of the Magdalena to facilitate this. On November 24, 1814, a constituent college, dominated by the notables, took control, a political change at the top that provoked intense popular opposition. Liévano Aguirre points to the contrast between "the college, controlled by the notables, and the enraged multitude that broke into the area of its meeting place and surrounded the building from the first day, hurling hostile cries at the Cartagena oligarchy." The notables had installed Dr. José María García de Toledo as governor of the Cartagena state, against whom the popular leader, Gabriel Gutiérrez de Piñeres, himself a member of the upper class, incited the *zambos* of the city. Accordingly, troops needed to fight the Santa Marta royalists had to be redeployed to hold back the popular classes inside the city itself to prevent a civil war between the white upper class and the colored majority. Bolívar, who at the end of 1814 had been caught in the conflict between the

20. Tovar, "Guerras de opinión," 197; Juan Jiménez (commander in La Ciénaga) to Viceroy Francisco de Montalvo, Portobelo, June 26, 1813, Governor Manuel Zegueira to Montalvo, Riohacha, September 5, 1814, Ayuntamiento to Montalvo, Santa Marta, January 8, 1814, Gonzalo Aramendi to Montalvo, Riohacha, January 17, 1814, Aramendi to Montalvo, no. 92, Valledupar, June 22, 1814, all in AHNC, Anexo, Guerra y Marina, tomo 117, fols. 919–22v, tomo 120, fols. 209–209v, 283–83v, 605–11; Cochrane, *Journal,* I, 104–105; Hamilton, *Travels,* I, 74–75; Fals Borda, *Mompox y Loba,* I, 139A, 141A; Cochrane, *Journal,* I, 57–59; Hamilton, *Travels,* 15, 20–21; Pablo Morillo, *Mémoires du General Morillo, Comte de Carthagène, Marquis de la Puerta: Rélatifs aux principaux événements de ses campagnes en Amérique de 1815 à 1821* (Paris, 1826), 60–61.

congress of the United Provinces based in the provincial town of Socorro and the city of Santa Fe, which he had taken on December 12, now found himself caught up in the Cartagena situation. The military commander in Cartagena, Castillo, fearing Bolivarian control of the city, refused to cooperate with Bolívar's efforts to renew the campaign in Venezuela. By March, 1815, Bolívar was determined to march against the city to prepare for a general campaign against Santa Marta. These differences benefited only the royalists, who took Mompós on April 29, 1815. The loss of this rich and important position cut off the coast from the interior. In that month, the Spanish expeditionary force under Morillo arrived on the Venezuelan coast. Morillo reached Santa Marta on July 23 and established the blockade of Cartagena on August 22. Royalist seizure of Tierrabomba cut off the fortress of San Fernando de Bocachica and led to the fall of Cartagena. Montalvo took up residence there and reestablished the Consulado on October 23, 1816, and the city's white militia force; he decided not to restore the battalion of *pardos libres* because of revolutionary recruitment among the colored population.[21]

The insurrection in the Cauca Valley was supported by the patriots of Santa Fe, but not exclusively motivated by their example. It derived its origins from local conditions. In the province of Popayán, for instance, whites constituted less than a quarter of the population.[22] The fears of landed proprietors and slave owners resulted from the fact that the Negro and mulatto population, the chief source of labor, was double the white. Gaspar Mollien, the French traveler, commented that "one hardly encounters anyone but Negroes along the entire cordillera between Cartagena and Pasto." Social tensions in these regions, with their marked racial aspect, certainly did not originate in the Independence period, and similarly, they did not terminate with the creation of the Colombian state in 1821. The social conflicts of the Independence period probably had their roots in eighteenth-century economic condi-

21. Blanco-Fombona, *Ultimos virreyes,* 57, 63; Liévano Aguirre, *Los grandes conflictos,* II, 879–86, 902–903; Blanco-Fombona, *Ultimos virreyes,* 64, 70–73, 77–89, 93, 100, 122.

22. Hermes Tovar Pinzón, "El estado colonial frente al poder local y regional," *Nova americana,* V (1983), 42–43. Tovar includes Pasto in this southern zone and gives the following proportions: free Negroes and mulattoes, 32,766; Indians, 27,764; whites, 21,066; Negroes, 18,761; total, 100,356 (12.5 percent of the population of the viceroyalty).

tions, such as the expansion of sugar refining in the Cauca Valley. The livestock haciendas depended largely upon slave labor: in fact, the value of the slave population represented one of the largest assets of these estates. The social and racial tensions of the Cauca Valley before 1810 were the context for the struggles thereafter, particularly since the traditional methods of political control through the Spanish colonial system had broken down at governmental level. The regional elites, who derived their power from control of land and labor, found themselves caught between royalist counterrevolution and revolt from below. Continued tensions in the valley after independence inhibited economic development. Slavery entered a long, terminal crisis. Loss of slaves, as a result of the fighting during the Wars of Independence, could seriously affect the value of properties.[23]

Similar conflicts affected the gold-producing sector of the Popayán economy. The sisters of the Valencia family of Popayán owned the mine of Yurmangín in the southern coastal zone. The slave-labor force rebelled early in the insurrection, and these proprietors, arguing that the prosperity of the province depended upon slavery, warned that the state itself would suffer if the mines were not worked. The slaves, however, not only persisted in their rebellious conduct, but sought to spread the insurrection. In November, 1813, the sisters appealed to the president of Quito to order troops from Tumaco to put down the slave rebellions.[24]

The town councils of Cali, Buga, Cartago, Anserma, and Toro supported in 1811 the insurrection of Santa Fe against the colonial regime and formed the Confederation of the Cauca Valley. These were, however, risings of the creole elites that had broad geographical repercussions among that social group. Nevertheless, the risings in the Cauca region took from the start a decidedly popular character, though it is difficult to ascertain to what degree

23. Gaspar Théodore Mollien, *Viaje por la República de Colombia en 1823* (Bogotá, 1944), 275; Germán Colmenares, *Historia económica y social de Colombia, II Popayán: Una sociedad esclavista, 1680–1800* (Bogotá, 1979), 269–71; Keith Christie, "Antioqueño Colonization in Western Colombia: A Reappraisal," *HAHR,* LVIII (1978), 260–83; José Escorcía, "Haciendas y estructura agraria en el Valle del Cauca, 1810–50," *ACHSC,* X (1982), 119–38.

24. Ignacia Valencia to Montes, Popayán, November 6, 1813, ANHE, PQ, Vol. 483 (1813), XI, doc. 23, fols. 23–23v.

popular participation was stimulated by elite leadership or example. According to the royalist military commander in Cartago, José Antonio Yllera, who was involved in the concertina warfare across the region in 1813, "unrest in the valley grows in momentum with every day, and the local populace thinks only of renewing their rebellion" (which had begun in 1811). Such activity obliged him to evacuate the area. Yllera warned that three hundred insurgents with eight pieces of artillery in Anserma were ready to attack royalist positions in the Cauca Valley by way of the mountainous passes of the Quindío and Barragán. These actions culminated in the seizure of Cartago by the revolutionary forces of Santa Fe and Antioquia. Such reports as these suggest collusion between local popular leaders within the valley zone and the creole leaders of the revolutions in the main cities. Yllera pointed to the revolutionary role of the dominant group in the city of Cali. Other sources commented on this as well, particularly with respect to Cali's rivalry with Popayán. Royalist authorities complained that the city of Popayán had been the first to witness bloodshed on account of its opposition to the revolution. "The city had been attacked thereafter by its subordinate cities and suffered all the miseries of war brought upon it by the hostility of Cali, which had been continually rained down upon it." In 1811–1812, "the traitors of Cali" occupied Popayán. The president of the republican government in Popayán was Joaquín Caicedo, member of the celebrated family that originated in Cali. His brother, Manuel José Caicedo, was provisor of the diocese. Their uncle was Bishop José de Cuero y Caicedo of Quito, who in 1809 had written to the leading citizens of Popayán asking them to support the Quito revolution. All of them, and a number of other clerics in Popayán, were singled out by Miguel Tacón, the royalist commander, as determined enemies of Spanish rule.[25]

25. José Antonio Yllera to Sámano, Buga, December 8, 1813, Yllera to José Esteban de Dorronsoro (teniente general del asiento), Cartago, December 2, 1813, Yllera to Sámano, Tulúa, December 8, 1813, all in ANHE, PQ, Vol. 484 (1813), XII, no. 55, fol. 60, no. 7, fols. 7–7v, no. 69, fols. 75–76; J. M. Rodríguez to Montes, Quito, October 2, 1815, ANHE, PQ, Vol. 512 (1815), III, exp. 11,364, fols. 10–16; ANHE, PQ, Vol. 510, exp. 11,332, fol. 181v; Miguel Tacón to Molina (president of Quito), Tumaco, November 23, 1811, ANHE, PQ, Vol. 468 (1811), IV, fols. 264–65v.

Revolutionary action in southern New Granada depended to a large extent on the survival of the second revolutionary regime in Quito. However, a further military intervention from royalist Peru extinguished that regime in November, 1812. The Consulado of Lima, bastion of the Peruvian counterrevolution, contributed the sum of 100,000 pesos toward this expeditionary army against Quito. Once the royalists had recovered the city, the president of the audiencia, Toribio Montes, began the counteroffensive into southern New Granada.[26] The royalists reoccupied the city of Popayán on June 30, 1813. However, the matter did not end there. The new governor, Colonel Juan Sámano, a confirmed soldier with no civil tact, made himself and his Peruvian troops immediately unpopular with the Popayán creole elite, who regarded themselves as a highly superior and cultured aristocracy. Indeed, the Popayán elite found itself caught between the dangerous revolutionaries of Santa Fe and the Cauca Valley on the one hand, and the rough, increasingly arbitrary, counterrevolution emanating from Quito and Lima on the other. They were squeezed and did not know which way to turn. Sámano pressured the *ayuntamiento* for thirty thousand pesos for the payment and maintenance of his force. Indeed, such requests for instant cash earned him the hostility of the pro-independence faction of the clergy. Sámano himself mistrusted everyone and suspected all of collusion with the enemy: the Dominican prior was "a well-known insurgent"; the Franciscan Joaquín Fernández de Soto was "one of the principal apostles of insurrection in the province, companion of the late Caicedo and fellow member of the revolutionary junta"; the diocesan provisor, Manuel Mariano Urrutia, was "by nature an intriguer and turbulent rebel." Urrutia took upon himself the task of openly confronting Sámano's authority in Popayán when the latter arrested the parish priest of El Trapiche, Belisario Gómez, whom the royalist governor considered to be "the most ardent protagonist of the revolutionary system since its beginnings." Such conflicts point to the evident tendency of the royalist military to blame the American clergy for the outbreak and sustenance of the insur-

26. Luis de Ariza and Gabriel Fernández de Urbina to Montes, Guayaquil, June 4, 1812, ANHE, PQ, Vol. 471 (1812), II, doc. 81, fols. 99–99v.

rection in New Granada, and in Popayán the inviolability of suspected insurgent clerics could not be guaranteed.[27]

Once they had recovered Popayán, the royalists attempted to pacify the Cauca Valley, and they formed detachments for the "expulsion of the bandits" from the area of Las Cañas. Even so, they feared at any time the recrudescence in the still unruly Cauca zone of the "insurrectionary movement . . . of the slaves." Furthermore, the threat of a royalist révanche from the south had encouraged the president of Cundinamarca, Antonio Nariño, to bring his main force to the valley. Since Sámano felt too exposed to challenge him, he abandoned Popayán on January 15, 1814, and withdrew to Pasto, leaving the Casa de Moneda and printing press in revolutionary hands. With Nariño's advance, a considerable number of Sámano's locally recruited forces deserted to the rebels.[28] After the capture of Nariño in Pasto, the royalist Teniente Coronel Aparicio Vidaurrazaga reoccupied Popayán on December 29, 1814, and renewed Sámano's controversial measures. The city apparently presented a dismal picture of impoverishment and disarray.[29] Vidaurrazaga's pressures on ecclesiastical immunity led to the protest of Provisor Urrutia and the parish priest of Tambo, Dr. Manuel María Rodríguez, a member of one of the senior families, in the spring of 1815. Vidaurrazaga arrested Rodríguez, in what was perceived to be a scandalous manner, as an alleged collaborator of

27. Sámano to cabildo, Popayán, November 4, 1813, Sámano to Montes, Popayán, November 9, 1813, Fray Pedro de Paredes to an anonymous cleric, Popayán, October 21, 1813, Sámano to Montes, Popayán, November 11, 1813, all in ANHE, PQ, Vol. 483 (1813), doc. 24, fols. 24–24v, doc. 44, fols. 45–47v, doc. 47, no. 3, fols. 50–50v, doc. 65, fols. 74–75. B. R. Hamnett, "The Counterrevolution of Morillo and the Insurgent Clerics of New Granada, 1815–1820," *Americas,* XXXII (1976), 597–617, studied this problem in the Bogotá context, with particular reference to Fernando Caicedo y Flores, to whom Pope Leo XII granted canonical recognition as Archbishop of Santa Fe in May 1827.

28. Ildefonso Gil de la Tejada to Montes, Buga, November 22, 1813, Sámano to Montes, Popayán, November 23, 1813, both in ANHE, PQ, Vol. 483 (1813), no. 131, fols. 152–52v, no. 134, fols. 156–57; Montes to Benito Pérez, Quito, April 7, 1814, in Sergio Elías Ortiz (ed.), *Colección de documentos para la historia de Colombia (época de la Independencia)* (Bogotá, 1964), primera serie, 52–53. Montes censured Sámano for this retreat.

29. Montalvo to Montes, Santa Marta, May 10, 1815, ANHE, PQ, Vol. 514 (1814), V, exp. 11,432; J. A. Balcázar Sánchez to Montes, Popayán, January 5, 1815, ANHE, PQ, Vol. 515 (1815), VI, no. 41, fols. 46–46v.

Nariño, whom he himself claimed to have opposed, and hauled him before a civil judge. Montes, when informed of such procedures, ordered his release to prevent an open breach between the civil and the ecclesiastical powers.[30]

The pressures of war, especially in view of the frequent changes of control in Popayán, fell heavily upon the city's elite, many of whom were prominent royalists. Few, however, found themselves in any way sympathetic to the new militarism of the counterrevolutionary army. Many were caught up in the escalating conflict and could not control their situations. Dr. José María de Mosquera y Figueroa, *procurador supernumerario* of the city council in 1810 and commander of the militia, contributed 42,000 pesos in loans, livestock, and food to the royalist cause. Nariño's forces inflicted heavy damage to his estates. In March, 1811, when the royalist commander, Governor Miguel Tacón, abandoned the city to the revolutionaries for the first time, he asked Mosquera to remain there to prevent a sack. He stayed there to welcome the Quito royalist forces in December, 1814, and contributed large sums of his own and from the estate of his business associate, Francisco José Arboleda, to the royalist cause, even loaning Negroes from the La Tota mine.[31] The Rodríguez family, which had so greatly incurred Vidaurrazaga's wrath, was strongly royalist. José María Rodríguez Gil del Valle, captain of Popayán militia forces, had fled to Pasto in 1811 to avoid being compromised by the revolutionary occupation of his city. He was the son of the regidor Francisco Antonio Rodríguez. Dr. José María made donations to the royalist cause in 1814 and played a significant role in the counterrevolution by recruiting loyal natives of the Patía region and contributing thereby to the capture of the revolutionary junta president, Caicedo, in Pasto. Vidaurrazaga in 1815, however, suspected him of insurgent sympathies because he was the

30. Rodríguez to Montes, Tambo, June 5, 1815, Rodríguez to Montes, Popayán, June 21, 1815, Provisor Manuel Mariano Urrutia, Quito, December 1, 1815, all in ANHE, PQ, Vol. 513 (1815), no. 4, exp. 11,410, fols. 136–231v. After removal from Popayán, Vidaurrazaga became subdelegate of Santa and Chancay.

31. Documentos que acreditan las erogaciones, suplementos y donativos que han hecho Dr. J. M. de Mosquera . . . , ANHE, PQ, Vol. 556 (1817), II, exp. 12,088, fols. 160–71v, cuaderno 1. See also Oidor Joaquín de Mosquera y Figueroa to the king, Madrid, January 31, 1818, in Ortiz (ed.), *Colección de documentos,* primera serie, 100–107.

brother of the parish priest of El Tambo, who resisted royalist violations of ecclesiastical immunity.[32]

Between 1810 and 1815, the various social groups involved in the conflicts of the epoch of the *patria boba* coexisted uneasily, each with distinct perspectives concerning the nature and purpose of the struggle. The breach between Antonio Nariño and the Congress of Cundinamarca exposed the degree to which such tensions led to political disintegration within the revolutionary camp. The continued royalist positions in Panama and Santa Marta in the north and Pasto and Quito in the south made this dissolution alarming. Once the royalist counteroffensive opened in the south in 1812–1813, the patriots had to devise some sort of political response as well as a military one, and they appealed for popular support to maintain revolutionary momentum. Nariño attempted to recruit support among the dissident hacienda slave population of the Western Cordillera for his campaign against the southern royalists in the autumn of 1813. Nariño's military efforts, however, were repeatedly obstructed by the resistance of the provincial authorities in the rival cities of Antioquia, Tunja, and Socorro to placing their forces under a unified command. Antioquia's military commander refused to compromise the sovereignty of the province. Nariño, imitating the royalist practice begun by Tacón and anticipating the policy to be pursued in Venezuela by Bolívar after his Carúpano decrees of 1816, offered slaves their liberty on condition that they serve in his army. Such actions provoked slave rebellions on estates and in mining zones. The situation in the west reached such a serious state of affairs that the patriot dictator of Antioquia, Juan del Corral, advocated a gradual abolition of slavery. Corral, a native of Mompós and closely related to the creole revolutionaries of that region, had become a hereditary city councilor in Antioquia in 1808 and deputy in the first congress of New

32. Rodríguez to Montes, Quito, October 2, 1815, ANHE, PQ, Vol. 512 (1815), III, exp. 11,364, fols. 10–16. Montes upheld Rodríguez's position. Upon the news of the Spanish expeditionary force's advance toward Neiva, Sámano moved north from Pasto in company with Ramón Zambrano, commander of the Pasto Militia Battalion, and reoccupied Popayán on June 30, 1816, after the rebels had failed to destroy the Casa de Moneda. Fernando Zambrano to Montes, Pasto, June 13, 1816, ANHE, PQ, Vol. 532 (1816), IV, no. 80, fols. 93–93v; Manuel de Pombo to Sámano, Popayán, July 2, 1816, ANHE, PQ, Vol. 533 (1816), VII, no. 26, fols. 29–30v.

Granada in July, 1810. When the Quito royalists recovered Popayán, the Antioquia legislature appointed Corral president-dictator on July 30, 1813, with the full support of the Antioquia Revolutionary Junta's president, José Miguel de Restrepo. Antioquia's response to the royalist advance down the Cauca Valley was the campaign to the south by the specially organized "Batallón Antioqueño" of some five hundred men formed at the cost of 337,518 pesos. The aim of this force was eventually to cooperate with Nariño's offensive towards Popayán and Pasto. Corral urged the Congress of the Union on December 12, 1813, to adopt a policy of emancipation of slaves to prevent royalist attempts to stir up slaves against patriot landowners. Manumission, however, was legislated to apply only within the province of Antioquia because of the general hostility to such a radical policy in Chocó and Popayán, the other centers of slave-manned gold-prospecting operations. In Antioquia, in any case, manumission applied only to the descendants of those in slavery at the time of promulgation. The slave trade into and out of the province was banned, and a progressive emancipation of all slaves was projected. The royalist counter-revolution of 1816 terminated this policy altogether. The Congress of the Union, then located in Tunja, resisted even recognizing the liberty Nariño had offered to combatant slaves.[33]

Popular participation in the struggles of the 1810s took different forms in different places. In the Pasto region, the popular class consistently fought on the royalist side. From the first instant, Pasto had opposed the revolutionary movement, whether launched from Quito in 1809 or from Bogotá in 1810. In response to this royalist sentiment, Tacón in 1811 unilaterally reduced Indian tribute by one peso to four pesos. Nevertheless, when the Quito royalists recovered the city, Montes restored the full tribute in October, 1814, in spite of Indian protests.[34] Patriot campaigns against the city, as in 1812, were met by mass organization to resist them, regardless of the insurrection of the towns farther down the

33. Roberto M. Tisnes Jiménez, *Don Juan del Corral: Libertador de los esclavos* (Cali, 1980), 18, 32, 34, 47, 51, 59, 101–102, 116–17, 157, 165–67, 183, 262–73, 276. Corral died on April 7, 1814 (Liévano Aguirre, *Los grandes conflictos,* II, 805–10).

34. Governor Tomás Miguel Santa Cruz to Montes, Pasto, February 27, 1815, ANHE, PQ, Vol. 516 (1815), VI, no. 142, fol. 163.

Cauca Valley. This opposition to the patriots did not in any way signify that either Pasto or its adjacent regions had a history of passivity before the official power. On the contrary, the south and the districts of Quito beyond Tulcán had a long tradition of resistance to the fiscal impositions of a central power. Indeed, the Quito populace itself had set the example by its long resistance during 1765 to tax innovations and to exclusive peninsular dominance. Otavalo and the other regions had rebelled in 1777, and Túquerres in 1800. The Indians of Pasto rose in 1780 to oppose the establishment of the aguardiente monopoly, and they were initially supported in their dissent by the *vecinos*. In Túquerres, in 1800, attempts to reinforce the tribute burden precipitated a protest movement among the Indians. A further revolt occurred in Barbacoas. Such rebellions were not revolutionary movements designed to overthrow the colonial system, but protests against specific impositions and evidence of local resentment at incursions by a remote central power tentatively attempting to poach new resources for itself. In these rebellions, many whites acted in collusion with the popular classes of society, in a common, multiethnic front against fiscal measures.[35]

The resistance of Pasto to the new republican order should be understood within this context of opposition to central-government innovations. The city, caught between the revolutionary forces of the Cauca Valley cities in the north and of Quito in the south, fell early in the insurrection and was sacked. *Pastuso* royalists, however, regrouped in the surrounding hills and waged a guerrilla struggle that finally enabled them to recover control. Nariño's surrender in Pasto in 1814 extinguished the revolutionary threat until the autumn of 1819. The loyalty of Pasto to the royal cause encouraged its leading citizens to petition the crown to elevate the region to a civil and military governorship and designate it as a diocese in its own right. They also requested the foundation of a college so that they could circumvent the expensive necessity of sending their sons to Popayán or Quito for their education. Fur-

35. Javier Lavina, "La sublevación de Túquerres en 1800: una revuelta antifiscal," *Boletín americanista*, XX (1978), 191–92, 195–96. According to this source, the Túquerres rebellion began on May 18 and lasted two days. See especially Moreno Yañez, *Sublevaciones indigenas*, 147–70, and (for the Otavalo rebellion of 1777) 359–79.

thermore, they requested exemption from recent taxes on official sealed paper and on strong drink. The city council requested, in addition, "that the Pasto Indians, our constant companions throughout the military struggle over the past five years in Quito and Santa Fe, should be exempted from tribute payments." The Council of the Indies replied on February 27, 1819, and conceded Pasto certain favors: a ten-year exemption from payment of *alcabalas,* exoneration of one-half the tribute payment for a period to be specified by the viceroy, and the right to found its own college-seminary.[36] Such concessions, though never implemented, may have helped to reinforce Pasto's royalist allegiance.

Regions such as Patía, which contained a number of escaped slave *palenques,* and Barbacoas continued to be royalist in sentiment throughout the 1810s. In Barbacoas, the local Negroes struggled against white proprietors. In effect, they were probably taking advantage of disturbed conditions throughout the south to improve their position and weaken the links that bound them to the political center. They rose in 1811 against the patriot regime in Santa Fe. In the summer of 1811, "the inhabitants of El Tambo and Timbío formed common cause with those of Patía. They abandoned their homes and . . . invaded the Valley of Patía, pillaging and robbing the local proprietors and even killing several patriot stragglers from the armies." Patriot authorities regarded such popular insurrections as "banditry" when they were directed against themselves; royalist authorities adopted exactly the same response. In the colonial period, the viceregal government, well aware of the warlike nature of the region's inhabitants, had left them well alone. Republicans, however, feared for the safety of their forces on campaign against Pasto, since the Barbacoas zone lay on their flank. Indeed, militia forces from Barbacoas assisted Miguel Tacón, royalist governor of Popayán, against the patriots in 1812. A series of coastal and coastal-hinterland positions from Barbacoas, Iscuandé, and Buenaventura to Tumaco and Esmeraldas long remained in royalist hands, in spite of periodic patriot actions there.[37] Despite

36. "Representación del Cabildo de Pasto ante Su Majestad sobre el mérito de la ciudad en las pasadas convulsiones," Sala Capitular del Ayuntamiento Constitucional de Pasto, June 13, 1814, in Ortiz (ed.), *Colección de documentos,* primera serie, 54–64; Consejo de Indias en sala segunda, Madrid, February 27, 1819, *ibid.,* 110–14.

37. J. M. Cabral to Dr. Miguel de Pombo, Popayán, August 4, 1811, in Sergio Elías

popular royalism among the castes, royalist military commanders, most of them property owners or local elites, had their fears of overzealous participation. Captain José María Rodríguez, of the leading Popayán family, played an important role in the organization of, in his own words, "the counterrevolution," in the pueblos of El Tambo and Patía. He claimed to have been obliged to hold back the *patianos* to prevent them from committing any excesses since their "sole objective was robbery and murder, scarcely compatible with the defense of the crown."[38]

Insurgent corsair activity along the coasts occasionally resulted in damage or occupation, and trade between Panama and Guayaquil, especially in textiles, was cut off, though such actions never altered the course of the war, especially because after 1816 the Spanish expeditionary force controlled the main areas of settlement in New Granada. Buenos Aires' corsairs attacked the royalist-held port of Guayaquil on February 8, 1816, and entered the Puerto de Dagua with three large ships in the hope of joining forces with the Cauca Valley insurgents and threatening Tumaco. A second attempt took place between February 17 and 29, and a third in June.[39] In January, 1819, however, Buenos Aires' corsairs reduced the port of Tumaco to ruins and threatened Iscuandé, the River Barbacoas, and the port of Esmeraldas until late in February, 1819, when their main thrusts were directed to the Bay of Guayaquil and the coast of Panama.[40]

Ortiz (ed.), *Colección de documentos para la historia de Colombia (época de la Independencia)* (Bogotá, 1966), tercera serie, 206–207; Nicolas de Quiñones y Cienfuegos (comandante de milicias disciplinadas de la ciudad de Barbacoas) to Gabriel de Torres (subinspector general del reino), Barbacoas, April 6, 1817, in Ortiz (ed.), *Colección de documentos*, primera serie, 93–97.

38. Rodríquez to Montes, Quito, October 2, 1815, ANHE, PQ, Vol. 512 (1815), III, exp. 11,364, fols. 10–16.

39. José de Maruri (jefe político y militar) to Montes, Tumaco, May 22, 1816, ANHE, PQ, Vol. 531 (1816), V, no. 139, fols. 164–64v; Vasco to Montes, Guayaquil, February 17, 1816, Vasco to Montes, Guayaquil, February 19, 1816, AHNE, PQ, Vol. 528 (1816), II, no. 115, fols. 140–40v, no. 192, fol. 222; Antonio Mingues to Montes, Barbacoas, June 6, 1816, ANHE, PQ, Vol. 532 (1816), VI, doc. 44, fols. 51–52. Iscuandé and Micay were defended by fifty militiamen.

40. *Vecinos* to Ramírez, Barbacoas, January 6, 1819, Andrés de Castro to Ramírez, Esmeraldas, February 24–25 and March 25, 1819, all in ANHE, PQ, Vol. 567 (1819), I, no. 11, fols. 11–11v, nos. 82, 86, 116, fols. 89, 93, 131.

The Llanos of Casanare

The royalist insurgency from Pasto, Barbacoas, Patía, etc., derived its strength from predominance in remote zones. The Spanish expeditionary force's failure to pacify the Llanos of Casanare enabled a patriot insurgency to develop there within three years of the fall of Santa Fe to Morillo, with appalling consequences for the restored royalist regime. Indeed, Viceroy Montalvo himself pointed out that the entire kingdom had been pacified militarily, *with the exception of the Llanos*. By September to October, 1817, the Bogotá regime had concluded that a military expedition into the Llanos was, as Sámano himself put it, "absolutely indispensible."[41]

The Llanos of Casanare became the base area of revolutionary resistance after the military triumph of the counterrevolution in 1815–1816, which led to a harsh political repression throughout the subsequent three years. The defeat of the armed forces of the regional revolutionary powers of Cartagena, Tunja, Santa Fe, and Cali left few possibilities of open resistance. Nevertheless, by 1817 conspiracies and limited insurgencies had become the patriot response to the counterrevolution. A guerrilla movement could take root because the royalist reconquest was not complete. The royalist armies, in spite of their punitive measures throughout the main settled areas, had made the classic error of failing to establish absolute military control over all territory. This failure enabled insurgent bands to recover the initiative on the eastern Llanos, a vast, open region linked geographically to the plains of Venezuela, which were still in a state of open rebellion. Of the territory of the viceroyalty of New Granada, only the Llanos of Casanare remained independent of royalist control in 1816. This remote region was distant from the political center, but nevertheless offered relatively easy access to pockets of insurgency in Boyacá by means of the valleys that led upward into the cordillera. There was, however, no attempt by the New Granada revolutionaries—in any case, a severely decimated group—to set up an insurgent provisional government in the Llanos. The whole region continued to be nomi-

41. Montalvo to Sámano, Cartagena, January 30, 1818, in Blanco-Fombona, *Ultimos virreyes*, 217; Sámano to Oidor Decano Juan Jurado, Santa Fe, September 12, 1817, AHNC, Anexo, Historia, tomo 23, fol. 119.

nally under the authority of the Venezuelan revolutionary authorities based in Angostura.[42]

Jane Loy's recent studies have highlighted the peculiarities of the Colombian Llanos. Miguel Izard's examination of the Venezuelan Llanos has similarly set the region and its people within a historical context. According to Izard, "the Llanos were always a zone of refuge," though "between the second half of the seventeenth and the first half of the eighteenth centuries they became a zone of great unrest, principally because the white oligarchy of the coast sought to bring the inhabitants and wealth of the Llanos under its control." This unsuccessful attempt "in itself let loose a long-lasting confrontation that would endure until the early twentieth century." Banditry had become endemic, and contraband was notorious. Insurgency in the Llanos had already anticipated the Caracas revolution of April, 1810, by several years, and after Venezuelan independence, conflict throughout the Llanos continued just as before. In Casanare, local *caudillos* operated independently of the supreme Venezuelan *caudillo* of the Llanos, José Antonio Páez. Their activities obliged the New Granadan royalists to maintain troops at the points of upward access into the cordillera and to send patrols down to the nearby lowlands. Morillo's expeditionary force failed to establish a position of control in the Llanos and ultimately withdrew from them because of the threat the *llanero* cavalry posed to communications.[43] The *llaneros,* as is well known, contributed decisively to the Bolivarian victory of 1819 in Boyacá and Cundinamarca. After the Spanish reconquest in 1816, several patriot chieftains fled to Casanare for safety. In that zone, a number of rebel bands were already operating under *caudillos* such as Juan Galea, Ramón Nonato Pérez, and the most celebrated of all, the Dominican friar Colonel Fray Ignacio Mariño. By the end of 1817, these bands controlled the entire Casanare zone and were beginning to threaten the royalist position in the Eastern Cordillera.

42. David Bushnell, *The Santander Regime in Gran Colombia* (Delaware, 1954), 10.

43. Miguel Izard, "Ni Cuartreros ni Montoneros, Llaneros," *Boletín americanista,* XXIII (1981), 88, 109, 113–18; Osvaldo Díaz Díaz, *Los Almeydas: Episodios de la resistencia patriótica contra el ejército pacificador de Tierra Firme* (Bogotá, 1962), 187–94; Izard, "Ni Cuartreros," 121–24.

Insurgency in the Eastern Cordillera

Continued revolt in the Llanos led to pockets of insurgency in the Eastern Cordillera. These, moreover, could be fueled by insurgent recruitment of disaffected troops from the royalist armies. Guerrilla bands were formed within the territory nominally under the control of the Spanish expeditionary force, particularly in regions with a tradition of opposition to the central power, such as Socorro, Tunja, Vélez, and the Cauca Valley. Leaders of these bands were generally persons of wealth and position within their particular provinces, and only rarely were they of lower-class origin. Colonel Juan José Neira, for instance, who operated in Guachetá, was one of the hacendados of the province of Tunja. He had led a band consisting of estate tenants and persons of station in an attempt to hold back Morillo's advance in 1816.[44]

Harsh royalist repression after the recovery of the viceregal capital rapidly alienated sympathies. Viceroy Montalvo himself put the number of persons executed at more than seven thousand, and these he described as "individuals from the principal families of the viceroyalty." Many had been put before the firing squad after being sentenced by the Consejo de Guerra Permanente (a permanent court martial) at Morillo's instructions. This policy of implacable terror had left the population restless and desperate. The cost of the armed forces operating in New Granada in 1816–1817, moreover, already exceeded three million pesos, a sum levied upon that territory itself. In other words, the financial demands of the counterrevolution and the Spanish army took as drastic a toll as the revolutionary turmoil of the preceding five years. Morillo continued to draw on the funds of the royal treasury, regardless of the viceroy's position as *supremo intendente general* of finance. Montalvo's complaints had been ignored. Well after the actual campaign of "pacification" had ceased, Morillo continued to assume that the expenses of the Spanish expeditionary army and those of the viceregal government were one and the same. Montalvo argued that, if Morillo had not interfered, but had instead left for Venezuela to rectify the situation there, the unrest throughout New Granada would have been considerably less. Morillo imposed large contributions on several provinces: thirty thousand

44. Díaz Díaz, *Los Almeydas,* 41–42, 138–41.

pesos on El Chocó, twenty thousnd pesos on Antioquia, and comparable sums on Socorro and Popayán, besides appropriations of horses and cash, and levies of fines in Santa Fe. These sums proceeded straight into the treasury of the expeditionary army.[45]

Furthermore, the reestablishment of the Audiencia of Santa Fe at the end of May, 1817, led to a series of major jurisdictional conflicts between the civilian magistrates and the military commanders that further discredited the counterrevolutionary regime and undermined its claim to legitimacy. The connection between conspiratorial activity in the capital and guerrilla activity in the countryside became apparent at this time. In the autumn of 1817, the Almeydas, landowners from the valley of Cúcuta, formed a band of some three hundred men (with only twenty firearms) in the mountains of Machetá. This band, like others formed more or less contemporaneously, cooperated with the insurgents of the Llanos. According to Osvaldo Díaz, "The ramifications of this guerrilla activity were so broad that scarcely a town of the northern Sabana and the slopes of the cordillera could not boast of some participation." These local insurgencies, moreover, incorporated not only former revolutionary soldiers and royalist defectors, but also many peasants and several priests sympathetic to the patriot cause.[46] This situation may not have been drastic in itself, but put together with the royalist failure to establish control of the Llanos, it became potentially disastrous.

Sámano, at that time *mariscal de campo* and commander of the 3rd Division of the expeditionary army, recognized the danger immediately. On September 12, 1817, Sámano began to press the Santa Fe government for instant subsidies to finance an expedition into the Llanos, a campaign he regarded as "absolutely indispensable." The cash he looked to, however, had been sent already to Maracaibo at Morillo's instructions to counter Bolívar's descent on the Venezuelan coast. Sámano requested fifty thousand pesos, which the Junta Superior de Hacienda Extraordinaria voted on October 19 to extend him as an urgent necessity. In mid-November, Sámano reported the presence of insurgents from the Llanos in Guateque and Machetá and identified the Valle de Tenza in the

45. Blanco-Fombona, *Ultimos virreyes,* 158, 141, 147–48, 152–53, 156.

46. Díaz Díaz, *Los Almeydas,* 57–59, 72–74, 81–82, 88–90, 95, 105, 116, 123–25.

cordillera slopes as a major zone of recruitment. Rebel bands took Chocontá, and the Almeydas operated from Machetá, a town only two or three days' journey from Santa Fe. These bands could apparently rely on the assistance of the villages of the whole region between Honda and Socorro. These risings marked in part a patriot response to the executions planned in Santa Fe for November 14. The public execution of conspirators aroused not only public revulsion in the capital, but also provoked a further and deeper round of conflicts between military actions and civilian jurisdiction. The viceroy and *oidores,* sitting together as the Real Acuerdo, protested to Sámano, military governor of the city, against the flagrant violation of normal legal procedure, since most of the accused were themselves civilians. Sámano, without consulting the Sala del Crimen of the audiencia, had reestablished Morillo's Consejo de Guerra Permanente to try those suspected of a conspiracy to revive the revolutionary movement in the city. Eight men and one woman were executed at 11:00 A.M. outside the audiencia offices in the Plaza Mayor, without either prior consultation with or even notification of the civil magistrates.[47]

In the countryside, the Spanish response to the local insurgencies was a cruel repression. Sámano described them as *bandolerismo,* but organized a type of counterinsurgency to combat them. This took the form principally of a series of *destacamentos volantes* dispatched to the affected zones. In their repression of the insurgency, the royalist commanders executed not only leaders but also peasant and Indian participants, and reduced villagers' crops to ashes. This was particularly the case in the Valle de Tenza, center of the greatest activity until December, 1817. The towns of Machetá, Tibiritá, Nemocón, and Chocontá lay at the center of the revolt and had been patriot since the first days of the independence movement. Sámano put Lieutenant Colonel Carlos Tolrá, already known for his actions in the counterrevolution in the Popayán region, in command of the mobile detachments, which were increased to six hundred men, predominantly experienced infantry-

47. Junta Superior, Santa Fe, October 19, 1817, Sámano to Jurado, Santa Fe, September 12, 1817, Sámano to Teniente Coronel Vicente Sánchez de Lima, Santa Fe, October 24, 1817, all in AHNC, Anexo, Historia, tomo 23, fols. 117–19, 124; Díaz Díaz, *Los Almeydas,* 95–105; Real Acuerdo de Justicia, Santa Fe, November 14, 1817, AHNC, Anexo, Historia, tomo 23, fols. 58–58v.

men riding as cavalrymen and with firearms. The Dragones de Granada, moreover, were made up of the fervently royalist inhabitants of Pasto and Patía. Tolrá's proclamation in Chocontá on November 23 established the death penalty for any local authorities guilty of collaboration with insurgency and for the collective punishment of any town guilty of the same.[48] Sámano was promoted to the office of viceroy.

The ferocity of the royalist military response seems to have shocked the patriot guerrillas, who, nevertheless, still retained the option of tactical withdrawal to the Llanos and later reactivation. Even so, rumors of discontent continued to arise from the zones of insurgent activity in 1817. In the autumn of 1818, for instance, the audiencia investigated a supposed conspiracy in the villages of the Guateque area in the Valle de Tenza, with apparently a woman at the center of it. The royalist campaign against the insurgent bands in the northern zones of Tunja province, however, placed major emphasis thereafter upon the remaining zone of rebel activity, the Llanos. In August, 1818, Bolívar sent a volunteer officer from the Cúcuta Valley, Francisco de Paula Santander, into the Llanos with the specific task of coordinating the rebel bands. The objective was to be a campaign by the main armed force, led by Bolívar himself, from the Llanos into the cordillera of Boyacá, with the aim of establishing military and political control over the entire Sabana of Cundinamarca. This strategy culminated in Bolívar's victory at the Puente de Boyacá in August, 1819, and the royalists' loss of the viceregal capital.[49]

The Rebellion of the Cauca Valley

The impact of Boyaća was profound in the interior. Salvador Jiménez de Enciso y Cobos Padilla, the royalist bishop of Popayán, lamented that "a rising has taken place in the Cauca Valley, led neither by members of the clergy nor by any of the decent classes of society, but by deserters and other evil-doers who had sought ref-

48. Díaz Díaz, *Los Almeydas,* 116, 123–25, 128–29, 133–34, 145, 152–53, 156, 170–71. Tolrá executed possibly some one hundred "infelices indios y campesinos," described by him as "insurgentes."

49. Audiencia of Santa Fe to Sámano, Santa Fe, October 1, 1818, AHNC, Anexo, Historia, tomo 24, fols. 309–10; Díaz Díaz, *Los Almeydas,* 133–34, 165–81.

uge in the mountains since the last revolution." This rising consisted of "armed groups of bandits" who preyed "upon the loyal and peaceful citizens." In the judgment of Popayán's royalist commander, Sebastián de la Calzada, "several rebels have dared to regroup and form armed bands with the sole object of robbery, as they had shown in the case of Llano Grande, where they sacked private properties and burned down the Royal Tobacco Office. . . . I am convinced that obscure figures lead these bands, since persons of station (*los nobles*) have taken no part in these criminal actions here in the Cauca Valley." Calzada was in fact speaking of a general insurrection throughout the valley, directed against the royalist position there. The governor of Popayán, Pedro Domínguez, perished, and the royalists were forced to abandon the city yet again and withdraw to Pasto.[50]

The intensity of the Cauca risings in the summer and autumn of 1819 may not have represented simply popular responses to the news of Boyacá, but more long-term factors such as hatred of the excesses of the royalist forces there since the reconquest. The governor of Popayán had already complained to Viceroy Montalvo in October, 1817, of what he described as "the terrorism and confusion brought about by Ruperto Delgado, commander of the First Numancia Battalion, and several of his subaltern commanders in their duties with their garrison forces in the towns of the Cauca Valley." Montalvo, himself critical of the arbitrary conduct of Morillo and Sámano, now heard of the "most serious excesses" committed by the army in the king's name, as well as flagrant usurpation of civil jurisdiction by the military and flouting of the rights of municipal councils in the towns under their charge. Army recruitment measures that excepted neither farmers nor married men had driven many families to seek refuge in the hills, where they encountered the remnants of the rebel bands and often joined their ranks. The governor of Popayán had warned in 1817 of the political consequences of alienating the local population through such disdainful treatment. This alienation was not limited to the lower

50. Bishop to Sámano, Popayán, September 8, 1819, in Ortiz (ed.), *Colección de documentos,* primera serie, 132–33; Sebastián de la Calzada to Sámano, Popayán, September 8, 1819, Calzada to Melchor Aymerich (president of Quito), Mercaderes, October 11, 1819, Aymerich to Calzada, Quito, October 23 and October 30, 1819, all in Oritz (ed.), *Colección de documentos,* primera serie, 134–35, 143–44, 148–49, 153–55.

classes. On the contrary, Delgado's arrest of town councilors in Cartago, Cali, Anserma, and Buga had outraged persons of local reputation. In Buga he had brushed aside civilian authority altogether. The military commanders, moreover, had put the burden of paying the army on the region itself. Troops consumed what livestock was left in the private estates after seven years of warfare; local artisans had been forced to work on military equipment with only an insignificant remuneration; labor gangs had been recruited and put to work on road construction. The results had been simmering discontent.[51]

It has often been wrongly concluded that Bolívar's victory at Boyacá led to rapid extinction of royalist rule in New Granada. Although the Cauca Valley remained a principal area of revolutionary support throughout the 1810s, the south's firm resistance—as much to Bolívar in 1819–1822 as to Nariño in 1810–1814—continued undiminished. The strong royalist position in Pasto enabled Calzada to recover the city of Popayán on January 24, 1820, a serious threat to the political solution Bolivarian forces thought they had accomplished with the fall of Santa Fe. This royalist counteroffensive in the south prepared the way for a campaign of reconquest along the Cauca Valley by March, 1820. Calzada, aware of the support Santander had given to the Cauca patriots, struck into rebel-held territory with three thousand troops to extinguish a "mass insurrection, which had taken the lives not only of Europeans but also of loyal and distinguished Americans in the valley." This campaign threatened to deprive the main patriot army of the possibility of extending the revolution southward into Quito and thence to the royalist stronghold of Peru.[52]

As had been the case with the Llanos of Casanare in 1816–1817, the royalist pacification in 1820 was incomplete, owing to lack of manpower and resources, insurgent strength in the east, and above all, the nature of the terrain. Calzada's campaign left the Chocó region unsubdued. The insurgency disintegrated in the Cauca Valley only to fester and rekindle in El Chocó, particularly in the Vega de Supía with its Negro slave population. The con-

51. Governor José Solís to Montalvo, Popayán, August 5, October 6, and October 20, 1817, AHNC, Anexo, Guerra y Marina, tomo 152, fols. 241–43, 246–48v, 251–52v.

52. Calzada to Aymerich, Popayán, January 24, 1820, Aymerich to Sámano, Quito, February 7, 1820, both in Ortiz (ed.), *Colección de documentos,* primera serie, 206, 207–10.

tinued insurrection in El Chocó meant not only that communications with one of the principal gold-producing zones remained beyond the reach of royal power, but also that other provinces were able to open new theatres of insurgency. Accordingly, just as the royalists believed they had pacified the Cauca Valley, the province of Antioquia renewed the revolutionary struggle.[53]

In contrast, the Pasto royalists contributed a royalist battalion for the war in Popayán in 1819 and 1820. Calzada had a low opinion of its composition: "they are all peasants, with no military training and no discipline: even worse than their unruliness is the fact that they have only a few rifles that are any use." The *pastusos* responded to the patriot victories of 1819 with a regional solidarity that cut across social groups. When they proposed to form a second battalion, hacienda owners offered their livestock for its sustenance, and an appeal was made for assistance from the twenty-six Indian towns of the city hinterland. This confrontational zeal extended into the year 1821, when Basilio García informed Mariscal de Campo Melchor Aymerich, president of Quito, that "enthusiasm for the royalist cause is general, not only in Pasto and its district, but throughout the province . . . the entire Valley of Patía, furthermore, is ready *en masse* for the enemy, should he appear, and the province of Almaguer is of the same mind." Nevertheless, enthusiasm had to be paid for, and soon enough the fiscal burden of warfare fell upon the *pastusos*. Ramón Zambrano levied a special 1 percent contribution in January, 1822, for the purpose of sustaining local troops. This tax did not exempt even the convents, where it was met with wounded indignation. The bishop of Popayán, in exile once more, commented on the warlike capacities and skilled marksmanship of the *pastusos,* particularly when called to defend their native soil, but warned of their extreme reluctance to fight for anything beyond it. Within their own territory, they were natural guerrilla warriors.[54]

53. Bishop of Popayán to the crown, Popayán, March 21, 1820, *ibid.,* 211–16.

54. Calzada to Aymerich, Mercaderes, October 11, 1819, Bishop of Popayán, Pasto, May 18, 1820, "Actas celebradas en Pasto por la Junta de Autoridades," Pasto, July 17–21, 1820, *ibid.,* 143–44, 217–18, 221–28; Basilio García to Aymerich, Pasto, January 1, 1821, García to Aymerich, Campo de Matabojoy, January 29, 1821, both in ANHE, PQ, Vol. 584 (1821), I, doc. 2, fols. 4–4v, 121–121v; Abadesa y Monjas del Convento de Conceptas to

It has been argued that Pasto's continued resistance to the new Colombian republic established in Bogotá placed the region effectively beyond the reach of central authority for much of the early 1820s.[55] Bolívar and his close associate, Antonio José de Sucre, were extremely preoccupied with what they saw as the deteriorating situation in the south. Sucre's Quito campaign, which culminated in his victory on the slopes of Pichincha on May 24, 1822, was designed to resolve the problem definitively; however, it did not. Initially, Bolívar's capitulation provisions for Pasto on June 8 permitted all royalist employees to remain in office in the city, as a means of preserving harmony, until the complete establishment of the new constitutional system of the Republic of Colombia. Accordingly, Ramón Zambrano, colonel of the royalist militia, became republican governor, without, however, a serious commitment to the patriot cause. When the financially hard-pressed Bogotá government sought to levy a tax on Pasto as part of its contribution to a forced assessment, the city rose in rebellion on October 28 with general popular support. Bolívar described Pasto as "bitterly hostile to the republic."[56] The new republican authorities in the Quito zone were alarmed at the prospect of isolation from Santa Fe in the face of a supposed *pastuso* and *patiano* advance on Tulcán and appealed for aid from the city of Quito to combat it. After yet another tenacious resistance, Pasto fell at the end of December.[57]

The new republican state found it as difficult as the former viceregency had to control the extent of national territory. The

---

Juan de la Cruz Mourgeon (captain general, jefe superior y político of the Kingdom of New Granada), Pasto, January 14, 1822, Bishop of Popayán to Mourgeon, Pasto, January 18, 1822, ANHE, PQ and RC, Vol. 596 (1822), I, doc. 418, fols. 160–60v, no. 219, fols. 244–45v.

55. Ospina Vásquez, *Industria y protección,* 127.

56. Bolívar, Cuartel General de Pasto, June 9, 1822, in [Simon Bolivar], *Decretos del Libertador* (Los Teques, 1983), I, 254–55; "Capitulación de Pasto, Cuartel General Liberatador en Pasto," June 8, 1822, in José M. de Mier, *La Gran Colombia* (Bogotá, 1983), V, 1676–79. See ANHE, PQ, Vol. 567 (1819), I, doc. 142, fols. 160–60v, on Zambrano in the Pasto resistance of 1819.

57. Manuel López Pardo to Governor Joaquín Gómez de la Torre, Cumbral, November 3, 1822, ANHE, RC, Vol. 603 (1822), VIII, no. 2, fols. 2–3v; Bolívar, Cuartel General de Pasto, January 13, 1823, in [Bolivar], *Decretos del Libertador,* I, 273–74.

towns of the Cauca Valley early in 1821 had maintained their revolutionary tradition, but this time in opposition to the republican state in Bogotá. The Cauca rebellion had seriously compromised the precarious patriot position in the south. Bolívar had threatened a punitive example. In the remote coastal zones of the south, republican commanders in 1823 reported local resistance from Esmeraldas to Tumaco and denounced it as the work of "facciosos" and "bárbaros, enemigos acérrimos de Colombia y de la tranquilidad pública." In Esmeraldas, local resistance seemed to have formed around the Casierras, a group of mountain chieftains. The local republican commander claimed to have Bolívar's authorization to make "an imposing example" of these dissidents by shooting them in whatever number he saw fit, since "the ferocity of their resistance defied any claim to leniency."[58]

Pasto itself remained for decades in sporadic opposition to the central power. The former royalist guerrilla commander, Colonel José María Obando, who had defected to Bolívar in Popayán on February 7, 1822, led the Pasto rebellion of 1839–1841 in opposition to the abolition of the convents. Similarly, the insurrection of May, 1851, formed part of a Catholic reaction to liberal anticlerical measures between 1849 and 1854.[59]

Conclusions

New Granada's long history of governmental weakness in outlying areas allowed insurgency movements to form and later flourish at sporadic intervals during the 1810s and 1820s. Regions such as the Caribbean hinterland, the Llanos of Casanare, Chocó, and the remote zones of the Pacific south were cases in point. It did not matter whether insurrectionary action was directed against roy-

58. Bolívar, Cuartel General de Bogotá, January 7, 1821, in [Bolivar], *Decretos del Libertador,* I, 221–22; Pedro José Villegas to Intendant Vicente Aguirre, Esmeraldas, February 13, 1823 (three letters), ANHE, RC, Vol. 607 (1823), I, no. 178, fols. 202–202v, no. 184, fols. 208–208v, no. 190, fols. 214–14v.

59. ANHE, RC, Vol. 596 (1822), I, doc. 229, fol. 254; Tulio Halperín Donghi, *The Aftermath of Revolution in Latin America* (New York, 1973), 9, 11; Orlando Fals Borda, *Subversion and Social Change in Colombia* (New York, 1969), 86. The Obando family were Pasto landowners who fulfilled administrative duties such as the lease of tribute and tithe collection and were connected to the Popayán elite.

alist or republican regimes; it took similar forms and was responded to in similar ways. The Pasto zone in the far south stood in constant opposition to the revolutionary system throughout the 1810s and early 1820s, and this fierce resistance delayed the establishment of a Bolivarian state in the New Granada region. When popular action supported the royalist cause, as in the case of risings of the Negroes of the southwestern regions of Patía and Barbacoas, royalist commanders feared the social implications of lower-class revolt as much as their republican counterparts. Whenever they could, both royalist and republican authorities sought to bring popular militancy under control and channel it into a subordinate role within their own movements. This common fear of lower-class autonomous action existed irrespective of the divisions within the elites concerning ideology and political forms. Such fears in themselves demonstrated the existence of spontaneous popular participation in the conflicts at the regional and local levels during the Wars of Independence. Participants and observers of opposing political views similarly commented on the repeated evidence of popular rebellions. Lower-class social groups probably saw in escalating violence and the disintegration of central authority the means to press for the improvement of their condition. In such a way, long-standing local tensions, such as those in the Cauca Valley, became to an extent subsumed within the broader civil struggles. In themselves, however, these local rebellions could not have generated a national movement. Without the superstructure of elite resistance to metropolitan rule, combined with the temporary collapse of peninsular Spain during 1808–1814, it is likely that they would simply have resembled the local rebellions of the colonial era. Since political independence, won between 1819 and 1822, did not involve any necessary commitment to the resolution of lower-class social grievances, the sources of tension that had generated spontaneous popular participation during the 1810s and early 1820s probably continued to simmer below the surface thereafter.

The survival of insurgent bands in the Llanos of Casanare kept the spirit of resistance alive, in spite of the apparently complete military victory of the Spanish expeditionary army in 1816. Savage Spanish reprisals combined with the arbitrary conduct of the military commanders, many of them detested even within the royalist camp, undermined the prestige of the Bourbon cause and threw into doubt the legitimacy of Spanish rule after what had seemed to be a successful campaign of reconquest.

Rivalry between Cali and Popayán led to outright conflict during the Wars of Independence. The Cauca Valley, like the Caribbean coastal zone, was an area of high concentration of Negroid population, where the livestock estates and sugar production were sustained by slave labor. The collapse of central authority after 1810 provided the opportunity for popular rebellion against the slave owners, who traditionally controlled town councils in the region and derived their social position from mastery of land and labor. Attention to the struggles within the elites, between those who wanted to preserve the empire and those who wanted to separate from it, or between the centralists and the regionalists, has tended to obfuscate the intense social conflicts that characterized these areas. In the Pasto zone, social relations were not torn apart by comparable ethnic tensions, mainly, of course, because the economic system there was entirely different from that prevalent in the Cauca Valley. A common opposition emerged to the intervention of outside power, which in this case was perceived to be the revolutionary regime of Santa Fe.

Bibliography

Archival Sources

Archives des Affaires Etrangères, Paris
Correspondance Politique Espagne: Volume 540.
Archivo Central del Cauca, Popayán
Signatura 7061.
Archivo Departamental, Cuzco
Real Audiencia: Ordinarias 51.
Archivo Diocesano, Cuzco
XII: 1, 12.
XVI: 3, 5, 42, 100.
Archivo General de Indias, Seville
Chile: Legajos 433, 438.
Contaduría: Legajos 1426–27, 1428A, 1428B, 1429, 1518–20, 1521A, 1521B, 1521C, 1567.
Contratación: Legajos 2901, 2902B.
Consulado de Cádiz: Libro 84.
Consulados: Libros 358, 494, 767, 786, 787.
Cuzco: Legajo 63.
Estado: Legajo 52.

Indiferente General: Legajos 535, 1337, 1586, 1707, 1885, 2046A, 2466–67, 2470–72, 2823–24.
Libros Manuscritos: 26.
Lima: Legajos 1039, 1052, 1489–91, 1494, 1499–1504.
Panamá: Legajo 257.
Quito: Legajos 269, 398–99, 574.
Santo Domingo: Legajo 1509.
Santa Fe: Legajos 286, 374, 384, 477–78, 514, 573, 576, 577A, 602, 636, 641–51, 653–54, 837–38, 939, 948A, 948B, 949, 956–57, 960, 1012, 1093, 1094–95, 1097–98, 1156, 1233, 1288.
Ultramar: Legajos 722, 723, 742, 833, 839–40.

Archivo General del Ministerio de Relaciones Exteriores, Lima
Sección Colonial: Libro 2–2.

Archivo General de la Nación, Lima
Aduanas: Legajos 5, 6, 161–62.
Superior Gobierno: Legajos 12, 13, 17.

Archivo General de Simancas
Guerra Moderna: Legajos 7280–82.

Archivo Histórico de Antioquía, Medellín
Tomo 709.

Archivo Histórico Nacional, Madrid
Estado: Libro 4; Legajos 2314, 2548, 2850, 2944.
Consejos, Consejo de Indias: Legajo 20494.

Archivo Histórico Nacional de Colombia, Bogotá
Anexo, Diezmos: Tomos 26, 35.
Anexo, Historia: Tomos 23–24.
Anexo, Guerra y Marina: Tomos 117, 120, 152.
Historia: Tomo 3.
Impuestos Varios (Cartas): Tomos 17, 22–23.
Juicios Criminales: Tomo 129.
Milicia y Marina: Tomos 123, 125–26.
Miscelánea: Tomos 116, 138.
Reales Cédulas: Tomo 17.
Real Hacienda: Libros de Cuentas, no. 2915.
República, Secretaría de Guerra y Marina: Tomo 1540.
Virreyes: Tomo 2.

Archivo Nacional de Historia del Ecuador, Quito
Presidencia de Quito: Vols. 468, 471, 483–84, 510, 512–16, 528, 531–33, 556, 564, 567, 584, 596.
República de Colombia: Vols. 509, 596, 603, 607.

Biblioteca Nacional, Lima

Sección Investigaciones Históricas: MSS C-557, D-6649, D-12361, D-12364–65, D-12431.
Biblioteca Nacional, Madrid
Sección de Manuscritos: MS 9728.
Biblioteca Nacional de Colombia, Bogotá
Libros Raros y Curiosos, Fondo Quijano Otero: MS 179.
Biblioteca del Palacio, Madrid
Sección Miscelánea Ayala: MSS 2816, 2867.
Duke University, William R. Perkins Library, Durham, N.C.
Manuscript Department: Duque de Montemar Papers.
Servicio Histórico Militar, Madrid
Document 5-2-12-11.

Published Primary Sources

Arbitraje de límites entre Perú y el Ecuador: Documentos anexos al alegato del Perú. 7 vols. Madrid, 1905.

Barriga, V. M., ed. *Memorias para la historia de Arequipa*. 3 vols. Arequipa, 1941.

Bermúdez Plata, Cristóbal. *Narración de la defensa de Cartagena de Indias contra el ataque de los ingleses en 1741*. Seville, 1912.

Blanco-Fombona, R., ed. *Ultimos virreyes de Nueva Granada: Relación de mando del Virrey Francisco Montalvo y noticias del Virrey Sámano sobre la pérdida del reino (1813–1819)*. Madrid, 1918.

[Bolívar, Simón]. *Decretos del Libertador*. 4 vols. Los Teques, 1983.

Campbell, John. *A Concise History of the Spanish America*. London, 1972.

Castro, Ignacio de. *Relación del Cuzco*. Edited by C. D. Valcárcel. Lima, 1978.

Cochrane, Charles Stuart. *Journal of a Residence and Travels in Colombia*. 2 vols. London, 1825.

García, José Joaquín. *Crónicas de Bucaramanga*. Bucaramanga, 1944.

González de Salcedo, Pedro. *Tratado jurídico político del contra-bando*. Madrid, 1729.

Great Britain, Public Record Office. *Calendar of State Papers, Colonial Series, 1719–1720*. London, n.d.

Hamilton, John P. *Travels Through the Interior Provinces of Colombia*. 2 vols. London, 1827.

Helmer, Marie. "Documents pour l'histoire economique de l'Amérique du Sud: Commerce et industrie au Pérou a fin du XVIIIme siecle." *Revista de Indias*, X (1950), 519–26.

Hernández de Alba, Guillermo, comp. *Archivo epistolar del sabio naturalista Don José Celestino Mutis.* 4 vols. Bogotá, 1968–75.

Jaramillo, Gabriel Giraldo, comp. *Relaciones de mando de los virreyes de la Nueva Granada: Memorias económicas.* Bogotá, 1954.

Juan, Jorge, and Antonio de Ulloa. *A Voyage to South America.* Edited and translated by John Adams. New York, 1964.

———. *Discourse and Political Reflections on the Kingdoms of Peru.* Edited by John J. TePaske. Norman, Okla., 1978.

Le Moyne, A[uguste]. *Viajes y estancias en América del Sur, La Nueva Granada, Santiago de Cuba, Jamaica y El Istmo de Panamá.* Bogotá, 1945.

Loayza, Francisco A. *Preliminares del incendio: documentos del año de 1776 a 1780 . . . anteriores y sobre la Revolución Libertadora que engendró y dio vida José Gabriel Túpak Amaru, en 1780.* Lima, 1947.

Mier, Jose M. de. *La Gran Colombia.* 7 vols. Bogotá, 1983.

Mollien, Gaspar Théodore. *Viaje por la República de Colombia en 1823.* Bogotá, 1944.

Moreno y Escandón, Francisco Antonio. "Estado del Virreinato de Santafé, Nuevo Reino de Granada . . . 1772." *BHA,* XXIII (1936), 547–616.

Morillo, Pablo. *Mémoires du General Morillo, Comte de Carthagène, Marquis de la Puerta: Relatifs aux principaux événements de ses campagnes en Amérique de 1815 a 1821.* Paris, 1826.

"Notas históricas. Fiestas que se celebran en Quito a fines del siglo XVIII." *Boletín de la Academia Nacional de la Historia* (Quito), VII (1923), no. 19, 262–66.

"Noticia de los movimientos de Quito en el año de 1765." *Museo Histórico* (Quito), III, no. 9 (1951), 37–54.

Ortiz, Sergio Elías, ed. *Colección de documentos para la historia de Colombia (época de la Independencia).* Primera serie. Bogotá, 1964.

———. *Colección de documentos para la historia de Colombia (época de la Independencia).* Tercera serie. Bogotá, 1966.

Oviedo, Vicente de. *Cualidades y riquezas del Nuevo Reino de Granada.* Edited by Augusto Cuervo. Bogotá, 1930.

Paz, Melchor de. *Guerra separatista, rebeliones de Indios en Sur América: la sublevación de Túpac Amaru.* 2 vols. Lima, 1952.

Posada, E., and P. M. Ibáñez. *Relaciones de mando: Memorias presentadas por los gobernantes del Nuevo Reino de Granada.* Bogotá, 1910.

"Proceso seguido a los sediciosos de 1780." *Revista del Archivo Histórico del Cuzco,* XII (1967), 204–35.

Reglamento para el comercio libre, 1778. Seville, 1978.

"Relación sumaria de las dos sublevaciones de la Pleve de Quito." *Boletín de la Academia Nacional de Historia* (Quito), XV (1937), 102–16.

Restrepo, José Manuel. *Historia de la revolución de la República de Colombia en la América meridional.* 8 vols. Bogotá, 1942–50.

Silvestre, Francisco. *Descripción del Reyno de Santa Fe de Bogotá, escrita en 1789.* Bogotá, 1950.

"Sublevación de Quito por la Aduana y los Estancos." *Museo Histórico* (Quito), II, no. 7 (1950), 25–37; III, no. 8 (1951), 16–31.

Urrutia M., Miguel, and Mario Arrubla, eds. *Compendio de estadísticas históricas de Colombia.* Bogotá, 1970.

Vargas, Pedro Fermín de. *Pensamientos políticos y memorias sobre la población del Nuevo Reino de Granada.* Bogotá, 1953.

Velasco, Juan de. *Historia del Reino de Quito.* 2 vols. Quito, 1971.

Wills, Guillermo. *Observaciones sobre el comercio de la Nueva Granada, con un apéndice relativo al de Bogotá.* 1831; rpr. Bogotá, 1952.

Secondary Sources

BOOKS

Alcácer, Antonio de. *Las misiones capuchinas en el Nuevo Reino de Granada, hoy Colombia (1648–1820).* Puente Común, Cundinamarca, 1959.

Ancízar, Manuel. *Peregrinación de alpha.* 2 vols. Bogotá, 1970.

Arcila Farías, Eduardo. *Comercio entre Venezuela y México en los siglos xvi y xvii.* México, 1950.

Arcila Robledo, Gregorio. *Las misiones franciscanas en Colombia.* Bogotá, 1950.

Barbier, Jacques A. *Reform and Politics in Bourbon Chile, 1755–1796.* Ottawa, 1980.

Bloch, Marc. *The Royal Touch: Sacred Monarchy and Scrofula in England and France.* Translated by J. E. Anderson. London, 1973.

Blossom, T. *Nariño: Hero of Colombian Independence.* Arizona, 1967.

Bourne, Ruth. *Queen Anne's Navy in the West Indies.* New Haven, 1939.

Brading, D. A. *Miners and Merchants in Bourbon Mexico, 1763–1810.* Cambridge, England, 1971.

Brown, Kendall W. *Bourbons and Brandy: Imperial Reform in Eighteenth-Century Arequipa.* Albuquerque, 1986.

Burkholder, Mark A., and D. S. Chandler. *From Impotence to Authority: The Spanish Crown and the American Audiencias.* Columbia, 1977.

Bushnell, David. *The Santander Regime in Gran Colombia.* Delaware, 1954.

Campbell, Leon G. *The Military and Society in Colonial Peru, 1750–1810.* Philadelphia, 1978.

Cárdenas Acosta, Pablo G. *El movimiento comunal de 1781 en Nueva Granada.* 2 vols. Bogotá, 1960.

Carrera Damas, Germán. *Boves: Aspectos socioeconómicos de la guerra de independencia.* Caracas, 1972.
Carvalho Neto, Pedro de. *Antología del folklore ecuatoriano, 1653–1963.* Quito, 1964.
Caycedo, Bernardo J. *D'Elhúyar y el siglo XVIII neogranadino.* Bogotá, 1971.
Chocano, Magdalena. *Comercio en Cerro de Pasco a fines de la época colonial.* Lima, 1982.
Colmenares, Germán. *Las haciendas de los Jesuítas en el Nuevo Reino de Granada, siglo XVIII.* Bogotá, 1969.
———. *Historia económica y social de Colombia, 1537–1719.* Cali, 1973.
———. *Historia económica y social de Colombia, II Popayán: Una sociedad esclavista, 1680–1800.* Bogotá, 1979.
———. *La provincia de Tunja en el Nuevo Reino de Granada: Ensayo de historia social (1539–1800).* Bogotá, 1970.
Colombia, Departamento Administrativo Nacional de Estadística. *División político-administrativa de Colombia.* 6th ed. Bogotá, 1967.
Davies, Keith A. *Landowners in Colonial Peru.* Austin, 1984.
de la Torre Reyes, Carlos. *La revolución de Quito del 10 de 1809.* Quito, 1961.
Descola, Jean. *La vida cotidiana en el Perú en tiempos de los españoles.* Lima, 1962.
Díaz Díaz, Osvaldo. *Los Almeydas: Episodios de la resistencia patriótica contra el ejército pacificador de Tierra Firme.* Bogotá, 1962.
Díaz-Trechuelo Spínola, María Lourdes. *La Real Compañia de Filipinas.* Seville, 1965.
Domínguez Ortiz, Antonio. *Sociedad y estado en el siglo XVIII.* Barcelona, 1976.
Dorta, Enrique Marco. *Cartagena de Indias: Puerto y plaza fuerte.* Bogotá, 1960.
Elliott, J. H. *Imperial Spain, 1469–1716.* New York, 1966.
Espinoza Claudio, César, and José Boza Monteverde. *Alcabalas y protesta popular: Cerro de Pasco, 1780.* Lima, 1981.
Fals Borda, Orlando. *Mompox y Loba: Historia doble de la costa.* 4 vols. Bogotá, 1980.
———. *Subversion and Social Change in Colombia.* New York, 1969.
Fisher, John Robert. *Commerical Relations Between Spain and Spanish America in the Era of Free Trade, 1778–1796.* Liverpool, 1985.
———. *Government and Society in Colonial Peru: The Intendant System, 1784–1814.* London, 1970.
———. *Silver Mines and Silver Miners in Colonial Peru, 1776–1824.* Liverpool, 1977.

Floyd, Troy S. *The Anglo-Spanish Struggle for Mosquitia*. Albuquerque, 1967.

García Baquero, Antonio. *Cádiz y el Atlántico (1717–1778)*. 2 vols. Seville, 1976.

Goebel, Julius. *The Struggle for the Falkland Islands: A Study in Legal and Diplomatic History*. New Haven, 1927.

González N., Omar. *Los Guajiros: Una cultura indo-hispana*. Caracas, 1973.

González Suárez, Federico. *Historia general de la República del Ecuador.* 7 vols. Quito, 1970.

Gredilla, A. Fedérico. *Biografía de José Celestino Mutis con relación de su viaje y estudios practicados en el Nuevo Reino de Granada*. Madrid, 1911.

Groot, José Manuel. *Historia eclesiástica y civil de Nueva Granada*. 5 vols. Bogotá, 1953–56.

Halperín Donghi, Tulio. *The Aftermath of Revolution in Latin America*. New York, 1973.

Hobsbawm, E. J. *Primitive Rebels: Studies in Archaic Forms of Social Movement in the 19th and 20th Centuries*. Manchester, 1958.

Howe, Walter. *The Mining Guild of New Spain and Its Tribunal General, 1770–1821*. New York, 1968.

Izard, Miguel. *El miedo a la revolución: La lucha por la libertad en Venezuela (1777–1830)*. Madrid, 1979.

Jensen, Arthur L. *The Maritime Commerce of Colonial Philadelphia*. Madison, 1963.

Julián, Antonio. *La perla de América: Provincia de Santa Marta*. Bogotá, 1951.

Kuethe, Allan J. *Cuba, 1753–1815: Crown, Military, and Society*. Knoxville, 1986.

———. *Military Reform and Society in New Granada, 1773–1808*. Gainesville, 1978.

Ladurie, Emmanuel Le Roy. *Carnival in Romans: A People's Uprising at Romans, 1579–1580*. Harmondsworth, Middlesex, England, 1981.

Lemaitre, Eduardo. *Breve historia de Cartagena*. Cartagena, 1958.

Lewín, Boleslao. *La rebelión de Túpac Amaru y los orígenes de la Independencia de Hispanoamérica*. Buenos Aires, 1943.

Liévano Aguirre, Indalecio. *Los grandes conflictos sociales y económicos de nuestra historia*. 7th ed. 2 vols. Bogotá, 1978.

McAlister, Lyle N. *The "Fuero Militar" in New Spain, 1764–1800*. Gainesville, 1957.

McGreevey, William Paul. *An Economic History of Colombia, 1845–1930*. Cambridge, 1971.

Maravall, José Antonio. *Las comunidades de Castilla: Una primera revolución moderna.* 2nd ed. Madrid, 1979.

Marchena Fernández, Juan. *La institución militar en Cartagena de Indias.* Seville, 1982.

———. *Oficiales y soldados en el ejército de América.* Seville, 1983.

Merino Navarro, José Patricio. *La armada española en el siglo XVIII.* Madrid, 1981.

Mörner, Magnus. *Notas sobre el comercio y los comerciantes del Cusco desde fines de la colonia hasta 1930.* Lima, 1979.

Moore, John Preston. *The Cabildo in Peru Under the Hapsburgs.* Durham, N.C., 1954.

Moreno Yañez, Segundo. *Sublevaciones indígenas en la Audiencia de Quito, desde comienzos del siglo XVIII hasta finales de la colonia.* Bonn, 1976.

Nash, Gary B. *The Urban Crucible: Social Change, Political Consciousness, and the Origins of the American Revolution.* Cambridge, Mass., 1979.

O'Phelan Godoy, Scarlett. *Rebellions and Revolts in Eighteenth Century Peru and Upper Peru.* Cologne, 1985.

Ortiz de la Tabla, Javier. *Comercio exterior de Veracruz, 1778–1821: Crisis de dependencia.* Seville, 1978.

Ospina Vásquez, Luis. *Industria y protección en Colombia, 1810–1930.* Medellín, 1955.

Palma, Ricardo. *Tradiciones peruanas.* Buenos Aires, 1942.

Pares, Richard. *War and Trade in the West Indies, 1739–1763.* Oxford, 1936.

Park, James William. *Rafael Núñez and the Politics of Colombian Regionalism, 1863–1886.* Baton Rouge, 1985.

Parsons, James J. *Antioqueño Colonization in Western Colombia.* 2nd ed. Berkeley, 1968.

Pérez, Joseph. *Los movimientos precursores de la emancipación en Hispanoamérica.* Madrid, 1977.

Pérez Ayala, José Manuel. *Antonio Caballero y Góngora, virrey y arzobispo de Santa Fe, 1723–1796.* Bogotá, 1951.

Phelan, John Leddy. *The Kingdom of Quito in the Seventeenth Century: Bureaucratic Politics in the Spanish Empire.* Madison, 1967.

———. *The People and the King: The Comunero Revolution in Colombia, 1781.* Madison, 1978.

Porras Troconis, G. *Cartagena hispánica, 1533–1810.* Bogotá, 1954.

Priestly, Herbert Ingram. *José de Gálvez, Visitor General of New Spain, 1765–1771.* Berkeley, 1916.

Rausch, Jane M. *A Tropical Plains Frontier: The Llanos of Colombia, 1513–1831.* Albuquerque, 1984.

[Real de Gandía, Segismundo del]. *Tribus que poblaron la costa y modo de*

civilizarlas: Conferencia dictada por el padre Segismundo del Real de Gandía en Santa Marta. Bogotá, 1912.
Restrepo, Vicente. *Estudios sobre las minas de oro y plata de Colombia.* 2nd ed. Bogotá, 1888.
Restrepo Tirado, Ernesto. *Historia de la provincia de Santa Marta.* 6 vols. Bogotá, 1953.
Riaño, Camilo. *La campaña libertadora de 1819.* Bogotá, 1969.
Rout, Leslie B., Jr. *The African Experience in Spanish America, 1502 to the Present Day.* Cambridge, 1976.
Rudé, George. *Ideology and Popular Protest.* London, 1980.
———. *The Crowd in History: A Study of Popular Disturbances in France and England, 1730–1848.* New York, 1964.
Ryden, Stig. *Don Juan José de Elhúyar en Suecia (1781–1782).* Madrid, 1963.
Safford, Frank. *The Ideal of the Practical: Colombia's Struggle to Form a Technical Elite.* Austin, 1976.
Sánchez, Gonzalo, and Donny Meertens. *Bandoleros, gamonales y campesinos: El caso de la violencia en Colombia.* Bogotá, 1983.
Santa Gertrudis, Juan de. *Maravilla de la naturaleza.* 2 vols. Bogotá, 1956.
Sharp, William. *Slavery on the Spanish Frontier: The Colombian Chocó, 1680–1810.* Norman, Okla., 1976.
Silva Santisteban, Fernando. *Los obrajes en el Virreinato del Perú.* Lima, 1964.
Suárez, Santiago Gerardo. *Las milicias: Instituciones militares hispanoamericanas.* Caracas, 1985.
Taylor, William B. *Drinking, Homicide, and Rebellion in Colonial Mexican Villages.* Stanford, 1979.
Tisnes Jiménez, Roberto M. *Don Juan del Corral: Libertador de los esclavos.* Cali, 1980.
Twinam, Ann. *Miners, Merchants and Farmers in Colonial Colombia.* Austin, 1982.
Vega, Juan José, and Alejandro Seraylan Leiva. *Historia general del ejército peruano.* Lima, 1981.
Vicens Vives, Jaime. *Approaches to the History of Spain.* 2nd ed. Berkeley, 1970.
Walker, Geoffrey J. *Spanish Politics and Imperial Trade, 1700–1789.* Bloomington, 1979.
Weston, Julian A. *The Cactus Eaters.* London, 1937.
Wilbert, Johannes. *Survivors of Eldorado: Four Indian Cultures of South America.* New York, 1972.
Young, Alfred, ed. *The American Revolution: Explorations in the History of American Radicalism.* Dekalb, 1976.

Zapatero, Juan Manuel. *La guerra del Caribe en el siglo XVIII*. San Juan, 1964.

ARTICLES AND ESSAYS

Acosta Saignes, Miguel. "Algunos conceptos . . . sobre el problema indígena en Venezuela." In *La Guajira: Su importancia,* edited by Manuel Matos Romero. Caracas, 1971.

Barbier, Jacques A. "The Culmination of the Bourbon Reforms, 1787–1792." *HAHR,* LVII (1977), 51–68.

———. "Imperial Policy Towards the Port of Veracruz, 1788–1808: The Struggle between Madrid, Cádiz and Havana Interests." In *The Economies of Mexico and Peru During the Late Colonial Period, 1760–1810,* edited by Nils Jacobsen and Hans-Jurgen Puhle. Berlin, 1986.

———. "Indies Revenues and Naval Spending: The Cost of Colonialism for the Spanish Bourbons, 1763–1805." *Jahrbuch für Geschichte von Staat, Wirtschaft und Gesellschaft Lateinamerikas,* XXI (1984), 171–88.

———. "Peninsular Finance and Colonial Trade: The Dilemma of Charles IV's Spain." *JLAS,* XII (1980), 21–37.

———. "Silver, North American Penetration and the Spanish Imperial Economy, 1760–1800." In *The North American Role in the Spanish Imperial Economy, 1760–1819,* edited by Jacques A. Barbier and Allan J. Kuethe. Manchester, 1984.

———. "Venezuelan 'Libranzas,' 1788–1808: From Economic Nostrum to Fiscal Imperative." *Americas,* XXXVII (1981), 457–78.

Barbier, Jacques A., and Herbert S. Klein. "Revolutionary Wars and Public Finances: The Madrid Treasury, 1794–1807." *Journal of Economic History,* XLI (1981), 315–39.

Bowman, Charles H. "Antonio Caballero y Góngora y Manuel Torres: La cultura en la Nueva Granada." *BHA,* LVIII (1971), 415–42.

Campbell, Leon G. "The Army of Peru and the Túpac Amaru Revolt." *HAHR,* LVI (1976), 31–57.

———. "The Changing Racial and Administrative Structure of the Peruvian Military Under the Later Bourbons." *Americas,* XXXII (1975), 117–33.

———. "Social Structure of the Túpac Amaru Army in Cuzco." *HAHR,* LXI (1981), 675–93.

Castañeda Delgado, Paulino, and Juan Marchena Fernández. "La iglesia americana en la segunda mitad del siglo XVIII." In *Historia general de España y América,* edited by Demetrio Ramos. Vol. XI. Madrid, 1989.

Christie, Keith. "Antiqueño Colonization in Western Colombia: A Reappraisal." *HAHR,* LVIII (1978), 260–83.

Dorta, Enrique Marco. "Ganadería y abastecimiento en Cartagena de Indias (1766)." *Revista de Indias,* XXX (1970), 473–502.

Escorcía, José. "Haciendas y estructura agraria en el Valle del Cauca, 1810–50." *ACHSC,* X (1982), 119–38.

Eugenio Martínez, María Angeles. "La competencia inglesa en el comercio del Nuevo Reino con Cartagena." *Temas Americanistas,* II (1983), 13–18.

Fisher, John Robert. "Imperial 'Free Trade' and the Hispanic Economy, 1778–1796." *JLAS,* XIII (1981), 21–56.

———. "Miners, Silver Merchants and Capitalists in Late Colonial Peru." *Ibero-Amerikanisches Archiv,* n.s., II (1976), 257–68.

———. "La rebelión de Túpac Amaru y el programa de la reforma imperial de Carlos III." *AEA,* XXXVIII (1971), 405–21.

———. "Royalism, Regionalism and Rebellion in Colonial Peru, 1808–1815." *HAHR,* LIX (1979), 232–57.

González, Margarita. "El estanco colonial del tabaco." *Cuadernos Colombianos,* VIII (1975), 636–708.

González Luna, María Dolores. "La política de población y pacificación indígena en las poblaciones de Santa Marta y Cartagena (Nuevo Reino de Granada), 1750–1800." *Boletín americanista,* XX (1978), 87–118.

Hamnett, B. R. "The Counterrrevolution of Morillo and the Insurgent Clerics of New Granada, 1815–1820." *Americas,* XXXII (1976), 597–617.

Holton, Robert J. "The Crowd in History: Some Problems of Theory and Method." *Social History,* III (1978), 219–33.

Hussey, Roland D. "Antecedents of the Spanish Monopolistic Overseas Trading Companies (1624–1728)." *HAHR,* IX (1929), 1–30.

Inglis, G. Douglas, and Allan J. Kuethe. "El Consulado de Cádiz y el Reglamento de Comercio Libre de 1765." In *Andalucía y América en el siglo XVIII,* edited by Bibiano Torres Ramírez and José Hernández Palomo. Vol. I of 2 vols. Seville, 1985.

Izard, Miguel. "Ni Cuartreros ni Montoneros, Llaneros." *Boletín americanista,* XXIII (1981), 83–142.

Kuethe, Allan J. "Guns, Subsidies, and Commercial Privilege: Some Historical Factors in the Emergence of the Cuban National Character, 1763–1815." *Cuban Studies,* XVI (1986), 123–38.

———. "More on the 'Culmination of the Bourbon Reforms': A Perspective from New Granada." *HAHR,* LVII (1978), 477–80.

———. "The Pacification Campaign on the Riohacha Frontier, 1772–1779." *HAHR,* L (1970), 467–81.

Kuethe, Allan J., and Lowell Blaisdell. "The Esquilache Government and the Reforms of Charles III in Cuba." *Jahrbuch für Geschichte von Staat, Wirtschaft und Gesellschaft Lateinamerikas,* XIX (1982), 117–36.

Kuethe, Allan J., and G. Douglas Inglis. "Absolutism and Enlightened Reform: Charles III, the Establishment of the Alcabala, and Commercial Reorganization in Cuba." *Past and Present,* no. 109 (November, 1985), 118–43.

Lavina, Javier. "La sublevación de Túquerres en 1800: Una revuelta antifiscal." *Boletín americanista,* XX (1978), 189–96.

Loy, Jane M. "Forgotten Comuneros: The 1781 Revolt in the Llanos of Casanare." *HAHR,* LXI (1981), 235–57.

Lucena Salmoral, Manuel. "Apuntes para un diálogo sobre el Virreinato del Nuevo Reino de Granada en 1776." In *Hispanoamérica hacia 1776.* Madrid, 1980.

McFarlane, Anthony. "Civil Disorders and Popular Protests in Late Colonial New Granada." *HAHR,* LXIV (1984), 17–54.

———. "Comerciantes y monopolio en la Nueva Granada: El Consulado de Cartagena de Indias." *ACHSC,* XI (1983), 43–69.

———. "El comercio exterior del Virreinato de la Nueva Granada: Conflictos en la política económica de los Borbones, 1783–1789." *ACHSC,* VI–VII (1971–72), 69–116.

———. "Riot and Rebellion in Colonial Spanish America." *Latin American Research Review,* XVII (1982), 212–21.

Málaga Medina, Alejandro, and Eusebio Quiroz Paz Soldán. "La Rebelión de Túpac Amaru en Arequipa." *Historia* (Arequipa), II (1983), 98–137.

Marchena Fernández, Juan. "La financiación militar en Indias: Introducción a su estudio." *AEA,* XXXVI (1979), 81–110.

Mora de Tovar, Gilma. "La política fiscal del estado colonial y el monopolio de la industria del aguardiente en la Nueva Granada durante el siglo XVIII." *Desarollo y Sociedad,* X (1983), 89–119.

Moscoso, Maximiliano. "Apuntes para la historia de la industria textil en el Cusco colonial." *Revista universitaria* (Cuzco), LI–LII (1962–63), 67–94.

Muller, Herman J. "British Business and Spanish America, 1700–1800." *Mid-America,* XXXIX (1957), 3–20.

Muñoz Pérez, J. "La publicación del Reglamento de Comercio Libre de Indias, de 1778." *AEA,* IV (1947), 615–64.

Navarro García, Luis. "Campillo y el nuevo sistema: Una atribución dudosa." *Temas americanistas,* II (Seville, 1983), 22–29.

O'Phelan Godoy, Scarlett. "Elementos étnicos y de poder en el mo-

vimiento tupacamarista, 1780–81." *Nova Americana,* V (1982), 79–101.
———. "Las reformas fiscales borbónicas y su impacto en la sociedad colonial del Bajo y el Alto Perú." *Historia y cultura,* XVI (1983), 113–28.
Ortiz de la Tabla, Javier. "El obraje colonial ecuatoriana: Aproximación a su estudio." *Revista de Indias,* CXLIX–CL (1977), 472–541.
———. "Panorama económico y social del corregimiento de Quito (1768–1775)." *Revista de Indias,* CXLV–CXLVI (1976), 83–98.
Palacio Atard, Vicente. "Areche y Guirior: Observaciones sobre el fracaso de una visita al Perú." *AEA,* III (1946), 271–376.
Pérez Ayala. "Aspectos desconocidos de la vida del virrey don Manuel de Guirior, co-fundador de la Biblioteca Nacional de Bogotá." *BHA,* XLIII (1956), 156–82.
Quiroz, Eusebio, *et al.* "La rebelión de 1780 in Arequipa." In *La emancipación americana en Bolivia y Perú,* edited by Carlos Urquizo Sossa. Vol. III of 3 vols. La Paz, 1976.
Restrepo Canal, Carlos. "El sitio de Cartagena por el Almirante Vernon." *BHA,* XXVIII (1941), 447–67.
Restrepo de García, Inés. "El ataque a Cartagena de 1741: Una lucha de mercados." *BHA,* LXIV (1977), 597–637.
Salas de Coloma, Miriam. "Los obrajes de Huamanga en la economía centro-sur peruana a fines del siglo XVIII." *Revista del Archivo General de la Nación,* VII (1984), 119–46.
Sanders, G. Earl. "Counter-contraband in Spanish America: Handicaps of the Governors of the Indies." *Americas,* XXXIV (1977), 62–71.
Super, John C. "Querétaro Obrajes: Industry and Society in Provincial Mexico, 1600–1810." *HAHR,* LVI (1976), 197–216.
Taussig, Michael. "The Evolution of Rural Wage Labour in the Cauca Valley of Colombia, 1700–1970." In *Land and Labour in Latin America,* edited by K. Duncan and I. Rutledge. Cambridge, 1977.
Thompson, E. P. "Eighteenth-Century English Society: Class Struggle Without Class?" *Social History,* III (1978), 133–65.
———. "The Moral Economy of the English Crowd in the Eighteenth Century." *Past and Present,* no. 50 (1971), 76–136.
Tovar Pinzón, Hermes. "El estado colonial frente al poder local y regional." *Nova americana,* V (1983), 39–77.
———. "Guerras de opinión y represión en Colombia durante la Independencia, 1810–1820." *ACHSC,* XI (1983), 187–232.
Vovelle, Michel. "Le tournant des mentalités en France 1750–1789: La sensibilité pre-révolutionnaire." *Social History,* II (1977), 605–29.

Whitaker, Arthur P. "The Elhúyar Mining Missions and the Enlightenment." *HAHR*, XXXI (1951), 558–85.

THESES AND DISSERTATIONS

Dilg, George Robertson. "The Collapse of the Portobelo Fairs: A Study in Spanish Commercial Reform, 1720–1740." Ph.D. dissertation, Indiana University, 1975.

Douglas, W. Clarke. "Patterns of Indian Warfare in the Province of Santa Marta." Ph.D. dissertation, University of Wisconsin, 1974.

Fisher, Margaret Ann. "The Role of the Spanish American Inheritance in European Diplomacy, 1659–1713." Ph.D. dissertation, University of Washington, 1972.

Grahn, Lance R. "Contraband, Commerce, and Society in New Granada, 1713–1763." Ph.D. dissertation, Duke University, 1985.

Minchom, A. M. "Urban Popular Society in Colonial Quito, c. 1700–1800." Ph.D. dissertation, University of Liverpool, 1984.

Montgomery, Sandra Cornell. "The Bourbon Mining Reform in New Granada, 1784–1796." M.A. thesis, Texas Tech University, 1984.

Pogonyi, Miklos. "The Search for Trade and Profits in Bourbon Colombia, 1765–1777." Ph.D. dissertation, University of New Mexico, 1978.

Tyrer, Robson B. "The Demographic and Economic History of the Audiencia of Quito: Indian Population and the Textile Industry, 1600–1800." Ph.D. dissertation, University of California, Berkeley, 1976.

Wibel, John F. "The Evolution of a Regional Community Within Spanish Empire and Peruvian Nation: Arequipa, 1780–1845." Ph.D. dissertation, Stanford University, 1975.

Contributors

✧✦✧

JACQUES A. BARBIER, professor of history at the University of Ottawa, is the author of *Reform and Politics in Bourbon Chile, 1755–1796* (1980) and coeditor of *The North American Role in the Spanish Imperial Economy, 1760–1819* (1984).

MAURICE P. BRUNGARDT, associate professor of history at Loyola University in New Orleans, is the author of "The United Fruit Company in Colombia," in Henry C. Dethloff and C. Joseph Pusateri (eds.), *American Business History* (1987).

DAVID CAHILL, assistant professor of Latin American History at the University of Bielefeld, is currently working on a study of the social history of the southern Peruvian sierra from 1750 to 1850.

JOHN FISHER, director of the Institute of Latin American Studies at the University of Liverpool, is the author of *Government and Society in Colonial Peru* (1970), *Silver Mines and Silver Miners in Colonial Peru* (1976), and *Commercial Relations Between Spain and Spanish America in the Era of Free Trade* (1985).

LANCE R. GRAHN, assistant professor of history at Marquette University, is currently working on a study of the role of contraband in New Granada under the early Bourbons.

BRIAN R. HAMNETT, reader in modern history at the University of Strathclyde, Great Britain, is the author of *Politics and Trade in Southern Mexico, 1750–1821* (1971), *Revolución y Contrarrevolución en México y el Perú, 1800–1824* (1978), *La política española en una época revolucionaria, 1790–1820* (1985), and *Roots of Insurgency: Mexican Regions, 1750–1824* (1986).

ALLAN J. KUETHE, professor of history at Texas Tech University, is the author of *Military Reform and Society in New Granada, 1773–1808* (1978) and *Cuba, 1753–1815: Crown, Military, and Society* (1986), and coeditor of *The North American Role in the Spanish Imperial Economy, 1760–1819* (1982).

ANTHONY MCFARLANE, lecturer in Latin American history at the University of Warwick, has written a considerable number of articles dealing with aspects of the social and economic history of Colombia during the late colonial and early independence periods, and the general phenomenon of late colonial rebellions in Spanish America.

JUAN MARCHENA FERNÁNDEZ, professor in the Department of American History at the University of Seville, is the author of *La institución militar en Cartagena de Indias* (1982), *Oficiales y soldados en el ejército de America* (1983), and *Financiación militar y flujos de capitales a fines del S. XVIII* (1989).

SANDRA MONTGOMERY KEELAN is a doctoral student at the University of North Carolina, Chapel Hill.

Index